THE HENRY L. STIMSON LECTURES SERIES

JOHN J. MEARSHEIMER

The Great Delusion

LIBERAL DREAMS AND INTERNATIONAL REALITIES

Yale

UNIVERSITY PRESS

NEW HAVEN AND LONDON

The Henry L. Stimson Lectures at the Whitney and Betty MacMillan
Center for International and Area Studies at Yale.

Yale University Press books may be purchased in quantity for
educational, business, or promotional use. For information, please e-mail
sales.press@yale.edu (U.S. office) or sales@yaleup.co.uk
(U.K. office).

Set in type by Westchester Publishing Services.
Printed in the United States of America.

Library of Congress Control Number: 2018941374
ISBN 978-0-300-23419-0 (hardcover : alk. paper)

A catalogue record for this book is available from the British Library.

This paper meets the requirements of ANSI/NISO Z39.48-1992
(Permanence of Paper).

10 9 8 7 6 5 4 3 2

CONTENTS

PREFACE

WHEN I BEGAN WORKING ON THIS BOOK ten years ago, I had two different ideas about what the topic might be. First, I was interested in explaining why post–Cold War U.S. foreign policy was so prone to failure, sometimes disastrous failure. I was especially interested in explaining America's fiascoes in the greater Middle East, which continued to accumulate, and the steady deterioration of U.S.-Russian relations, which culminated in a major rupture over Ukraine in 2014. This subject was all the more interesting because there was so much optimism in the early 1990s about America's role in the world. I wanted to figure out what went wrong.

Second, I aspired to write a book about how liberalism, nationalism, and realism interact to affect relations among states. I have long considered nationalism a remarkably powerful force in international politics, but I had never examined that topic in detail. I had written a good deal about realism, however, and explored its differences with liberalism in several earlier works. I thought that it would be interesting to write a book comparing and contrasting these three "isms," especially since I knew of no article or book that did this.

As I thought about the relationship between liberalism, nationalism, and realism, I came to realize that this trichotomy provided an ideal template for explaining the failures of U.S. foreign policy since 1989, and especially since 2001. At that point, my two reasons for writing this book fit together rather neatly.

My basic argument is that the United States was so powerful in the aftermath of the Cold War that it could adopt a profoundly liberal foreign policy, commonly referred to as "liberal hegemony." The aim of this ambitious strategy is to turn as many countries as possible into liberal democracies while also fostering an open international economy and building formidable international institutions. In essence, the United States has sought to remake the world in its own image. Proponents of this policy, which is widely embraced in the American foreign policy establishment, believe it will make the world more peaceful and ameliorate the dual problems of nuclear proliferation and terrorism. It will reduce human rights violations and make liberal democracies more secure against internal threats.

From the beginning, however, liberal hegemony was destined to fail, and it did. This strategy invariably leads to policies that put a country at odds with nationalism and realism, which ultimately have far more influence on international politics than liberalism does. This basic fact of life is difficult for most Americans to accept. The United States is a deeply liberal country whose foreign policy elite have an almost knee-jerk hostility toward both nationalism and realism. But this kind of thinking can only lead to trouble on the foreign policy front. American policymakers would be wise to abandon liberal hegemony and pursue a more restrained foreign policy based on realism and a proper understanding of how nationalism constrains great powers.

The deeper roots of this book go back to my days as a graduate student at Cornell University. In the fall of 1976, I took the Field Seminar in Political Theory taught by Professor Isaac Kramnick. The class, which introduced students to the writings of seminal thinkers like Plato, Machiavelli, Hobbes, Locke, Rousseau, and Marx, had a greater impact on me than any other course I have ever taken. Indeed, I still have my notebook from that class, and over the years I have consulted it at least fifty times.

Three aspects of that seminar made it central to my intellectual development. First, I learned much about all sorts of isms, including liberalism, nationalism, and realism, and the course lent itself to contrasting them against each other. Second, it taught me that theory is indispensable for understanding how the world works. The reason I have referred back to the course notebook so many times is that I remembered particular arguments those theorists made that had significant implications for contemporary political issues. Third, I learned that one may talk and write about important theoretical issues in simple, clear language that is accessible to non-experts. Although it was often hard to figure out exactly what the famous theorists on our reading list were saying, Professor Kramnick's ability to spell out their theories in straightforward language not only made them easy to understand but also made it clear why they are important.

The Great Delusion is intended to be theoretical at its core. The premise underlying the book is that theory is essential for understanding policy issues. But in the spirit of Isaac Kramnick, I have gone to great lengths to spell out my arguments as clearly as possible so that any well-educated and interested reader can grasp them. To put it bluntly, my aim is to be a great communicator, not a great obfuscator. Only the reader, of course, can determine whether I have succeeded.

I could not have written this book without the help of many very smart people. My greatest debt is to four individuals whose fingerprints are all over it: Eliza Gheorghe, Mariya Grinberg, Sebastian Rosato, and Stephen Walt. They not only made critically important conceptual points that caused me to alter particular arguments, but also spotted contradictions that I had missed and gave sage advice on how to reorganize chapters as well as the book's overall structure.

The manuscript went through five major drafts before I turned it over to Yale University Press. In November 2016, after the second major draft, I had a book workshop featuring six scholars from outside the University of Chicago—Daniel Deudney, Matthew Kocher, John Owen, Sebastian Rosato, Stephen Walt, and Alexander Wendt—who were kind enough to read the entire manuscript and spend eight hours critiquing it in detail. Their feedback, both at the workshop and in subsequent email and phone exchanges, led me to make numerous changes, some of them fundamental.

Other participants at that book workshop, including my good friend Thomas Durkin, gave me sage advice on how the pursuit of liberal hegemony threatens civil liberties at home and facilitates the growth of a national security state. I also had the good fortune of having all my international relations colleagues at the University of Chicago—Austin Carson, Robert

Gulotty, Charles Lipson, Robert Pape, Paul Poast, Michael J. Reese, and Paul Staniland—participate in the discussion. They too offered excellent comments that helped me tighten some arguments and forced me to alter others.

I owe a special debt of gratitude to Sean Lynn-Jones, who read the entire manuscript and gave me a detailed set of comments that helped me refine the final version of the manuscript. I am especially grateful to my editor at Yale University Press, William Frucht, who did a superb job of editing that final version. He pushed me hard to tighten particular arguments while he streamlined virtually all of them in ways that helped make the book more reader friendly. Liz Schueler, with some help from John Donohue, did a fine job of copyediting, and Karen Olson handled the logistics efficiently and cheerfully.

Many other individuals helped me—some in small ways, some in big ways—produce this book. They include Sener Akturk, Zeynep Bulutgil, Jon Caverley, Michael Desch, Alexander Downes, Charles Glaser, Burak Kadercan, Brian Leiter, Jennifer A. Lind, Gabriel Mares, Max Mearsheimer, Nicholas Mearsheimer, Rajan Menon, Nuno Monteiro, Francesca Morgan, Valerie Morkevičius, John Mueller, Sankar Muthu, David Nirenberg, Lindsey O'Rourke, Joseph Parent, Don Reneau, Marie-Eve Reny, Michael Rosol, John Schuessler, James Scott, Yubing Sheng, Tom Switzer, and the two anonymous reviewers for Yale University Press.

I would like to thank Ian Shapiro, the Henry R. Luce Director of the Mac-Millan Center for International and Area Studies at Yale, who invited me to give the Henry L. Stimson Lectures for 2017. The three lectures that I gave at Yale are, in effect, the central ingredients of this book. I would also like to express my appreciation to the University of Chicago, which has been my intellectual home for more than thirty-five years and has generously supported the research that went into producing not only this book but virtually everything I have written since I started there as an assistant professor in 1982. In addition, I want to thank the Charles Koch Foundation for helping to fund my research and the book workshop. I especially appreciate the support of William Ruger, its vice president for research.

I have been fortunate over the years to have top-notch administrative assistants who not only have helped me deal with the everyday logistical demands of being a professor and scholar but also have done significant amounts of research for me. Megan Belansky, Emma Chilton, Souvik De, Elizabeth Jenkins, and Michael Rowley have all served me well and have contributed in important ways to the making of this book. I am also grateful for all the support I received on the home front from my family, especially from my wife, Pamela, who never complained about the endless hours I spent writing and rewriting the book manuscript.

Finally, I would like to dedicate this book to all the students I have taught over the years, going back to when I taught my first course at Mohawk Valley Community College in upstate New York in 1974. I am using the term *student* here in its broadest sense, to include people who have not formally taken a course with me but have told me that my work has helped shape their thinking. I love teaching because I get great satisfaction from imparting knowledge to students and from helping them come up with their own theories about how the world works.

At the same time, I have learned an enormous amount over the years from interacting with students. This is especially true of seminars, where I have often gone into class thinking one way about an article or book on the syllabus and left thinking about it differently because of something a student said. Teaching large lecture courses has also been an important learning experience, as it has forced me to organize my thoughts on big topics and figure out how to present them in a clear and accessible way.

All of this is to say that teaching and working with students over the years has helped shape my thinking about international politics in ways that are reflected in every page of this book. For that I am forever grateful.

THE GREAT DELUSION

The Impossible Dream

LIBERAL HEGEMONY IS AN AMBITIOUS STRATEGY in which a state aims to turn as many countries as possible into liberal democracies like itself while also promoting an open international economy and building international institutions. In essence, the liberal state seeks to spread its own values far and wide. My goal in this book is to describe what happens when a powerful state pursues this strategy at the expense of balance-of-power politics.

Many in the West, especially among foreign policy elites, consider liberal hegemony a wise policy that states should axiomatically adopt. Spreading liberal democracy around the world is said to make eminently good sense from both a moral and a strategic perspective. For starters, it is thought to be an excellent way to protect human rights, which are sometimes seriously violated by authoritarian states. And because the policy holds that liberal democracies do not want to go to war with each other, it ultimately provides a formula for transcending realism and fostering international peace. Finally, proponents claim it helps protect liberalism at home by eliminating authoritarian states that otherwise might aid the illiberal forces that are constantly present inside the liberal state.

This conventional wisdom is wrong. Great powers are rarely in a position to pursue a full-scale liberal foreign policy. As long as two or more of them exist on the planet, they have little choice but to pay close attention to their position in the global balance of power and act according to the dictates of realism. Great powers of all persuasions care deeply about their survival, and there is always the danger in a bipolar or multipolar system that they will be attacked by another great power. In these circumstances, liberal great powers regularly dress up their hard-nosed behavior with liberal rhetoric. They talk like liberals and act like realists. Should they adopt liberal policies that are at odds with realist logic, they invariably come to regret it.

But occasionally a liberal democracy encounters such a favorable balance of power that it is able to embrace liberal hegemony. That situation is most likely to arise in a unipolar world, where the single great power does not have to worry about being attacked by another great power since there is none. Then the liberal sole pole will almost always abandon realism and adopt a liberal foreign policy. Liberal states have a crusader mentality hardwired into them that is hard to restrain.

Because liberalism prizes the concept of inalienable or natural rights, committed liberals are deeply concerned about the rights of virtually every individual on the planet. This universalist logic creates a powerful incentive for liberal states to get involved in the affairs of countries that seriously violate their citizens' rights. To take this a step further, the best way to ensure that the rights of foreigners are not trampled is for them to live in a liberal democracy. This logic leads straight to an active policy of regime change, where the goal is to topple autocrats and put liberal democracies in their place. Liberals do not shy from this task, mainly because they often have great faith in their state's ability to do social engineering both at home and abroad. Creating a world populated by liberal democracies is also thought to be a formula for international peace, which would not just eliminate war but greatly reduce, if not eliminate, the twin scourges of nuclear proliferation and terrorism. And lastly, it is an ideal way of protecting liberalism at home.

This enthusiasm notwithstanding, liberal hegemony will not achieve its goals, and its failure will inevitably come with huge costs. The liberal state is likely to end up fighting endless wars, which will increase rather than reduce the level of conflict in international politics and thus aggravate the problems of proliferation and terrorism. Moreover, the state's militaristic behavior is almost certain to end up threatening its own liberal values. Liberalism abroad leads to illiberalism at home. Finally, even if the liberal state were to achieve its aims—spreading democracy near and far, fostering economic intercourse, and creating international institutions—they would not produce peace.

The key to understanding liberalism's limits is to recognize its relationship with nationalism and realism. This book is ultimately all about these three isms and how they interact to affect international politics.

Nationalism is an enormously powerful political ideology. It revolves around the division of the world into a wide variety of nations, which are formidable social units, each with a distinct culture. Virtually every nation would prefer to have its own state, although not all can. Still, we live in a world populated almost exclusively by nation-states, which means that liberalism must coexist with nationalism. Liberal states are also nation-states. There is no question that liberalism and nationalism can coexist, but when they clash, nationalism almost always wins.

The influence of nationalism often undercuts a liberal foreign policy. For example, nationalism places great emphasis on self-determination, which means that most countries will resist a liberal great power's efforts to interfere in their domestic politics—which, of course, is what liberal hegemony is all about. These two isms also clash over individual rights. Liberals believe everyone has the same rights, regardless of which country they call home. Nationalism is a particularist ideology from top to bottom, which means it does not treat rights as inalienable. In practice, the vast majority of people around the globe do not care greatly about the rights of individuals in other countries. They are much more concerned about their fellow citizens' rights, and even that commitment has limits. Liberalism oversells the importance of individual rights.

Liberalism is also no match for realism. At its core, liberalism assumes that the individuals who make up any society sometimes have profound differences about what constitutes the good life, and these differences might lead them to try to kill each other. Thus a state is needed to keep the peace. But there is no world state to keep countries at bay when they have profound disagreements. The structure of the international system is anarchic, not hierarchic, which means that liberalism applied to international politics cannot work. Countries thus have little choice but to act according to balance-of-power logic if they hope to survive. There are special cases, however, where a country is so secure that it can take a break from realpolitik and pursue truly liberal policies. The results are almost always bad, largely because nationalism thwarts the liberal crusader.

My argument, stated briefly, is that nationalism and realism almost always trump liberalism. Our world has been shaped in good part by those two powerful isms, not by liberalism. Consider that five hundred years ago the political universe was remarkably heterogeneous; it included city-states, duchies, empires, principalities, and assorted other political forms. That world has given way to a globe populated almost exclusively by nation-states. Although many factors caused this great transformation, two of the main driving forces behind the modern state system were nationalism and balance-of-power politics.

The American Embrace of Liberal Hegemony

This book is also motivated by a desire to understand recent American foreign policy. The United States is a deeply liberal country that emerged from the Cold War as by far the most powerful state in the international system.[1] The collapse of the Soviet Union in 1991 left it in an ideal position to pursue liberal hegemony.[2] The American foreign policy establishment embraced that ambitious policy with little hesitation, and with abundant optimism about the future of the United States and the world. At least at first, the broader public shared this enthusiasm.

The zeitgeist was captured in Francis Fukuyama's famous article, "The End of History?," published just as the Cold War was coming to a close.[3] Liberalism, he argued, defeated fascism in the first half of the twentieth century and communism in the second half, and now there was no viable alternative left standing. The world would eventually be entirely populated by liberal democracies. According to Fukuyama, these nations would have virtually no meaningful disputes, and wars between great powers would cease. The biggest problem confronting people in this new world, he suggested, might be boredom.

It was also widely believed at the time that the spread of liberalism would ultimately bring an end to balance-of-power politics. The harsh security competition that has long characterized great-power relations would disappear, and realism, long the dominant intellectual paradigm in international relations, would land on the scrap heap of history. "In a world where freedom, not tyranny, is on the march," Bill Clinton proclaimed while campaigning for the White House in 1992, "the cynical calculus of pure power politics simply does not compute. It is ill-suited to a new era in which ideas and information are broadcast around the globe before ambassadors can read their cables."[4]

Probably no recent president embraced the mission of spreading liberalism more enthusiastically than George W. Bush, who said in a speech in March 2003, two weeks before the invasion of Iraq: "The current Iraqi regime has shown the power of tyranny to spread discord and violence in the Middle East. A liberated Iraq can show the power of freedom to transform that vital region, by bringing hope and progress into the lives of millions. America's interests in security, and America's belief in liberty, both lead in the same direction: to a free and peaceful Iraq."[5] Later that year, on September 6, he proclaimed: "The advance of freedom is the calling of our time; it is the calling of our country. From the Fourteen Points to the Four Freedoms, to the Speech at Westminster, America has put our power at the service of principle. We believe that liberty is the design of nature; we believe that liberty is the direction of history. We believe that human fulfillment and excellence come in the responsible exercise of liberty. And we believe that freedom—the freedom we prize—is not for us alone, it is the right and the capacity of all mankind."[6]

Something went badly wrong. Most people's view of U.S. foreign policy today, in 2018, is starkly different from what it was in 2003, much less the early 1990s. Pessimism, not optimism, dominates most assessments of America's accomplishments during its holiday from realism. Under Presidents Bush and Barack Obama, Washington has played a key role in sowing death and destruction across the greater Middle East, and there is little evidence the mayhem will end anytime soon. American policy toward Ukraine, motivated by liberal logic, is principally responsible for the ongoing crisis between Russia and the West. The United States has been at war for two out of every three years since 1989, fighting seven different wars. We should not be surprised by this. Contrary to the prevailing wisdom in the West, a liberal foreign policy is not a formula for cooperation and peace but for instability and conflict.

In this book I focus on the period between 1993 and 2017, when the Clinton, Bush, and Obama administrations, each in control of American foreign policy for eight years, were fully committed to pursuing liberal hegemony. Although President Obama had some reservations about that policy, they mattered little for how his administration actually acted abroad. I do not consider the Trump administration for two reasons. First, as I was finishing this book it was difficult to determine what President Trump's foreign policy would look like, although it is clear from his rhetoric during the 2016 campaign that he recognizes that liberal hegemony has been an abject failure and would like to abandon key elements of that strategy. Second, there is good reason to think that with the rise of China and the resurrection of Russian power having put great power politics back on the table, Trump eventually will have no choice but to move toward a grand strategy based on realism, even if doing so meets with considerable resistance at home.

The Centrality of Human Nature

When scholars assess liberalism's effect on international politics, they usually begin by analyzing a cluster of theories widely seen as the liberal alternatives to realism. *Democratic peace theory* maintains that liberal democracies do not go to war with each other, but not that they are more peaceful than non-democracies. According to *economic interdependence theory,* countries with significant economic relations rarely fight with each other, because the costs of war are prohibitive for both sides. *Liberal institutionalism* claims that states that join international institutions are more likely to cooperate with each other, because they will be constrained by the organization's rules, which is almost always in their long-term interest to obey.

I will carefully assess each of these theories. But before I do, it is essential to put aside matters of international relations and address more basic questions: what liberalism is and what its intellectual foundations are. My aim, in other words, is to begin with the assumptions and logics that sit at the core of liberalism itself—and determine whether they make sense. It is enormously important when evaluating theories to examine their foundational assumptions about human nature. John Locke, one of liberalism's founding fathers, put the point well: "To understand political power right . . . we must consider what state all men are naturally in."[7]

What is the "state all men are naturally in"? What distinguishing characteristics do all humans have in common? Answering this question is important not only for understanding liberalism but also for understanding nationalism and realism. The more closely any ism accords with human nature, the more relevance it will have in the real world. So I have to spell out my own views about human nature and explain how the common characteristics operate together to affect political life. This ultimately means coming up with a sparse theory of politics that can be used to evaluate and compare liberalism, nationalism, and realism.

We need to answer two principal questions about human nature. First, are men and women social beings above all else, or does it make more sense to emphasize their individuality? In other words, are humans fundamentally social animals who strive hard to carve out room for their individuality, or are they individuals who form social contracts? Second, have our critical faculties developed to the point where we can reach some rough moral consensus on what defines the good life? Can we agree on first principles?

My view is that we are profoundly social beings from the start to the finish of our lives and that individualism is of secondary importance, which is not to say that it is unimportant. Second, it is impossible to reach a common understanding about first principles, even though there can be widespread agreement within different groups. But because there are no universal truths regarding what constitutes the good life, the disagreements among individuals and groups can be profound.

Liberalism downplays the social nature of human beings to the point of almost ignoring it, instead treating people largely as atomistic actors. But liberals wisely emphasize that it is not possible to approach any universal agreement on questions relating to what constitutes the good life. Thus liberalism is one for two in answering the key questions about human nature. Both nationalism and realism, meanwhile, are in sync with human nature, which explains not only why they trump liberalism when they are at odds with it but also why they are the main driving forces behind international politics. Nationalism and realism pay little attention to individuals and rights and instead see the world in terms of distinct nation-states, re-flecting the fact that humans are principally social beings who have funda-mentally different views of what constitutes the good life.[8]

These differences notwithstanding, all three isms have one important feature in common: a profound concern about survival. Nations, I argue, are deeply committed to having their own state because it is the best way to ensure their survival, which can never be taken for granted. States in the international system are also intensely influenced by concerns about survival, which is why they carefully monitor the balance of power and ultimately seek hegemony. Finally, survival is a defining aspect of liberalism. After all, that theory is predicated on the belief that individuals sometimes disagree so strongly about first principles that they try to kill each other. A crucial purpose of the state is to act as a constable and maximize each person's prospects of survival.

Political Liberalism

I have yet to define the term *liberalism* in any detail. It is important that I do so now, because it can mean different things to different people. The same is true of nationalism and realism. It is essential to settle on clear definitions of all these terms, because that is the only way to make coherent arguments about how they relate to each other and how they interact to influence international politics. Precise definitions allow scholars to impose order on a messy and complicated body of facts. They also help readers decide whether an author's arguments are compelling, and if not, where and why not.

Definitions are neither right nor wrong in the sense of being true or false. We are free to define our core concepts as we see fit. This is not to say, however, that there is no way to discriminate among definitions. The primary criterion for assessing any definition's worth is how useful it is for understanding the phenomenon under study. I have chosen definitions that I hope serve that purpose.

Political liberalism, in my lexicon, is an ideology that is individualistic at its core and assigns great importance to the concept of inalienable rights.[9] This concern for rights is the basis of its universalism—everyone on the planet has the same inherent set of rights—and this is what motivates liberal states to pursue ambitious foreign policies. The public and scholarly discourse about liberalism since World War II has placed enormous emphasis on what are commonly called human rights. This is true all around the world, not just in the West. "Human rights," Samuel Moyn notes, "have come to define the most elevated aspirations of both social movements and political entities—state and interstate. They evoke hope and provoke action."[10]

Political liberalism is also built on the assumption that individuals sometimes differ intensely about bedrock political and social issues, which necessitates a state that can maintain order if those disputes threaten to turn violent. Relatedly, liberals place great emphasis on tolerance, a norm that encourages people to respect each other despite their fundamental disagreements. But while they agree on all of these matters, liberals are divided by some fundamental differences.

Political liberalism, in fact, comes in two varieties: what some call *modus vivendi liberalism* and *progressive liberalism*, a terminology I use throughout this book.[11] There are basically two important differences between them, the first of which concerns how they think about individual rights. Modus vivendi liberals conceive of rights almost exclusively in terms of individual freedoms, by which they mean the freedom to act without fear of government intrusion. Freedom of speech, freedom of the press, and the right to hold property are representative examples of these rights. The government exists to protect these freedoms from threats that might emanate either from within the broader society or from outside it. Progressive liberals prize the same individual freedoms, which are sometimes called negative rights, but they are also deeply committed to a set of rights that are actively promoted by the government. They believe, for example, that everyone has a right to equal opportunity, which can be achieved only with active government involvement. Modus vivendi liberals are intensely opposed to this notion of positive rights.

This discussion of individual rights leads to the second important difference between modus vivendi and progressive liberalism. They differ sharply on the role the state should assume, beyond keeping the peace at home. Modus vivendi liberals, in line with their emphasis on protecting individual freedoms and their skepticism about positive rights, maintain that the state should involve itself in society as little as possible. Unsurprisingly, they tend to be dismissive about governments' ability to do social engineering. Progressive liberals take the opposite view. They prefer an activist state that can promote individual rights, and they have much more faith in the capacity of governments to do social engineering.

While there is little doubt that both kinds of political liberalism receive great attention in the world of ideas, in practice, progressive liberalism has triumphed over modus vivendi liberalism. The complexities and demands of life in the modern world leave states with no choice but to be deeply engaged in social engineering, including promoting positive rights. This is not to deny that some states are more involved in this enterprise than others, or that a state's depth of involvement can vary over time. Still, we live in the age of the interventionist state, and there is no reason to think this will change anytime soon. Thus, for all intents and purposes, political liberalism in this book is synonymous with progressive liberalism.

Three further points about my definition of liberalism are in order. First, two other isms are sometimes categorized as liberal political ideologies: *utilitarianism* and *liberal idealism*. One is free to treat them as variants of political liberalism, of course, but I do not, because they operate according to different logics from modus vivendi and progressive liberalism. In particular, neither utilitarianism nor liberal idealism pays much attention to individual rights, which are at the heart of liberalism. Jeremy Bentham, the intellectual father of utilitarianism, called natural rights "rhetorical nonsense, nonsense upon stilts."[12]

E. H. Carr's famous book *The Twenty Years' Crisis*, written in the late 1930s, is widely considered a classic critique of liberalism as it applies to international politics.[13] In fact, his target is not rights-based liberalism of the sort I discuss here. Carr cares little about either modus vivendi or progressive liberalism, which at the time were not highly regarded isms. Instead he takes dead aim at liberal idealism and utilitarianism, which were much more influential in 1930s Britain.[14] Carr and I thus mean different things when we talk about liberalism, and there is not much overlap in our critiques.

None of this is to say that liberal idealism and utilitarianism are unimportant or that they are useless for understanding life in the international system. But they are different theories from political liberalism, and assessing their relevance to state behavior would require a separate study.

Second, the terms *liberalism* and *democracy* are often used interchangeably, or linked together in the phrase "liberal democracy." But the two concepts are not the same, and it is important to distinguish between them and explain how they relate to each other. I define democracy as a form of government with a broad franchise in which citizens get to choose their leaders in periodic elections. Those leaders then write and implement the rules that govern the polity. Liberalism, on the other hand, is all about individual rights. A liberal state privileges the rights of its citizens and protects them through its laws.

It is possible to have an illiberal democracy in which the elected majority tramples on the rights of the minority. This is sometimes referred to as a tyranny of the majority, and one can certainly point to real-world examples. States that are liberal, however, are almost always democratic as well, because the concept of inalienable rights clearly implies the right to have a voice in one's own governance through elections. Markus Fischer puts the point well: "The relation between liberalism and democracy is asymmetrical: liberalism implies democratic institutions to a large degree, whereas democracy entails liberal rights only to a minimal extent."[15]

One might argue, however, that liberal states are anti-democratic when minorities make rights-based arguments that obstruct the majority's decisions. While there is no question this sometimes happens, I do not consider this behavior anti-democratic, because the outcome in such cases is based on laws or rules the citizenry democratically adopted. Thus the term *liberal state*, as used in this book, means a liberal democracy.[16]

Third, some readers might see this book as a sweeping attack on liberalism and conclude I am hostile to that political ideology. That would be wrong. It is essential to distinguish the way liberalism operates inside a country from the way it functions in the international system. My views about liberalism are different for each of these realms.

Within countries, I believe liberalism is a genuine force for good, and it is highly desirable to live in a country that privileges and protects individual rights. I consider myself especially fortunate to have been born and lived all my life in liberal America. Liberalism at the international level, however, is a different matter. States that pursue ambitious liberal foreign policies, as the United States has done in recent years, end up making the world less peaceful. Moreover, they risk undermining liberalism at home, an outcome that should strike fear into the heart of every liberal.

A Road Map

My views on human nature and politics are developed at length in chapter 2. There I lay out my basic theory of politics, which I will use in subsequent chapters to analyze liberalism, nationalism, and realism. In chapter 3, I describe political liberalism, paying careful attention to the similarities and differences between modus vivendi and progressive liberalism, and explain why political liberalism today is largely progressive liberalism. I also briefly consider utilitarianism and liberal idealism and explain why I do not consider them liberal theories.

In chapter 4, I take up the key problems with political liberalism. I examine the relationship between liberalism and nationalism, as well as the limits of liberal claims about universal rights. By this point I will have paid hardly any attention to how liberalism relates to international politics. My aim in the first half of the book is simply to understand what liberalism is about.

I begin zeroing in on how liberalism affects the international system in chapter 5, where I consider in detail the relationship between liberalism and realism. My central argument is that on the rare occasions when states are in a position to adopt liberal hegemony, it usually leads to failed diplomacy and failed wars. I also explain how nationalism and realism—not liberalism—are largely responsible for creating a modern international system that is almost wholly populated with nation-states. Finally, I assess the likelihood of a world state, which, if it materialized, would profoundly change the relevance of liberalism for international politics.

The core argument in chapter 6 is that a state pursuing liberal hegemony does not simply court failure, it suffers significant costs in doing so. Such states invariably end up fighting endless wars, which serve to increase rather than reduce international conflict. I also describe how this liberal militarism usually ends up inflicting huge costs on the target state while endangering liberalism at home.

I make the case in chapter 7 that even if a liberal foreign policy were to achieve its principal goals—spreading liberal democracy widely, creating an open world economy, and building lots of impressive international institutions—that would not lead to a more peaceful world. There would still be security competition with serious potential for war. The reason is that each of the three theories underpinning the expectation that liberal hegemony will radically transform international politics—democratic peace theory, economic interdependence theory, and liberal institutionalism—has fundamental flaws. I conclude in chapter 8 with some observations about the future trajectory of American foreign policy. I assess the prospects that the United States will abandon liberal hegemony and adopt a more restrained foreign policy based on realism, coupled with recognition of the fact that nationalism sharply limits the ability of great powers to directly intervene in the politics of other states. I also offer some cautious observations on President Trump's likely effect on American foreign policy during his tenure in the White House.

To sum up, the discussion about human nature in chapter 2 focuses on the traits of *individuals,* the analysis of political liberalism in chapters 3 and 4 concentrates on how it relates to a country's *domestic politics,* and the discussion in chapters 5–8 concerns how that ism relates to *international politics.* This basic template, of course, reflects the three levels of analysis—individual, unit, and system—that ultimately concern all students of international relations.[17]

2

Human Nature and Politics

BELIEFS ABOUT HUMAN NATURE ARE the building blocks of theoretical arguments in politics, and liberalism is no exception. Its core claims are based
on a set of assumptions about human nature, meaning those attributes that
are common to all people, as opposed to those that vary among individuals.
Thus, to assess liberalism, we must first describe what it says about human
nature and determine whether those claims square with what we know
about the human condition.

The conservative French thinker Joseph de Maistre maintained that
"there is no such thing as *man* in the world. In my lifetime I have seen
Frenchmen, Italians, Russians, etc.; thanks to Montesquieu, I even know
that *one can be Persian*. But as for *man,* I declare that I have never in my life
met him; if he exists, he is unknown to me."[1] Of course, there are important differences among peoples as well as people, and those differences are
central to the arguments in this book. Yet certain features are permanent
and distinctive in almost every person, and these can provide the micro-
foundations for a simple theory of politics that can then be employed to
evaluate liberalism and its relationship to nationalism and realism. My
main aim in this chapter is to present my own thinking about human nature and politics.

I begin with two simple assumptions, the first of which concerns our
critical faculties. There is no question humans have an impressive capacity
to reason. Still, this capacity has significant limits, especially when it comes
to answering essential questions about what constitutes the good life.

Almost everyone agrees that survival is the most important individual goal, because without it you cannot pursue any other goal. But beyond that, there is often intractable disagreement about the answers to the important ethical, moral, and political questions that all societies confront, and which have profound implications for daily life. Those differences over first principles sometimes become so passionate that they create the potential for deadly conflict. That lurking possibility of violence, which leads individuals to fear each other and worry about their survival, applies to relations among societies as well as among individuals.

My second assumption is that humans are profoundly social beings. They do not operate as lone wolves but are born into social groups or societies that shape their identities well before they can assert their individualism. Moreover, individuals usually develop strong attachments to their group and are sometimes willing to make great sacrifices for their fellow members. Humans are often said to be tribal at their core. The main reason for our social nature is that the best way for a person to survive is to be embedded in a society and to cooperate with fellow members rather than act alone. This is not to deny that individuals sometimes have good reasons to act selfishly and take advantage of other group members. On balance, however, cooperation trumps selfish behavior. Social groups are survival vehicles.[2]

One might wonder how it is possible to have a functioning society when it is so difficult for individuals to agree about fundamental beliefs. There is unquestionably a tension between my two core assumptions, which is why social groups sometimes break apart and also why there never has been and probably never will be a unified global society. Nevertheless, people are obviously capable of living together in social groups for sustained periods, as the planet has been populated with them since human beings first appeared.

For a society to hold together, there must be substantial overlap in how its members think about the good life, and they must respect each other when, inevitably, serious disagreements arise. These differences notwithstanding, it is possible within a social group to have considerable agreement about first principles, mainly because the members share a common culture, which includes a variety of beliefs about ultimate values. Most people have been socialized since birth to venerate their culture, which means being socialized to respect certain core principles. Culture is a kind of glue that helps hold individuals together inside a society.

But culture alone is not enough. To stay intact, a society also must have political institutions that govern behavior within the group. It needs rules that stipulate how the group's members are expected to live together, as well as the means to enforce those rules. This commonly takes the form of a juridical system based on what has become known as "the rule of law." Social groups also need political institutions to help them survive in the face of threats from other groups. These institutions must control the means of violence both to enforce the rules within the society and to protect it from external threats.

With political institutions comes politics, which is crucial to daily life in any society. Politics is essentially about who gets to write the rules that govern the group. This responsibility matters greatly because the members of any society are certain to have some conflicting interests, as they will never completely agree about first principles. Given that basic fact of life, whichever faction writes and interprets the rules can do so in ways that serve its interests rather than its rivals', or reflect its vision of society rather than its rivals'. Of course, power matters greatly in determining which faction wins this competition. The more resources an individual or faction possesses, the more likely it is to control the governing institutions. In short, in a world where reason takes you only so far, the balance of power usually decides who gets to write and enforce the rules.

Given the absolute necessity of politics for the functioning of social groups, when I say that humans are naturally social beings, I am in effect saying they are also political beings. This obviously includes hunter-gatherers, who are sometimes wrongly portrayed as operating alone in a Hobbesian world. In fact, they lived together in small groups in which power, rules, and factions—that is, politics—were unavoidable. The political and social dimensions of the human condition go hand in hand. Questions about what constitutes the good life are axiomatically about political as well as social matters. Although I frequently use the term *social group* in this book, it is shorthand for what is effectively a sociopolitical group.

Politics is vitally important in the relations between self-governing social groups. There are no higher political institutions, however, that can write and reliably enforce rules that might govern their behavior toward each other. The power to write rules, which matters so much inside a society, thus matters much less at the intergroup level. Still, power itself matters greatly in dealings among groups, because possessing superior power allows a group to get its way when it is at odds with another group. Above all else, it allows a group to fend off threats to its survival from other groups. Independent social groups thus compete with each other for power. Politics among groups is all about gaining relative power.

Social groups have a propensity to expand, because greater size usually augments their power relative to rival groups and thus enhances their prospects for survival. Groups can also be bent on expansion for other reasons. They might believe, for example, that they have found the true religion or political ideology, and go on a crusade to export their prized blueprint to other societies. Groups mainly expand by conquering other groups, although occasionally groups with common interests join together voluntarily. Conquerors usually try either to dominate the vanquished group and rob it of its autonomy or else absorb it into its own society. Sometimes they try to wipe out the defeated group. There are limits as to how far any group can expand because the potential victims almost always have powerful incentives to resist and ensure their own survival.

In sum, I begin with two simple assumptions about human nature: there are significant limits on our ability to reason about first principles, and we are social animals at our core. Taken together, these assumptions tell us three important facts about the world. First, it is populated with a great number of social groups, each with its own distinctive culture. There is no reason to think that situation will change in the near or distant future. In effect, the crucial universal traits of humankind lead us to a world distinguished by its particularism.

Second, social groups have no choice but to build political institutions, which means politics and power are at the center of life within societies as well as among them. Third, survival is of overriding importance for individuals as well as social groups. It runs like a red skein through human history.

Before examining the main components of my argument in detail, I need to define some important concepts.

Key Definitions

Much of the subsequent discussion revolves around five basic concepts: culture, groups, identity, political institutions, and society. At least two of them—culture and identity—are difficult to define, mainly because they are so sweeping. Not surprisingly, those terms are employed in various ways in both the scholarly literature and public discourse. Thus it is essential to explain as precisely as possible how I am using them.

I should note that these concepts are closely linked and hard to disentangle. For example, one might argue that culture, identity, and society are all part of a seamless web. They certainly overlap. Still, I have tried to define each one carefully and show how they relate to each other, in the hope that this will make my core arguments easier to understand.

A *society* is a large group of people who interact with each other on a continual basis in organized and routine ways. The members of a society are interdependent, leading some people to use the words *society* and *community* interchangeably. All societies have their own discrete culture, and they usually occupy a particular piece of territory. Many are sovereign political entities, which means they largely control their own destiny. Some societies, however, are not sovereign but are part of a larger political order.

Culture gives meaning to the patterns of relationships that are the essence of any society. Cultures exist only in the context of societies. In my vocabulary, culture is the set of shared practices and beliefs that are at a society's heart. Those practices include customs and rituals, dress, food, music, routines, symbols, and the language people speak. They also include the subtle gestures, mannerisms, and communications by which people interact and make their way through daily life. The French sociologist Pierre Bourdieu called these a "habitus."[3] A society's beliefs, on the other hand—consisting of its political and social values, views about morality and religion, and stories about its history—deal explicitly with first principles. They guide how a particular society decides what constitutes the good life. Culture also includes the civil institutions, like churches and soccer stadiums, that reflect those practices and beliefs.

Culture gives every society distinct characteristics that separate it from other societies. Sometimes, however, particular features are shared across cultures, although there is never a complete overlap. The reason cultures are distinct is that peoples around the world have remarkably diverse life experiences and histories. The environment, in other words, heavily shapes human behavior. Yet people also have agency; they possess critical faculties with which to determine how best to lead their lives. But people in different societies often come to different conclusions about first principles, which is another reason for variation among cultures. None of this is to deny that cultures evolve and change, sometimes drastically. History marches on, constantly bringing new circumstances and new ideas, to which different cultures respond in different ways.

When Western elites talk about "global society" or "human society," the implication is that there has been a profound leveling of cultural differences across the planet. While there is no question that the Industrial Revolution, globalization, and the worldwide influence of Britain and the United States have had something of a leveling effect over the past two centuries, they have not led to anything like the universal culture that is a prerequisite for a global society. The proliferation of McDonald's and Starbucks and the ability of so many of the world's elites to speak English hardly amount to cultural sameness. There is an abundance of distinct cultures in the world, and they underpin a wide variety of societies. Heterogeneity, not homogeneity, is the prevailing state of global culture. Thus, *global society* and *human society* are not useful terms.

A *group* is a collection of individuals who regularly interact with each other, have a sense of comradeship, share many of the same ideas, and have a common purpose. Although a society obviously qualifies as a group, the concept is elastic enough to include all sorts of clusters of people. My focus, however, is on large social groups that have their own political institutions. As it is used in this book, *group* is synonymous with *society*.

Identity is a profoundly social concept that involves a person's or group's sense of self. Who am I? Or who are we?[4] Identity is largely defined in relation to the "other." At the individual level, it involves how a person thinks about himself in relation to other individuals or groups. This can involve multiple identities, of course, because people can belong to multiple groups. My focus here is on how individuals within a society relate to each other. For sure, an individual's identity is deeply influenced by his society's culture, because it provides a set of practices and beliefs that all members must relate to daily, and encourages members to think of themselves as similar. Nevertheless, each member's identity will invariably be shaped by important differences with others. Individuals in any society have different abilities and preferences and can affiliate with a host of different groups, and these things influence how they think about themselves in relation to others. A person's identity is not defined simply.

What about societies themselves? Any large group's sense of itself depends on how its practices and beliefs distinguish it from other societies. In other words, a society's culture and its identity are inextricably bound up with each other. In this book I pay particular attention to nations, the dominant social group on the planet, and to the concept of national identity. An individual's identity in the modern world is heavily influenced, but not completely shaped, by her nation's culture.

Finally, *political institutions* are the governing bodies that create rules to regulate daily life and maintain order. Though they operate at different levels, within any society there must be an overarching political authority. No society could survive for long without effective political institutions. Of course, in preliterate societies, customary practices and norms take the place of written rules and formal governing institutions.[5] My focus in this book, however, is on more modern societies.

Let me now turn to my key assumptions about human nature.

The Limits of Reason and the Good Life

Humans have the capability to reason or think critically, a faculty that distinguishes them from all other animals and has allowed them to dominate the planet. It has also allowed them to establish an impressive body of theories about how the world works. Yet there are significant limits on our ability to reason, which have important consequences for social and political life. One such limitation, our inability to agree about what constitutes the good life, sometimes leads individuals as well as social groups to hate and try to hurt others, which in turn causes the others to worry about their survival.

It is important to distinguish between our preferences and the best strategies for achieving them. This difference is reflected in the following two questions. First, are our preferences rational, and do those goals promote our survival or make some other kind of sense? Second, are we acting strategically to achieve our goals? These two kinds of rationality are sometimes referred to as substantive and instrumental rationality, respectively. My main concern is with substantive rationality, which is more important for understanding politics. Yet instrumental rationality also matters in my story, because it is directly tied to the ability of governments to effectively perform social engineering. There is certainly no consensus on that issue.

In terms of our preferences, the key questions are: What can reason tell us about the good life? What does it say about how we should behave and arrange our lives, how a society should be organized, and what rules should govern its members' conduct? What can our critical faculties tell us about the bedrock ethical, moral, and political questions that confront all individuals and societies? How do we distinguish between right and wrong? All of these questions deal with first principles: the essential guidance for how we think and act.

To put the questions in more concrete terms: What does reason tell us about which religion, if any, provides the true guide to how we should lead our daily lives? Can we reason our way to the ideal political system? Can our critical faculties resolve debates about abortion, affirmative action, or capital punishment? Can they settle conflicts between individual rights, such as when one person's freedom of speech clashes with another's right to privacy? What does reason say about whether we should treat outsiders differently from members of our own society, or when it is permissible to make war on other countries? These are just a few of the many questions related to how societies should be organized and how their members should behave.

Because we are an intensely social species, we cannot avoid wrestling with such questions. We have little choice but to try to figure out how to live with each other and develop a shared sense of the common good, even if that process never leads to a lasting consensus. Leo Strauss exaggerated only slightly when he wrote, "All political action has then in itself a directedness towards knowledge of the good: of the good life, or of the good society."[6] Sometimes people have little opportunity to express their views on pivotal questions, and sometimes they try to avoid dealing with them. But every society must address them in some fashion.

Take, for example, the matter of devising a body of moral principles to guide individual behavior. No social group can function effectively without widespread agreement on what constitutes moral behavior. The rules that facilitate cooperation in any society are rooted in its moral code. Even Judge Richard Posner, one of the world's leading legal theorists and no fan of basing legal decisions on moral principles, acknowledges that morality "is a pervasive feature of social life and is in the background of many legal principles."[7]

"Reason Rules the World"

Many people believe there is an objective set of first principles that almost every individual can ascertain.[8] In other words, reason gives humans the capacity to figure out, in broad outline, what constitutes the good life. If some of us have difficulty figuring this out on our own, we can engage with others to clarify our thinking. The assumption is that reason, because it privileges facts and logic and is little influenced by cultural or social forces that might interfere with systematic thinking, leads nearly everyone toward the same truths.[9]

Faith in reason was especially pronounced during the Enlightenment, the era in European history from roughly 1650 to 1800 that is sometimes called the Age of Reason.[10] Many European intellectuals at the time, horrified by the long religious wars that ensued from the Protestant Reformation, wanted to believe that religion was a fading force and that the growth of science and education would provide people with the tools to recognize the essential truths about the good life. The power of reason would triumph over faith and settle many of the great questions of the day that religion had been unable to answer. Objective truth about the good life was thought to be possible.

The French philosopher Nicolas de Condorcet captured this optimistic outlook when he wrote in his 1794 book *Sketch for a Historical Picture of the Human Mind* that his object "will be to show, from reasoning and from facts, that no bounds have been fixed to the improvement of the human faculties; that the perfectibility of man is absolutely indefinite; that the progress of this perfectibility . . . has no other limit than the duration of the globe upon which nature has placed us."[11] The British philosopher William

Godwin went so far as to argue in 1793 that "man is perfectible" and that our understanding of justice would eventually be so advanced that there will be no need for government.[12] Most Enlightenment thinkers' claims were more modest, but almost all of them had faith in the ability of human reason to significantly improve the human condition.

Confidence in the power of our critical faculties has weakened over the past two centuries.[13] Although science made giant strides during that period, there has been little progress in working out a coherent and universally accepted understanding of what represents the good life. Individuals continue to have different core values and varying notions of what is the best society, and these conflicting ideals are usually irreconcilable. The political philosopher Alasdair MacIntyre captured how little progress has been made in achieving agreement about first principles: "The most striking feature of contemporary moral utterance is that so much of it is used to express disagreements; and the most striking feature of the debates in which these disagreements are expressed is their interminable character. I do not mean by this just that such debates go on and on and on—although they do—but also that they apparently can find no terminus. There seems to be no rational way of securing moral agreement in our culture."[14]

Yet many people, when pressed, still maintain there are universal principles and that they know what they are. The power of this belief in objective truth often surfaces when a person is accused of being a moral relativist—someone who believes there are no right or wrong answers to life's big questions. Most will deny it vehemently: relativists are sometimes accused of being nihilists, which means they are willing to tolerate almost any form of behavior, and the evil of nihilism is one of the few moral standards that command nearly universal agreement. Yet different people will answer the same questions in different ways and there is no mechanism for choosing among their responses. Often the more specific the question, the more intractable the disagreements. It is impossible to determine which person has the correct answer; it is all a matter of personal preference or opinion.

The smart fallback position for dodging the relativism charge is to maintain that there is an objective set of first principles and I know what they are, but I cannot persuade everyone else to recognize them. Those who disagree with me are simply wrong but refuse to admit it. This line of argument, which many people pursue either explicitly or implicitly, allows them to escape the charge of relativism.

What does this viewpoint say about our collective ability to use reason to arrive at a universal, or even widely shared, understanding of the good life? It tells us that people who believe their critical faculties can help them find moral truth are deluding themselves. Reason alone cannot answer these foundational questions. Reason does not rule the world, and it has limited value in helping large numbers of individuals reach a consensus regarding their core preferences.

How Little We Agree

To illustrate the limits of reason, consider what it tells us about religion, which is profoundly concerned with ethical and moral questions. There is no way our critical faculties can determine which of the world's many religions provides the best rule book for guiding individual conduct, or whether atheism provides better guidance. We have no objective reason for choosing, for instance, Catholicism over Protestantism or vice versa.[15] This explains in good part why Catholics and Protestants murdered each other in huge numbers during the Reformation. Other religions show the same diversity. Consider the divide between Shia and Sunni Muslims or the divisions among Conservative, Orthodox, Reform, and Ultra-Orthodox Jews.

The historical record shows that religions have a powerful tendency to fragment over time. Certain members grow dissatisfied with existing interpretations of the original wisdom and break away. In Christianity, for instance, the first great schism occurred in 1054, when the Christian world broke into two parts: Roman Catholicism and Eastern Orthodoxy. The second major break came in 1517 with the Reformation, when Martin Luther promulgated his Ninety-Five Theses criticizing the practices of the Catholic Church. This brought a division not simply between Catholics and Protestants but the myriad churches in the Protestant world: Anglicans, Baptists, Calvinists, Evangelicals, Lutherans, Methodists, Puritans, Quakers, and others.

In an important study of the Reformation and its consequences, the historian Brad Gregory explains that the reformers' initial aim was to repair what they thought were important doctrinal flaws in Catholicism. Their intention was to think critically about first principles. Instead, Gregory writes, they "unintentionally introduced multiple sources of unwanted disagreement" and found that "doctrinal controversy was literally endless." This led not just to the proliferation of different Christian religions but to the privatization of religion in Western liberal states, which in turn helped promote secularization. Thus we are faced today with "the proliferation of secular and religious truth claims along with related practices that constitute contemporary hyperpluralism."[16] In short, the history of religion offers little support for the claim that our critical faculties can help us reach broad agreement on core principles.

Some might think the American legal system is a domain where reason and deliberation lead to widespread agreement about right and wrong. Many Americans surely think that justice is ultimately based on a well-defined and well-established inventory of moral principles. Nothing could be further from the truth. Many of the main bodies of Anglo-Saxon legal theory reject the notion that the law is or should be based on universal moral principles. They include critical legal studies, law and economics, legal positivism, legal realism, and liberal legalism.

Legal realists, for example, focus on how judges decide cases, especially those in which the existing laws are indeterminate. They believe judges have considerable leeway in adjudicating these so-called hard cases, and that their decisions are ultimately determined by "judgments of fairness or consideration of commercial norms."[17] Judges, in other words, are pragmatic: they pay careful attention to how their decisions will play out in the real world. This is not to deny that the judge's own moral code influences her decision, but that is much different from saying she bases the decision on universal moral principles.

Law and economics is based on a similar logic.[18] Proponents of this approach maintain that judges should decide hard cases largely on the basis of economic efficiency, not widely recognized moral principles. This is a utilitarian approach to the law that emphasizes doing what is best for as many people as possible. Of course, not all judges considering the same case would agree on a single outcome. Who is the ultimate decider matters in the law and economics story as much as in legal realism.

There are certainly legal scholars who believe judges should rely on universal moral principles. Natural law theorists fit in this category. Probably the most famous proponent of this position is Ronald Dworkin, who asserts that "adjudication is characteristically a matter of principle rather than policy," even while acknowledging that this is a minority view. "Anglo-American lawyers," he writes, "have on the whole been skeptical about the possibility of a 'right answer' in any genuinely hard case." They are skeptical for good reason: lawyers and judges rarely agree about first principles or on how to apply them in difficult cases. For Dworkin, "the root principle" on which courts should base their decisions is that "government must treat people as equals," by which he means the government should actively work to promote equality by providing everyone with equal resources to compete, even if that means restricting liberty. This is a legitimate point of view, but it is not widely shared.[19]

The problem is that it is virtually impossible to come up with a moral code that everyone (or almost everyone) in the legal field accepts. Dworkin admits as much when he writes, "Any judge's opinion about the best interpretation will therefore be the consequence of beliefs other judges need not share."[20] A judge may think he has found moral truth, but he is not likely to find many colleagues who agree with him. Most will side with Oliver Wendell Holmes's claim that "absolute truth is a mirage."[21]

That judges disagree about right and wrong explains why conservatives and liberals engage in bitter political fights over Supreme Court appointments. People on both sides of the ideological divide understand that the Court regularly gets important cases where the law is unclear and where the judges' opinions matter greatly. They do not want their ideological adversaries to dominate the Court, so they try hard to block the other side's candidates. Senator Barack Obama's 2005 statement explaining his vote against John Roberts as chief justice reflects this thinking:

> The problem I face ... is that while adherence to legal precedent and rules of statutory or constitutional construction will dispose of 95 percent of the cases that come before a court ... what matters on the Supreme Court is those 5 percent of cases that are truly difficult. In those cases, adherence to precedent and rules of construction and interpretation will only get you

through the 25th mile of the marathon. That last mile can only be deter-mined on the basis of one's deepest values, one's core concerns, one's broader perspectives on how the world works, and the depth and breadth of one's empathy. In those 5 percent of hard cases, the constitutional text will not be directly on point. The language of the statute will not be perfectly clear. Legal process alone will not lead you to a rule of decision. . . . [I]n those difficult cases, the critical ingredient is supplied by what is in the judge's heart.[22]

What do economists have to say about the good life? Most economists assume that individuals are capable of using their critical faculties to maximize their utility, but this assumption concerns instrumental, not substantive, rationality. On the latter score, which is what we care about here, economists rarely claim that reason can be employed to choose pref-erences or utilities. Instead they assume individual preferences as givens and concentrate on finding the optimal strategy to achieve whatever prefer-ences are on the table. Economics, as Irving Kristol once remarked, "has many useful and important things to tell us, but it really has nothing to say about the larger features of a good society."[23]

Finally, a word is in order about how Leo Strauss thought about our abil-ity to divine the good life, which he took to be the main purpose of political philosophy. The common view of Strauss, a highly influential political phi-losopher, is that he believed that the best and brightest in any society can discern a coherent body of natural laws and rights. These chosen few would use their superior intellect to discover eternal truths, which would help them govern wisely.

This is not an accurate interpretation of Strauss's thinking. Probably the best evidence he did not think this way is that in all of his voluminous writ-ings, he never set out what those purported moral truths are. This lacuna prompted C. Bradley Thompson and Yaron Brook to "challenge Strauss's students to explicate and defend a systematic, secular, rationally demon-strable moral code as objectively *true*."[24] Their challenge went unanswered. This missing body of absolute truths is unsurprising, however, because Strauss himself talks explicitly about "our inability to acquire any genuine knowledge of what is intrinsically good or right."[25] Political philosophy, for Strauss, is all about the pursuit of truth with no promise that anyone will ever discover it. He writes: "Philosophy is essentially not possession of the truth, but quest for the truth. The distinctive tract of the philosopher is that 'he knows that he knows nothing,' and that his insight into our ignorance concerning the most important things induces him to strive with all this power for knowledge. . . . It may be that as regards the possible answers to these questions, the pros and cons will always be in more or less even balance, and therefore that philosophy will never go beyond the stage of discussion or disputation, and will never reach the stage of decision."[26] This is hardly an optimistic view of what our critical faculties can do, even with abundant intellectual horsepower.

A close look at Strauss's writings suggests that he believes reason's strong suit is not discovering truth but calling into question existing moral codes and other widely held beliefs. He comments at one point that "the more we cultivate reason, the more we cultivate nihilism: the less are we able to be loyal members of society."[27] This belief in reason's deconstructive power helps explain why Strauss thinks political philosophers are a danger to their own society and also why he believes political philosophy reached a dead end with Nietzsche.[28] In other words, even though political philosophy is deeply concerned with the noble pursuit of the good life, it is ultimately a self-destructive enterprise because it privileges reason.

Why Truth Is So Elusive

It seems apparent from this evidence, which could easily be amplified, that there are significant limits to what reason can tell us about the good life. Why is this so? Why do people have such difficulty agreeing on first principles? There are two main causes: first, our critical faculties alone cannot provide a universal set of answers to the pivotal questions all of us must confront; and second, the factors other than reason that shape our preferences are often resistant to reason and may even be outside our conscious awareness.

An individual's thinking about the good life is largely shaped by three factors. First and foremost is socialization. Starting at birth, our parents and the broader society bombard us with messages about right and wrong. The principles we are taught largely reflect our society's cultural norms. But because all societies have evolved in different circumstances, they have distinct cultures. The same is also true of families. This means that individuals vary markedly in their thinking about the good life, depending on the circumstances in which they are raised. The social psychologist Jonathan Haidt concludes, "Children somehow end up with a morality that is unique to their culture or group."[29]

The second factor that influences our moral thinking is the set of innate sentiments hardwired into each of us at birth. We are born with a discrete bundle of attitudes or passions that are driven by feelings that are largely independent of the software package that society programs into us over our lifetimes. We are not born as blank slates. All humans, in other words, have different inclinations toward life's big questions even before their families and societies begin shaping how they think.

These innate feelings are hard to measure: we have limited knowledge about how the human brain works. Nevertheless, we see evidence all around us of individuals who were raised in the same family and socialized in similar ways, yet have different personalities and widely dissimilar views about what constitutes the good life. This is not to deny the power of socialization, but if it were the sole driving force, there would be more homogeneity of thought inside families and societies.

Reason is the final factor influencing an individual's core principles. It involves a mental process different from that of sentiment and socialization, both of which rely on intuition. With intuition, individuals make decisions without consciously working through the matter at hand. The person thinks she instinctively knows the correct position to take. Sometimes this position comes quickly, as a visceral response to seeing or hearing about a situation; other times it is a matter of slowly realizing how one feels about an issue, perhaps after repeated exposure to it. Often this realization comes with a sense of having always felt this way but only now coming to acknowledge it consciously. Whether fast or slow, however, sentiment and socialization naturally push individuals to believe they are well equipped to offer insights on a host of issues. Reason, however, operates fundamentally differently.

Reasoning is a process by which humans make a concentrated effort to put aside their intuitions and employ facts and logic to analyze problems and make decisions. An individual employing reason tries to address problems in a systematic and disciplined way without letting his biases or emotions interfere with his thought process. Reasoning is a time-consuming mental activity because it rejects spontaneous responses and instead requires careful construction and evaluation of arguments.[30] Of course, an individual can engage in deliberation, which is where he and others collectively employ their critical faculties to analyze a difficult issue. Reason is a more disciplined form of inference than intuition, and it often provides a more transparent way of answering questions than either sentiment or socialization.[31]

The effort to exclude emotions is often not successful. As Antonio Damasio makes clear, it is impossible to completely separate your critical faculties from your biases and emotions, which, he argues, actually help individuals make well-reasoned decisions.[32]

Despite its elevated ranking, reason is the least important of the three ways we determine our preferences. It certainly is less important than socialization. The main reason socialization matters so much is that humans have a long childhood in which they are protected and nurtured by their families and the surrounding society, and meanwhile exposed to intense socialization. At the same time, they are only beginning to develop their critical faculties, so they are not equipped to think for themselves. By the time an individual reaches the point where his reasoning skills are well developed, his family and society have already imposed an enormous value infusion on him. Moreover, that individual is born with innate sentiments that also strongly influence how he thinks about the world around him. All of this means that people have limited choice in formulating a moral code, because so much of their thinking about right and wrong comes from inborn attitudes and socialization.

Some social psychologists argue that reason has very little to do with the formation of an individual's views about the good life. What reason does best, they claim, is provide a rationale for opinions largely formed by our intuitions.[33] This perspective is stated in its starkest form by the famous British philosopher David Hume, who maintained that "the rules of morality . . . are not conclusions of our reason." For him, "Reason is, and ought only to be the slave of the passions, and can never pretend to any other office than to serve and obey them."[34] There is a place for reasoning in Hume's story, but it comes after the moral code has been established, and its main job is to find clever ways to justify it. This is what instrumental rationality is all about. There is obviously little substantive rationality in Hume's account.

Hume overstates the case. Reason has its limits, but it does more than simply help us rationalize deeply held beliefs. For instance, it tells us that survival is our paramount goal, because we cannot pursue our other goals if we do not survive. And even if it has limited utility in determining what those other goals might be, it can still be useful. Reason can help arbitrate when different intuitions come into conflict. It can also help an individual adjust his first principles when they lead to foolish or destructive behavior. Situations of this sort are not unusual, because occasionally a person's surroundings change and she finds that accustomed ways of thinking about her environment no longer make sense. Finally, there are exceptional individuals who are committed to examining their deepest convictions in coldly analytical ways. Reason can lead such people to new ways of thinking about the world, which others may then follow. We do have agency. We are not mere prisoners of our sentiments and socialization.

Of course, not everyone is committed to rigorous self-examination, but even if they were, there are no grounds for thinking that unfettered reason would lead to universal agreement on what constitutes the good life. Pure reason can take you only so far.

One might argue that education—not just for a society's elite but for every citizen—is the solution to this problem. That was the view held by John Dewey, an early twentieth-century American philosopher who believed that with the proper education, "the average individual would rise to undreamed heights of social and political intelligence."[35] Dewey was well aware that societies are beset with conflicting views on core political and social issues, but he thought democracy coupled with education could resolve these "conflicting claims." He wrote, "The method of democracy—inasfar as it is that of organized intelligence—is to bring these conflicts out into the open where their special claims can be seen and appraised, where they can be discussed and judged. . . . The more the respective claims . . . are publicly and scientifically weighed, the more likely it is that the public interest will be disclosed and be made effective."[36]

The belief that more education will produce consensus about the public interest is intuitively attractive, but on close inspection it falls apart. Because humans are social beings, they tend to form strong bonds with fellow group members. Their loyalty makes it difficult for them to challenge prevailing group wisdoms. The power of groupthink—strong but not absolute—means that most people are not inclined to step outside their social group and act autonomously. Even when they try to act like hard-headed rationalists, they tend to proceed from assumptions based on years of socialization.

There is little reason to think that providing citizens with more education will help them reach broad agreement about the principles that should govern their lives together. In fact, the opposite is more likely. Some forms of education explicitly instruct students in a particular moral view. Madrasas run today by Islamist extremists, the Marxist universities of the former communist world, or the religiously based higher education offered at European and American universities before the twentieth century endorsed official views of the moral life. In some cases these represented (or represent) little more than indoctrination. These forms of education only reinforce existing differences among societies.

Where education exposes people to a variety of perspectives, it typically pushes students to be tolerant, if not respectful, of opposing viewpoints. Education of the sort Dewey prescribes widens rather than narrows one's horizons. In most Western universities, for instance, most educators avoid telling students what to think about value-laden questions, because they are not in the business of proselytizing.[37] In essence, the more education people get, the more complicated the world appears and the more difficult it becomes to believe in, much less discover, timeless truths.

Finally, Dewey's ideal of education invariably involves teaching students to think critically. This is why we refer to our capacity to reason as our critical faculties. Educators (at least good ones) teach their students to ask hard questions and challenge received wisdoms, including their own. It is no accident that the motto of Britain's Royal Society, which describes itself as "the oldest scientific academy in continuous existence," has as its motto: "Take nobody's word for it."[38] The result is that a high-quality education makes students exceptionally good at criticizing purported truths but gives them little training to discover truth other than empirically verifiable fact. Education hones our ability to reason but ultimately makes it more, not less, difficult to reach agreement on first principles.

Where does this leave us? Rousseau said long ago, "I would have wished to be in a country where the sovereign and the people could have only one and the same interest, so that all movements of the machine always tended only to the common happiness."[39] Of course, he was wishing for a state of affairs that can never be, because no group of people can ever achieve that level of agreement on foundational questions. For better or worse, our critical faculties are incapable of leading us to universal truths or categorical laws. We live in a world where relativism is a fact of life, even if most of us do not think of ourselves as relativists.

Our Social Essence

How should we think about the relationship between individuals and their societies? One way, commonly identified with liberalism, is to privilege the individual by arguing that she comes before society, which is effectively an artificial construct that is voluntarily created by a collection of individuals. Individuals in their natural state, so the argument goes, are free agents who develop their identities largely on their own. They choose to form societies and governments for their mutual benefit, but the social groups they form are essentially aggregates of individuals and do not meaningfully shape their members' identities. They are equivalent to marriages of convenience.

This is a mistaken view of human nature. Individuals are social beings from the beginning. The idea that anyone starts life in the state of nature as a socially disconnected individual and lives that way for any period of time is obviously wrong.[40] We all begin life as helpless infants and remain highly dependent on others for at least the first ten years of our lives, during which the people around us deeply influence how we think about and deal with the world. It can be no other way. Our individualism, which is inextricably bound up with our ability to reason, takes at least a few years to develop.

Even if we withdraw to a desolate island, we cannot escape the fact that others have already socialized us in profound ways. Think about Robinson

Crusoe, who was shipwrecked and stranded alone on the Island of Despair for twenty-eight years. His thinking and behavior on that island were heavily shaped by everything he learned growing up in York, England. Daniel Defoe, who wrote *Robinson Crusoe,* said as much in later reflections on the book: "Man is a creature so formed for society, that it may not only be said that it is not good for him to be alone, but 'tis really impossible he should be alone."[41]

It also seems clear, as Defoe hints, that we like interacting with other people. The evidence is overwhelming that humans are psychologically disposed to want to be part of a society. Humans are hardwired to want frequent interactions with other humans, including people outside their immediate families. Hardly anyone moves to a remote area and cuts off all contact with the outside world. Even Ted Kaczynski, the infamous Unabomber, continued to interact with American society, albeit in limited and wicked ways.

The Survival Imperative

Survival is the foremost reason that humans naturally operate in groups larger than the family unit.[42] For starters, individuals need sexual partners, not only to satisfy their desires but also to help create and sustain families and the species more generally.[43] The need to reproduce is common to all species, and for primates that necessitates looking for sexual partners beyond one's immediate family. Of course, having children means that families not only grow in size but also become connected with other families. This pattern facilitates the growth of social groups.

Groups are also more efficient than individuals or single families at providing food and life's other necessities. The people who constitute any sizable group inevitably have a variety of skills and aptitudes, which will allow them to create a division of labor. This kind of specialization and cooperation makes it easier to satisfy the basic needs of daily life, and also facilitates greater prosperity. Furthermore, if a family is alone and runs into serious hardship, say the death of one or both parents, the children have nobody to turn to for help. But if they are embedded in a social group, they have a large support network that can step in and provide assistance. Finally, belonging to a group can help protect a person from someone or some group that might want to harm him, as there is strength in numbers. Large size, however, does not guarantee survival.

A social group, then, is a survival vehicle. By cooperating with each other, members maximize their prospects of not only staying alive but also remaining able to pursue their interests, including their interest in reproducing. Of course, there is no assurance they will survive inside a society, but their chances are generally much better within a group than if they go it alone. Even though there are particular situations in which individuals have a strong incentive to eschew cooperation and act selfishly, the imperative to cooperate more often than not trumps the urge to take advantage of others in the group.

The Importance of Culture

Every society has its own distinctive culture, with different practices and beliefs. Two societies might speak different languages, worship different gods, and have different moral codes, customs, and historical narratives. "Society," Emile Durkheim writes, "is not a mere sum of individuals. Rather, the system formed by their association represents a specific reality which has its own characteristics."[44]

This cultural variety, which militates against the formation of a global society, is due in good part to geography. The planet is huge and the circumstances people face in its countless regions vary greatly, causing groups around the world to develop distinctive routines and ways of thinking. But the diversity also exists because people, using their critical faculties, reach different conclusions about what constitutes the good life. It is not just the environment that shapes culture; individuals have agency. This simple fact of life makes it difficult—though not impossible—to build consensus within a social group. While it is sometimes possible to generate substantial agreement across different societies regarding their practices and beliefs, enough important differences almost always remain to keep those societies functioning as independent entities. This inability to make societies identical explains why the world has been and always will be populated by a vast array of social groups with unique cultures.

Culture is enormously important in shaping how individuals think and behave. The social group that a person is born into is forever a part of his identity. As Antonio Gramsci put it, we are all the product of historical processes that have deposited in us "an infinity of traces, without leaving an inventory."[45] We have little choice regarding the culture in which we are reared and in which our identity is deeply bound up. The cultural software that the society provides to an individual in those critically important formative years heavily influences how he thinks about himself and the world around him, and how he acts in his daily life.

An individual can reject the culture she was born into, either by attempting to change it or by joining a different society.[46] Transforming a society's culture not only is exceedingly difficult—cultures have deep roots—but doomed to only partial success. Even an individual who succeeds still cannot change the fact that she was shaped in large part by the culture she seeks to transform, and that even in defiance she remains in many ways its prisoner. Similarly, someone who leaves an old life brings to his new life cultural baggage that will continue to shape his identity in important ways.

Think about an immigrant coming to the United States. No matter how fervently he embraces American culture and rejects the values and traditions of the old country, his identity will always be heavily influenced by the culture of his youth. Hans Morgenthau and Leo Strauss, for example, left Europe as young men in the 1930s and came to the United States, where they became major figures in American intellectual life. Yet their thinking about the world remained deeply influenced by German intellectuals such as Martin Heidegger, Friedrich Nietzsche, Carl Schmitt, and Max Weber, whom they had read as students and fledgling scholars in Europe.[47]

Culture is important for another reason: it is the glue that helps hold a society together. Humans may be social animals, but the people who make up a society are individuals as well as community members. Despite all the socialization they undergo, they are capable of thinking for themselves, and often do. Sometimes they do not cooperate with others to solve important problems but instead act in selfish and harmful ways. More importantly, as we have seen, people in any social group have difficulty reaching shared agreement about first principles. Centrifugal forces of varying intensity are at work in every society and are sometimes strong enough to make it violently fly apart.

Culture plays an essential role in keeping those centrifugal forces at bay. First, within social groups there is usually considerable (though never complete) agreement about first principles because the members share similar daily lives and have a common history. Most of them, having been heavily socialized since birth to venerate their culture, will have a sense (to quote Edmund Burke) that their society is "a partnership not only between those who are living, but between those who are living, those who are dead, and those who are to be born."[48] Group members also tend to respect each other and develop powerful group loyalties that help them get along despite their differences. Members are likely to feel they are part of a common enterprise in which people work together for the good of the collective. Most members strongly identify the group's survival with their own, giving them a powerful incentive to cooperate and to agree to disagree even on major issues.

Yet there are limits to what culture can do to hold a society together. Sometimes a single issue exposes such deep divisions that it threatens to tear the society apart. (Think about the slavery issue in the United States before the Civil War.) Sometimes radically new circumstances undermine a society's key practices and beliefs, revealing deep disagreements among the members as they attempt to reformulate their views on what constitutes the good life. (Think about Germany after its devastating defeat in World War I.) Sometimes unanticipated stresses are so great that the society loses coherence. (Think of Chinese society after European colonization during the nineteenth century.)

When substantial numbers of people in a society reject important aspects of their culture or act selfishly because they believe they are no longer part of a common enterprise, it is difficult for the community to survive unless those dissatisfied persons are either mollified or made to leave. In brief, individuals may naturally operate within social groups, but their level of commitment to the collectivity can vary enormously. Attachment obviously promotes group solidarity, while disillusionment, if sufficiently widespread, leads to the demise of the group and the birth of new ones in its place.

That centrifugal forces are at play in every society and occasionally lead to its unraveling tells us that culture alone is not enough to hold a society together. There are three other ways to keep a society intact. One is to create a foreign bogeyman sufficiently fearful to motivate the society's members to work together to defend against the threat. Another is to unify a majority by defining a treacherous "other" within the society itself. But the most important way societies prevent disintegration is by building formidable political institutions, for which there is no substitute.

Political Institutions and Power

Societies need political institutions in order to deal with other groups and to help their members live together peacefully and productively. Within the group, individuals constantly interact with each other and sometimes compete over matters like resources and money. They engage in sharp disputes about broader societal goals and how best to achieve them. Thus those individuals, as well as the factions and social organizations they form, need rules that define acceptable and unacceptable conduct and also dictate how disputes will be settled.[49]

Social groups also need mechanisms to interpret and enforce these rules. They need a way to adjudicate disputes and punish rule breakers. In some cases they have to prevent or stop violence among their members. They need some person or body responsible for organizing and administering daily life to ensure that no member endangers other members' survival. Simply put, they need authorities. Social groups have a powerful incentive to move beyond anarchy and create hierarchy.[50]

Societies also need political institutions for another reason: to help shield them from other social groups that might have an incentive to attack and maybe destroy them. In this their aim is not to transcend anarchy but to determine how best to survive in a world where a group that gets into trouble has no higher authority to turn to. Such a group will need some sort of military force to maximize its prospects for survival. All of this is to say the society's political institutions should control the means of violence, not only to enforce the rules at home but also to protect against foreign enemies. Those institutions will have to deal with the outside world on more mundane matters as well, because survival, while vitally important, is not a group's only concern.

To this point, I have portrayed political institutions as largely neutral instruments that favor no individual or faction over others—suggesting that there are no politics in my story. In fact, political institutions are not impartial bodies. The rules that govern social groups reflect a particular vision of the good life and invariably favor some individuals' or factions' interests more than others'. Therefore, it matters greatly who writes, interprets, and enforces the rules, because whoever does these things can shape daily life in ways that reflect her interests and views about the good life. There will almost always be fierce competition within any social group to determine who controls its political institutions. Politics is a staple of everyday life in any society.

At its deepest level, politics is a conflict over first principles, which is not to deny its more mundane side. Political competition revolves around conflicting visions of how society should be organized or how the individuals and factions within it should interact with each other. This competition is usually intense and sometimes it involves chicanery, coercion, and violence. As former president Bill Clinton once remarked, politics is a "contact sport" that inevitably produces winners and losers, although their positions are not guaranteed to be permanent.[51]

At a more practical level, politics in any society is all about competing for control of the governing institutions. Here is where power, which is based on resources like money, social capital, and access to media, matters. The more powerful a person or faction, the more likely it is to prevail in the political arena, which will then allow it to shape the society's political institutions in ways that enhance its own interests and power.[52] In other words, the mighty get to determine, in Harold Lasswell's famous words, "who gets what, when, how."[53] Winners are not prevented from pursuing policies that benefit almost everyone in the group, although how much each person profits is another matter. The institutions that govern any society are not simply fairminded arbiters or night watchmen: they are political actors at their core.

Politics among Social Groups

The interactions among social groups are also political. While the balance of power matters in intergroup relations as well as in intragroup relations, there is an important difference between the two realms. Within a society, who writes and interprets the rules matters greatly. But rules do not matter nearly as much in interactions among social groups, because there is no superior authority to enforce them. Social groups operate in an anarchic setting.[54] More importantly, there is no higher authority policing intergroup behavior to make sure one group does not threaten another group's survival. This is not to say survival is guaranteed inside a society, because it is not. But within a group there are political institutions with substantial coercive power that can protect the group's members.[55]

The importance of power in anarchy is not that it determines who writes the rules, because rules do not matter much in intergroup relations, but that it is the best means for societies to protect themselves against violent threats from another society. They want abundant material resources, especially military ones, to maximize their prospects of survival in the face of existential threats. In the absence of a higher political authority, fear is a powerful motivator. Social groups also want power because it allows them to pursue other goals as well. They understand Thucydides's maxim: in an anarchic system, "the strong do what they can and the weak suffer what they must."[56] No society can ever be too powerful relative to its competitors.

The Imperative to Expand

Social groups are strongly inclined to grow at the expense of other groups. Not every society has the ability to expand, but the incentive is ever present. There are several possible motives for enlargement, one of which is ideology. The leaders of a society may think they have discovered the true religion or the ideal political system and want to export it to other societies, because they think it would benefit humankind. A more likely impulse, however, is economic. A group might want to seize another group's land or raw materials, or simply incorporate the other group's economy into its own so as to make itself larger and wealthier.

But the main reason societies seek to expand is survival. Because groups can have different interests and profound disagreements about core principles, there is always the possibility one group will threaten another group's survival. That threat can take different forms. One group might try to kill everyone in a rival group. Or it may leave the target society intact but deny it autonomy. The aggressor controls the resources of the conquered group and heavily influences its politics, or even enslaves it. Finally, the target society may simply be absorbed into the victor's society. All of these outcomes are disastrous for any society, and fear of them leads societies to fear each other and to worry about their survival.

One of the best ways for a society to increase its survival prospects is to become more powerful. The best insurance is to be much more powerful than all the others. The strong do not always defeat the weak, but they do more often than not. Thus, for purposes of maximizing security, social groups have a strong incentive to incorporate or dominate—even eradicate—other groups. Doing so not only makes a society more powerful but also eliminates potential rivals. It should be clear from this discussion that it is difficult to separate the economic and survival motives, because wealth is one of the key prerequisites of military power.

The discussion so far has emphasized expansion at the end of a rifle barrel. But there is another way for a group to expand: it can form a social contract with a like-minded group. It is possible, although highly unlikely, that two societies would voluntarily join together because they have similar cultures, agree in good part on core values, and have few conflicting interests. A union might promise greater prosperity for both societies. Egypt and Syria coming together to form the United Arab Republic in 1958 is an example of this kind of union. But unsurprisingly the new country fell apart after only three years. It is also possible, although extremely unlikely, that two social groups might think about the good life in different ways, but one is able to convince the other to accept its way of thinking and join together to form a larger whole. The most likely reason for two societies to merge is a common threat that makes unification into a more powerful entity seem like a good bet to increase their prospects of survival.[57]

These voluntary associations are hard to engineer. Social groups rarely give up their independence to become part of a larger whole. Expansion is almost always the result of one society coercing or conquering another. Societies tend to have markedly different cultures that generally entail fundamental differences over first principles, making it hard for any group to persuade another to abandon its way of life and accept a new set of practices and beliefs. Any society bent on expanding its borders will in all likelihood have to do it by force.

Yet there are limits to what can be achieved by force. Coercion and conquest sometimes work well, but certainly not all of the time. One problem an expansionist group faces is that the target is likely to resist its advances, often with fanatical zeal. Even if the attacking forces defeat an opponent, the victim still might find subtle and sophisticated ways to resist integration.[58] Moreover, as a society grows, its potential for disintegration increases, simply because a greater population brings a greater possibility of profound differences about what constitutes the good life. The more different the cultures that are merged, the more severe these value differences are likely to be.[59]

Furthermore, even if a society conquers and absorbs many other groups, it still faces significant limits on additional enlargement. One problem is that there is an abundance of groups on the planet and few of the remaining ones would go down without a fight. And because those groups are spread out around the globe, any group bent on dominating all the others will find that distance makes it harder and harder to project power—a problem that is made worse by large bodies of water, mountain ranges, and deserts.[60] Any society can expand only so far before the law of diminishing returns sets in.

These barriers to expansion go a long way toward explaining why there is no global society, and thus why the international system is anarchic.

Survival and the Human Condition

My bottom line is straightforward. Our critical faculties cannot provide definitive answers to questions regarding the good life, and so there will always be serious disagreements about these issues, which matter greatly to both individuals and societies. These differences sometimes lead to such a deep hostility that one or both parties are moved to act aggressively. The fact that many people believe universal truth exists and that they have found it only makes the situation worse, as thinking in terms of absolutes makes it hard to promote compromise and tolerance. If almost everyone were a self-acknowledged moral relativist, it would foster a live-and-let-live zeitgeist that would help make the world a more peaceful place. But people are not like that, and the fact that those who disagree with you may be inclined to kill you means that individuals as well as societies will fear each other and worry about their survival.

Fortunately, human social groups are configured to address the twin problems of fear and survival. The prevailing culture in any society contains a package of practices and beliefs to which members are introduced when they are young, and which they hear about for the rest of their lives. Most of these principles are accepted by most members most of the time, which has the effect of reducing but not eliminating conflict over them. Culture works like glue—it is essential to a society's cohesion—but it is not sufficient by itself. Societies also construct political institutions that write rules and maintain order, which fosters some tolerance and helps prevent their members from killing each other when they clash over important issues. Yet the potential for conflict never goes away completely.

Simply put, the fact that we live in a world populated by social beings with impressive but limited critical faculties is the taproot of human conflict.

To be crystal clear, I am not arguing that individuals are naturally bad or evil. The political philosopher Carl Schmitt maintained that ultimately every theory of politics revolves around the assumption that humans are either essentially good or essentially bad, and some famous thinkers did in fact base their theories on such assumptions.[61] Rousseau, for example, argued that humans are essentially good in their natural condition but are corrupted by society.[62] Reinhold Niebuhr, on the other hand, believed that humans are born with original sin, which means they are primed to misbehave in various ways for the rest of their lives.[63]

One problem with Schmitt's perspective is that good and bad are vague concepts whose meaning is hard to pin down. To the extent that we can wrap our heads around them, surely everyone has some of both traits. Anyway, if one does employ this distinction, what explains why people are naturally good or bad? Attributing it to original sin or something similar does not provide an explanation that we can evaluate through any sort of evidence.

I am also not arguing that humans are naturally aggressive, as some sociobiologists claim, or that they possess an *animus dominandi,* as Hans

Morgenthau famously asserted.[64] For sure, some people fit this model, but there are also many who do not. The human species is a variegated lot; we are not all type A personalities. Moreover, one could argue that natural selection leads first and foremost to cooperation, not aggression. Individuals have powerful incentives to cooperate with others, especially fellow members of their group, to maximize their survival prospects. Of course, humans sometimes behave aggressively—and the propensity for aggression certainly varies from one person to the next—but in my story it is often because they have fundamental disagreements about first principles, not because aggression is a hardwired first reaction to any given situation. They may also act aggressively because their environment encourages them to do so. For example, they may be members of a social group, operating in an anarchic system, that is bent on expanding to maximize its chances of survival. The same individuals might be much less aggressive in a hierarchic system.

The great isms of liberalism, realism, and nationalism do not operate in a state of mathematical abstraction: they work the way they do because humanity is the way it is. When we turn to examine liberalism (which I will do in the next chapter) it will be in light of the ideas about human nature and politics that I have just outlined.

3

Political Liberalism

WE CAN THINK OF POLITICAL LIBERALISM as coming in two variants: modus vivendi liberalism and progressive liberalism. They share a common view of human nature, which emphasizes individualism as well as the limits of our critical faculties to discover collective truths about the good life. Both stress the importance of inalienable rights (rights that cannot be taken away or voluntarily given up), tolerance, and the need for a state to maintain public order.

There are two key differences between modus vivendi and progressive liberals: they think differently about the content of individual rights and about the role of the state. For modus vivendi liberals, rights are all about individual freedom to act without government interference. Freedom of the press and the right to own property are two examples. Progressive liberals also prize individual freedoms, but they also believe in rights that call for the government to help its citizens. They think all individuals have a right to equal opportunity, which requires social engineering by the state to ensure that right is realized. Modus vivendi liberals do not recognize that right and are generally skeptical about the benefits of social engineering. They tend to have a minimalist view of how much the state should interfere in the daily lives of its citizens, while progressive liberals favor a more activist government.

One might think that modus vivendi and progressive liberals fundamentally disagree about the power of our critical faculties to determine first principles. Progressives tend to emphasize that reason facilitates extreme tolerance in liberal societies and can even help us move toward universal consensus on moral matters. Modus vivendi liberals clearly reject those claims and instead emphasize reason's limits. And while they recognize the importance of tolerance, they are more inclined than progressive liberals to see its limits too. But closer inspection reveals no meaningful difference between the two strains of liberalism on these matters. Progressive liberals cannot back up their optimistic claims for what reason can tell us about the good life, and they ultimately end up sounding like modus vivendi liberals.

Concerning our ability to reason, progressive and modus vivendi liberals think differently about the effectiveness of social engineering, which involves using one's critical faculties for instrumental purposes, not for determining ultimate goals. Progressive liberals have more faith in instrumental rationality than do modus vivendi liberals. Thus the taproot of progressivism is not reason in the service of determining first principles or promoting tolerance, but an expansive view of individual rights coupled with a belief in the state's ability to do social engineering.

A glance at how contemporary liberal societies are organized makes it clear that progressive liberalism has triumphed over modus vivendi liberalism. This is not to deny that liberal democracies contain a substantial number of modus vivendi liberals, or argue that progressive liberalism is intellectually superior. But progressive liberalism has won the day in real-world influence. Contemporary liberal societies cannot be organized along the lines prescribed by modus vivendi liberalism because the structural forces that buffet modern states demand the kind of interventionist policies that are at the core of progressive liberalism. Political leaders operate in a world that is too complicated for modus vivendi liberalism's laissez-faire approach to governing. Because there is today no substitute for an interventionist state, political liberalism is now synonymous with progressive liberalism.

The best starting point for examining political liberalism is to define the features that modus vivendi and progressive liberalism have in common. This is liberalism's hard core. Next I will analyze both variants of political liberalism, emphasizing their differences, and then explain why progressive liberalism is now the dominant form. Finally, I will briefly examine a pair of theories—utilitarianism and liberal idealism—that are sometimes labeled liberal, but are not (even if one of them has the word *liberal* in its name), because they do not share political liberalism's emphasis on natural rights. They operate according to fundamentally different logics than either modus vivendi or progressive liberalism. Utilitarianism and liberal idealism may be important theories, but they are not *liberal* theories, and so they fall outside the scope of this book.

Political Liberalism

The liberal story begins with atomized individuals in the state of nature, where they are said to have a common set of traits. In this "state of perfect freedom" they are all endowed with a set of inalienable rights and they are all equals. John Locke, one of liberalism's founders, describes the state of nature as "a state also of equality, wherein all the power and jurisdiction is reciprocal, no one having more than another; there being nothing more evident than that creatures of the same species and rank, promiscuously born to all the same advantages of nature and the use of the same faculties, should also be equal one amongst another without subordination or subjection."[1]

This emphasis on individualism represented a radical break with the writings of premodern political philosophers such as Aristotle, Aquinas, Augustine, Machiavelli, and Plato, all of whom assumed that humans are naturally political or social beings. As Alexis de Tocqueville put it, "Our ancestors had no word for *individualism,* a word we have coined for our own use because, in their time, there was no individual who did not belong to a group or who could consider himself to be entirely alone."[2] Nor did these "ancestors" think that all individuals should be seen as equals. They thought that some men are born with superior talents and thus deserve to rule the less capable.[3]

Political liberalism's second foundational assumption concerns our ability to reason. There is no question humans possess impressive critical faculties. But as we have seen, their ability to reason has only limited use for determining what constitutes the good life. Reason alone does not dictate how people think about life's big questions but is subordinate to sentiments and socialization. Even when individuals deliberately set out to make well-reasoned judgments about first principles, or make moral deductions from those principles, there are at least some disagreements, save for the universal agreement (among liberals) that all individuals are naturally bestowed with a set of rights.

When individuals differ over first principles, they sometimes end up hating and trying to harm each other. This basic logic is laid out in the writings of Thomas Hobbes, who, though he was not a liberal theorist, articulated some of the seminal ideas underpinning liberalism.[4] At first glance, Locke appears to take a different view: he begins his *Second Treatise* by extolling the virtues of reason, making it seem like the state of nature, unlike the one depicted in Hobbes's *Leviathan,* is an idyllic place. Locke quickly changes his story, however, and ends up portraying the state of nature as rather nasty and brutish, in good part because of the "variety of opinions and contrariety of interests, which unavoidably happen in all collections of men."[5]

The threat of conflict sits at the heart of political liberalism. The key question is what can be done to ameliorate that danger.

The Liberal Formula for Maintaining Order

Political liberals have a three-pronged strategy for dealing with the possibility of deadly conflict. First, they emphasize that everyone's set of inalienable rights includes the right to life, which means not only the right to survive but also the freedom to live the good life as one sees fit. People have the right to choose whatever lifestyle they want, as long as it does not infringe on the rights of others. This specifically includes "freedom of conscience," the right to live according to one's religious beliefs. Rights are designed to maximize the amount of freedom individuals have in their daily lives. The most famous sentence in America's Declaration of Independence succinctly captures this first prong of political liberalism: "We hold these truths to be self-evident, that all men are created equal, that they are endowed by their Creator with certain unalienable Rights, that among these are Life, Liberty and the pursuit of Happiness."

The second prong in the strategy is to purvey the norm of toleration. If individuals have the right to pursue their own way of life, others have an affirmative duty to recognize this right.[6] The norm of toleration tells us that we should accept that others will sometimes disagree with us about core principles, and that even if we intensely dislike or despise what others think or say, we may not punish or kill them for their views. Instead, everyone will adopt a live-and-let-live approach to life, resolve their conflicts peacefully, and maintain a healthy respect for the law. At best, individuals might come to respect opposing viewpoints about the good life and think that fundamental differences make for a healthy society.[7] We come together, one might argue, by accepting our differences. But it is imperative that people at least tolerate those with whom they have profound disagreements.

But tolerance has its limits. Some people feel so passionately about particular aspects of the good life that they cannot abide disagreement. They find it impossible to believe that other worldviews can be held in good faith—the people who hold those views, they imagine, must be deliberately turning away from the truth and are perhaps evil. This intolerant mind-set makes them a threat not just to their antagonists but to liberal society itself. The fact that not everyone will be committed to value pluralism brings us to the third prong in the liberal strategy: a strong state that sits above society and maintains order. The state is well suited for this task because, as Max Weber famously said, it holds a "monopoly of the legitimate use of physical force within a given territory."[8]

The state, to maintain order, assumes three principal roles. Most importantly, it acts as a night watchman that protects individual rights and prevents mortal combat between people or factions with conflicting views. Liberalism, to borrow Thomas Carlyle's phrase, is "anarchy plus a constable."[9] The state also writes the rules that define acceptable and unacceptable conduct while going to great lengths not to trample on individual rights. These rules allow individuals or groups to interact in civil ways as each pursues its own version of the good life. Finally, the state acts as an arbiter when serious disputes arise, to ensure that conflicts do not lead to violence.[10] The state, in other words, functions as rule maker, umpire, and night watchman.

The liberal state obviously performs more functions than those aimed at keeping domestic order. Progressive liberals want the state to promote equal opportunity for its citizens and engage in other forms of social engineering as well. Modus vivendi liberals would surely object, but even they mostly agree that the state has to manage its economy and conduct foreign policy. A host of other matters, such as education, social security, housing, and labor relations, also require the attention of even a laissez-faire government, if it hopes to avoid economic depression, chaos, and unrest. In short, modern liberalism cannot work without a strong state.

Still, political liberals of all persuasions have mixed views about the state's role. Although they know the state is essential for preserving order and allowing civil society to flourish, they also recognize its powerful potential to trample on individual rights. As the political theorist Judith Shklar put it in an important essay on liberalism: "The fear and favor that have always inhibited freedom are overwhelmingly generated by governments, both formal and informal. And while the sources of social oppression are indeed numerous, none has the deadly effect of those who, as agents of the modern state, have unique resources of physical might and persuasion at their disposal."[11] Nevertheless, as the quintessential liberal Thomas Paine wrote, government is in the final analysis a "necessary evil."[12]

Liberals thus look for ways to limit the state's power. For example, liberal states can set up a political order built around checks and balances; or they can adopt federalism, where the central government delegates substantial power to regional authorities. Because liberal countries are invariably democracies, there is always the risk that the majority will tyrannize the minority. One way to minimize this danger is to write a clearly articulated bill of rights into the constitution.

It is important to emphasize that, outside of its night-watchman function, a liberal state seeks to stay out of the business of telling people what kind of behavior is morally correct or incorrect. It encourages (and sometimes requires) toleration and works to ensure the prosperity and security of its citizens. The central aim, however, is to allow people, as much as possible, to live according to their own principles. Liberalism is distinct from republicanism, which emphasizes an individual's duties and obligations and favors a state that actively promotes civic virtue. It is also fundamentally at odds with Aristotle's view that "the end of politics" is to produce "citizens of a certain sort—that is, good people and doers of noble actions."[13] A purely liberal state is soulless: it creates few emotional bonds between citizens and their government, which is why it is sometimes said that getting people to fight and die for a liberal state is especially difficult.[14]

It should be apparent by now that the liberal story envisions a distinct boundary between the state and civil society.[15] The state is the product of a social contract drawn up by a large body of individuals who go to considerable lengths to make sure the government they create does not interfere too much in their lives. The goal is to limit the amount of what Herbert Spencer called "ministerial overseeing," so as to maximize people's freedom to lead their own version of the good life.[16] Modus vivendi liberals and progressive liberals disagree on what is the appropriate amount of ministerial oversight.

Liberalism also seeks to minimize the importance of politics as much as possible. As I noted earlier, politics at its most basic level is about conflicts over fundamental questions regarding the good life. This is what makes it an adversarial enterprise. Liberalism tries to ameliorate political conflict by giving individuals abundant freedom to live their lives as they see fit, thus removing at least part of the reason for fighting over first principles. As Markus Fischer notes, "Liberalism has pacified political life by emptying it of much of its meaning."[17] Or as Stephen Holmes puts it, liberalism seeks "to remove from the public agenda issues that are impossible to resolve by either argument or compromise."[18]

Yet even as they try to attenuate politics, liberals acknowledge the importance of allowing individuals to freely engage in economic activity. Their ultimate aim is to create a world where economics overshadows politics.[19] This line of thinking, clearly reflected in the writings of John Locke, was pushed forward in its most comprehensive form by Adam Smith. He argues for doing as much as possible to keep the government from interfering in the economy so that individuals can pursue their own self-interest, which he claims will ultimately work to the benefit of the entire society. The "invisible hand," he maintains, will guide the market to create increasing abundance, whereas the state, if it tried to guide the economy, would be more of a hindrance than a help. It is no exaggeration to say that capitalism and liberalism go hand in hand.

Liberals understand that there will always be serious political disputes between individuals and between factions. Those quarrels, however, are settled by the state, which writes the rules and enforces them. The state is the ultimate arbiter in a process built around peaceful conflict resolution. Predictably, political liberalism places much emphasis on courts and the rule of law, since it aims to deal with political problems in the legal system, not the political arena. John Gray captures this point in his assessment of John Rawls's thinking: "The central institution of Rawls's 'political liberalism' is not a deliberative assembly such as a parliament. It is a court of law. All fundamental questions are removed from political deliberation in order to be adjudicated by a Supreme Court. The self-description of Rawlsian doctrine as political liberalism is supremely ironic. In fact, Rawls's doctrine is a species of anti-political legalism."[20]

There are limits, however, on the ability of liberal states to minimize politics. The most important limit is that the state is unable to be neutral, mainly because it writes the rules that govern much of daily life, and many of those rules deal with first principles. Given the inevitable sharp differences over what constitutes the good life, it matters enormously which faction in a society gets to write the rules. This means there will be marked competition to win high office. This competition is likely to be especially intense in liberal states because they are also democracies, which carries at least the theoretical possibility of a transfer of power through an election. Authoritarian states actually have less room for politics because iron control from the top either stamps out or limits public competition for office. In short, politics is guaranteed to be part of daily life in liberal states, simply because there is no way of completely eliminating deep disagreements over first principles.

The liberal formula for separating the state from civil society and trying to reduce the influence of politics marks a fundamental break with previous thinking about the optimum political order. In the writings of ancient philosophers such as Aristotle and Plato, political institutions and civil society were woven closely together; actively participating in politics was a necessary element of a good life. Engaging in the public sphere was considered a noble enterprise, and thus it was a mark of distinction to be a prominent public figure. Even Machiavelli, who emphasized the harsh and cruel side of politics in *The Prince,* saw the state and civil society as a seamless web. He stressed that clever political strategies could serve the pursuit of noble political goals, especially republicanism.[21] Liberalism offers a much different way of thinking about politics and the good life.

Liberalism's Paradoxes

Two paradoxes embedded in liberalism merit discussion before we examine the differences between modus vivendi and progressive liberalism. The first paradox concerns tolerance. In any liberal society, some people will reject liberalism and would overturn the political order if given the opportunity. If a substantial number of people held this view, they would surely present a mortal threat to liberalism. It would make little sense in these circumstances for liberals to practice toleration toward their enemies, since a live-and-let-live approach could destroy the regime.

Liberals, of course, are aware of this danger, which means liberalism has a sense of vulnerability at its core that naturally provokes a tendency toward intolerance among liberals. This logic explains in good part why Locke, who wrote a famous essay on the virtues of toleration, was intolerant in his writings toward atheists and Catholics. He believed Catholics could not be trusted because of their allegiance to the pope and their own intolerance, and that atheists could not be trusted because their pledges were not backed up by divine sanction. Both groups were thus, in his mind, a threat to liberalism.[22] In practice, the level of threat varies, and this intolerance is usually kept at bay.

Liberalism tends toward intolerance for another reason as well. Most liberals consider liberalism superior to other kinds of political order and believe the world would be a better place if it were populated solely by liberal regimes. There is a sense of both vulnerability and superiority wired into liberalism that fosters intolerance despite the theory's emphasis on purveying tolerance to maintain domestic harmony.

There is another seeming contradiction at liberalism's core. The theory contains both a particularist and a universalist strand, which stand in marked contrast to each other. The universalist strand springs from liberalism's deep-seated commitment to individual rights. There are no boundaries or borders when it comes to human rights: they apply to every person on the planet. To be clear, the claim is not that individuals *should* have those rights but that all people axiomatically *do* have them. There are no meaningful limits to our ability to reason when it comes to comprehending rights. One might say this is the pacific dimension of liberalism, because respect for the rights of others should promote tolerance and discourage violent behavior.

The particularist strand, on the other hand, stems from the liberal belief that it is impossible to get unanimous agreement on what constitutes the good life. Here we see the limits of reason at play. Some people will agree some of the time, but not all of them all of the time—and their disagreements will sometimes be so passionate that they are motivated to harm each other. One might call this liberalism's conflictual dimension, which underpins the need for the state to function as night watchman.

Political liberalism thus has a universalist strand that emphasizes the power of reason, inalienable rights, and nonviolence as well as a particularist strand that stresses the limits of reason, disagreements about first principles, and the fractious nature of politics. How do these opposing components of liberalism relate to each other? And which one is dominant?

The overall theory seems to privilege the particularist strand, but this does not mean the universalist strand is of little consequence. The reason is straightforward. If liberalism's story about rights were truly compelling, there would be no need for a strong state to maintain order. A pervasive respect for individual rights would guarantee toleration and largely eliminate the need for a higher authority to prevent murder and mayhem. But virtually every liberal theorist recognizes the limits of tolerance and thus the need for a state to keep the peace. Passionate and potentially deadly disputes over what defines the good life will always be with us. Tolerance by itself is not enough, which is another way of saying the particularist strand ultimately has more explanatory power in the liberal story than the universalist one.

Modus Vivendi Liberalism

The main arguments put forth by both modus vivendi and progressive liberals are fully consistent with the above description of political liberalism. The aim in this section and the next one is to examine the fine points of each variant and show how they differ.

A number of political theorists who qualify as modus vivendi liberals would not necessarily agree with every detail of the composite picture sketched below. John Locke is a quintessential modus vivendi liberal, as are Adam Smith and Friedrich Hayek. Two contemporary political theorists who fit in this category are John Gray and Stephen Holmes. Many other liberal theorists make arguments that fit squarely with modus vivendi liberalism but promote other ideas that are at odds with it. These people—John Stuart Mill is one—are hard to put in the modus vivendi camp. Where appropriate, I will draw on the writings of these modus vivendi liberals to illustrate my main points.

Modus vivendi liberals are deeply pessimistic about our ability to reach agreement on core principles. "Rational inquiry," Gray writes, "shows that the good life comes in many varieties. . . . Reason can enlighten us as to our ethical conflicts. Often, it shows them to be deeper than we thought, and leaves us in the lurch as to how to resolve them."[23] This pessimism is magnified by the fact that individuals often make decisions without the aid of reason. As Holmes notes: "All classical liberals were perfectly aware that most human behavior is noncalculating, habitual, and emotional and that most human goals are nonmaterial."[24] Reason, it seems, does not point us to any objective truth about what political order is best.

Modus vivendi liberals believe the essential function of rights is to give individuals maximum personal freedom to pursue their own interests. Their emphasis is almost exclusively on negative rights—those that protect individuals from being constrained by others, including the government. They pay great attention to the right to own and exchange property, an emphasis that helps explain why liberalism is closely tied to capitalism. Finally, although modus vivendi liberals believe that all individuals are equal, they do not believe that this equality requires the government to level the playing field for its citizens.

Tolerance is obviously central for modus vivendi liberals. Although they advocate a live-and-let-live approach to daily life, coexistence has its limits. They believe in the importance of a strong state that can maintain order, but beyond that they would, as much as possible, prevent the state from interfering in civil society.

This perspective is hardly surprising, since modus vivendi liberals oppose state efforts to foster equality of opportunity, which would entail significant government action. Creating equal opportunity would involve redistributing resources, which would surely have adverse consequences for private property and also impinge on personal freedom. More generally, modus vivendi liberals do not like the idea of the state interfering in society to promote any kind of individual rights. Instead, the paramount goal should be simply to protect rights that might be threatened. Nor do they believe the state should try to manage the economy unless absolutely necessary. The preference instead is to build an economy based on unrestricted competition in open markets.

The pessimism of modus vivendi liberals about our critical faculties goes beyond simply saying we cannot agree on first principles. They also tend to think the state cannot act intelligently to achieve ambitious goals. Governments, they argue, do not make meaningful progress; they hinder it. In essence, modus vivendi liberals question whether states are instrumentally rational, which predisposes them to believe that almost all forms of government-directed social engineering are likely to fail. There is no place for an expansive welfare state in modus vivendi liberalism.

Ultimately, modus vivendi liberalism is not an optimistic or progressive theory of politics.[25] The state is supposed to take a laissez-faire approach to governing: its goal should be simply to keep disagreements from turning deadly and to allow people as much freedom as possible to live as they see fit.

Progressive Liberalism

Progressive liberals tell a more hopeful story about political life. One might think from reading some of their works that this is because they are more sanguine about the capacity of human reason to answer critical questions regarding the good life. Some even appear to say that we can discover absolute truths. Others suggest that reason promotes deep tolerance among citizens in a liberal society, thus largely removing the threat of violence. But on close inspection, these claims do not hold up, and the progressive liberals who make them invariably backtrack and end up admitting, like modus vivendi liberals, that we cannot use our critical faculties to reach a universal consensus on what constitutes the good life.

What really gives progressive liberals a more hopeful outlook than modus vivendi liberals is how they think about individual rights and the state's ability to do social engineering in the service of those rights. They have a more expansive view of rights, especially regarding their belief that everyone has a right to equal opportunity. They also believe that governments have both a responsibility and the ability to pursue policies that ensure that outcome. Their faith in governments' capacity to act in instrumentally rational ways sets them apart from modus vivendi liberals, who have no such faith. Progressive liberals also recognize the need for the state to act as a night watchman, since they understand that it is not possible to achieve consensus on first principles.

Progressive liberalism has its roots in the Enlightenment, which, as Isaac Kramnick notes, "valorized the individual and the moral legitimacy of self-interest," but also trumpeted the importance of "unassisted human reason, not faith or tradition."[26] As Jeremy Waldron put it, "The relationship between liberal thought and the legacy of the Enlightenment cannot be stressed too strongly. The Enlightenment was characterized by a burgeoning confidence in the human ability to make sense of the world, to grasp its regularities and fundamental principles, to predict its future, and to manipulate its powers for the benefit of mankind."[27]

The most prominent progressive liberals over the past fifty years include Ronald Dworkin, Francis Fukuyama, Steven Pinker, and John Rawls. Fukuyama's famous 1989 article "The End of History?," which argued that with the fall of communism the question of the ideal form of government had largely been answered in favor of liberal democracy, is an outstanding example of this genre. Rawls, of course, was one of the most influential political philosophers of modern times, while Dworkin was a giant among legal philosophers. Pinker is probably the most famous proponent of the claim that the triumph of reason and liberal values has played a key role in reducing violence around the world. Going back further in time, the French philosopher Nicolas de Condorcet fits in this category, as does Immanuel Kant, who wrote: "Have courage to use your own reason—that is the motto of Enlightenment."[28]

The Power of Reason

Many progressive liberals believe reason, coupled with certain discoverable principles, is the key to making the world a better place, a conviction reflected in Dworkin's comment that "liberalism cannot be based on skepticism."[29] There are actually two variants of progressive liberalism, each with a different take on what our critical faculties can tell us. Let us call them bounded and unbounded progressives.

The unbounded progressives have the most faith in reason. They claim that when we collectively discover first principles and couple them with universal respect for individual rights, it effectively takes violent conflict off the table. Bounded progressives, while they have more faith in reason than modus vivendi liberals, do not think people around the world can reach a consensus on questions about the good life. But they do believe people in liberal societies are smart enough to accept those differences and not fight over them. Abundant tolerance, accompanied by peaceful conflict resolution and respect for the law, governs daily life wherever liberalism reigns.

Both kinds of progressivism have an unrealistic understanding of what our critical faculties can do for us. It is not possible to argue (at least not successfully) that there are truths about first principles that virtually everyone accepts. Nor is there any basis for believing that reason alone can produce profound tolerance in liberal societies, which is not to say that liberal institutions cannot socialize people to be highly tolerant, respect the law, and settle their conflicts peacefully. Moreover, a careful examination of their writings shows that progressive liberals themselves recognize the limits of reason, in effect undermining their own optimistic claims.

Unbounded Progressivism

The writings of Dworkin, Fukuyama, and Pinker contain arguments that fit with unbounded progressivism. As I noted earlier, Dworkin pays much attention to the question of whether it is possible for Supreme Court justices to come up with "right answers" for the "hard cases" that invariably make their way to them. Specifically, he is concerned with whether there are universal moral principles that can provide objectively correct answers in these cases, rather than answers that depend on particular justices' value preferences. He believes that there is a set of liberal "constitutive princi-ples" that justices can employ to help get the right answers. "The occasions when a legal question has no right answer in our own legal system," he writes, "may be much rarer than is generally supposed." He goes on to say that "in a complex and comprehensive legal system it is antecedently un-likely that two theories will differ sufficiently to demand different answers in some case and yet provide equally good fit with the relevant legal materi-als." It is also worth noting that after saying liberalism cannot be grounded on skepticism, Dworkin argues that liberalism's "constitutive morality pro-vides that human beings must be treated as equals by their government, not because there is no right and wrong in political morality, but because that is what is right."[30] One could point to other examples of Dworkin mak-ing the case for universal truths.

In his famous writings about the end of history, Fukuyama appears to make even bolder claims. History's end, goes the argument, means "there would be no further progress in the development of underlying principles and institutions, because all of the really big questions had been settled."[31] With the triumph of Western liberal democracy over all other political forms, Fukuyama writes, we have reached the "endpoint of mankind's ide-ological evolution." In the "universal homogeneous state, all prior contra-dictions are resolved and all human needs are satisfied. There is no struggle or conflict over 'large' issues and consequently no need for generals or statesmen; what remains is primarily economic activity." Given a world where people have no meaningful disagreements over first principles, their biggest problem is likely to be "boredom." It hardly needs mention-ing that boredom has not yet descended upon us.

Finally, Pinker, who emphasizes what he calls "the escalator of reason," has the earmarks of an unbounded progressive. "Believe it or not," he tells us, "we *are* getting smarter." And "smarter people are more liberal." One important implication of "our psychological commonality is that however much people differ, there can be, in principle, a meeting of the minds." The reason is simple: "When cosmopolitan currents bring diverse people into discussion, when freedom of speech allows the discussion to go where it pleases, and when history's failed experiments are held up to the light, the evidence sug-gests that value systems evolve in the direction of liberal humanism."[32]

The case for unbounded progressivism is ultimately unpersuasive. There has never been anything approximating a universal consensus on what constitutes the good life, and no good reason to think there ever will be. The argument that we can use our critical faculties to divine universally accepted truths regarding first principles simply cannot be sustained. This is not to deny that individuals can come up with beliefs they deem ultimate truths, but getting everyone else to accept their views is another matter. Nor is it to deny that it is possible to get large groups of people to reach a consensus on public issues that matter to them. But even that is difficult, and it falls far short of universal agreement. Waldron drives this point home in his critique of Dworkin's views on truth in the legal realm: "None of this talk about objectivity . . . makes the slightest dent on the fact that different judges asking and answering the objective questions of value that Dworkin's jurisprudence requires will come up with different answers." In other words, "the answers will differ depending on the person, not depending on the law."[33]

Given reason's obvious limits, it is unsurprising that unbounded progressives themselves ultimately retreat from their bold assertions and begin to sound like modus vivendi liberals. Unfortunately, their bouncing back and forth on this critical matter is untenable. One has to choose between the opposite approaches. Either one believes universal truths about first principles are attainable or one does not.

Fukuyama's writings about the end of history provide what is probably the best example of this phenomenon. As noted, he argues in his well-known 1989 article that all of the big questions have been settled and that little remains to fight about. But while he repeats these claims in his 1992 follow-up book, he also contradicts himself with numerous statements that could easily come from a modus vivendi liberal. In his book, for example, Fukuyama makes much of "the intellectual impasse in which modern relativism has left us," which he says "does not permit defense of liberal rights traditionally understood." At another point, he writes: "The incoherence in our current discourse on the nature of rights springs from a deeper philosophical crisis concerning the possibility of a rational understanding of man. . . . Today, everybody talks about human dignity, but there is no consensus as to why people possess it." One cannot talk about "the relativist impasse of modern thought" and yet argue there is broad agreement on first principles.[34]

Elsewhere in his book, Fukuyama warns about the dangers ahead, but these do not include boredom. He writes, for example: "Looking backward, we who live in the old age of mankind might come to the following conclusion. No regime—no 'socio-economic system'—is able to satisfy all men in all places. This includes liberal democracy. . . . Rather, the dissatisfaction arises precisely where democracy has triumphed most unboundedly: it is a dissatisfaction *with* liberty and equality. Thus those who remain dissatisfied will always have the potential to restart history." More pointedly, he notes, "Modern thought raises no barriers to a future nihilistic war against liberal democracy on the part of those brought up in its bosom." Along the same lines, he posits that "it is not clear that there will be any end to new and potentially more radical challenges to liberal democracy based on other forms of inequality." And possibly his most striking claim is that "we have no guarantees and cannot assure future generations that there will be no future Hitlers or Pol Pots."[35]

Stephen Holmes succinctly sums up the consequences of taking these contradictory positions: "Fukuyama does not seem to understand that all these pre-emptive concessions amount to an admission of defeat."[36]

This tendency to employ opposing views about the power of reason also appears in Kant's work, which explains why some scholars classify him as a modus vivendi liberal, while others see him as a progressive. Both Deborah Boucoyannis and Kenneth Waltz, for instance, say Kant is a modus vivendi liberal, while Michael Desch and John Gray portray him as a progressive liberal.[37] The reason for this confusion, as Waltz points out, is that Kant's writings give you ammunition to support both perspectives.[38]

In sum, the unbounded progressives' profound optimism about our ability to reason is undermined by their own writings and also by their failure to offer a compelling explanation for why human nature has changed so profoundly in just a few centuries.

Bounded Progressivism

With the second variant of progressive liberalism, reason does not yield consensus about life's big questions, but it does produce deep tolerance of opposing views. Rawls is the most important bounded progressive. He makes it clear that he believes citizens in liberal societies do not have "a comprehensive conception of the good." There is no agreement, he maintains, about "universal principles having validity in all parts of moral and political life."[39] Indeed, he expects citizens in a liberal society to be "profoundly divided by reasonable religious, philosophical, and moral doctrines."[40] Moreover, he does not expect all of the "reasonable comprehensive doctrines" found in a liberal society to be "liberal comprehensive doctrines."

Nevertheless, Rawls firmly believes not only that citizens in a liberal state have "a certain moral character" but that they are eminently sensible, which means they will not fight over their "irreconcilable comprehensive doctrines" but will instead be "constrained by their sense of what is reasonable." In the end, "public reason" will lead them to reach compromise solutions and respect each other's views. "As reasonable citizens" they will "offer to cooperate on fair terms with other citizens." This deeply embedded norm of toleration in liberal societies, he writes, will lead to "reasonable pluralism," if not a "realistic utopia."[41]

The two variants of progressive liberalism differ markedly in their emphasis on tolerance. For bounded progressives, tolerance acts as a magic elixir and is obviously of central importance. It is less important for unbounded progressives, who assume, at least much of the time, that broad agreement on first principles may make it unnecessary. There is little need to worry about tolerating difference in a world with no meaningful differences. Any society will surely harbor a few oddballs who do not recognize the truth, but unbounded progressives will not be inclined to tolerate their misguided views. Instead they will want to coax or coerce them into seeing the light.

Bounded progressivism is intuitively more attractive, simply because it acknowledges the difficulty of reaching universal agreement on foundational questions. Still, there are problems with its expectation that tolerance in liberal societies will trump the intense passions generated by fundamental disagreements over first principles.

For starters, there is little evidence that citizens in liberal societies are as tolerant as Rawls and other bounded progressives claim, and much evidence that they are not. The political philosopher George Klosko, who directly engages Rawls's claims about tolerance, argues that "the evidence shows many liberal citizens are remarkably intolerant"—an argument he supports with abundant evidence. Klosko notes that this point "should not be surprising to anyone familiar with research in American public opinion."[42] I will say more about this in the next chapter, when I discuss the overselling of individual rights. But suffice it to say here that there is no empirical basis for bounded progressivism's claims about deep tolerance.

Rawls does not argue that people have a natural inclination toward reasonableness or tolerance. He clearly believes the world is populated by non-liberal as well as liberal societies, and that people living in non-liberal societies are not reasonable by the standards of liberal societies. For example, he talks about "decent societies" as well as "outlaw states" that are "aggressive and dangerous." Regarding the beliefs of those individuals who populate decent societies, he writes: "I do not say they are reasonable, but rather they are not fully unreasonable." One would assume people living in outlaw states, at least most of them, are mostly unreasonable. The simple fact that huge numbers of people in the world are not reasonable by Rawls's own standards can only mean he does not believe people are naturally reasonable.[43]

This point is reinforced by Rawls's views on the history of the concept of tolerance. Specifically, he acknowledges that intolerance, not tolerance, was commonplace before Locke and others began formulating liberal theory in the seventeenth century; until then, "intolerance was accepted as a condition of social order and stability." There was, Rawls writes, a "centuries-long practice of intolerance." Thus the prevalence of reasonableness and tolerance in liberal societies cannot be a product of human nature. Something else must account for it.[44]

Where do reasonableness and tolerance come from in liberal societies? On what basis does Rawls claim that liberal citizens have a "certain moral character"? He does not say much about these important questions. His main claim seems to be that "reasonable pluralism," which has tolerance deeply embedded in it, is largely the result of the socialization that takes place over time inside liberal societies. It is "the long-term outcome of a society's culture in the context of . . . free institutions."[45] But this line of argument fails to say where the serious commitment to tolerance came from in the first place as well as who is responsible for purveying that norm. One might suppose the state is principally responsible for shaping its citizens' behavior, but Rawls does not make that argument, and he tends to play down the role of the state in his theory. Moreover, it is hard to believe that the state—or any institution—could purvey a norm like tolerance so effectively that it would largely eliminate violent conflict over competing views of the good life. In short, Rawls provides no good answer for how reasonableness, one of the main driving forces in his theory, comes to flourish in liberal societies. Not surprisingly, he offers little empirical support for his bold claims about tolerance.

Nor is it surprising that Rawls, like the unbounded progressives, occasionally makes arguments that contradict his fundamental claims about the peacefulness of liberal societies and leave him sounding like a modus vivendi liberal. For example: "Certain truths, it may be said, concern things so important that differences about them have to be fought out, even should this mean civil war."[46] He also notes that because large numbers of people reject liberalism, there are "important limits to reconciliation," adding that "many persons . . . could not be reconciled to a social world such as I have described. For them the social world envisaged by political liberalism is a nightmare of social fragmentation and false doctrines, if not positively evil."[47] Furthermore, Rawls fully accepts that liberal states sometimes face a supreme emergency that requires liberalism to be abandoned or at least seriously curtailed.[48]

Where does this leave us? While there is no question that progressive liberals sometimes make bold claims about the power of our critical faculties, those claims do not stand up to close inspection. Although the claims of bounded progressives are more limited, the two versions share the same flaws. Neither provides a persuasive explanation for why reason can offer final answers to questions about the good life or promote prodigious tolerance in liberal societies. Instead, theorists in this tradition make their cases mainly by assertion. Second, both bounded and unbounded progressives sometimes make arguments that contradict their assertions about how reason ameliorates conflict and leave them sounding like modus vivendi liberals.

In the end, there is no meaningful difference between modus vivendi and progressive liberalism on the pacifying effects of reason. The real difference between these two variants of political liberalism involves how they think about individual rights and social engineering by the state.

Rights and Social Engineering

Modus vivendi and progressive liberals hardly differ on the centrality of individual rights. But they disagree over what those rights are and how to strike a balance when they come into conflict. Modus vivendi liberals emphasize negative rights, which largely involve freedom from government interference in individual action. Freedom to assemble, freedom of the press, and freedom of speech are good examples. The right to acquire and exchange private property is an especially important right for modus vivendi liberals, as reflected in the writings of Locke and Smith.[49]

This emphasis on individual freedom is also reflected in the writings of Friedrich Hayek, a canonical modus vivendi liberal. The first sentences of the first chapter of Hayek's *The Constitution of Liberty,* for example, read: "We are concerned in this book with that condition of men in which coercion of some by others is reduced as much as possible in society. This state we shall describe throughout as a state of liberty or freedom."[50]

Unsurprisingly, many modus vivendi liberals have an intense dislike of positive rights, which require a serious effort by the state to help its citizens. Positive rights make individuals subject to government actions, which aim to provide them with a good or service to which they have a right. These efforts have little to do with freedom from government interference and may even entail the opposite. A good example of a positive right, and the one that modus vivendi liberals especially loathe, is the right to equal opportunity. This involves the government taking action to maximize the likelihood that every person has the same level of resources to compete for success. The aim is not to guarantee equal outcomes, just equal opportunity.

Hayek reveals modus vivendi liberalism's hostility toward the notion of equal opportunity when he writes: "Equality of the general rule of law and conduct . . . is the only kind of equality conducive to liberty and the only equality which we can secure without destroying liberty. Not only has liberty nothing to do with any other sort of equality, but it is even bound to produce inequality in many respects."[51] Modus vivendi liberals not only believe there is no such thing as an inalienable right to equal opportunity but also think the state is ill equipped to provide it, and as Hayek notes, efforts to do so may even cause inequality. Governments, they maintain, should not be in the business of promoting positive rights, which they feel are not even legitimate rights.

Progressive liberals are committed to the same set of basic freedoms that are at the core of modus vivendi liberalism. But then they add other rights. Equal opportunity is a dominating theme in the writings of both Dworkin and Rawls,[52] for whom it is synonymous with fairness, which they believe is what justice is all about. And they care greatly about justice. Rawls's most famous book is titled *A Theory of Justice*, and Dworkin uses "Liberalism and Justice" as the title for the section in *A Matter of Principle* where he "explores the present state of liberal theory."[53] Modus vivendi liberals rarely talk about justice.

Progressive liberals believe in other positive rights as well, such as the right to health care, the right to a decent education, and the right to live free of poverty. To some extent, these rights are linked with equality of opportunity, as it is hard to achieve success if you grow up impoverished or lack a good education or good health. One could also argue, of course, that these are important rights independent of what they mean for equal opportunity.

One problem with promoting positive rights, however, is that they sometimes conflict with negative rights.[54] This is especially true of equal opportunity, which often conflicts with the right to private property. Any meaningful effort to foster equal opportunity involves a significant redistribution of a society's resources. That means taking money, which is private property, from the rich and transferring it to the poor. Progressive liberals hardly hesitate to tax the rich to foster equal opportunity, which is not to say they do not recognize the right to property. They do, but they do not accord that right the same importance that modus vivendi liberals do. Rawls does not emphasize individual property rights in his writings, especially compared with Locke and Smith, for whom it is sacrosanct.

The two kinds of liberalism also have fundamental differences—directly related to their different views of rights—over the role of the state and social engineering. Modus vivendi liberals, who want the state to maintain order while doing everything possible to maximize individual freedom, do not want social engineering, and they certainly do not want a welfare state built around positive rights. Progressive liberals recognize the need for a state to act as a night watchman, but they also want it to promote positive rights for the purpose of enhancing individual welfare. This, in their view, is the best way to promote the overall well-being of society. (That is what makes them progressive liberals.) Their state will rely heavily on experts, many in its direct employ, and others who serve as consultants from their positions in academia or think tanks. Many of these experts will be social scientists, since after all the state is doing social engineering.[55]

While progressive liberals are certainly interested in building an interventionist state that can affect civil society in profound ways, they remain wary of big government. They do not lionize the state the way a philosopher like Hegel does, mainly because they recognize that it has the potential to turn into a leviathan and threaten individual freedoms.[56] In short, progressive liberals have a conflicted view of the state: they fear it even while treating it as a major force for good.

Progressive liberals' great faith in the ability of states to do social engineering says, in effect, that they place a high premium on instrumental rationality. They believe people can use their critical faculties to come up with smart strategies for achieving ambitious social goals. Modus vivendi liberals have little faith in government social engineering, which is to say they have less confidence in the state's ability to act in instrumentally rational ways. This clear difference about the sway of instrumental rationality notwithstanding, modus vivendi and progressive liberals agree on substantive rationality: that reason cannot help us divine collective truths about the good life.

As I noted earlier, politics is always at play in a liberal society. Because the state must make at least some rules and laws that deal with first principles, it matters to the citizenry who among them runs the government. People living in a state dominated by progressive liberals will care more about this because the progressive state will insert itself more in civil society. The intensity of political competition is likely to be greater in states where progressive rather than modus vivendi liberals are in charge. In such circumstances, modus vivendi liberals will have a powerful incentive to engage in politics so as to limit the interventionist state.

The bottom line is that the key differences in political liberalism's two variants are how they think about rights and the role of the state. Over the past two centuries the balance of power between them has shifted decisively in favor of progressive liberalism.

The Triumph of Liberal Progressivism

In its original form, political liberalism was synonymous with modus vivendi liberalism. But that variant gradually fell out of favor, partly because a laissez-faire approach to governing led to extreme economic inequality and widespread poverty. Moreover, for reasons I will discuss, it was an unsuitable blueprint for administering an industrialized nation-state. Utilitarianism and liberal idealism emerged in good part as responses to modus vivendi liberalism's shortcomings. Progressive liberalism was also an alternative to modus vivendi liberalism, and by the early twentieth century it was the dominant form of political liberalism in American and British politics. Its king of thought is John Rawls.

The key indicator of liberal progressivism's triumph is that the interventionist state, committed in its liberal form to fostering economic opportunity as well as other positive rights, is here to stay. Yet progressive liberalism has not won such a decisive victory as to render modus vivendi liberalism irrelevant. Modus vivendi liberalism has a substantial following in every liberal society, and its advocates sometimes have a significant influence on public discourse. But in practice, the best its proponents can do is to curb the excesses of the interventionist state.[57] There is virtually no hope of replacing it with a state that eschews social engineering and positive rights.

Progressivism in America

The American case shows us why. Liberal progressivism was a powerful force in U.S. politics in the late nineteenth and especially the early twentieth centuries.[58] The Republican Party, which was the dominant party until the 1932 presidential election, was closely identified with progressivism. Several constitutional amendments in this era—to authorize the federal income tax, elect senators by popular vote, give women the vote, and prohibit the sale of alcohol—emerged from progressive initiatives. Even Herbert Hoover, contrary to the conventional wisdom, was deeply committed to social engineering when he was secretary of commerce from 1921 to 1928, and as president from 1929 to 1933.[59] There is no question, however, that liberal progressivism has had its ups and downs and that its adherents' initial optimism has waned over time. But overall the U.S. government has remained deeply engaged in social engineering.[60] Franklin D. Roosevelt's New Deal (1933–38) and Lyndon B. Johnson's Great Society (1964–65) were extremely ambitious attempts at social engineering, aimed at promoting positive rights.

To understand how thoroughly progressivism has triumphed, consider how liberalism relates to the major political parties in the United States today. The Democratic Party's ruling ideology is clearly progressive liberalism, and it acts accordingly when it controls the key levers of power in Washington. If you listen to Republicans, you might think they follow the dictates of modus vivendi liberalism. That is usually true of their rhetoric, but it is not how they govern. In office, Republicans act like Democrats. For example, the annualized growth of federal spending since 1982 grew more under Republican presidents (Reagan, Bush 41, and Bush 43) than Democrats (Clinton and Obama). It grew by 8.7 percent under Reagan between 1982 and 1985, but only 1.4 percent under Obama between 2010 and 2013.[61]

Reagan also signed into law in 1986 the Emergency Medical Treatment and Active Labor Act, which prohibits hospitals from turning away people who come to an emergency room for treatment. It does not matter whether those individuals are American citizens, what their legal status is, or whether they can afford the treatment. In effect, this law says that health care is a human right. In fact, Reagan said as early as 1961 that "any person in the United States who requires medical attention and cannot provide it for himself should have it provided for him."[62] Further evidence that Republicans recognize this right comes from the often-repeated slogan "repeal and replace." They understand they cannot simply eliminate the Affordable

Care Act but must substitute another system that aims to provide Americans with decent health care. Republican presidents oversaw the beginnings of the Interstate Highway System, the Environmental Protection Agency, and the Department of Homeland Security. Republicans, in short, are deeply committed to the interventionist state and the extensive social engineering that comes with it.

The United States does have a political party that is genuinely committed to modus vivendi liberalism, and it is appropriately called the Libertarian Party. It is dedicated to promoting civil liberties and laissez-faire capitalism and to abolishing the welfare state. Its party platform takes dead aim at positive rights: "We seek a world of liberty; a world in which all individuals are sovereign over their own lives and no one is forced to sacrifice his or her values for the benefit of others."[63] The Libertarian Party has never won a single seat in Congress and never come close to winning the White House. Its candidate in the 2016 presidential election received 3.3 percent of the vote. Even if the Libertarians ever did gain power, they would surely find themselves prisoners of the interventionist state and its ambitious social programs.

Why Progressivism Won

Progressivism won out over modus vivendi liberalism because the profound changes that began sweeping across the world in the early nineteenth century forced states to build large-scale institutions dedicated to social engineering. For liberal democracies, this engineering included intervention in civil society to promote rights. These new roles were facilitated by the states' increasing capacity to handle them. For example, improvements in communications and transportation made it increasingly easy for governments to penetrate civil society. Walter Lippmann, writing in 1914, captured the spirit of the times: "We can no longer treat life as something that has trickled down to us. We have to deal with it deliberately, devise its social organization, alter its tools, formulate its method, educate and control it."[64]

Three major forces drove progressive liberalism's ascendancy. The first was the Industrial Revolution, which started in England in the eighteenth century and continues even today to generate enormous economic and social change. Among other things, it led to the rise of large-scale enterprises—manufacturing companies, financial firms, trade associations, research universities, and labor unions, to name a few—that profoundly affected the lives of millions of people. John Dewey put the point well: "The new technology applied in production and commerce resulted in a social revolution. The local communities without intent or forecast found their affairs conditioned by remote and invisible organizations."[65]

Another consequence of industrialization, the aforementioned growth in communication and transportation networks, occurred not just at the national level but at the international level as well. The Industrial Revolution helped fuel globalization, which meant that major economic developments in any one country inevitably affected other countries in the system and made the world increasingly interdependent. Industrialization also led to child labor, worker exploitation, and environmental damage. Given these and other hugely consequential developments, the state had no choice but to get seriously involved in managing various aspects of society, including the economy.[66] Given the sheer size of the relevant enterprises, the speed at which technology changes, and the global nature of industrial capitalism, the necessary levels of planning and regulating were far beyond the capacities of local governments.

Much to the chagrin of modus vivendi liberals, relying on the invisible hand to work its magic in the economy is not a feasible strategy. Liberal countries might be wedded to capitalism and a market economy, but that does not prevent the interventionist state from closely regulating not only its own economy but the international economy as well.[67] These tasks involve making and implementing policies that unavoidably affect individual rights.

The second key force behind the triumph of progressive liberalism is nationalism, which, like industrialization, became a dominating force in international politics during the nineteenth century. I will discuss nationalism at length in the next chapter, but suffice it to say here that all states have powerful reasons (administrative, economic, and military) to foster in their people a strong sense of nationhood, which requires extensive social engineering. This task never ends, not only because newly born citizens have to be socialized but also because some states allow large-scale immigration.

Moreover, most states are multinational, which means they have to work assiduously to forge a common identity among their different groups.

At the same time, nationalism creates powerful bonds between citizens and the state, leading people to expect their government to reward their loyalty by providing for their welfare. This demand reinforces the nation-state's inclination toward intervention, which includes, in liberal democracies, the promotion of rights. Democracy further bolsters this interventionism. Voters demand that politicians put forward policies that promote their welfare, and politicians who make bold promises and deliver on them are likely to get elected and reelected. This popular pressure causes most politicians to favor, or at least not fervently oppose, policies that promote equal opportunity and other positive rights.

The third major force behind progressive liberalism's dominance is the changing nature of warfare and the need to maintain a large peacetime military establishment. Modern militaries invariably contain large numbers of individuals in uniform as well as numerous civilian employees, and rely on a vast and constantly changing arsenal of sophisticated weaponry that today, for several states, includes massively destructive nuclear weapons. They depend as well on manufacturing, logistics, and services from private businesses, creating what Dwight Eisenhower called the military-industrial complex. The state has no choice but to manage this behemoth, because the military is an integral part of the state.[68] The need to fill the ranks of the military with healthy and well-educated citizens gives the government a powerful incentive to provide for the welfare of its citizenry. And it must then provide for the welfare of those citizens who end up wearing a uniform.[69]

When these modern militaries fight major wars, especially "total wars" like the two World Wars, the state ends up interfering in almost every aspect of daily life. The government has little alternative if it hopes to mobilize the resources necessary to win. The result, however, is that the state discovers its ability to do social engineering on a grand scale. As the sociologist Morris Janowitz notes regarding World War II: "A society that could mobilize for total war was defined as one that could mobilize for social welfare. Thus it was the actual performance of the central government during the war that was crucial in the thrust toward a welfare state. In essence, the political elites gained the knowledge and the confidence that they could manage the welfare state."[70]

Even when states become involved in protracted conflicts that do not involve the clashing of mass armies, like the Cold War and the so-called global war on terror, they still interfere profoundly in civil society. During the Cold War, for example, blatant racism against African Americans in the United States made it difficult for American policymakers to promote the U.S. political system internationally as superior to communism. As the legal historian Mary Dudziak notes, "At a time when the United States hoped to reshape the postwar world in its own image, the international attention given to racial segregation was troublesome and embarrassing." The need to rectify this problem played an important role in propelling the civil rights movement, as Richard Nixon explicitly acknowledged when he was vice president under Eisenhower.[71] In other words, "civil rights reform was *in part* a product of the Cold War," because that change was "consistent with and important to the more central mission of fighting world communism."[72]

When wars end, the returning soldiers often make demands on the state. For example, veterans who come from groups that have been denied the right to vote are likely to demand it. As the historian Alexander Keyssar notes: "Nearly all of the major expansions of the franchise that have occurred in American history took place either during or in the wake of wars. The historical record indicates that this was not a coincidence: the demands of both war itself and preparedness for war created powerful pressures to enlarge the right to vote. Armies had to be recruited, often from the so-called lower orders of society, and it was rhetorically as well as practically difficult to compel men to bear arms while denying them the franchise; similarly, conducting a war meant mobilizing popular support, which gave political leverage to any social groups excluded from the polity."[73]

Returning soldiers also make claims for pensions, health care, and educational benefits. After the American Civil War, for example, the Bureau of Pensions, which handled military pensions, "became one of the largest and most active agencies of the federal government." As the sociologist Theda Skocpol notes, "By the early twentieth century . . . many American voters and citizens appear to have wanted to extend this policy precedent into more widely available old-age pensions."[74] In 1930, the Bureau of Pensions became part of the new Veterans Administration, which today has roughly 350,000 employees and a budget of over $150 billion. Following World War II, countless American veterans went to college on the G.I. Bill, which also benefited veterans of the wars in Korea, Vietnam, Afghanistan, and Iraq.[75]

In short, national security considerations force liberal states not only to engage in large-scale social engineering but also to promote individual rights. Both efforts foster progressive liberalism. In the modern world, modus vivendi liberalism cannot survive contact with an enemy. Political liberalism today is effectively synonymous with progressive liberalism, and modus vivendi liberalism can only hope to shape progressivism, not replace it.

Before turning to a critique of political liberalism, I want to briefly examine utilitarianism and liberal idealism, which are sometimes portrayed as liberal theories but, at least under my definition, are not.

Utilitarianism

Jeremy Bentham is the intellectual father of utilitarianism, although he is hardly the only luminary in that tradition, which includes James Mill, his son John Stuart Mill, Henry Sidgwick, and many others. Advocates of this ism maintain that the primary goal of politics is to find ways of promoting the overall happiness of society. Happiness is the utility in this theory, and the key goal for leaders is to promote policies that contribute to "the greatest happiness of the greatest number."[76]

Utilitarianism treats all citizens as equals in the sense that no individual's desires are favored over another's. John Stuart Mill is something of an exception, as he argues for privileging intellectual over physical pleasures. Very importantly, the stark individualism central to political liberalism is absent from utilitarianism. People are instead treated as social beings from the start, and the "general well-being" of the collectivity is political leaders' main concern.[77] Given that utilitarians reject the liberal emphasis on individualism, it is not surprising they also reject the liberal conception of natural rights. Bentham's downright hostility toward inalienable rights led him to criticize both the American Declaration of Independence and the French Declaration of the Rights of Man and of the Citizen.[78]

None of this is to say rights do not matter for utilitarians, because they do. But they are determined by the government; they are not natural rights. Furthermore, the primary purpose of rights is to promote the general welfare, not to give individuals maximum freedom to pursue their own interests. In other words, rights are important for maximizing collective utility, not because individual freedom is a good in itself. This means not only that individual rights are doled out by the state but also that they can be circumscribed when they no longer serve the common good. This is a far cry from how political liberals think about rights.

Leaders play an essential role in the utilitarian story, as they are principally responsible for assessing their constituents' desires and then cutting deals with groups and individuals to maximize the "aggregate stock of happiness of the community."[79] In effect, bargaining is at the core of utilitarianism, which means there will have to be trade-offs between the interests of different actors as well as between rights. There is a clear sense in utilitarianism that virtually all interests are, as Deborah Boucoyannis puts it, "negotiable, divisible, and exchangeable."[80]

The utilitarian world is not one where individuals are fervently committed to first principles or moral truths. Its people are mainly concerned with finding happiness, while the government is concerned with determining what pleases them so as to design policies to achieve that end. Some people may have strong passions about life's big questions, but not many can have them, simply because passionate beliefs would make it difficult to make the trade-offs necessary for maximizing everyone's happiness. While reason has little to do with determining what makes people happy, reason matters greatly for figuring out the best way to maximize collective utility. Utilitarians therefore place great emphasis on instrumental rationality. Bentham makes this distinction clear: "It is by hopes and fears that the *ends* of action are determined; all that reason does is to find and determine the means."[81]

Utilitarians are generally optimistic about the prospects of creating a peaceful and prosperous society. Much of their optimism comes from the belief that most people are intelligent and reasonable and thus capable of doing the right thing. James Mill succinctly summarizes this perspective: "When various conclusions are, with their evidence, presented with equal care and with equal skill, there is a moral certainty, though some few may be misguided, that the greatest number will judge right, and the greatest form of evidence, whatever it is, will produce the greatest impression."[82] In other words, public opinion is a powerful force for good. Moreover, utilitarians have a progressive view of history, which further reinforces their belief that people will realize they have a harmony of interests. As John Stuart Mill notes, utilitarianism is "grounded on the permanent interests of man as a progressive being."[83]

The state's principal role in utilitarianism is to manage the bargaining process. The government must be concerned with important matters like determining how wealth and resources are distributed and which rights should be privileged over others. This is not a laissez-faire state that depends on the invisible hand to produce favorable outcomes: the hand here is visible, interventionist, and actively engaged in social engineering. Utilitarians, however, do not place much emphasis on the state acting as a night watchman, mainly because they do not believe there are profound differences about what constitutes the good life. Instead, the state's main function is to ensure that everyone gets a fair shake and ends up maximizing their pleasure.[84]

In sum, utilitarianism differs in essential ways from political liberalism and thus falls outside this book's purview.

Liberal Idealism

Liberal idealism is another ism that some classify as a liberal theory. Its founding father is the British philosopher T. H. Green,[85] whose many followers in Britain included Bernard Bosanquet, L. T. Hobhouse, J. A. Hobson, and D. G. Ritchie. The two key liberal idealists who wrote about international politics were Gilbert Murray and Alfred Zimmern. The leading liberal idealist in the United States in the early twentieth century was John Dewey, who was deeply influenced by Green's writings.[86] This theoretical approach has been carried on in the contemporary Anglo-Saxon world by scholars such as Gerald Gaus, Stephen Macedo, and Jack Crittenden, who writes in *Beyond Individualism* (1992): "The view of liberalism that I am offering here—liberalism beyond individualism—is . . . a continuation of the 'revisioning' of liberalism undertaken by T. H. Green and his disciples . . . and by John Dewey in America."[87]

Why Liberal Idealists Are Liberals in Name Only

There is little doubt that liberal idealists are literally idealists, as the label indicates, but they are not political liberals. There is no room in their theory for liberalism's unambiguous individualism and its accompanying belief in inalienable rights. Liberal idealists emphasize that human beings are first and foremost social animals. According to Green, men in "detachment from social relations . . . would not be men at all."[88] Or, as Dewey put it, only by working "for the common good can individual human beings realize their true individualities and become truly free."[89]

Green's and Dewey's comments make it clear that although liberal idealists are committed to maintaining as much individual freedom as possible, they see individuals above all else as social beings. This view is what attracted them to Hegel, who was clearly an important influence on virtually all the early thinkers in this tradition. Hegel, of course, has an organic view of society, although he also cares much about individual rights. As is clear from his famous tract *The Philosophy of Right*, he believes individual freedom and social unity are not at odds with each other but can be joined together to produce a vibrant body politic.[90]

A few liberal idealists—Hobhouse and Hobson being the most prominent—agree with Hegel that it is possible to design an organic society that allows its citizens to take maximum advantage of their individual rights. But that merger of opposites is not possible. Liberalism and liberal idealism look at the relationship between individuals and their society in contradictory ways. Any country committed to promoting social unity has to place significant limits on freedom or rights. It is not that rights have no place in liberal idealism but that they must be circumscribed in important ways if the society is to foster interdependence and cooperation among its citizens rather than egoistic behavior designed to maximize individual utility.[91]

Given the primacy of society in liberal idealist thinking, coupled with the increasing influence of nationalist sentiment in Europe during the latter half of the nineteenth century, it is not surprising that patriotism figures prominently in the writings of many liberal idealists. They treated it as a force for good, as a highly effective means of unifying a society. Bosanquet, for example, claims that patriotism is "an immense natural force, a magical spell," which grows from "family and kindred—the tie of blood," while Green extols what two contemporary British scholars call "cosmopolitan nationalism."[92] For Green, "the love of mankind . . . needs to be particularized in order to have any power over life and action."[93]

E. H. Carr maintains that one reason for the liberal idealists' blithe view of nationalism was that there were not many nations at the time, so they "were not yet visibly jostling one another."[94] While Carr is probably correct, nationalism was also widely admired because it was seen to embody popular sovereignty, which is closely tied to democracy.[95] It played a key role before and after the turn of the century in toppling dynastic rulers all across Europe. Dewey, who was deeply committed to "nationalizing education," captures this perspective when he writes: "The upbuilding of national states has substituted a unity of feeling and aim, a freedom of intercourse, over wide areas for earlier local isolations, suspicions, jealousies and hatreds. It has forced men out of narrow sectionalisms, into membership in a larger social unit, and created loyalty to a state which subordinates petty and selfish interests."[96]

Over time, and surely after World War I, liberal idealists grew more aware of nationalism's dark side. In 1916, Dewey contrasted the "good aspect of nationalism" with its "evil side"; two years later, Zimmern used "True and False Nationalism" as the title of a chapter of a book about promoting international peace.[97] Nonetheless, liberal idealists continued to view nationalism, on balance, as a positive force. In the same book, for example, Zimmern writes: "Nationalism rightly understood and cherished is a great uplifting and life-giving force, a bulwark alike against chauvinism and against materialism—against all the decivilising impersonal forces which harass and degrade the minds and souls of modern men."[98] Given liberal idealism's organic conception of society, it fits neatly with nationalism.

One point of agreement between political liberals, especially modus vivendi liberals, and liberal idealists concerns their fear of a too-powerful state. Hegel revered the state, calling it "the actuality of concrete freedom."[99] The state also plays a central role in nationalism, as we will see in the next chapter. Given liberal idealism's close links with both Hegel and nationalism, one would expect liberal idealists to favor a formidable state with abundant capacity to intervene in civil society for the common good. In fact, they embrace the notion of a strong state only reluctantly and tend to worry that a state with too much power will bring serious trouble. This is one reason liberal idealists do not fully embrace Hegel's teachings.[100]

Why Liberal Idealists Are Idealists

The idealism embedded in the liberal idealists' worldview is reflected in their deep-seated belief that politics is about the pursuit of moral goodness. What matters for them is the "moral progress of man," not the utilitarian goal of maximizing happiness.[101] Green contemptuously described utilitarianism as "Hedonistic fatalism."[102] He began his famous lectures on political obligation by saying: "My purpose is to consider the moral function or object served by law, or by the system of rights and obligations which the state enforces, and in so doing to discover the true ground or justification for obedience to law."[103]

Other liberal idealists shared Green's emphasis on morality, although none could ever state what exactly the "moral ideal" looks like or what was involved in the "perfecting of man."[104] Probably the best answer is Hobhouse's claim that "the ideal society is conceived as a whole which lives and flourishes by the harmonious growth of its parts, each of which in developing on its own lines and in accordance with its own nature tends on the whole to foster the development of others."[105] Still, this is a rather vague prescription for future political life. Thus, it is not surprising that Green acknowledged his inability to nail down what human perfectibility would look like: "But while . . . it is impossible for us to say what the perfecting of man, of which the idea actuates the moral life, in its actual attainment might be, we can discern certain conditions which, if it is to satisfy the idea, it must fulfill."[106]

Liberal idealists also have a deep-rooted belief in reason as the key tool for realizing moral goodness. Utilitarians also privilege reason, but there is a subtle difference. Utilitarians tend to be elitists, in the sense that they have great faith in the mental faculties of the governing elites who are principally responsible for crafting the bargains at the heart of the utilitarian enterprise. Liberal idealists appear to have more faith in the common people's ability to use their critical faculties in smart ways. As A. D. Lindsay writes in his introduction to Green's *Principles of Political Obligation*: "Green and his fellow-idealists had . . . a profound belief in the worth and dignity of the ordinary man."[107] Liberal idealists are invariably champions of democracy, while most utilitarians' enthusiasm is more restrained.

Perhaps the most eloquent liberal idealist on how reason can help build the ideal society is Dewey, who was especially bullish on ordinary people's capabilities. He believed that given the right educational opportunities, "the average individual would rise to undreamed heights of social and political intelligence."[108] If those regular people were then brought together, "the cumulative intelligence of a multitude of cooperating individuals" would take society to even greater heights.[109] He condemns violence as a tool of social change and instead extols "intelligence as an alternative method of social action."[110] For Dewey, "organized intelligence" can solve "the crisis in democracy" by resurrecting "democratic ideals" in pursuit of "genuine democracy."[111]

Finally, the idealism of Green and his followers is reflected in their belief in nationalism as ultimately a benign force. Even in the aftermath of World War I, which was linked with nationalism in many people's minds, the dark side of that ism was largely shunted aside by liberal idealists. This approach is reflected in the writings of Murray and Zimmern, who were deeply committed to fostering international peace in the interwar period.[112] They hoped to construct an international society in which the great powers would cooperate to improve each other's lot. Nationalism was a major force for good in their story, as reflected in Zimmern's comment that "the road to internationalism lies through nationalism; and no theory or ideal of internationalism can be helpful in our thinking or effective in practice unless it is based on a right understanding of the place which national sentiment occupies and must always occupy in the life of mankind."[113] More generally, for Zimmern and other liberal idealists, the power of reason kept passionate disagreements at bay, allowing states in the international system, like individuals in a society, to realize a natural harmony of interests.

Thus, Murray and Zimmern saw no need for a commanding League of Nations that would transcend anarchy and police the great powers through military might and the force of law, any more than they saw the need for a powerful state to keep individuals and groups from killing each other. Instead, as Jeanne Morefield puts it, they saw the League as "a natural extension of humanity's tendency toward social cohesion."[114] This view may be fairly described as idealistic, if not utopian.

It should be clear that liberal idealism differs in fundamental ways from political liberalism. Not only do liberal idealists view humans as essentially social animals, they also do not believe in natural rights and assign nationalism an important place in their story. They believe reason can help facilitate moral progress, leading the way toward some kind of "ideal society." These beliefs conflict with the core notions that underpin political liberalism—an ideology that merits an extended critique of its own.

4

Cracks in the Liberal Edifice

TWO OF POLITICAL LIBERALISM'S MOST salient features are also its two significant flaws: the prominence it accords individualism, and the weight it places on inalienable rights. Contemporary liberalism, as we saw, is largely synonymous with progressive liberalism, although modus vivendi liberalism still affects the contours of political life. My criticisms of political liberalism in this chapter apply equally to both variants, as there is little daylight between them regarding the importance they ascribe to individualism and rights. In this chapter I am concerned with assessing liberalism as a political ideology. A liberal democracy's foreign policy, and international relations more generally, are reserved for later chapters.

The first problem with liberalism is that it wrongly assumes that humans are fundamentally solitary individuals, when in fact they are social beings at their core. This commitment to far-reaching individualism leads political liberals to downplay nationalism, which is an especially powerful political ideology with profound influence inside every country in the world. Liberalism's fate is therefore bound up with nationalism. Although these two isms differ in important ways, they can coexist inside a country's borders. But when they are at odds, nationalism wins almost every time. In short, nationalism places serious limits on liberalism's influence, including its emphasis on natural rights.

Liberalism's second problem is that its story about individual rights is not persuasive. The claim that rights are inalienable and that this is "self-evident," that almost everyone should be able to recognize both the universality and importance of rights, is not compelling. The influence of rights in people's daily lives is nowhere near as profound as liberals seem to think, which is not to say rights are of no concern at all. But their impact is limited, even in places like the United States, where liberalism is deeply wired into the culture.

These shortcomings are by no means fatal. Nor do they cripple this ism in any meaningful way, as it still has a number of important virtues. What these flaws show, however, is that liberalism's ability to shape daily life inside any country will encounter limits. And as I will argue in the next chapter, those limits are even more pronounced in the international system. Here I will stay within the nation-state, concluding with a discussion of the possibility that liberal countries might be intrinsically unworkable because the factions within them have strong incentives to capture the state permanently and prevent rival factions from taking the reins of power. While this argument should not be taken lightly, mature liberal democracies have certain features that go a long way toward ameliorating this problem, but they are not foolproof.

The Nationalism Problem

Liberalism's most important shortcoming is its radical individualism. In focusing almost exclusively on individuals and their rights, it pays little attention to the fact that human beings are born into and operate in large collectivities, which help shape their essence and command their loyalties. Most people are at least partially tribal from the start to the finish of their lives, a point that is largely absent from the liberal story.[1]

The nation is the highest-level social group of real significance for the vast majority of people around the world. Nations are large collections of people who have much in common and who also have a powerful allegiance to the group. Individuals live as members of a nation, which fundamentally shapes their identities and behavior. Nations, which privilege self-determination and worry about their survival, want their own state.[2] At the same time, states themselves have powerful reasons for wanting their people to be organized into a nation, which leads them to play a critical role in fusing the nation and the state together. Thus it is no surprise that the world is populated with nation-states, the embodiment of nationalism.

If liberalism and nationalism are both powerful forces in our world, what is the relationship between them? Three points are in order. First, nationalism is at play in every country, which is reflected in the fact that we live in a world of nation-states. Liberalism, however, is not a powerful force everywhere. True liberal democracies have never made up a majority of states in the international system. Second, given nationalism's pervasiveness, liberalism must always coexist with nationalism. It is impossible to have a liberal state that is not a nation-state and thus nationalist to its core. Liberalism, in other words, operates within the confines of nation-states. Finally, liberalism invariably loses when it clashes with nationalism.

What Is Nationalism?

Nationalism is a theory that explains how people around the world are organized socially and politically. It holds that the human population is divided into many different nations composed of people with a strong sense of group loyalty. With the possible exception of the family, allegiance to the nation usually overrides all other forms of an individual's identity. Furthermore, members of a nation are deeply committed to maximizing their nation's autonomy, which means they prefer to have their own state. As Ernest Gellner famously put it, nationalism "holds that the political and the national unit should be congruent."[3] This is not to say that every national group can have its own state, but that is the ultimate goal, given their yearning for self-determination. States, meanwhile, have powerful incentives to govern people who are organized into nations, which leads political leaders to work hard to foster nationalism. Nationalism is both a bottom-up and a top-down phenomenon.

In popular discourse, nationalism is sometimes said to reflect "ancient hatreds," which implies it has plagued the planet for most of recorded history. This perception is false: nationalism is a recent phenomenon. It first emerged in Europe, and by extension North America, in the second half of the eighteenth century, although it was incubating in Europe before then.[4] Liberalism actually came onto the European scene roughly a century before nationalism. Moreover, although nationalism can lead to hatred among peoples, that is only one facet of a complicated phenomenon that has positive as well as negative attributes.

The best starting point for understanding nationalism is to describe the basic characteristics of a nation and show how it differs from prior social groups. I will then discuss the essential functions that nations perform for their members, why nations want their own state, and why states want to govern their own nation. These complementary incentives work to fuse the nation and state together, which accounts in good part for why nationalism is such a powerful force. I will also describe how the modern state differs from the political forms that preceded it.

What Is a Nation?

Nations have six fundamental features that, taken together, distinguish them from the other kinds of large groups that inhabited the planet before nations came on the scene.[5]

A SENSE OF ONENESS

A nation is a large community of people with a powerful sense of oneness, even though each member knows only a small number of fellow nationals. Benedict Anderson's famous description of a nation as an "imagined community" nicely captures this feature.[6] A nation is imagined in the sense that no person knows more than a tiny fraction of the other members, and yet almost all of them identify as part of a community. They have a strong sense of loyalty to the community's other members, which means they tend to feel mutually responsible for each other, especially in dealing with the outside world. That the bonds among fellow nationals are tight tends to make the boundaries between different nations clear and firm.[7]

In addition to this sense of solidarity, a nation's members also tend to treat each other as equals.[8] They view themselves as part of a common enterprise, and although the group contains leaders and followers, the people at the top and those at the bottom are ultimately all members of the same community. Anderson captures this point when he notes that even though there will always be different kinds of "inequality and exploitation in any society, the nation is always conceived as a deep, horizontal comradeship."[9]

Before the coming of nations, the bonds among members of the large social groups that populated Europe were not tight. Those earlier groups tended to be quite fluid, which meant that identities were relatively malleable. Consider the historian Patrick Geary's discussion of social life in Europe after the collapse of the Roman Empire: "The fourth and fifth centuries saw fundamental changes in the European social and political fabric. In the process, great confederations like those of the Goths disappeared, to reemerge transformed into kingdoms in Italy and Gaul. Others like the Hunnic Empire or the Vandal kingdom seemed to spring from nowhere, only to vanish utterly in a few generations. Still other, previously obscure peoples, such as the Angles and the Franks, emerged to create enduring polities."[10] Such fluidity is unthinkable in the age of nationalism, in which nations tend to be tightly integrated, permanent entities separated by clear boundaries.[11] It is hard to imagine any contemporary nation disappearing or even undergoing the sort of rapid transformation in its identity that Geary describes.

Furthermore, there was no sense of equality within those earlier social groups. While there is not strict equality in a nation, there was a marked reduction in the gap between elites and their people. Pre-national Europe was largely agricultural and comprised two main classes: the aristocracy and the peasantry. The gulf separating them was huge, under the Roman Empire, during the Middle Ages, and in the era of dynastic states that preceded the appearance of nation-states.[12]

But by the late eighteenth century, the chasm had narrowed significantly, in good part because elites and their publics came to communicate in the same language and see themselves as part of a shared enterprise with a common destiny. The historian of France David Bell captures this transformation when he writes that "neither Virgil nor Richelieu or Mazarin envisioned taking entire populations—from elegant courtiers to impoverished sharecroppers, from well-polished intellectuals to urban beggars—and forging them all, in their millions into a single nation, transforming everything from language to manners to the most intimate ideas."[13] This melding of people in a society (which has its limits) inclines them to feel like equals.

None of this is to deny that individuals have other identities and loyalties besides national allegiance. Everyone has multiple identities: they almost always belong to a variety of organizations and groups, and have multiple interests, friendships, and commitments. Nevertheless, aside from family ties, a person's highest loyalty is almost always to his nation, and that commitment usually overrides others when they conflict. Marxists, for example, emphasize that individuals identify most strongly with their social class, be it capitalists, the bourgeoisie, or the working class, and that this identification surpasses national identity. This thinking, clearly reflected in the *Communist Manifesto,* explains why some Marxists believed the working classes of Europe would not take up arms against each other when their governments went to war in 1914.[14] They discovered that while social class is often a powerful form of identity, it is not in the same league as nationalism, which tends to fuse classes together by providing them with a higher loyalty. As the historian Michael Howard puts it, "The appeals for class unity across international frontiers were scattered to the winds once the bugles began to blow in 1914," and the workers of the world fought with their fellow nationals against rival nation-states.[15] In short, national identity is not the only identity an individual possesses, but it is generally the most powerful.

Nor is it to deny that individuals in a nation sometimes act in selfish ways and take advantage of other members. We all face situations where there is much to be gained by acting like the proverbial utility maximizer. And selfish behavior sometimes leads to bitter, even deadly, disputes between fellow nationals. Nevertheless, this kind of egoistic behavior takes place within a nation, where individuals have obligations to the wider community and where there are powerful reasons to act in ways that benefit the collective. When those two logics conflict, most people privilege loyalty to their nation over loyalty to themselves.

A DISTINCT CULTURE

What separates nations from each other is culture. Each nation has a distinct set of beliefs and practices that are shared by its members and that distinguish it from other nations. The practices involve things like language, rituals, codes, music, and symbols, while beliefs involve matters like religion, basic political and social values, and a particular understanding of history. The members of a nation tend to act and think in similar ways in their daily lives, and this helps foster strong bonds among them.

But it would be impracticable for all of the individuals who make up a nation-state to share the same practices and beliefs. There is instead a substantial commonality, which varies from case to case. It makes sense to distinguish between thick and thin cultures, which reflect the amount of cultural diversity a nation has. Thick cultures have significant cultural homogeneity, while thin cultures are more diverse. Nation-states that are largely composed of a single nation, such as Japan and Poland, have thick cultures. Those that have a core nation and minority nations, such as Canada, India, and Spain, have thin cultures.[16] In other words, there is a thin national identity at the level of the state, but the core and minority nations also have their own identities.[17] Most societies' elites would like to mold a thick national identity, but that is usually not practical in societies containing two or more nations. Nevertheless, research shows that members of thick and thin cultures have roughly the same "degree of strong identity and pride in membership in the state."[18]

It is impossible to generalize about which cultural features allow us to distinguish one nation from another. Language might seem like a good marker, but different nations often speak the same language. Just think of all the countries in Central and South America that speak Spanish. The same is true of religion. Catholicism, after all, is the dominant religion in Austria, France, Italy, Portugal, and Spain, just to name a few examples, and Islam dominates throughout the Arab world. Beliefs and practices that cut across cultures show that different cultures' defining features may overlap substantially. Germany and Austria are a good example. Nevertheless, they have differences as well, seemingly minor to outsiders but which the members of each nation invariably rivet on. Sigmund Freud famously called this phenomenon the "narcissism of minor differences."[19]

One might also think that culture is synonymous with ethnicity, which is sometimes defined as a set of ancient, fixed characteristics of a group that have been carried forward to the present. According to this primordialist perspective, a nation's roots are its bloodlines: its common descent from relatives who lived long ago. But large social groups, and nations in particular, have evolved in ways that contradict that definition of ethnicity, which is why I do not employ the term in this book.

Cultures are not fixed because individual identities are not hardwired into people at birth. Instead, they are socially constructed and are more fluid than primordialists recognize. Elites often play a key role in shaping a nation, as reflected in this comment by a prominent Italian leader in 1861, when Italy was being unified: "We have made Italy. Now we have to make Italians."[20] If I did use the word *ethnicity*, I would use it in Max Weber's sense, to mean "a subjective belief in . . . common descent," or the belief that a particular people share a common cultural tradition.[21] Those definitions are consistent with my story.

In essence, the real basis of nationhood is psychological, not biological, which is why Walker Connor says "the essence of a nation is intangible."[22] A nation exists when a large number of people think of themselves as members of the same unique social group with a distinct culture. In other words, a nation is a large group that considers itself a nation[23] and that has tangible beliefs and practices that matter greatly for its common identity. Once nations are formed, they are exceptionally resistant to fundamental change, partly because individuals are heavily socialized into a particular culture from birth, and typically accustomed to and committed to its beliefs and practices.

There is another important reason for the durability of national loyalties: the movement from oral to written traditions. Until the nineteenth century, most people learned about their social group's history by word of mouth. Few people could read, and for them there were few popular history books. It was reasonably easy to change stories about the past to accommodate newcomers as well as shifting circumstances. But once a group's history is written in books, it is difficult to change the story to suit new conditions. As the political scientist James Scott notes, "The key disadvantage of monuments and written texts is precisely their relative permanence."[24] In a literate world, people's identities inside large social groups become more fixed, and boundaries become less fluid. The movement from an oral to a literate culture not only created tighter bonds within Europe's burgeoning nations but also made those communities more robust and resistant to change.

A SENSE OF SUPERIORITY

Regardless of what other nations do, people take pride in their own nation because it is a home to them. But they also think about how their nation compares with other nations, especially those they interact with frequently.

Chauvinism usually follows.[25] Most people think their nation is superior to others. It has special qualities that merit its being privileged over other nations. The German nationalist Johann Fichte captures this perspective with his comment that "the German alone . . . can be patriotic; he alone can for the sake of his nation encompass the whole of mankind; contrasted with him from now on, the patriotism of every other nation must be egoistic, narrow and hostile to the rest of mankind."[26] Lord Palmerston, Britain's liberal foreign secretary in 1848, was no less chauvinistic: "Our duty—our vocation—is not to enslave, but to set free: and I may say, without any vain-glorious boast, or without great offence to anyone, that we stand at the head of moral, social and political civilization. Our task is to lead the way and direct the march of other nations."[27]

Unsurprisingly, this sense of specialness leads some nations to think they have been singled out by God. This belief has a rich tradition in the United States, going back to the Puritans, who believed, as many Americans have over time, that there is a special covenant between God and the United States, and that God has given it special attributes that make its people smarter and nobler than other peoples. Of course, one does not have to believe in God to believe in American exceptionalism. Woodrow Wilson, for example, made no reference to God when he said: "The manifest destiny of America is not to rule the world by physical force. . . . The destiny of America and the leadership of America is that she shall do the thinking of the world."[28] Nor did Secretary of State Madeleine Albright appeal to God when she famously said in 1998: "If we have to use force, it is because we are America. We are the indispensable nation. We stand tall. We see further into the future."[29] Americans, as Reinhold Niebuhr noted, generally believe they are "tutors of mankind in its pilgrimage to perfection."[30] All of this is to say Americans are nationalists to the core, even though this is not how most of them think of themselves.

Nations sometimes go beyond feeling superior to other nations and end up loathing their competitors. I call this hypernationalism: the belief that other nations are not just inferior but dangerous, and must be dealt with harshly or even brutally. In such cases, contempt and hatred of "the other" suffuses the nation and creates powerful incentives to eliminate that threat with violence.[31] Yet nations do not always loathe each other; sometimes they get along quite well.

A DEEP HISTORY

History matters greatly for all nations, although they tend to emphasize creating myths rather than getting the facts right. Nations invent heroic stories about themselves to denigrate the achievements of other nations and buttress their claim that they are special. "Chauvinist mythmaking," as Stephen Van Evera notes, "is a hallmark of nationalism, practiced by nearly all nationalist movements to some degree."[32] Those myths, he argues, come in different varieties. Some are meant to glorify past behavior, while others are invented to whitewash instances where the nation acted foolishly or shamefully. Other myths malign rival nations by making them look inferior or blaming them for the home nation's past or present problems. But even when some myth proves impossible to sell, the usual response is to defend the nation anyway, because "it is my nation, right or wrong."

Nations also employ myths to argue that they have ancient roots, which explains in part why ethnicity is occasionally defined in terms of timeless features. Most people want to believe their nation has a long and rich tradition, even though few do. History is altered or rewritten to remedy the problem. This phenomenon was commonplace in nineteenth-century Europe, when nationalism was sweeping the region and history was becoming a scholarly enterprise. Patrick Geary describes the result: "Modern history was born in the nineteenth century, conceived and developed as an instrument of European nationalism. As a tool of nationalist ideology, the history of Europe's nations was a great success, but it has turned our understanding of the past into a toxic waste dump."[33] Mythmaking and nationalism go hand in hand, which is why Ernest Renan said, "Historical error is an essential factor in the creation of a nation."[34]

SACRED TERRITORY

Nations invariably identify with specific geographical spaces, which they treat as sacred territory.[35] People form a deep emotional attachment with land they perceive as their rightful homeland. The principal aim is to establish sovereignty over that territory, which is inextricably bound up with the nation's identity. And if any part of that imagined homeland is lost, the nation's members are almost always committed to recovering it. A good example is China's attitude toward Taiwan. It is widely and deeply believed among mainland Chinese that Taiwan is a part of China and must eventually be reintegrated, even though the Taiwanese have developed their own identity in recent decades and want Taiwan to be treated as a sovereign nation-state. Successive governments in Beijing have emphasized that they would go to war if Taiwan declared itself an independent country, even though a war would likely do significant damage to China's economy.[36] All nations, not just China, are obsessed with exercising authority over the territory they believe is an integral part of their hallowed homeland.

The large social groups that came before nations also cared about controlling territory, but they rarely viewed it as sacred space. Territory mattered largely for economic and military reasons. Prime real estate, which included much of the land in Europe, contained valuable resources, including manpower, that were essential for building a powerful economy and a formidable military force. Some territory was also strategically important: it provided defensible borders or access to an important waterway or ocean. This instrumental view meant that leaders could treat their territory as divisible under the right circumstances. But a nation's territory holds enormous intrinsic value as part of its cultural heritage, which means it is indivisible.[37]

SOVEREIGNTY

Finally, nations aim to maximize their control over their own political fate, which is another way of saying they are deeply concerned about sovereignty, or how political authority is arranged inside a state as well as among states. In domestic terms, sovereignty denotes where supreme political authority lies within a state.[38] The sovereign holds the ultimate authority to formulate and execute domestic as well as foreign policy.[39]

There can be only one sovereign within a state, as sovereignty is indivisible. In the dynastic states that populated Europe between roughly 1500 and 1800, sovereignty rested exclusively with the king or queen and was said to be conferred on the crown by God. Thus it was commonplace during that period to talk about the "divine right of kings." But this perspective on sovereignty is incompatible with nationalism. In a nation-state, supreme authority resides in the people or the nation. The people are not subjects who owe allegiance to a monarch but citizens with the rights and responsibilities that come with being members of a nation. As such, they are all equals.

This notion of popular sovereignty is clearly reflected in the French constitution of 1791, which states: "Sovereignty is one, indivisible, inalienable, and imprescriptible; it belongs to the Nation; no group can attribute sovereignty to itself nor can an individual arrogate it to himself."[40] That challenge to monarchial authority would have confounded Louis XV, who said, "The rights and interests of the nation, which some dare to regard as a separate body from the monarch, are necessarily united with my rights and interests, and they repose only in my hands."[41] (This is simply a more prolix version of his predecessor's famous outburst, "L'etat, c'est moi!") Before the coming of nationalism, writes the international relations scholar Robert Jackson, "sovereign rulers were preoccupied with territory but were largely indifferent to the peoples that occupied it, provided they accepted their authority."[42] Kings and queens often felt they had more in common with their fellow sovereigns than the populations under their control.

The notion of popular sovereignty must be qualified, though, because it is virtually impossible for a nation to collectively make policy decisions, in an emergency especially, but also in normal times. Speed and efficiency demand that in an existential crisis, supreme authority rests with a single person or at most a few people.[43] In more ordinary circumstances, decisions can be made by either autocrats or democratically elected leaders. The key feature in all of these circumstances, however, is that the decider or deciders have a close bond with their people and believe they are acting on the people's behalf. As the political theorist Bernard Yack writes, "Even authoritarian and totalitarian nationalists invoke popular sovereignty to justify their demands for extreme forms of national assertion."[44] The dynastic sovereigns did not consider themselves servants of the populations they controlled, but instead acted to serve either their own interests or what they perceived to be the state's interests.

Internationally, sovereignty means that the state wants the ability to make its own decisions on both domestic and foreign policy, free from outside interference. That viewpoint applies to both dynastic states and nation-states.

Of course, various structural forces in the international system will limit a sovereign state's menu of options, but sovereignty demands that other states not purposely intrude in its politics. States are deeply committed to self-determination, and nations, which are inextricably bound up with the state, care greatly about self-determination, both in dealing with other nation-states and inside their own states.

This emphasis on self-determination, coupled with the sense of oneness integral to nationalism, points us to the democratic impulse embedded in this ism.[45] Robespierre captured the link between democracy and nationalism when he wrote: "It is only under a democracy that the state is the fatherland of all the individuals who compose it and can count as many active defenders of its cause as it has citizens."[46] This is not to say nationalism is the principal cause of democracy, because it is not, but it is an important contributing factor. It is no accident that over the past two centuries, democracy has spread across large portions of the globe at the same time that nationalism was gaining sway around the world. Note, however, that I am talking about nationalism's relationship with democracy, not with liberalism. Liberalism and nationalism sometimes clash in fundamental ways.

In sum, nations have six core features that, taken together, distinguish them from the kinds of large social groups that dominated the landscape before nations came on the scene. These features are a powerful sense of oneness, a distinct culture, a marked sense of specialness, a historical narrative that emphasizes timelessness, a deep attachment to territory, and a strong commitment to sovereignty or self-determination.

The Essential Functions of a Nation

Nations serve their members in two critically important ways: they facilitate survival and fulfill important psychological needs. In this they are no different from their predecessors, although the actual mechanics vary somewhat between them.

Nations are primarily survival vehicles. Their underlying culture allows members to cooperate easily and effectively, which in turn maximizes their chances of securing life's basic necessities. Take language, for example. The fact that a nation's people mostly speak the same language makes it easy for them to communicate and work together to achieve important goals.[47] The same is true of a nation's customs and rituals, and its behavioral norms. Cooperation also facilitates building reliable security forces that can protect individual members if they are threatened by another member or an outsider. A nation's culture and sense of oneness help it create clear boundaries with other nations, which also help identify and protect against outsiders. Finally, nations care greatly about self-determination, in part because it allows them to make the decisions they think are necessary to protect them from rival nations.

But nations are more than survival vehicles. For most people, they also fulfill important emotional needs. We are all social animals and have little choice but to belong to groups, but there are many social groups.[48] What makes a nation so special is that it provides an existential narrative. It gives its members a strong sense that they are part of an exceptional and exclusive community whose history is filled with important traditions as well as remarkable individuals and events. Their culture, in other words, is special. Members want to live together to carry on those traditions, "validate the heritage that has been jointly received,"[49] and share a common destiny.

Furthermore, nations promise their members that they will be there for future generations the way they were there in the past. In this sense, nationalism is much like religion, which also does an excellent job of weaving the past, present, and future into a seamless web that gives members a sense they are part of a long and rich tradition.[50] This veneration of the nation acts as a formidable bonding force that enhances its cohesiveness and boosts its prospects for survival.

Why Nations Want States

So far I have paid little attention to the political dimension of nationhood, but as I explained in chapter 2, all large social groups, including nations, need political institutions from the beginning to survive. For a nation, the best possible situation is to have its own state.

What, then, is a state? Some scholars use the term to describe almost all of the higher political institutions that have existed over time. For example, Charles Tilly writes in his seminal book *Coercion, Capital, and European States, AD 990–1992,* "States have been the world's largest and most powerful organizations for more than five thousand years."[51] Such a broad definition, however, fails to capture important differences among the widely varying political forms that have existed in Europe and other regions throughout history. Instead, I restrict the term *state* to the particular political entity that began to take shape in Europe during the early 1500s and eventually spread across the globe. It differs significantly from its many predecessors, which include (to name just a few) city-states, empires, tribes, principalities, duchies, theocracies, and feudal monarchies. The state in my story takes two forms: the dynastic state, which predominated from about 1500 to 1800, and the nation-state, which replaced it.

A state is a political institution that controls a large territory with well-defined borders and has the ability to employ force to break or discipline the individuals and groups living within those borders.[52] Within these borders, in other words, the state has "exclusive supreme command, enabling it within this territory, to overrule the lower administrative echelons as well as disregard private property."[53] Decision making is centralized in a state: power is concentrated at the center. In practical terms, this means a state has a permanent bureaucracy, a system of rules and laws, and the capacity to levy taxes on the people living within its borders. Most importantly, the central administration controls the lawful tools of violence. The state, of course, looks outward as well as inward, and thus engages in diplomacy, economic intercourse, security competition, and war with other states.

The concept of sovereignty was conceived just as dynastic states were emerging in Europe, which is why they are sometimes referred to as sovereign states. Sovereignty was vested in the crown in those dynastic states, but with the coming of the nation-state, it became lodged in the people. Although sovereignty is all about who has supreme political authority, not actual political power, in the real world authority and power are closely linked. Who possessed ultimate authority mattered greatly in the emerging states, because those people could become remarkably powerful, which meant they would have a huge influence on the people who fell under their purview.

Before the dynastic state came on the scene, both political authority and political power in Europe were much more decentralized. It was often difficult to tell where sovereignty resided. During the Middle Ages (roughly 500 to 1500 AD), writes the political sociologist William Sewell, "The social system was both corporate and hierarchical. . . . People belonged to a whole range of constituted solidarity units, sharing communities of recognition in a simultaneously negotiated fashion with overlapping collections of other persons."[54] The Catholic Church had some authority, but so did kings, the local nobility, towns, cities, and even guilds. Political authority was, as Robert Jackson puts it, "diverse, dislocated, and disjointed."[55] The difficulty of determining who had supreme authority was abetted by the fact that no political entity in Europe was significantly more powerful than its competitors.

One might think that medieval kings had significant political power. But the most powerful political actors were usually the resident nobles and the bishops who ran the local churches. Central authorities were generally no match for these local forces, which had much more influence on an individual's daily life than did monarchs. As the historians Joseph Strayer and Dana Munro note, "Kings were neither especially dignified nor especially important. In most regions of Europe they did not receive the primary allegiance of their peoples and could not determine the political destinies of their countries. . . . The personal bond between a man and his lord was far stronger than the vague idea of allegiance to the state."[56]

The situation began to change in the early 1500s with the emergence of the dynastic state, which was committed to asserting political control over all people within its borders. This meant weakening the authority of the Catholic Church in Rome as well as that of local authorities. Nevertheless, it took time for the dynastic state to centralize control within its borders, because the technology of the day did not permit easy projection of power by the crown. Road systems across Europe were primitive, communication could travel no faster than a horse or a ship, and the capacity to make multiple copies of documents was just beginning to develop.[57] Not until some three hundred years after the first states began appearing in Europe did it make sense to talk about concentrated power at their centers.

By the late 1700s, however, the state was much better positioned to confront the local authorities inside its borders. Not surprisingly, the newly emerging nations paid this development much attention. Each wanted its own nation-state.

Nations covet a state for two reasons, the first of which is self-determination. Like any large social group, nations prefer to run their own affairs and determine their own fates as much as possible. The best way to achieve those ends is for a nation to control the political institutions that shape its daily life. In the modern world, that translates into having one's own state. Of course, not every nation can fulfill this ambition, and nations that cannot are not necessarily doomed to disappear. As the political philosopher Yael Tamir notes, "The right to self-determination can be realized in a variety of different ways: cultural autonomies, regional autonomies, federations, and confederations." But she acknowledges that "unquestionably a nation-state can ensure the widest possible degree of national autonomy and the maximum range of possibilities for the enjoyment of national life."[58] Nations push from the bottom up to establish states they can dominate and run.

Nations also want their own states because this is the best way to maximize their survival prospects. Nations face a variety of threats to their existence, starting with the intrusive nature of the modern state. The dynastic state did not interfere much in the daily lives of the people within its borders. It mainly collected taxes and looked for relatively small numbers of young men who might serve in the army. Otherwise, people were pretty much left alone under the purview of local cultural and political institutions. But as the state became more deeply involved in its citizens' lives, that changed drastically. States had a powerful incentive to mold their people into a single culture with a common language and a shared history.[59]

This impulse to homogenize the culture, which is synonymous with nation-building, presents a grave danger for any minority group in a multinational state, simply because the majority is likely to ensure that the emerging common culture is defined by its own language and traditions. Minority cultures are likely to be pushed aside and maybe even disappear. As Walker Connor points out, states that engage in nation-building are invariably in the business of nation-breaking as well.[60] The best way for a nation to avoid that fate is to have its own state. This logic explains why so many multinational states have broken apart over the past two centuries.[61]

Another reason members of minority nations worry about their survival is that they might be killed in a civil war. A good example is the Hutu genocide against the Tutsis in Rwanda in 1994. A murderous campaign against a minority group might happen for a number of reasons. It might be driven by resentment over the minority's disproportionate influence in the economy, or the minority might be seen as a fifth column, like the Armenians in Turkey during World War I.[62] It is always safer to have your own state than to be on the short end of the power balance in a fractious multinational state.

Finally, national survival was a matter of great concern for subject peoples during the age of imperialism, and fear of conquest played an important role in spreading the modern state system beyond Europe.[63] Between the early sixteenth century and the early twentieth, the European great powers created empires covering large portions of the globe. The indigenous people who became subjects of those far-flung empires often saw their cultures badly damaged by the imperial powers, which frequently restricted the natives' education, destroyed their economies, conscripted their young men, confiscated their farmland, and even forced native peoples into virtual (or actual) slavery. Local populations, spurred on by their elites, eventually began to see themselves as nations and to think about self-determination. In most cases, the only way to achieve that end was to break away from the empire and establish an independent nation-state.

These persuasive reasons for a nation to want its own state have contributed greatly to the development of the nation-state. The converse is true as well: dynastic states had compelling reasons to turn themselves into nation-states, as states benefit greatly when their people are organized into nations.

Why States Want Nations

Nationalism is essential for economic as well as military success, both of which matter greatly for a state's survival. Governing elites also foster nationalism through their efforts to make their populations governable—never an easy task.

In the industrial age, states that want to compete economically have no choice but to create a common culture, as Ernest Gellner argues in his classic work *Nations and Nationalism*. Industry requires laborers who are literate and can communicate with each other. This means states need universal education as well as a common language. Industrial societies, in other words, demand a high degree of cultural homogeneity; they require a nation. The state plays the leading role in fostering that shared culture, especially through education, where it plays a central role in determining what is taught in the classroom. "The monopoly of legitimate education," Gellner writes, "is now more important, more central than is the monopoly of legitimate violence."[64]

There are also compelling national security reasons for states to promote nationalism.[65] As Barry Posen notes, "Any argument that one can make for the economic function of literacy and a shared culture is at least as plausible for a military function, particularly in mass warfare."[66] There is an abundance of evidence showing that educated soldiers perform far better in combat than illiterate ones. And compared with those with different languages and cultures, soldiers who speak the same language and share many of the same practices and beliefs are more easily molded into an effective fighting force.[67]

There is another way in which nationalism is a huge force multiplier. Because nationalism creates tight bonds between a people and their state, leaders in wartime—especially in times of extreme emergency—can usually get their citizens to steadfastly support the war effort and put on a uniform and fight.[68] Nation-states can raise large militaries and sustain them for long periods of time. None of the great powers in World War I, for example, ran out of soldiers. During each year of that unbelievably bloody conflict, the governments routinely replaced their many thousands of lost soldiers with a new crop of eligible males. (In the end, the war killed about nine million in uniform and seven million civilians.) This does not mean armies never collapse after years of deadly fighting, as the Russian army did in the fall of 1917 and the German army did a year later. The French army mutinied in the spring of 1917. Nor is it to deny that public support for a nation-state's war may quickly evaporate.

Nationalism, however, does more than increase the size of a country's military forces. It also makes soldiers, sailors, and airmen more reliable and committed to fighting for their country. In the age of the dynastic state, desertion was a major problem for military commanders both before and during battles. Rulers built their armies with mercenaries and "the criminal, the vagabond, and the destitute" from their own societies, and these soldiers felt little loyalty to the country for which they were fighting.[69] By far a greater motivation was to avoid getting killed. Desertion is much less of a problem when soldiers are drawn from a nationalistic population: they are primed to defend their country by putting themselves in harm's way. Napoleon captured this shift when he proclaimed, "All men who value life more than the glory of the nation and the esteem of their comrades should not be members of the French army."[70]

Nationalism can have a profound effect on the outcome of a war when one side uses it to build a powerful military while its opponents do not. After French nationalism in the wake of the 1789 Revolution helped Napoleon create the mightiest army in Europe, Carl von Clausewitz, who fought against it as an officer in the Prussian military, described its prowess: "This juggernaut of war, based on the strength of the entire people, began its pulverizing course through Europe. It moved with such confidence and certainty that whenever it was opposed by armies of the traditional type there could never be a moment's doubt as to the result."[71] Other countries could hope to survive only if they built an army like the French army, and the only way to do that was to cultivate a nation-state.[72]

Finally, there is a two-pronged logic behind governing a state that works to promote nationalism. First, leaders of all kinds desire popular allegiance. They want their people to be as united as possible and feel loyal to the state, which is not easy to achieve given that no society can ever reach a thoroughgoing consensus about what constitutes the good life. By fostering a common culture and tight bonds between the people and their state, nationalism can be the glue that holds otherwise disputatious people together.

Consider Britain and France in the sixteenth and seventeenth centuries, when states were just emerging as a political form and both countries were riven with conflicts between Catholics and Protestants. In his book *Faith in Nation*, Anthony Marx explains how the ruling monarchs in London and Paris diligently worked to end those conflicts and construct a common culture in their respective countries. Their aim, he notes, was not simply to generate greater cohesion in the populace but also to build loyalty between the people and their rulers.[73] They were largely successful in both cases, although they did not go so far as to create nations, which came later.

Nevertheless, their efforts explain why Britain and France were among the earliest dynastic states to evolve into nation-states.

States also have powerful incentives to shape their societies in ways that make day-to-day governance easier. Political leaders and bureaucrats alike abhor complexity, because it makes it difficult for them to make sense of the world around them and manage it to their state's advantage. They especially dislike trying to run a country where a variety of local cultures have their own boundaries, educational systems, measures, property systems, rules, and languages. To remedy this problem, governing elites engage in social engineering aimed at making it easier to gain knowledge about their country, which, in turn, makes it easier to administer. The key to success is to eliminate heterogeneity, which, according to James Scott, involves complementary processes: simplification and legibility. "A thoroughly legible society," Scott writes, "eliminates local monopolies of information and creates a kind of national transparency through the uniformity of codes, identities, statistics, regulations, and measures." But the "most powerful" of all "state simplifications" is "the imposition of a single, official language."[74] Making a society more homogeneous means transcending local cultures and building a unified nation, even if that is not the intent.

In sum, just as nations have powerful reasons to want their own states, states invariably try to mold their populations into nations. The complementary logics at the root of nationalism work to meld nations and states together into nation-states and have made them the dominant political form in the world. This is one of the realities that liberalism must deal with.

Living with the Dominator

The best starting point for understanding the relationship between liberalism and nationalism is to list their main differences. There are five key ones. First, liberalism focuses on the individual and pays little attention to social groups. Nationalism does the opposite: it rivets on the social group, which of course is the nation. The individual, while not irrelevant, is subordinate to the nation, which provides him with a powerful sense of participation in an enterprise with a timeless and grand tradition.

Second, natural rights and toleration are central components of liberal theory. Nationalism pays them little attention, although a nation-state can certainly have its own set of rights and preach toleration.

Third, liberalism has a particularist strand, which stems from its assumption that there are no final truths about the good life, and a universal strand, derived from its emphasis on inalienable rights. A certain tension exists between these strands. Nationalism does not have a universalist strand; despite its universal appeal, it is particularist all the way down.

Fourth, although the state is of central importance for both theories, its relationship to the wider public is different in each. With liberalism, the state's main functions are to act as a night watchman, arbitrate disputes, and do significant social engineering for the purposes of promoting individual rights and managing the various problems that attend daily life in a modern society. Modus vivendi liberals are opposed to social engineering, especially for the purpose of fostering positive rights, but that is a battle they have lost. Liberalism cultivates hardly any emotional attachment to the state among its citizens, even despite their enormous dependence on it. This functional view of the state explains why it is hard to motivate people to fight and die for a purely liberal state. The nationalist state also maintains order and does substantial social engineering, but it inspires powerful allegiance. People are willing to fight and die for it.

Fifth, liberalism and nationalism view territory differently. Nationalists tend to think of the land they live on, or aspire to live on, as sacred. It is their fatherland or motherland, and so worth making great sacrifices to defend. Where the land's borders are located matters greatly. Liberalism has no room for hallowed territory; it pays little attention to where countries draw their borders, which squares with the emphasis liberals place on universal rights. In the liberal story, land is most important as private property that individuals have an inalienable right to own and sell as they see fit.

The Potential for Coexistence

Despite these differences, there is abundant evidence that these two isms can coexist inside a country. It is important to emphasize, however, that liberalism always operates within the context of a nation-state. Liberalism without nationalism is impossible. We live in a world of nation-states—a world of omnipresent nationalism. Liberalism, of course, is not omnipresent. The international system contained few liberal democracies until after World War II.[75] Although their numbers have grown substantially since then, they have never accounted for even half the countries in the world. Freedom House, for example, reports that they represented 34 percent of the total in 1986 and 45 percent in 2017, but that the trend line is moving downward.[76] The key point, however, is that all of them are not simply liberal democracies but liberal nation-states. A purely liberal state is not feasible. Liberalism requires "the non-liberal underbelly of national community."[77]

Stephen Holmes captures this point when he writes: "Liberals have succeeded in realizing some of their ideals . . . only because they have compromised with the realities of national sovereignty erected on a preliberal basis. Liberal rights are meaningful only within the confines of pre-existing, territorially-bounded states, and only where there exists a rights-enforcing power."[78] To quote another political theorist, Will Kymlicka: "The freedom which liberals demand for individuals is not primarily the freedom to go beyond one's language and history, but rather the freedom to move around within one's societal culture, to distance oneself from particular cultural roles, to choose which features of the culture are most worth developing, and which are without value."[79]

We can get a good sense of how liberalism relates to nationalism from the literature on American national identity. It was once commonplace for scholars to argue that the United States is a deeply liberal country while paying little attention to American nationalism. This perspective is reflected in Louis Hartz's classic 1955 book *The Liberal Tradition in America*. He maintains that the United States was born a liberal country and never had a feudal tradition, unlike its European counterparts. Lacking a significant political right or left, it has instead veered toward an illiberal liberalism. But Hartz says little about American nationalism. In this he follows in the footsteps of Alexis de Tocqueville and Gunnar Myrdal, who also wrote important books on American identity that largely ignore nationalism.[80]

This was a "misleading orthodoxy," as Rogers Smith points out in his important book *Civic Ideals*.[81] American identity does not revolve only around liberalism, as Hartz seemed to think, but is inextricably bound up with nationalism. Political elites in the United States, Smith argues, "require a population to lead that imagines itself to be a 'people,'" which is another way of saying a nation.[82] He emphasizes that conceptions of peoplehood, which are particularist at their core, are at odds with liberalism's emphasis on "universal equal human rights."[83] Moreover, Smith notes that it is impossible to have a purely liberal state.[84]

Among modern scholars, it appears that Smith's view of the importance of "peoplehood" has won the day. For example, the importance of nationalism in American political life is clearly reflected in Anatol Lieven's *American Nationalism* and Samuel Huntington's last book, *Who Are We?* Huntington's great concern was that America's national identity is withering away and that eventually it will be left with only its liberal creed, which by itself cannot sustain the United States for long.[85]

Finally, as David Armitage reminds us, the American Declaration of Independence did not just emphasize the universality of individual rights. It also paid much attention to the idea of "one people" establishing sovereignty, which, of course, is what the colonists were doing at the time. He calls the Declaration "the birth certificate of the American nation." (I would modify this slightly and call it the birth certificate of the American nation-state.) Between these "two distinct elements," Armitage maintains, the founders and their successors paid more attention to "the assertion of popular sovereignty to create a new state" than to "ideas of individual rights." He argues that the Declaration's substantial universal appeal is based more on the sovereignty dimension than the rights one.[86]

On a related matter, some scholars make a distinction between civic nationalism and cultural or ethnic nationalism. For them, the word *civic* is a euphemism for *liberal,* which essentially means they are talking about fashioning a nation based almost exclusively on liberal values. In other words, they are asserting that one may have a nation without a culture based on a widely accepted package of distinct practices and beliefs. Liberalism alone can do the job. Scholars who make this argument usually hold up the United States and the countries of Western Europe as successful examples of this phenomenon.[87] The notion of civic nationalism captures Hartz's description of the United States.

Civic nationalism is not a useful concept. While liberal values can be a component of a nation's culture, they cannot be the sole basis of national identity. Civic nationalism is not a meaningful notion in good part because social groups like nations invariably have a variety of deeply rooted practices and beliefs that matter greatly in their members' daily lives. It is virtually impossible for a nation to function effectively without a multifaceted culture.[88] This is why most scholars who write about American culture today emphasize nationalism as well as liberalism. The American nation, like all nations, has a rich culture, which includes a variety of practices and beliefs. This makes Americans not simply liberals but liberal nationalists. When someone self-identifies as an American, she is effectively saying she is an American nationalist.

Why Nationalism Dominates

It should be clear by now that nationalism is a more powerful force than liberalism. Nationalism is pervasive, while liberalism is not. Liberalism always has to operate in the context of a nationalist state. Still, it would be wrong to think that liberalism matters for little. Even though it almost always loses in a direct conflict with nationalism, liberalism is a powerful ideology.

The two isms are not always at loggerheads. There should be little conflict between them in a society that largely comprises one nation and has a thick culture. In such cases, which include the United States, nationalism should not get in the way of creating a vibrant civil society with considerable room for individual rights and freedom from state interference. The same logic should apply in multinational states where the core nation and the minority nations respect each other's rights and are tolerant of each other's differences. Present-day Canada and India, with their thin national cultures, fit in this category.

Liberalism and nationalism conflict when there is deep hostility between the different groups in a multinational country. In those circumstances, it is almost impossible for liberalism to take hold in the face of national animosities. When relations between groups are filled with anger and hatred, tolerance and equal rights are extremely difficult to promote. Usually in such instances, the most powerful national group discriminates against the weaker group in an illiberal way. Israel's behavior toward the Palestinians is a good example, and with the rise of Hindu extremism, India is in danger of becoming an illiberal democracy.[89]

These circumstances favor nationalism for two reasons. First, liberals oversell the importance of individual rights, which is at the heart of their theory. Most people care about rights, but it is not a burning issue for them, and its influence in daily political life is much more limited than liberals recognize. It is especially limited when the rights conflict with the passions aroused by nationalist animosities. Second and more importantly, nationalism is more in sync with human nature than liberalism, which mistakenly treats individuals as utility maximizers who worry only about their own welfare, rather than as intensely social beings.[90] Nationalism, which is predicated on the correct belief that individuals invariably have a strong sense of loyalty toward their own group, is better at addressing several critically important human needs.[91] This is why it is a ubiquitous force in the modern world and liberalism is not.[92]

It is because liberalism fails to provide individuals with a sense of community that it cannot provide the glue to hold a society together. It does not make them feel they are part of a large and vibrant group that is special and worthy of esteem, which is important to people psychologically as well as for keeping a society intact. This problem derives partly from liberalism's particularist strand—that it rivets on atomistic individuals who have rights but few duties and obligations—and partly from its universalist strand: its emphasis on inalienable rights, which apply to all people, not just the members of a particular group.

In fact, liberalism does not simply fail to provide the bonds to keep a society intact; it also has the potential to eat away at those bonds and ultimately damage the society's foundations. The taproot of the problem is liberalism's radical individualism and its emphasis on utility maximization. It places virtually no emphasis on the importance of fostering a sense of community and caring about fellow citizens. Instead, everyone is encouraged to pursue his own self-interest, based on the assumption that the sum of all individuals' selfish behavior will be the common good. This self-regarding behavior is somewhat countered by contemporary liberalism's emphasis on ensuring equal opportunity for everyone, although not all liberals support that goal. In brief, liberalism not only contributes little to building societies but also has features that undermine social cohesion.

Nationalism, in contrast, is all about community and members' responsibilities to the collectivity. Unlike liberalism, it works toward creating a sense of belonging. It satisfies individuals' emotional need to be part of a large group with a rich tradition and a bright future. Moreover, nationalism is well suited to holding a society together, except in multinational states where the constituent nations are hostile to each other.

Liberalism also does a poor job of tying the individual to the state. In the liberal story, the state is the product of a social contract among individuals, and its main task is to protect them from each other and allow each to pursue her own notion of the good life. Although the state works to promote equal opportunity for its citizens, some liberals contest that mission, and the liberal state, by definition, has limited capacity to interfere in its citizens' lives. Individuals in the liberal story are not expected to have a deep emotional attachment to their state, and it is hard to imagine them putting their lives on the line for it.[93] Nationalism, on the other hand, creates strong bonds between individuals and their state. Many people are strongly inclined to fight and die, if necessary, for their nation-state.

Finally, the vast majority of people in the modern world care greatly about territory. Their identity is bound up in land they consider sacred. This perspective, of course, is central to nationalism and accounts for much of its appeal. Liberalism ignores the link between identity and territory. Uday Mehta maintains that "political theorists in the Anglo-American liberal tradition have, for the most part, not only ignored the links between political identity and territory, but have also conceptualized the former in terms that at least implicitly deny any significance to the latter and the links between the two."[94] Land is important to liberalism as private property, but that is a different matter.

All of this is to say that liberalism can have an important role in shaping daily life, but it almost always plays second fiddle to nationalism.

Overselling Individual Rights

The liberal case for rights rests on two claims. First, the overwhelming majority of people around the world recognize what those rights are and think they are universal and inalienable, meaning they apply equally to everyone in the world and cannot be given or taken away. Second, people across the board believe individual rights are truly important and should be privileged in the political arena. There are good reasons to doubt both of these suppositions. Rights are not insignificant, one can certainly argue that they should be universal and inalienable, and even if that is visibly not true everywhere, they are still of great importance in particular countries, where they form part of a well-established tradition. The 1689 English Bill of Rights, for example, which arose mainly out of the politics of the Glorious Revolution, gained legitimacy by invoking "ancient rights and liberties."[95]

Privileging the concept of inalienable rights creates theoretical as well as evidentiary problems. When you look carefully at the underlying logic, there are three reasons to be skeptical that any widely agreed-upon body of rights can exist; and when you look closely at the historical record, it provides considerable evidence to back up that skepticism.

False Universalism

For starters, liberalism assumes there is no possibility of a worldwide consensus on what constitutes the good life. Particular societies may reach substantial agreement on first principles, but they will never achieve universal agreement, save for the belief that everyone has a basic right to survival. At the same time, however, liberals maintain that there is some objectively correct set of individual rights, and that it is possible to discern what those rights are, how they relate to each other, and that they are inalienable.

How can this be, since individual rights are all about first principles? They are profoundly important for defining how people think about and act toward their fellow humans. Thus it is hard to believe, given the limits of our critical faculties, that there can be anything close to universal agreement on whether rights are inalienable, what they should be, and which ones should take precedence. There is a fundamental disagreement between modus vivendi and progressive liberals over whether individuals have a right to equal opportunity, and over positive rights more generally. Well-informed, well-meaning citizens disagree profoundly over whether there is a right to abortion or to affirmative action. These are matters that deal with the good life, and they show that we should not expect reason to provide collective truths.

To take this a step further, placing rights at the core of any political system is tantamount to saying that the best political order is a liberal one. It is difficult to imagine how it is possible to privilege rights in the absence of a liberal or at least quasi-liberal state. Political liberals are sometimes surprisingly intolerant toward illiberal groups or states, thinking that the only legitimate political order is a liberal one. This belief has long been widespread in the United States, as Louis Hartz makes clear in *The Liberal Tradition in America*. It is also on display in John Rawls's *The Law of Peoples*, where he makes it clear that the best world is one populated solely with liberal democracies.[96] John Locke also emphasized that liberal societies cannot tolerate groups that do not play by liberal rules.

Thus when liberals talk about inalienable rights, they are effectively defining the good life. They make no meaningful distinction between these two subjects. But if it is an axiom of liberalism (backed up by observation) that you cannot get universal agreement on first principles, then it follows that you cannot get a planetary consensus on individual rights.

I noted in the previous chapter that there is a paradox in political liberalism, which stems from the fact that its core holds a particularist as well as a universalist strand. The particularism, of course, comes from the liberal belief that there is no truth regarding the good life, while the universalism is tied to the concept of inalienable rights. These two dimensions, I emphasized, are in tension with each other. But under my analysis here, that paradox disappears, because liberalism properly understood is particularist all the way down. There can be no universal agreement about individual rights, just as there is no universal agreement about the good life, because there is no meaningful difference between those two realms.

Trumping Rights

There is a second theoretical problem with liberal thinking about rights: other considerations sometimes push them into the background. People will usually privilege political stability, which involves their personal security and welfare, over rights when the two come into conflict. For example, if rights, and liberal democracy generally, lead to disorder, which might mean privation or death, individual rights are unlikely to matter much in practice, even among a public that in principle genuinely favors them.

This logic is likely to apply in multinational states where there are deep-seated animosities among the rival groups. In such instances, many people will prefer an authoritarian leader who can keep the other factions at bay. There will also be cases, however, where a country is in turmoil for some reason and adopting a liberal democratic system would only make the problem worse. Finally, individual rights sometimes take a backseat to concerns about an external threat. Countries facing existential threats over long periods tend to become garrison states—also known as national security states—that often trample on individual rights.[97]

The final theoretical problem regarding rights concerns nationalism. According to the liberal story, rights apply equally to everyone, everywhere. But this flies in the face of nationalism, in which the concept of sovereignty means that each state is free to determine for itself which rights matter and how much they matter. Nation-states are likely to be jealous defenders of their self-determination, and it is hard to imagine them reaching a universal consensus on the correct package of rights.

Furthermore, nationalism is all about privileging one's own group over others. In an international system composed almost wholly of nation-states, most people will favor their fellow nationals over outsiders. In practice, countries are unlikely to accord the "other" the same rights given to their own people, and where nationalism turns ugly, they will have little difficulty trampling on the rights of foreigners they dislike or hate. In brief, nationalism, which is particularist to the core, presents a serious threat to the notion of inalienable rights.

One can make the case that it is dangerous to think in terms of universal rights in a world of nation-states. Doing so risks giving people the impression that there is some higher authority—maybe some international institution—empowered to protect their rights. In fact, there is no such entity; states protect an individual's rights, not some superior authority. Hannah Arendt saw the problem: "The Rights of Man . . . had been defined as 'inalienable' because they were supposed to be independent of all governments; but it turned out that the moment human beings lacked their own government and had to fall back upon their minimum rights, no authority was left to protect them and no institution was willing to guarantee them."[98] She maintained that stateless people and unwanted minorities residing inside nation-states live in grave danger, because there is no enforcement mechanism to defend their rights, including the right to life, if they come under attack. "The abstract nakedness of being nothing but human," she argued, "was their greatest danger."[99]

Arendt's solution was to eschew talk of universal rights and instead emphasize "nationally guaranteed rights." In this she aligned herself with Edmund Burke, who "opposed the French Revolution's Declaration of the Rights of Man" and instead made the case that rights "spring 'from within the nation.'" For Arendt, as for Burke, "It was much wiser to rely on an 'entailed inheritance' of rights which one transmits to one's children like life itself, and to claim one's rights to be the 'rights of an Englishman' rather than the inalienable rights of man."[100] Her opposition to this universalist strand of liberalism was driven in good part by concerns about survival.

Natural Rights and History

If reason tells us that everyone possesses a set of inalienable rights, as liberals claim, then it seems reasonable to expect that at least some important premodern thinkers would have understood this basic fact of life. That is not the case. Aristotle and Plato, as well as Machiavelli, apparently had no concept of natural rights. Hobbes and Locke did not begin developing the foundations of liberalism until the seventeenth century. Others, such as Benjamin Constant, Kant, and Montesquieu, followed in their footsteps, but many other political philosophers paid little attention to the liberal story about individual rights, and some, such as Burke and Bentham, explicitly challenged it. Thus it is not even possible to make the less sweeping claim that once the leading thinkers recognized the importance of natural rights, a solid consensus emerged. There has never been universal agreement that rights are inalienable or that they are fundamental to political life.[101]

Furthermore, liberals themselves disagree about which rights matter most and how to weigh them when they come into conflict. The problem is especially complicated when promoting equality is thrown into the mix.[102]

John Rawls maintains that "applying liberal principles has a certain simplicity," but this is only sometimes true.[103] Think about hate speech. Liberals who are absolutists regarding free speech believe it should be tolerated even if they find it abhorrent. Other liberals, however, want to ban it because it can seriously hurt those who are targeted, who have the right to be protected from verbal abuse just as they have a right to be protected from physical abuse.[104] There is no indisputable way to determine how to rank these different rights. As John Gray notes, "All regimes embody particular settlements among rival liberties."[105]

Hobbes's and Locke's thinking about individual rights was significantly shaped by contingency and history. The hate-filled conflict between Catholics and Protestants that raged in their day, coupled with the deep socioeconomic changes taking place in Britain, deeply influenced the foundational ideas of liberalism. In short, political ideologies are not created by reason alone. They tend to develop at critical points in history, and liberalism is no exception.

Even the staunchest advocates of individual rights are usually willing to limit, even disregard, rights in a supreme emergency. When an individual's or a country's survival is at stake, rights cannot be allowed to get in the way of doing whatever is necessary to endure. John Stuart Mill, for example, maintains that "the sole end for which mankind are warranted, individually or collectively, in interfering with the liberty of action of any of their number, is self-protection."[106] Michael Walzer, who argues that countries should fight wars under a strict moral code of conduct, follows in Mill's footsteps. At the end of his famous tract on just war theory, he writes that all the rules go out the window "when we are face-to-face not merely with defeat but with a defeat likely to bring disaster to a political community."[107] John Rawls too maintains that "political liberalism allows the supreme emergency exemption."[108]

Countries or regions that have experienced great upheaval usually show a yearning for political stability that trumps any desire to create a liberal democracy. For example, a recent survey of Arab youth in the Middle East found that 53 percent of the respondents believe that "promoting stability in the region is more important than promoting democracy." Only 28 percent disagreed.[109] Consider too the case of President Paul Kagame, an authoritarian leader who seriously limits free speech in Rwanda, which experienced genocide in 1994. His main aim is to limit hostilities between the Hutus, who perpetrated the genocide, and the Tutsis, who were its principal victims. Kagame has enjoyed great success, and not surprisingly he has been elected to three terms as president despite his illiberal policies.[110]

Russia's strong preference for order over rights and democracy today is hardly surprising given what happened there in the 1990s, when its attempt to embrace Western-style democracy failed miserably, creating corruption and disorder on a grand scale. Since the early 2000s, Russia has become steadily more authoritarian, largely restoring order in the process. A March 2014 poll conducted by the All-Russian Public Opinion Center showed that "seventy-one percent of Russians say they are ready to sacrifice civil freedoms to maintain stability, order and personal well-being."[111]

Finally, if individual rights are recognized and highly regarded by almost everyone, it should be reasonably easy to spread liberalism to other countries. But it is not. People are easily persuaded to respect their own rights, but convincing them that others' rights are equally important is a difficult task. It is much easier to advance a bare-bones version of democracy that demands nothing more than free and fair elections in which the winners take office. It took a long time for liberalism to take root throughout the West, which is where it got started and has had the greatest impact.[112] Of course, this is why the United States and its European allies are committed to spreading its values beyond the West.[113]

Even within the West, however, the commitment to individual rights is softer than most people realize. In the United States, leaders have violated individual rights when they thought the country was facing an extreme emergency. Probably the best-known example of this phenomenon is Abraham Lincoln's actions during the Civil War (1861–65), when, among other things, he suspended habeas corpus, censored the mail, instituted military tribunals, and arrested individuals "who were represented to him as being or about to engage in disloyal and treasonable practices."[114] Moreover, as Clinton Rossiter makes clear in *Constitutional Dictatorship*, the Civil War is not the only time America's political leaders seriously limited rights in circumstances they felt were highly dangerous. One might expect there was a huge outcry, or at least significant protests, from the American people when their rights were curtailed. But they did not protest, mainly because the public's support for individual rights in the United States is sometimes surprisingly soft.

The best evidence of the American people's flexible commitment to liberalism is that they tolerated slavery until the Civil War, and then tolerated blatant racism in both the North and the South until the mid-1960s. Racism today is less socially acceptable but has hardly vanished. There was widespread discrimination against immigrants throughout the nineteenth century and well into the twentieth. This too rests a few inches underground today. Aristide Zolberg describes U.S. policy toward Chinese immigrants in the latter half of the nineteenth century as the "only successful instance of 'ethnic cleansing' in the history of American immigration."[115] The Europeans who began moving to the United States in large numbers in the 1830s also faced marked discrimination well into the twentieth century.[116] Probably no group had it worse than the Irish, who were despised by the ruling WASP elites. And there is no greater instance of discrimination against a European ethnic group than what happened to German Americans during World War I.[117] Although America was a thoroughly liberal country in principle from its inception, for most of its history it has hardly been a paragon of liberal virtue in practice.

Fortunately, this illiberal behavior toward African Americans and immigrants has mostly disappeared from public view, and the United States now strives to be a liberal country in practice as well as in theory. But the American public's support for individual rights is not especially deep. While the discourse about rights is pervasive in contemporary America, that has been the case only since the 1950s. Before then, Americans did not pay much attention to individual rights.[118]

The present interest in rights notwithstanding, according to the political scientist Gerald Rosenberg, many Americans understand little about the real meaning of inalienable rights, including that they are supposed to apply universally.[119] Rosenberg shows that most equate rights with their own preferences. They tend to make rights claims that support their own interests but pay little attention to claims that do not. Thus it is unsurprising that Americans are willing to curtail important rights when it suits them. Rosenberg concludes, after examining a variety of public opinion surveys, that "Americans view the right to a free press as meaning only the ability to publish what people prefer to read. If the American public does not like the content, then the press should not be able to publish it." Regarding free speech, he finds that "Americans are both deeply committed to free speech in the abstract *and* strongly opposed to free speech for unpopular groups." Both cases, he emphasizes, provide "a good deal of empirical support for the notion of rights as preferences."[120] It seems clear that many Americans are not deeply committed to the principle of universal rights. If that is true, it is hard to imagine that a passionate commitment to inalienable rights exists elsewhere, since no country has as rich a liberal tradition as the United States.

The bottom line is that the universal strand of liberalism is nowhere near as powerful as liberals believe. Liberal claims about the importance of individual rights are much less compelling than liberals seem to believe, and might even be dead wrong. This circumscribed view of rights has direct implications for toleration and the state, the other two mechanisms that foster peace and prosperity in a liberal society. The more that citizens respect individual rights, the easier it is to promote tolerance and peaceful conflict resolution, and thus reduce the work the state has to perform to keep order. But if respect for rights is thin, it will be more difficult to promote tolerance, and the state's role in maintaining peace at home will loom larger.

The Authoritarian Temptation

There is a potentially devastating argument against liberalism that needs to be addressed. James Madison identified it long ago, in *Federalist No. 10*.[121] I do not think this argument ultimately reveals a fatal flaw in the theory, but it surely explains why it is often difficult to establish and maintain a liberal political order.

The taproot of the problem is that because there are always some sharp differences over first principles in every country, there will always be factions competing for power. As we saw, it matters greatly who governs the state because the faction in charge gets to write the rules, and in any society, whoever writes the rules gets to determine in part what constitutes the good life. There is no such thing as a neutral state that merely acts as an umpire among rival factions. One faction, or some combination of factions, has to run the government, and in the process it will shape society in important ways.

Thus each faction in a liberal democracy has a strong incentive to take over the state and not relinquish power to a rival faction. In the Middle East, this phenomenon is commonly referred to as "one man, one vote, one time."[122] Two motivating logics are at play here. Obviously, the faction that seized control would get to write the rules and not have to worry about losing a future election to a rival faction that might rewrite the rules. Additionally, each faction has good reason to think that every other faction understands this logic, and thus any faction that trusts another faction risks being played for a sucker. It is better to move first and capture the state for the long term before another faction beats you to the punch. This kind of behavior, which might seem unavoidable, would destroy a liberal democracy, even if the rival factions have no animus toward liberalism per se.

Still, liberal democracy is not doomed to fail because of this incentive structure. A well-ordered liberal state has specific features that help insulate it from collapse, although it may remain an uneasy standoff between factions. Five key considerations work together to attenuate the problem.

The first feature is balance-of-power behavior among various factions. If no single faction is especially powerful, it makes little sense for any faction to try to capture the state, because that move would almost certainly lead to a civil war. And if one faction *is* especially powerful, it can afford to play by the rules, get elected, and run the state over the long term in ways that it sees fit. It has no need to take control permanently. The one potentially dangerous situation is where there is an especially powerful faction that thinks it will lose its power over time. This creates incentives to undermine liberal democracy before the decline happens. The logic of this situation resembles that of preventive war. But even in this case, the rival factions will surely balance against the powerful, albeit declining, faction.

The second consideration is the presence of crosscutting cleavages, which are common in liberal states. Most people have multiple interests that contribute to their political views. At the same time, there is a diverse array of issues that can motivate a faction, which means that not every faction in a society is concerned with the same issue.[123] These two facts, when put to-gether, mean that different individuals will sometimes find themselves in competing factions on one issue but on the same side on another. This outcome complicates the problem for any faction that might try to capture the state and put an end to liberal democracy.

The third factor is organic solidarity, to borrow Durkheim's term.[124] The divisions of labor within a liberal society create extensive economic inter-dependence. People are intertwined at the economic level in profound ways. They depend on their fellow citizens in order to make a living and prosper, and most importantly, to survive. A civil war, which might ensue if one faction tried to conquer the state, would undermine that solidarity and gravely harm the entire society.

The fourth consideration is nationalism. Liberal democracies are ulti-mately nation-states with deeply rooted cultures. Their citizens share cer-tain practices and beliefs, and this works to ameliorate differences among them. One of those key beliefs, at least for most people, is sure to be a deep-seated faith in the virtues of liberal democracy in general and their own liberal democratic state in particular. Being liberal, in other words, is part of one's national identity. Citizens will still have fundamental differences over first principles, which means there will always be factions. Still, the *fact* of liberal democracy as an element of national identity can serve as a kind of glue, even if the theory cannot provide this glue.

The fifth feature is the deep state.[125] A liberal democracy, like any mod-ern state, is highly bureaucratized, meaning it contains a good number of large institutions populated by career civil servants. Some of those bureau-cracies are principally concerned with protecting the nation and the state against threats from within and without, which invariably means they have significant power to safeguard the existing political order. These institutions tend to operate autonomously, largely insulated from politics, which means that they usually do not identify with any particular faction. British civil servants, for example, devotedly serve both Conservative and Labor govern-ments. Sometimes, however, a faction can capture a bureaucratic state, as the Nazis did in Germany during the 1930s.

Finally, at least three of these attenuating factors generally get stronger with time, which suggests that mature liberal democracies should be more resilient than fledgling ones. The more time passes, the more interdependent a society's members become; the more they will be exposed to nation-building; and the stronger the deep state will become. In sum, the presence of competing internal factions does not mean that liberal states are doomed to fall apart.

On the international stage, however, things may be quite different.

5

Liberalism Goes Abroad

THE PREVIOUS TWO CHAPTERS FOCUSED ON describing and analyzing political liberalism as it applies to politics at home. It is time to shift gears and address the question at the heart of this book: what happens when a powerful state adopts a liberal foreign policy? In other words, what happens when a country that is deeply committed to individual rights and doing social engineering to promote those rights employs that template in the wider world?

That formidable state will end up embracing liberal hegemony, a highly interventionist foreign policy that involves fighting wars and doing significant social engineering in countries throughout the world. Its main aim will be to spread liberal democracy, toppling authoritarian regimes in the process, with the ultimate goal of creating a world populated solely by liberal democracies. In effect, a state pursuing liberal hegemony aims to remake the international system in its own image. It will also work to foster an open world economy and build international institutions to deal with both economic and security issues.

When a liberal country finds itself in a position to pursue this ambitious policy, it will almost always do so, in large part because the perceived benefits are so great. Not only does this policy hold out the promise of protecting the rights of people all around the world, it is also said to make the world more peaceful and protect liberalism at home from its enemies. Moreover, liberal hegemony provides the foreign policy elite with many attractive career opportunities, since trying to dominate the globe is a labor-intensive enterprise. Finally, that elite is likely to think it has the know-how to interfere effectively in the politics of other countries. This combination of per-ceived benefits and faith in the ability to realize them invariably leads powerful liberal states to pursue liberal hegemony.

The prominence that liberalism accords to the notion of inalienable or universal rights means that a foreign policy based on liberal principles re-quires careful monitoring of other countries' human rights performance. When the rights of foreigners are threatened, a powerful state pursuing liberal hegemony will likely feel compelled to intervene to protect the rights of those individuals. That state is apt to conclude that the best way to ame-liorate, even eliminate, the threat to individual rights is to make sure that as many people as possible live in a liberal democracy, where respect for individual rights is of great importance. This logic leads straight to an ac-tive policy of regime change aimed at toppling autocracies and replacing them with liberal democracies.

Liberals believe there is another important reason to promote the spread of liberal democracy: it facilitates peace. Liberalism, goes the argument, helps foster a deep commitment to individual rights that transcends state borders, and this in turn fosters tolerance among peoples living in differ-ent countries and also inspires them to settle their conflicts peacefully. States come to see themselves as part of an international community based on transnational respect for rights, and that powerful sense of community limits the pernicious effects of nationalism and helps states transcend balance-of-power politics. All of this makes for a more pacific world in which problems like nuclear proliferation and terrorism are effectively taken off the table. Some liberals argue that liberalism also helps further peace by enhancing economic prosperity, which of course is an end in itself.[1]

The final incentive for liberal democracies to move toward a world popu-lated by like-minded states is that this would effectively eliminate their principal ideological competitors, who might at some point threaten their survival. To use Woodrow Wilson's famous words, it would "make the world safe for democracy." While there is no question that spreading democracy around the world is an exceptionally ambitious undertaking, liberals be-lieve it is doable. In their story, people are hardwired to prize individual rights, and most liberals are confident about their ability to do social engi-neering at home as well as abroad.

I take issue with this story on two counts. First, liberal great powers are seldom in a position to pursue liberal hegemony. They normally have little choice but to act according to realist principles, because they are usually in competition with one or more other great powers. This argument is consistent with basic liberal logic, which effectively says that in the absence of a world state, states bent on survival have little choice but to compete for power. Liberalism has to have a night watchman if it is to work: it demands a hierarchic political system such as exists inside the state itself. But the international system is anarchic, not hierarchic. As long as liberal states operate in either bipolarity or multipolarity, they have no choice but to act toward each other according to realist logic.

Second, circumstances sometimes arise where the balance of power is so favorable to a liberal state that it is free to pursue liberal hegemony. This situation is most likely to occur in unipolarity, which is defined as the presence of only one great power in the system, thus rendering great-power security competition impossible. The United States found itself in this position when the Cold War ended and the Soviet Union collapsed, and unsurprisingly, it embraced liberal hegemony.[2] As the American case shows, this policy invariably goes badly awry, and the aspiring liberal hegemon usually ends up paying a big price for having pursued it.

Turning a country into a liberal democracy is extremely difficult, not only because foreign cultures have deep roots and are hard to manipulate, but also because many people around the world do not privilege individual rights. Moreover, nationalism, which is all about self-determination, leads countries to resist foreign interference in their domestic affairs. Finally, even if one country is pursuing liberal hegemony, others are likely to act according to balance-of-power logic, which means the liberalizer will meet stiff resistance from them. In short, liberalism as foreign policy is a source of trouble.

When it comes to politics among states, liberalism is no match for nationalism and realism. Those two isms together have played the leading role in shaping the modern international system, and their influence is likely to continue. Of course, the appearance of a world state, which would turn the state system hierarchic, would make liberalism a much more potent force in international politics. But there is hardly any chance that will happen.

Anarchy is here to stay, and as long as it does, liberalism cannot provide a sound basis for a state's foreign policy.

The Case for Liberal Hegemony

The critical actor in political liberalism's optimistic story about foreign policy is the individual, not the state. Liberalism's stark individualism is what makes it a universal ideology, which profoundly affects how liberals think about international relations. In particular, liberalism's core assumption that every individual, regardless of where she lives, is born with the same set of rights invariably leads liberals to see the world in universalist terms.

A liberal state, of course, does significant domestic social engineering to protect and promote the rights of its citizens. But because those rights are universal, that same state feels a genuine sense of responsibility to intervene, perhaps even militarily, on behalf of people in other countries if it sees their rights violated. Michael Doyle goes so far as to argue that "nonliberal governments are in a state of aggression with their own people," an idea that appears to call for intervention in the politics of every country that is not a liberal democracy and would lead to a remarkably ambitious foreign policy.[3]

The importance liberalism accords individual rights inexorably leads to the belief that the best way to guard those rights is for every country to be a liberal democracy. No political system compares to liberalism when it comes to promoting and protecting individual rights, and it is hard even to envision how rights could be privileged in a political order that is not at least somewhat liberal. We should therefore expect a liberal state to pursue a foreign policy that emphasizes advancing liberal democracy. That task will obviously involve regime change, sometimes by military force, as well as heavy-duty social engineering to transform the target state. When you consider that the ultimate aim is to spread liberalism all around the world, it becomes clear that a liberal foreign policy is extremely ambitious and highly interventionist.

Liberal states, of course, are also nation-states, which means that nationalism helps shape their approach to dealing with the world in important ways. One particular aspect of nationalism—a deep-seated sense of superiority over other nations—helps reinforce a liberal state's belief that it can affect fundamental change all over the world. This combination of nationalist chauvinism and liberal idealism is plainly reflected in the frequent claims of American policymakers who see the United States as having special qualities that enable it to instruct and transform other less fortunate countries.

Causing Peace

Liberals want to spread liberal democracy not just to protect the rights of individuals but also because they believe it is an excellent strategy for causing peace. The reason is simple: liberal democracies do not fight wars with each other. In the liberal story, states are much like the individuals who live inside them: they sometimes have irreconcilable differences. Given that any two states may at some point have a deep-seated disagreement over an issue both care intensely about, how is it possible to construct a peaceful world? There is no higher authority to maintain order in the international system, as there is inside a liberal state. How can liberalism be a pacifier in a world without a night watchman?

The answer is found in the all-important concept of individual rights. Not only is everyone bestowed with those rights, but there is also (at least in liberal societies) a deep-rooted and widespread respect for the rights of others. This respect, which is inextricably bound up with tolerance, transcends national borders. Liberal states understand that not just their own people but foreigners as well have inalienable rights, which must be respected at all times.[4]

This transnational respect for individual rights fosters a powerful sense of community among liberal states, where trust among them is commonplace. It is striking how often the word *community* appears in liberal discourse. In addition to the familiar term *international community,* one often hears reference to the transatlantic community, the European Community, and security communities more generally. When Woodrow Wilson spoke about power, a word liberals usually avoid, he would sometimes use the phrase "community of power."[5] Liberals also use cognate phrases like *international society, family of nations, common humanity,* and *collective security.*

Liberal societies develop a powerful norm of peaceful conflict resolution. Disputes between them—even bitter ones—are not settled by threats of force or war but by arbitration and compromise. Clausewitz's famous dictum that war is an extension of politics by other means does not apply in a liberal world, because liberal states do not consider war a legitimate way of settling their disagreements. Yet war remains an acceptable instrument for protecting human rights abroad and for spreading liberal democracy around the world. Doyle points out that liberal democracies are inclined to wage wars against non-democracies with "imprudent vehemence."[6] For liberals, as R. H. Tawney notes, "war is either a crime or a crusade. There is no half-way house."[7]

Realist logic is thus severely attenuated in a world of liberal states. Because they have no intention of attacking each other, they no longer have to worry about their survival and so need not compete with each other for power. As John Ikenberry notes, "There is an optimist assumption lurking in liberal internationalism that states can overcome constraints and cooperate to solve security dilemmas, pursue collective action, and create an open, stable system."[8]

Liberalism also dominates nationalism, which has a different take on individual rights, not to mention a dark side that sometimes pushes states to hate and fight each other. A committed nationalist would see someone in another nation as not entitled to the same rights as his fellow nationals. Liberals naturally reject this particularist perspective and instead emphasize that rights apply equally to people everywhere. They talk about human rights, not national rights, and the former trump the latter. This effectively neutralizes hypernationalism.

John Rawls, for example, focuses explicitly on "peoples" in his major treatise on international relations, showing that he understands the world is divided into different nations. (*Peoples* is a euphemism for *nations* in his story.) Yet when liberal peoples deal with each other, the nasty side of nationalism is almost completely absent. "Just peoples," he writes, "are fully prepared to grant the very same proper respect and recognition to other peoples as equals."[9] The individuals who make up these just peoples are driven by "common sympathies" that overwhelm any nation's sense of superiority over another.[10] This liberal take on nationalism is captured in Bertrand Russell's reflection about his own thinking on the relationship between those two isms: "I grew up as an ardent believer in optimistic liberalism. I both hoped and expected to see throughout the world a gradual spread of parliamentary democracy, personal liberty, and freedom for the countries that were at that time subject to European Powers, including Britain. I hoped that everybody would in time see the wisdom of Cobden's arguments for Free Trade, and that nationalism might gradually fade into a universal humanism."[11]

The final dimension of the argument that liberalism undermines nationalism and realism concerns the important concept of sovereignty. There is no question the state plays a prominent role in political liberalism, even in the writings of someone like Rawls, who focuses largely on peoples or nations. Yet the state does not have a hard shell around it. Modern liberalism appears to have a more relaxed attitude toward sovereignty than either nationalism or realism. In the liberal story, state borders are soft and permeable, because rights transcend those boundaries, meaning not only that people living in different countries have deep ties and common interests but also that liberal states have the right and responsibility to intervene in other countries' affairs if they violate their citizens' rights. Norms about individual rights overshadow the norm of sovereignty in a world of liberal states.[12]

A vibrant international community of liberal states, which by definition will be tolerant toward each other and deeply committed to settling their disputes peacefully, will defang nationalism and largely eliminate security competition and war. States will have little need for nuclear weapons. Deterrence will be an irrelevant concept. Terrorism should be much less of a problem, given that liberal democracies naturally enjoy significant legitimacy among their peoples. And those like-minded states should have little difficulty coordinating their efforts to deal with any terrorist threats that do arise. Thus the more liberal states there are, the better, and the ideal world would be populated only with liberal states.[13]

Protecting Liberalism at Home

A third reason liberals are attracted to regime change has to do with self-preservation. As I noted in chapter 3, liberalism has a core vulnerability in that there are always, in any liberal society, some people who reject liberalism and would overturn the political order if they could. A liberal state will always have internal enemies, although the severity of the threat varies. That problem is exacerbated when there are non-liberal countries that can join forces with those domestic anti-liberals and increase the threat to the liberal order. The problem is especially acute when there is a close ideological link between internal and external enemies. This threat gives liberal states a powerful incentive to eliminate the external enemy by transforming it into a liberal democracy. Of course, the problem would go away if all states were liberal.

The international relations scholar John Owen maintains that this link between internal and external enemies motivates not just liberal democracies but all states to pursue "forcible regime promotion" in countries governed by rival ideologies. "Precisely because the threat is transnational," he writes, "the government can degrade it by attacking it abroad as well as at home. By suppressing an enemy ideology abroad, it can remove a source of moral and perhaps material support for enemy ideologues at home."[14] Both sides understand this logic, which gives each an added incentive to knock off the other side's regime as quickly as possible.

The bottom line is that liberal states have three reasons for adopting a policy of regime change: protecting the rights of foreigners, facilitating peace, and safeguarding liberalism at home. But such an ambitious strategy is often out of reach. To pursue it, a state must be especially powerful and have the wherewithal to topple foreign regimes, sometimes with military force, at a reasonably low cost. It must also have the expertise and patience to manage the difficult task of building a stable liberal democracy to replace the ousted regime. Modern liberalism, however, is deeply committed to social engineering, not only for the purpose of fostering and protecting individual rights, but also because the complexities of contemporary life force states to be deeply involved in managing their societies. Many liberals think of regime change as a feasible policy that will reap huge benefits.[15]

Although a state that pursues liberal hegemony will be mainly concerned with protecting individual rights and spreading liberal democracy around the world, it will also pursue two other noteworthy missions: building international institutions and advancing economic intercourse among states.

These goals follow from the twin claims that international institutions and economic interdependence promote peace. In chapter 7, I will examine these theories at length, along with the claim that liberal democracies do not fight against each other, with an emphasis on determining whether any of them puts forward a compelling case. Here I will focus on explaining how constructing institutions and facilitating an open international economy can be considered key elements of a liberal foreign policy.

In fact, both tasks complement that policy. International institutions are essentially rules defining the rights and obligations that should guide state behavior. States are expected to obey these rules even when they believe that doing so is not in their interest. In addition to placing a high premium on the rule of law and safeguarding rights, institutions are designed to peacefully settle disputes between countries. All of these endeavors are part of the liberal canon.

It is hardly surprising that a liberal foreign policy favors market-based economies and calls for furthering international trade and investment. The right to own and exchange property is one of the cardinal tenets of political liberalism, and economic globalization provides abundant opportunity for individuals to pursue their self-interest. Moreover, liberals are determined to use economics to limit the damage caused by political disagreements. An open international economy, they believe, not only generates prosperity—which is a good in itself that inclines people toward peace and liberalism—but also makes states economically dependent on each other. These trading and investment relationships are a strong disincentive to fighting: Why would you go to war against a state on which your prosperity depends?

I should say a few words about a mission to which I give scant attention but which is occasionally identified with liberal foreign policy. Some liberals and others argue that states should promote global justice by adopting redistributive policies that reduce the sharp economic inequalities among states. They should, as one advocate puts it, "seek to influence the global distribution of resources and wealth" to advantage poorer countries.[16] This goal complements the liberal commitment to promoting equal opportunity among individuals inside liberal states. No liberal state has ever shown serious interest in helping other states gain economic advantages at its expense just to fight global injustice, and there is little reason to think any ever will.[17]

Elites, the Public, and Liberal Hegemony

Finally, it is important to note that liberal hegemony is largely an elite-driven policy. The foreign policy establishments in liberal states are generally more internationalist than their publics, which tend to be more nationalist. In particular, the foreign policy elites tend to be much more committed to defending individual rights abroad than the average citizen. This is not to say these publics do not have liberal instincts or to suggest that the elites are not nationalists. But there is little doubt that foreign policy elites are more interested in pursuing liberal goals abroad than are their broader publics.

There are a variety of reasons for this phenomenon. For starters, liberal elites tend to be better educated than the average citizen. They typically spend years attending colleges and universities, which have become remarkably international in recent decades. Most campuses today contain large numbers of foreign students as well as faculty born and raised in other countries, and native-born students are also given the opportunity to study abroad. The top colleges and universities have become thoroughly liberal places where nationalist sentiments are seldom on display.

Furthermore, elites in modern societies often spend a good deal of time hobnobbing with fellow elites from other countries. Academics, professionals, business leaders, journalists, policymakers, and think tankers all travel abroad, meet their foreign counterparts, and often form close friendships with them. Thus, the foreign policy elites in today's world tend to be decidedly cosmopolitan. This is not to say they all match Samuel Huntington's caricature of the men and women at the World Economic Forum in Davos, Switzerland, "who have little need for national loyalty" and see "national boundaries as obstacles that are thankfully vanishing."[18] But some are not far off.

Additionally, foreign policy is *le domaine réservé* of the state, generally carried out without much public involvement. Of course, groups of citizens can take strong positions on particular issues, organize protests, or press their representatives to vote a certain way on foreign policy–related matters.

But overall, the public's direct involvement in day-to-day foreign policy is limited. Elites run it, and they have a material interest in pursuing activist policies like liberal hegemony. Trying to run the world generates numerous high-level positions both inside and outside the government, whereas a more restrictive foreign policy would generate less work. As Stephen Walt puts it, liberal hegemony "is a full-employment strategy for the foreign policy establishment."[19]

Taken together, these two benefits—liberal hegemony's promise to protect individual rights around the world, prevent war, and thwart illiberal elements on the home front, as well as its promise of interesting, consequential, and well-paying job opportunities—help explain why liberal elites are so deeply committed to an expansive foreign policy, even after it runs into serious trouble.

Given that the foreign policy elite are so invested in pursuing liberal hegemony, it is hardly surprising that they have constructed a comprehensive narrative outlining its purported benefits, which they disseminate through think tank reports, public speeches, op-eds, and other forms of mass outreach. They fervently believe in this ambitious mission, which they envision as a noble one; and they do an excellent job of selling it to the public at large and to the young men and women who aspire to join the foreign policy establishment. As Walt notes, they are especially effective in marketing their message at the public policy schools that prepare future leaders for public service.

In sum, a liberal foreign policy is mainly concerned with maximizing the number of liberal democracies in the world. It is also concerned with the ancillary tasks of building international institutions and promoting an open international economy. But what are the prospects that a state will adopt such a policy? And if it does, can it be successful?

Liberalism Prescribes Realism

No great power can pursue liberal hegemony when there is at least one other great power in the system, which there typically is. As long as the system is either bipolar or multipolar, a powerful state must act according to realist principles. It cannot afford to privilege individual rights in its foreign policy, because the world is too dangerous to let protecting the rights of others come at the expense of one's own security. In fact, liberalism properly understood says that rival great powers have little choice but to compete for power so as to maximize their prospects for survival in a threatening world. Liberalism only works if there is a higher authority, like the state, that can maintain order, but there is no higher authority in the international system. Once there is no night watchman, liberalism devolves into realism.

I will begin by laying out realism's core logic. My main goal is to show why states compete for power, and sometimes fight wars, in the absence of a world state. I will explain why liberalism depends on hierarchy and why it effectively becomes realism in any world with two or more great powers. Then I will explore what happens in those rare situations in which there is a single great power in the system and that sole pole embraces liberal hegemony.

Realism 101

Realists maintain that international politics is a dangerous business and that states compete for power because the more power a state has, the more likely it is to survive. Sometimes that competition becomes so intense that war breaks out. The driving force behind this aggression is the structure of the international system, which gives states little choice but to pursue power at each other's expense.[20]

The basic theory is built on five assumptions, which describe the system's basic architecture.[21] First, states are the main actors on the world stage and there is no centralized authority above them. International institutions like the League of Nations or the United Nations are of secondary, if not tertiary, importance because they have little coercive leverage over states. States are like balls on a billiard table, though of varying size. Thus, the international system is anarchic, which is not to say it is chaotic or disordered, only that there is no ultimate arbiter.

The second and third assumptions deal with capabilities and intentions, the two key factors states consider when assessing each other. All states have some offensive military capability, although the great powers obviously have much more. Realists tend to focus on great powers because they have the biggest impact on international politics; but even among great powers, some have more capability than others. The third assumption is that states can never know for certain whether a potential rival's intentions are benign or hostile. They can sometimes make reasonable guesses, but they can never be sure.[22]

The reason for this uncertainty is that intentions are in the heads of policymakers and thus impossible to see or measure. Capabilities, on the other hand, are usually visible and reasonably easy to gauge. During the Cold War, for example, the United States could view and count the Soviet inventory of tanks, attack submarines, and nuclear-armed missiles, but it was impossible to see into the mind of Joseph Stalin or Nikita Khrushchev. One might concede the Soviet case and counter that the United States has surely known since at least the start of World War II that Britain has peaceful intentions toward it. There is no question that American policymakers have long viewed Britain as a friendly country, but that is because of its capabilities: it was too weak to threaten the United States. It depended on Washington to help protect it from Nazi Germany during World War II and the Soviet Union during the Cold War. If, over the past seventy-five years, Britain had been three or four times more powerful than it actually was, the United States would have worried greatly about its intentions, which would have been difficult to discern. In such cases, intentions are inferred from capabilities.

One might argue that policymakers can make their intentions clear through their words, but talk is cheap. Leaders sometimes misrepresent their views or simply lie. Even if one is confident that he knows another state's present intentions, it is impossible to know its future intentions. We have no idea who will be running any country (including our own) in the years ahead, and anyway those future leaders will be operating in circumstances that differ, perhaps drastically, from the present ones. None of this is to say that leaders have or will have malign intentions, only that you cannot know for sure.

Fourth, survival is every state's primary goal. States always have other aims as well—one reason it is difficult to know their intentions—but survival must always take priority. If a state does not survive, it cannot pursue any other goals. What exactly does survival mean? It obviously means the physical survival of the state. No state wants to be conquered and eliminated the way Korea and Poland once were. It also means states want to maintain their territorial integrity as well as their sovereignty. They do not want another state to be able to dictate important aspects of their domestic or foreign policy, as the Soviet Union did with the countries of Eastern Europe during the Cold War.

Fifth, states are rational actors. They have the ability to devise strategies that maximize their prospects for survival. States, in other words, are instrumentally rational. Because international politics is a complicated business, the strategies sometimes fail, even disastrously, but the point is that they are consciously devised to advance some goal. The theory makes no judgments on whether a state's goals are rational, with the one exception of survival.

None of these assumptions by itself portrays the competitive and dangerous world usually associated with realism. It is when they are brought together that trouble ensues. The five assumptions together tell us that states exhibit three kinds of behavior. First, they tend to fear each other. The level of fear varies, but there is always some residual fear among the great powers, partly because no state can be sure another state will not have formidable offensive capabilities and hostile intentions. Think about the United States looking at a rising China today, or Britain looking at a rising Germany in the decades before World War I. American leaders cannot know China's future intentions with high certainty, just as British policymakers could not be sure of Germany's intentions before 1914. Such situations create fear that trouble lies ahead. To compound matters, China will also fear that the United States might have aggressive intentions toward it, just as Germany distrusted Britain's intentions before the Great War.

There is another reason states fear each other: if they get into trouble, there is no higher authority they can turn to for help. When a threatened state dials 911, there is nobody at the other end to answer the phone and send help. Because of the anarchic structure of the international system, states have a powerful sense there is always potential for serious trouble.

Given this 911 problem, states recognize that they operate in a self-help system, where they must do all they can to provide for their own security. They can always form alliances with other states, but they can never be completely sure those allies will be there for them in times of trouble. Even close allies drift apart over time: states do not have permanent friends.[23] Lord Palmerston told the British Parliament in 1848: "It is a narrow policy to suppose that this country or that is to be marked out as the eternal ally or the perpetual enemy of England. We have no eternal allies, and we have no perpetual enemies. Our interests are eternal and perpetual, and those interests it is our duty to follow."[24]

Finally, states understand that the best way to survive in an anarchic system in which they can never be certain about the intentions of other states is to be as powerful as possible relative to their competitors. States therefore aim to maximize the military assets they control and make sure other states do not gain power at their expense, while also looking for opportunities to shift the balance of power in their favor. This zero-sum competition for power, which sometimes leads to war, is what makes international politics a ruthless and treacherous business.

Being powerful does not guarantee survival, but it markedly increases a state's prospects of deterring potential attackers, and of winning the war in the event deterrence fails. Having formidable fighting forces is also important because circumstances might arise where a great power feels compelled to initiate a war, either to enhance its security or for other reasons. The ideal situation for any state is to be the hegemon, which effectively means being the only great power in the system.[25] In that circumstance, no other state has the military wherewithal to coerce or defeat the dominant power in a war.

In short, great powers are trapped in an iron cage where they have little choice but to compete for power, because power is the means to survival in an anarchic system where conflict is an ever-present possibility.

Realism's Wide-Ranging Relevance

Though closely identified with the state system that began to emerge in Europe roughly five hundred years ago, realism can also be used to explain international politics in antiquity and the Middle Ages. Thucydides, who is widely regarded as the father of realism, wrote his history of the Peloponnesian War (431–401 BC) long before the first states began to appear in

Europe during the early 1500s.[26] Markus Fischer shows how realism explains many important aspects of politics among the various political entities that populated Europe during the Middle Ages.[27] Realism is a timeless theory, simply because the international system has always been anarchic and there has never been a way to discern the intentions of its constituent units with certainty.

Realist logic also applies to other realms besides international politics. It goes a long way toward explaining behavior in any situation where there is a danger that the actors will use violence against each other, and there is no higher authority to impose order and provide protection. The theory can be used, for example, to explain the behavior of illegal drug dealers anywhere in the world, as well as illicit transactions among alcohol bootleggers in the United States during the era of Prohibition. Neither drug dealers nor boot-leggers can call the police or go to court if they are cheated. Unsurprisingly, they usually bring guns to the table when dealing with each other, and violence, or the threat of it, is part of their daily lives.

Realist logic also applies in frontier areas that are outside the reach of the state, because there is no 911 that an individual can call if she is threat-ened with violence. In that setting, it makes good sense for people to be well armed and to shoot first and ask questions later if someone comes toward them in menacing ways. The growing reach of the various political enti-ties that have populated the planet since the beginning of human history seems to explain in good part why violence around the world has steadily declined over time. As Steven Pinker notes, "The reduction of homicide by government control is so obvious to anthropologists that they seldom docu-ment it with numbers."[28]

Finally, the story Thomas Hobbes tells in *Leviathan* is largely consistent with structural realism. Individuals in the state of nature, which is an anar-chic system, cannot know each other's intentions, and they all have the capa-bility to kill each other. That basic structure gives them powerful incentives to fear each other, and sometimes even kill other people to enhance their own survival prospects. For Hobbes, the key to preventing individuals from killing each other is to create a powerful state—a leviathan—that can impose order from above. Absent that state, "without a common power to keep them all in awe," life in an anarchic world is "solitary, poore, nasty, brutish, and short."[29]

Realism, Rights, and the International Community

Because states do whatever they deem necessary to guarantee their survival, rights are not an important part of the realist story. Realism certainly has no room for the concept of inalienable rights, although states can reach agreements that confer certain rights on all of them. In practice, however, maximizing power will always take precedence over respecting those rights. Great powers typically respect rights only when it is in their strategic interest to do so, or when doing so is of little strategic consequence. They join forces with autocrats when it suits their interests and overthrow democratically elected leaders if they are seen as threats.

One might think the realist story contains one inalienable right, the right to survive. The survival assumption, after all, lies at realism's core. But states tend to think they alone have the right to survive. They do not apply the right to other states. It is not that states are committed to threatening the survival of rival states, but they will do just that if they deem it necessary. Realism, unlike liberalism, is a particularist theory from top to bottom. It has no story about natural rights.

For this reason, realists do not assign much importance to the so-called international community, which is based on a deep respect for inalienable rights. For them, that community is a rhetorical device that powerful states use to sound high-minded when they are pursuing their interests, and that weak states invoke when they have no other recourse. States may certainly cooperate to form military alliances and create other kinds of international institutions for their mutual benefit. But they do so for self-regarding reasons, not because they think other countries share common values or noble motives.

Given that liberalism and realism say such different things about individual rights, how is it possible that liberalism is indistinguishable from realism at the international level? The main reason is that liberalism needs a higher authority or night watchman to work, and the international system has none. There is no world state; there is only anarchy, leaving individual countries little choice but to compete for power.

Liberalism and International Anarchy

Political liberalism starts with the assumption that individuals find the state of nature a dangerous and potentially deadly place, mainly because those individuals invariably have irreconcilable differences over first principles. Liberals deal with this problem by arguing that everyone has an incontrovertible set of rights that should be respected by others and by promoting the norms of peaceful conflict resolution and tolerance, which follow logically from their belief in universal rights. But rights and tolerance are not enough to keep peace in the state of nature. The individual's survival is still at risk. The solution is a social contract, which results in a state that can maintain order.

When political liberalism is applied to world politics, the focus shifts from individuals to the interactions among states.[30] When states, not individuals, are the unit of analysis, the same basic logic applies.

There is a marked similarity between states in the liberal story and states in the realist story. The five key assumptions that underpin realism turn out to apply equally to liberalism. Both theories assume that states operate in international anarchy and that survival is their principal goal. Both recognize that all states have some offensive military capability, and each assumes that states are instrumentally rational actors. Furthermore, uncertainty about intentions, which is a critically important assumption in realism, is an essential feature of liberalism as well. Specifically, states can never be sure that other states will not develop hostile plans for pursuing their goals, especially if those goals, or first principles, are disputed.[31]

Where liberalism differs from realism is in its emphasis on natural rights, tolerance, and norms of peaceful conflict resolution, all of which are supposed to provide the necessary ingredients for making the world more peaceful. But that formula does not work according to liberalism's own logic, which says that these factors alone are not enough to cause and maintain peace. Individuals must also come together, leave the state of nature behind, and create a state. They must move from anarchy to hierarchy. At the international level, this means that political liberalism cannot work as advertised unless there is a world state. As long as the international system is anarchic, liberalism is no different from realism in that realm. Without a world state, despite all its talk about rights, tolerance, and settling disputes peacefully, liberalism provides no way to move beyond balance-of-power politics.

A few prominent liberal thinkers have actually made this point. John Locke, for example, states it in synoptic form in *The Second Treatise*: "In a commonwealth the members of it are distinct persons still in reference to one another, and as such are governed by the laws of the society, yet, in reference to the rest of mankind, they make one body which is, as every member of it before was, still in the state of nature with the rest of mankind." He adds that this commonwealth, "therefore, contains the power of war and peace, leagues and alliances, and all the transactions with all persons and communities" outside it.[32] Stephen Holmes, a contemporary liberal, makes essentially the same point when he writes: "Liberal rights are meaningful only within the confines of pre-existing, territorially bounded states, and only where there exists a rights-enforcing power. To the extent that no enforcing power operates between states or across borders, liberal rights are futile."[33] This point is also a central theme for G. Lowes Dickinson, who introduced the term *anarchy* into the international relations literature, and in an important essay on liberalism and realism written by Deborah Boucoyannis.[34]

International anarchy alone makes it strategically foolish for a state to pursue a liberal foreign policy unless it is far more powerful than every other state in the system. But there is another reason why such a policy makes little sense. As I explained in the previous chapter, the liberal story oversells rights. There is little evidence that most people think individual rights are inalienable or that they matter greatly in daily political life. Rights do matter to some extent, but liberals exaggerate their influence on politics, which makes spreading democracy an especially difficult task.

As I also noted in the previous chapter, the importance people accord to individual rights has direct implications for the norms of tolerance and peaceful conflict resolution as well as for the role of the state. The less regard there is for inalienable rights, the more difficult it is to foster tolerance and persuade people to settle their disagreements peacefully, and the more a powerful state is needed to maintain order. If the universalist strand of liberalism is a less potent force than most liberals recognize, this makes it all the more important to have a formidable world state. The international system, however, remains anarchic.

In sum, liberalism properly understood does not trump realism. Until we have a world state, any clear-headed thinker who is deeply committed to liberal principles should approach international politics like a realist. Liberalism can be a powerful force for good inside states, but not when states are dealing with the wider world.[35]

Nationalism and the Limits of Social Engineering

The imperative to act according to realist dictates notwithstanding, a liberal state will sometimes find itself so secure that it can embrace liberal hegemony without having to worry about the balance of power. In a unipolar world, the sole great power in the system does not have to fear another great power threatening it, because there are none. Weaker liberal countries are free to join with the liberal unipole to try to spread democracy around the globe. In the wake of the Cold War, the United States and its West European allies, especially Britain, found themselves in just this benign strategic situation, which allowed them to join together to pursue liberal hegemony.

It is important to note that a unipole, liberal or not, can pursue strikingly different foreign policies. Nuno Monteiro points out that the dominant power has three basic choices: it can retreat from the world stage, knowing that it is both powerful and secure; it can remain a central player in international politics and seek to maintain the status quo; or it can attempt to change the status quo in ways favorable to itself.[36] The structure of the international system does not determine which strategy is optimal; that decision is largely a function of domestic politics. A powerful liberal democracy that finds itself in unipolarity will reflexively pursue liberal hegemony, at least initially, because remaking the world in its own image is baked into its DNA and the costs will appear manageable.

A liberal great power operating in either bipolarity or multipolarity cannot pursue liberal hegemony, because of the presence of other great powers. Nevertheless, it might occasionally ignore balance-of-power politics when it should not and selectively pursue liberal policies. The likely outcome of this limited form of liberal interventionism is the same as when a unipole pursues liberal hegemony: failure. Promoting individual rights and turning other countries into liberal democracies is an exceedingly difficult undertaking that rarely succeeds and often backfires.

One reason is that any country so targeted will have a deep-rooted culture that is hard to manipulate and reorder. Short of a social revolution, it is difficult even for local elites to make fundamental changes in their own societies. It is even harder for foreigners to come into a country they do not know well and transform it into a liberal democracy, or even just get it to stop abusing its citizens' rights. This problem is compounded by most people's soft commitment to individual rights. In the midst of political turmoil, they are more likely to be concerned with fostering stability. And then there is the remarkably powerful force of nationalism, which further complicates the task of spreading liberalism. I argued earlier that liberalism and nationalism could operate effectively together inside a state, although nationalism is almost always dominant. Once the focus shifts to the international system, nationalism tends to overwhelm liberalism at almost every turn.

Nationalism is in large part about identity. Individuals see the world comprising a wide variety of different peoples and nations, and invariably feel a special attachment to their own people. They usually feel far less connected with foreign nationals. This is one reason most people are much more inclined to treat their fellow nationals as equals deserving of rights than they are to respect the rights of foreign nationals.[37] Outsiders are distinctly different in ways that matter to people, and sometimes they are viewed with contempt, if not hatred. Life in the international system exacerbates this problem. Security competition and occasional war between countries not only strengthen this sense of difference but also foster hypernationalism. Even when outsiders are treated with respect, they are rarely seen as equals.

There is substantial evidence of this kind of thinking in the United States, the paradigmatic liberal country. For example, in his study of how Americans think about rights, Austin Sarat found that they "do not perceive the interrelatedness of their own freedom and the freedom of others; they value their own freedom but not the freedom of others."[38] It is difficult to get Americans to fight and die solely to protect the rights of other peoples, including the all-important right to life. The only instance where U.S. troops engaged in combat for humanitarian purposes alone was in Mogadishu, Somalia, in 1993. After eighteen Americans were killed in battle, President Clinton quickly withdrew all U.S. combat forces. He and his lieutenants were so unnerved by what happened in Somalia that they refused to commit troops the following year to stop the Rwandan genocide, even though the mission would have involved few U.S. casualties.[39]

When foreigners murder Americans, it is of much more concern to the average American than when those same foreigners murder each other or people from other countries.[40] The outcry in the United States when the Islamic State (ISIS) beheaded two American journalists in 2014 is one of the events that persuaded President Obama to go to war against ISIS.[41] Americans had been appalled by the widespread carnage and destruction wrought by ISIS, but they cared more about the deaths of their fellow Americans. Meanwhile, Americans who murder foreigners, especially nonwhite foreigners, are rarely treated as harshly as Americans who murder their fellow citizens. For example, Lieutenant William Calley, who commanded the U.S. soldiers involved in the infamous My Lai massacre in Vietnam in March 1968, served only three and a half years under house arrest before he was freed, and he enjoyed overwhelming support from the public after his role was revealed in the media. Nobody else in his unit was convicted of a criminal offense, even though somewhere between 350 and 500 civilians, mostly women and children, were murdered.[42] Calley and those under his command surely would not have received such benevolent treatment if they had butchered that number of unarmed American civilians. As John Mueller notes: "Although Americans are extremely sensitive to American casualties, they seem to be remarkably *in*sensitive to casualties suffered by foreigners including essentially uninvolved—that is, innocent—civilians."[43] John Tirman, who has done a major study on this subject, concurs: "One of the most remarkable aspects of American wars is how little we discuss the victims who are not Americans."[44] Of course, this kind of thinking is not peculiar to the United States. All nations think this way, and it cuts directly against liberalism's universalist dimension.

This division of the world into distinct and often mutually suspicious nations has significant consequences for the social engineering enterprise at the heart of a liberal foreign policy. Nationalism is all about self-determination, and people who live in a nation-state will want to shape their own politics without interference from an outside power. They will not want foreigners telling them how to conduct their lives, even if the intervening forces have noble intentions. In most cases, the target state will fiercely resist the liberal crusaders, and this resistance may even take the form of terrorism. Liberalism is not an easy sell in alien lands.

In addition to the difficulties the liberalizer faces inside the target country, it is likely to meet resistance from other states as well. Some countries may have compelling reasons to check the liberalizer's efforts to spread its ideology. Most other countries will be motivated by realism because, unlike the liberalizer, they do not face a permissive threat environment. They are thus likely to worry that if the liberalizer succeeds in its efforts to turn other countries into liberal democracies, it might gain new allies and shift the balance of power in its favor. Russia, for example, was deeply suspicious of the American-led effort to promote democracy in Eastern Europe through the so-called color revolutions. The February 22, 2014, coup in Ukraine, which the Americans helped facilitate and which toppled a pro-Russian leader, precipitated a major crisis between Moscow and the West.[45]

There are also likely to be at least a few countries—Rawls calls them "outlaw states"—that oppose the spread of liberalism because they are deeply hostile to liberalism in principle.[46] Rawls acknowledges that "many persons" in the world reject liberalism. "For them," he writes, "the social world envisaged by political liberalism is a nightmare of social fragmentation and false doctrines, if not positively evil."[47] All of these reasons mean that spreading liberal democracy around the world is destined to fail much more often than it succeeds.

What about the two ancillary missions that are part of a liberal foreign policy: building international institutions and promoting an open international economy? These two missions are more likely to succeed because, unlike democracy promotion, they are consistent with a realist foreign policy as well as a liberal one.

Realists believe that institutions are important instruments of statecraft. The United States, for example, relied heavily on the North Atlantic Treaty Organization (NATO), the European Community, the International Monetary Fund (IMF), the World Bank, and other institutions in waging the Cold

War. Facilitating economic intercourse is generally consistent with realism. Realists enthusiastically supported globalization during the Cold War, which certainly worked to America's advantage. The nub of the dispute between liberals and realists regarding both institutions and economic interdependence has to do with whether they promote world peace. Liberals believe they ameliorate conflict; realists do not.[48]

Modus Vivendi Liberalism: What If?

Up to this point, I have assumed that progressive liberalism dominates modus vivendi liberalism. We have no reason to think this situation will change. This suggests that there is hardly any chance modus vivendi liberalism will provide the template for a liberal state's foreign policy.

But this conclusion may be too pessimistic. As I will argue in chapter 8, there is a chance (small, but not trivial) that the United States will move toward a more restrained foreign policy in the wake of all the failures its pursuit of liberal hegemony has produced. That more limited and wiser strategy would be based on realist logic, coupled with an informed understanding of how nationalism affects the behavior of great powers. It would bear a marked resemblance to a foreign policy based on modus vivendi liberalism. A few words are therefore in order regarding what that liberal foreign policy would look like, not just because it overlaps with restraint but also because it differs from liberal hegemony.

A liberal foreign policy centered on the modus vivendi variant would be much less interventionist than one grounded on progressivism.[49] For sure, it would privilege inalienable rights, which would generate incentives to intervene abroad when the rights of foreigners are seriously threatened. That interventionist impulse, however, would be offset by the fact that modus vivendi liberals are deeply opposed to social engineering, which they do not like in principle and which they think fails more often than not. Their belief that activist governments cannot do much good at home, much less in foreign countries, leads modus vivendi liberals to reject the notion that liberal states should promote regime change around the world so as to help spread liberal democracy. Such a policy, after all, involves social engineering on a grand scale. Instead, they emphasize the importance of paying heed to the principle of self-determination.

Given this mind-set, modus vivendi liberals are reluctant to sanction human rights interventions in another country unless there is wholesale killing either by the government or by a rebel group. In those rare instances, they would aim to deal with the problem as quickly as possible and then return home without getting bogged down trying to reorder the target state's politics. Of course, a quick exit is difficult. There is a powerful temptation to stay and clean up the mess the intervention created, and then fix the underlying political and social problems that compelled it in the first place. Modus vivendi liberals understand this slippery slope, and it reinforces their opposition to intervening abroad.

Modus vivendi liberals are inclined to reject an interventionist foreign policy for another reason as well. Within their own country, they favor a state that mainly keeps order and guarantees individual freedoms. They do not want a powerful state interfering in their daily lives, which is one reason they intensely dislike social engineering, especially for the purpose of fostering positive rights. A liberal country with an interventionist foreign policy invariably ends up building a formidable state, which then is powerfully inclined to interfere in civil society. Modus vivendi liberals deeply fear this kind of national security state, so they favor a small military establishment and a highly restrained foreign policy. Although they consider liberalism the best political order, they prefer a live-and-let-live policy toward the rest of the world, which is one reason they are called modus vivendi liberals.

Progressive liberalism, however, has been the dominant form of political liberalism for well over a century now, and it is the driving force behind liberal hegemony. Nevertheless, nationalism and realism have had a much more profound influence in shaping international politics. Perhaps the best way to capture just how powerful nationalism and realism are compared with liberalism is to consider the remarkable transformation over the last five hundred years in the basic architecture of the international system.

The Making of the Modern International System

There were no states in Europe before 1500. The region instead housed a variety of political entities, including empires, city-states, duchies, principalities, urban federations, and various religious organizations. Sovereignty in Europe was associated with many different kinds of political units.[50] Nor were there any states outside Europe.

The first states—England, France, and Spain—began to take form in the early sixteenth century, and over the next three hundred years the dynastic state became the principal political actor in Europe. After 1800, those dynastic states slowly gave way to nation-states, and that political form eventually spread across the globe until today, the international system is made up almost exclusively of nation-states. As David Armitage notes, "The great political fact of global history in the last 500 years is the emergence of a world of states from a world of empires. That fact—more than the expansion of democracy, more than nationalism, more than the language of rights, more even than globalization—fundamentally defines the political universe we all inhabit."[51]

This extraordinary change, from a heterogeneous world system to a homogeneous one, obviously had many causes. The two main driving forces, however, were nationalism and realism, which interacted in important ways to help create the modern state system. The emphasis each of those isms places on the state and survival links them in ways that promoted the proliferation of nation-states.[52]

Realism and the Rise of the Modern State

A good way to understand how nationalism and realism have combined to shape the international system is to begin with an explanation of how the preoccupation with survival, which is at the core of balance-of-power politics, helped create nation-states and spread that political form around the world. Before there were states, the political entities that populated Europe engaged in almost constant security competition, which sometimes led to war.[53] The states that began to emerge in the early sixteenth century were, of course, deeply immersed in that pit of never-ending conflict. All of the political units in Europe cared greatly about their survival, as they faced an ever-present danger of being erased from the map.

Staying alive in that cutthroat world largely depended on military performance, where, unsurprisingly, the most powerful actors tended to prevail. Charles Tilly famously tells the story of how the state proved superior to all other organizational forms at building military power and winning wars.[54]

Military success depends in good part on having money to finance an army and a navy as well as enough people to fill out a large and effective fighting force. But those resources have to be extracted from the population, which means it is better to have a large population than a small one. States proved to be superior to all other political forms at extracting resources from the resident population and translating them into military might. Hence the state ultimately ran its competitors out of the European system, because the others could not build sufficient military power to compete with the state on the battlefield. Survival came to depend on having a state.

This logic deeply informs Machiavelli's *The Prince*. At the time he was writing, in the early sixteenth century, Italy was not a unified state. The Italian peninsula was populated with small city-states that fought among themselves and often fell prey to Austrian and French aggression. "This barbarian domination," he wrote, "stinks to everyone" and had brought Italy into a state of "slavery and disgrace." He thought the taproot of the problem was that Italy was divided: "For I do not believe that divisions ever do any good; on the contrary, when the enemy approaches, of necessity divided cities are immediately lost, because the weaker party always joins the external forces and the other will not be able to rule."[55]

Machiavelli understood that the best way to fix this problem would be to transcend Italy's city-state system and create a single Italian state that could stand up to Austria and France and keep them at bay. The brutal and frank advice he offered to some future Italian prince was principally aimed at helping that leader unify Italy and "redeem her from these barbarous cruelties and insults."[56] Italians would have to imitate their larger and more powerful neighbors and create a state of their own if they hoped to survive. This unification, however, did not happen until 1870.

Machiavelli wrote at a time when the dynastic state was just emerging in Europe. While that early version of the state was good for extracting resources from its population, it elicited little loyalty from the people living within its borders. Sovereignty was lodged in the crown, not in the population, which is why Machiavelli addressed a prince and instructed him on how to manipulate his people. That situation changed drastically in the wake of the French Revolution (1789), when France transformed itself into Europe's first nation-state. The arrival of nationalism in France meant that many French people began to feel a powerful allegiance to their state and were even willing to fight and die for it. Nationalism was a huge force multiplier that allowed Revolutionary and Napoleonic France to create a remarkably powerful mass army that overran most of Europe. Twenty-three years (1792–1815) and six great power coalitions were required to defeat it.[57]

The other European states eventually realized that if they hoped to survive in the European arena, they had little choice but to imitate France and become nation-states. Prussia's actions during the Napoleonic Wars provide a clear example of this phenomenon. After Napoleon's forces decisively defeated the Prussian army in battles at Jena and Auerstedt in October 1806, Prussia's leaders realized that overcoming their fear of nationalism and using it to turn their army into a much more formidable fighting force was their only hope for getting out from under Napoleon's yoke. They took the necessary steps, and Prussia subsequently played an important role in helping to defeat Napoleon's armies and end his reign of relentless aggression.[58]

By the early twentieth century, every state in Europe was effectively a nation-state. Sovereignty no longer resided in the crown but was lodged in the people.[59] The logic of power politics, with its emphasis on survival, had been critical in helping the dynastic state best its competitors, and then in helping the nation-state put the dynastic state out of business.

Nations and States

Nationalism also played a crucial role in making the present-day international system. Much of this story has been told in chapter 4, so just a brief synopsis is necessary here. For a variety of reasons that lie outside the scope of this book, nations began to appear in Europe and North America in the latter half of the eighteenth century, when dynastic states were the dominant political unit. What makes nations so special is that they are the highest form of social group in the contemporary world. They function as survival vehicles that allow their members to work together to secure the basic necessities of life. But nations also worry about their survival, since they operate in a world of rival nations that might have incentives to harm them.

The best way for a nation to guarantee its survival is to have its own state, which is not to say nations are condemned to ruin if they do not control a state. But it certainly maximizes their prospects of survival. Thus, from the start, nations had an irresistible incentive to have their own state, which eventually led to the rise of nation-states. Moreover, given that those states operate in international anarchy, each nation wanted its own state to be especially powerful, so as to guarantee the nation's long-term survival. In essence, nationalism reinforced basic realist logic, which by itself was shaping the modern world in profound ways.

This logic also applies outside Europe, where many of imperialism's victims were deeply concerned about their culture's long-term survival. Over time, it became clear to the subject peoples that the best way to deal with this threat was to rise up, break away from the empires that controlled them, and establish their own states. This process played out in numerous places during the twentieth century and explains in good part why the sun eventually set on all of the European empires, as well as why the world is now entirely populated with sovereign nation-states.

Not only do nations want their own state, but states also have powerful incentives to make sure their people constitute a nation. As discussed above, states gravitate to nationalism because it has become an indispensable source of military power. But central governments also cultivate their own nation-states for reasons unrelated to security. Not only does it make good economic sense to have a national culture with a common language and educational system, it also makes sense administratively. It is much easier to run a country whose citizens are part of a standardized culture and also feel a strong bond with the state. States want nations and nations want states, and the result is that nation-states have become the dominant political form on the planet.

One way to see the brute power of nationalism is to consider what happens when it comes up against other universal ideologies besides liberalism. Marxism, for example, has some striking similarities with liberalism. As John Gray puts it: "Both were enlightened ideologies that looked forward to a universal civilization."[60] Class analysis is the driving force behind Marx's universalism: he and his followers maintain that social classes transcend national groups and state borders. Most importantly, they argue that a powerful bond exists among the working classes in different countries, created by capitalist exploitation. This line of thinking led some Marxists to believe that the workers across Europe would not take up arms against each other at the start of World War I. Of course, they were wrong. Those workers fought and died in huge numbers for their respective nation-states.

The Soviet Union was the quintessential communist country in the twentieth century. But it contained many distinct nations, which remained firmly intact despite government efforts to weaken them, and nationalism ultimately played a key role in the unraveling of the Soviet Union.[61] Furthermore, as Benedict Anderson notes, "Since the end of World War II every successful revolution has defined itself in *national* terms," including those in Marxist countries like China and Vietnam. Anderson also emphasizes there are a number of cases where communist countries fought wars with each other, and "none of the belligerents has made more than the most perfunctory attempts to justify the bloodshed in terms of a recognizable *Marxist* theoretical perspective." Those wars were not supposed to happen, according to Marxist theory, but they did. Anderson goes on to quote the eminent Marxist scholar Tom Nairn, who argues that "the theory of nationalism represents Marxism's great historical failure."[62]

The bottom line is that the contemporary nation-state system is largely the product of the interplay between nationalism and balance-of-power politics, both of which privilege the state and are motivated by concerns about survival. Liberalism has certainly played a role in creating the modern world, but its influence has been secondary at best.

Is a World State Possible?

You might agree with my case against political liberalism as a foreign policy but argue that the solution is obvious: we need a world state. Some scholars argue that we are moving toward a world state, in large part because nation-states cannot deal with many of the economic, regulatory, security, and environmental challenges the world now faces. Once that new political order is in place, realism will no longer matter, the dark side of nationalism will be put under wraps,[63] and the world state will have a liberal political system.

Realism would be neutralized because the international system would no longer be anarchic; it would be hierarchic.[64] Balance-of-power logic does not apply under hierarchy, because there is a night watchman to protect weaker states. International politics would be transformed into domestic politics on a grand scale, leaving liberalism free to blossom. Most people around the globe would surely retain some allegiance to their present nation, but none of those nations, by definition, would have its own state. There would be only one super-sized state, and people everywhere would presumably have some sort of universal identity linked with that state, which would override, or at least dampen, their long-standing nationalisms. But even if that proved not to be the case, the überstate would work to keep those rival nations from fighting.

There is not going to be a world state anytime soon. For starters, there is virtually no chance that any nation with its own state will voluntarily give it up. And it is hard to imagine that those nations clamoring for a state will abandon that aspiration. Nations are obsessed with self-determination and thus unlikely to be willing to put their fate in the hands of a superstate over which they have at best limited control.

One might argue that globalization is causing nations to converge toward some universal culture that can serve as the foundation of a world state. There is little evidence to support this belief, and abundant evidence that even in the age of the Internet, deeply rooted cultures remain distinct in ways that are widely recognized and often celebrated. Furthermore, generating a universal culture would mean getting most of humankind to reach broad agreement on what constitutes the good life. Given that it is impossible to achieve such a consensus, there is no prospect of a universal culture, meaning that there will likely be no viable world state with a liberal political system.

The other conceivable route to a world state is via conquest. One especially powerful nation-state would have to take the offensive and subjugate the other countries. This is also not going to happen. The planet is simply too big for one country to conquer all or even most of it, especially when you consider the difficulty of projecting military power across oceans. The conqueror would face fierce resistance from its potential subject peoples, who would have powerful incentives to ally with each other to contain and ultimately destroy the aggressor. The United States, the most powerful state in recorded history, has never even hinted at using force to create an American-dominated world state. The reason is simple: it is an impossible task.

If my analysis is wrong and a world state becomes a reality, it would probably not be a liberal state. Not only is liberalism foreign to many countries, it is also time-consuming and difficult to grow in new places. To keep all the centrifugal forces within that world state at bay—and there would be many—the center would have to rule with an iron fist. Even then it might not be able to prevent major outbreaks of violence. This is one reason why many liberals have little enthusiasm for a world state. Both Kant and Rawls, for example, opposed the idea because they thought it would be either despotic or, as Rawls put it, "a fragile empire torn by frequent civil war."[65]

Anarchy Is Here to Stay

If we have no world state in our future, it means international anarchy is here to stay, and the great powers have little choice but to act according to realist dictates. Survival demands no less. At times, however, a favorable balance of power will allow a state to pursue liberal hegemony, in which case failure is likely. Liberalism has many virtues as a political system, but when it is applied to international politics, the resulting policies do not succeed.

We can take this criticism of liberalism a step further and argue that pursuing liberal hegemony imposes huge costs—not only on the liberal state but also on the target state. Moreover, a powerful state acting according to liberal dictates is likely to end up fostering instability around the world. A liberal foreign policy, in other words, is likely not only to fail but also to backfire.

6

Liberalism as a Source of Trouble

THE COSTS OF LIBERAL HEGEMONY BEGIN with the endless wars a liberal state ends up fighting to protect human rights and spread liberal democracy around the world. Once unleashed on the world stage, a liberal unipole soon becomes addicted to war.

This militarism arises from five factors. First, democratizing the globe is a vast mission that provides abundant opportunities to fight. Second, liberal policymakers believe they have the right, the responsibility, and the know-how to use military force to achieve their goals. Third, they often approach their task with missionary zeal. Fourth, pursuing liberal hegemony undercuts diplomacy, making it harder to settle disputes with other countries peacefully. Fifth, that ambitious strategy also undermines the notion of sovereignty, a core norm of international politics that is intended to limit interstate war.

The presence of a powerful state prone to fighting war after war increases the amount of conflict in the international system, creating instability. These armed conflicts usually end up failing, sometimes disastrously, and mainly at the expense of the state purportedly being rescued by the liberal goliath. One might think liberal elites would learn from their failures and become averse to using military force abroad, but that seldom happens.

Liberal hegemony promotes instability in other ways as well. Formidable liberal democracies also tend to embrace ambitious policies short of war that often backfire and poison relations between them and the target countries. For example, they often interfere in the politics of other countries. They are also inclined when engaging diplomatically with an authoritarian country to disregard its interests and think they know what is best for it. Finally, liberalism abroad tends to undermine liberalism at home, because a militaristic foreign policy invariably fosters a powerful national security state prone to violating its citizens' civil liberties.

My argument is that a country that embraces liberal hegemony ends up doing more harm than good to itself as well as other countries, especially those it intends to help. I will illustrate this argument by focusing on American foreign policy since Bill Clinton was elected to the White House in November 1992. With the end of the Cold War in 1989 and the collapse of the Soviet Union in 1991, the United States emerged as by far the most powerful country on the planet. Unsurprisingly, the Clinton administration embraced liberal hegemony from the start, and the policy remained firmly intact through the Bush and Obama administrations.

Not surprisingly, the United States has been involved in numerous wars during this period and has failed to achieve meaningful success in almost all of those conflicts. Washington has also played a central role in destabilizing the greater Middle East, to the great detriment of the people living there. Liberal Britain, which has acted as Washington's faithful sidekick in these wars, also bears some share of the blame for the trouble the United States has helped cause. American policymakers also played the key role in producing a major crisis with Russia over Ukraine. At this writing, that crisis shows no signs of abating and is hardly in America's interest, let alone Ukraine's. Back in the United States, Americans' civil liberties have been eroded by an increasingly powerful national security state.

Liberal Militarism

Because liberals so often speak about the evils of war and the importance of moving beyond power politics to create a peaceful world, it might seem odd to describe them as militarists. But many are militarists, deeply committed to a remarkably ambitious foreign policy agenda and not shy about using military force to advance it.[1]

One of liberalism's core missions is to protect people whose rights are being seriously violated. The urge to intervene in other countries is especially powerful when large numbers of those foreigners are being killed. This undertaking is clearly reflected in Responsibility to Protect (R2P), a norm that grew out of the failure of the so-called international community to prevent the Rwandan genocide in 1994 and the Srebrenica massacre in 1995.[2] R2P mandates that states have a responsibility not only to protect their own populations from serious human rights violations like ethnic cleansing and mass murder, but also to protect people in other countries from these crimes. In essence, nations are told to be on the lookout for major human rights abuses around the globe and, when they arise, to move quickly to stop them. A powerful liberal state with the military wherewithal to intervene in such circumstances is strongly encouraged to go to war to protect the victims.

This task of defending individual rights easily morphs into the more ambitious strategy of removing the source of the problem by actively promoting liberal democracy in other countries. Liberal states, by definition, are committed to protecting their citizens' rights, and this strategy, so the argument goes, will also lead to a more peaceful world and help protect liberal democracy from its internal enemies. Liberalism is also said to facilitate economic prosperity, which not only is a positive end in itself but also contributes to peace. In short, spreading liberalism is thought to make the world safer, more peaceful, and more prosperous.

As we can see from countless comments by American liberals, proponents of this worldview tend to be deeply committed to it. In the midst of World War I, for example, Elihu Root, who had been both secretary of state and secretary of war under President Theodore Roosevelt, stated, "To be safe democracy must kill its enemy when it can and where it can. The world cannot be half democratic and half autocratic." In the midst of the Vietnam War, Secretary of State Dean Rusk declared that the "United States cannot be secure until the total international environment is ideologically safe." As Christopher Layne notes, "These are not isolated comments. . . . American statesmen have frequently expressed this view."[3]

This missionary zeal is hardly limited to policymakers. John Rawls, for example, writes, "It is characteristic of liberal and decent peoples that they seek a world in which all peoples have a well-ordered regime. . . . Their long-range aim is to bring all societies eventually to honor the Law of Peoples and to become full members in good standing of the society of well-ordered peoples."[4] This ambitious agenda does not axiomatically lead to war, and Rawls is careful to make clear that he is not advocating armed crusades to spread liberal democracy across the planet.[5] Still, there is no question that war is often seen as a viable and even attractive option for promoting liberalism. This penchant for employing force to achieve liberal goals is reflected in the writings of John Owen, a prominent liberal interventionist, who comments that "liberal ideas cause liberal democracies to tend away from war with one another, and . . . the same ideas prod these states into war with illiberal states." Moreover, he writes, "all individuals share an interest in peace, and should want war only as an instrument to bring about peace."[6]

The Bush Doctrine, developed during 2002 and used to justify the March 2003 invasion of Iraq, is probably the best example of this kind of liberal interventionism. In the wake of the 9/11 attacks, the Bush administration concluded that to win what it termed the "global war on terror" it must not only defeat al Qaeda but also confront Iran, Iraq, and Syria. The regimes in these so-called rogue states were assumed to be closely tied to terrorist organizations like al Qaeda and were bent on acquiring nuclear weapons, which they might even give to terrorists.[7] In short, they were mortal enemies of the United States. Bush proposed to use military might to turn those countries and others across the Middle East into liberal democracies. He put the point succinctly in early 2003, just before the United States attacked Iraq: "By the resolve and purpose of America, and of our friends and allies, we will make this an age of progress and liberty. Free people will set the course of history, and free people will keep the peace of the world."[8]

There is no question that President Bush and his lieutenants were also motivated to topple Saddam Hussein from power because he was a brutal dictator who trampled on the rights of his citizens. But that was a long-standing problem that, by itself, could not cause the United States to get rid of Hussein and replace him with a democratically elected leader. What drove the United States to invade Iraq was the perceived need to deal with the proliferation and terrorism. And the best way to do that, the Bush team thought, was to turn all the countries in the greater Middle East into liberal

Still, the aim of "big stick diplomacy" is to either avoid or terminate a war. If a state facing a hostile rival abjures diplomacy, war becomes more likely and harder to terminate once it starts.

Liberal democracies have little difficulty conducting diplomacy with illiberal states when they are acting according to realist dictates, which is most of the time. In those circumstances, liberal democracies do whatever is necessary to maximize their survival prospects, and that includes negotiating with authoritarian leaders. They sometimes even support or form alliances with murderous dictators, as the United Stated did in World War II when it worked with Joseph Stalin to defeat Nazi Germany, or when it cooperated with Mao Zedong after 1972 to contain the Soviet Union. Occasionally they even overthrow democratic regimes they perceive as hostile. Liberal democracies go to great lengths to disguise such behavior with liberal rhetoric, but in fact they are acting contrary to their own principles. Such is the influence of realpolitik.

Diplomacy gets shortchanged, however, when a unipolar state is able to push aside balance-of-power logic and adopt a liberal foreign policy. Such a state is strongly inclined to eschew diplomacy with its illiberal foes, for reasons that by now should be familiar. Although tolerance is a core principle of liberalism, it tends to get pushed aside when a liberal state confronts a rival that violates its citizens' rights. After all, rights are inalienable. Since authoritarian states regularly shortchange—and sometimes trample on—the rights of their people, liberal states freed from the shackles of realism are likely to treat them as deeply flawed polities not worthy of diplomatic engagement.

Countries pursuing liberal hegemony often develop a deep-seated antipathy toward illiberal states. They tend to see the international system as consisting of good and evil states, with little room for compromise between the two sides. This view creates a powerful incentive to eliminate authoritarian states by whatever means necessary whenever the opportunity presents itself. One consequence of this loathing is that liberal states find it hard to engage in limited wars with illiberal foes and instead are inclined to pursue decisive victories against them. Unconditional surrender becomes the order of the day, as it is virtually impossible to countenance compromising with evil.[12] Of course, nationalism, which usually generates hatred between states at war with each other, reinforces this tendency for wars to escalate to their extreme.

This eliminationist mentality is perhaps best reflected in Woodrow Wilson's thinking about how to deal with Germany and the other defeated powers after World War I. Since peace could not be achieved by an "arrangement or compromise or adjustment of interests," he argued, there could not be "any kind of bargain or compromise with the governments of the Central Empires." Wilson associated compromise with balance-of-power politics, what he contemptuously called the "old order of international politics," and which he felt had to be "utterly destroyed." The goal had to be "the overcoming of evil, by the defeat once [and] for all of the sinister forces that interrupt peace and render it impossible." In late 1919 he said of the Treaty of Versailles, "I hear that this treaty is very hard on Germany. When an individual has committed a criminal act, the punishment is hard, but the punishment is not unjust. This nation permitted itself, through unscrupulous governors, to commit a criminal act against mankind, and it is to undergo the punishment."[13]

The bottom line is that when a liberal democracy is free to act abroad according to its foundational principles, it finds it difficult to engage in diplomacy with an illiberal opponent, increasing the likelihood that the two sides will attempt to settle their differences violently. Liberal intolerance, sometimes accompanied by liberal loathing, leads a liberal unipole freed from balance-of-power politics into endless wars.

Liberalism and Sovereignty

There is a final reason why states pursuing liberal hegemony become warlike: liberalism undermines sovereignty. Respect for sovereignty is the most significant norm in international politics, and its purpose is to minimize war and facilitate peaceful relations among states. Consider, for example, the United Nations Charter. The first sentence of Article I states that the goal of the United Nations is "to maintain international peace and security." The first sentence of Article II says that "the Organization is based on the principle of the sovereign equality of all its members."

Sovereignty means that states have the ultimate authority over what happens inside their borders, and that foreign powers have no right to interfere in their politics.[14] All states are equal in this regard, which means that weak as well as powerful countries are supposed to be free to make their own policies, domestic and foreign, without outside influence from other states. This notion of state sovereignty, which has become the cornerstone of international law, means that countries are not supposed to invade each other, at least not without permission from the United Nations Security Council.

There is no question, however, that norms have a limited impact on state behavior. Sovereignty has been violated many times.[15] As any realist can tell you, when matters of vital security are at play, states will do what they think is in their self-interest, regardless of whether it violates prevailing norms or the written rules of international institutions.[16] Nonetheless, almost all leaders care about legitimacy and thus pay careful attention to well-established norms, as they do not want to be seen by other states as wantonly disregarding rules that enjoy widespread respect and support. This is especially true of sovereignty because of its centrality to international politics. In at least some cases where policymakers are not sure whether invading another country makes good strategic sense, the norm of sovereignty is likely to influence the final decision.

Sovereignty began to emerge as a norm when states first started forming in Europe in the early 1500s, but it did not achieve prominence until the Treaty of Westphalia, which helped bring an end to the incredibly bloody Thirty Years' War of 1618–48,[17] which by some estimates killed one-third of Germany's population.[18] Much of the conflict in Europe during that era was motivated by religious differences. Catholic and Protestant countries invaded each other with the hope of converting the target state. The norm of sovereignty was designed to put an end to this behavior by ruling such armed interventions out of court. Sovereignty may have helped put an end to those deadly religious wars, but it did not stop the European states from engaging in balance-of-power politics, which led them to violate the norm whenever they thought their vital interests were at stake. Nor was the concept of sovereignty meant to apply outside Europe, an exception that left the European great powers free to build empires throughout the world. So sovereignty had little effect on the behavior of European states for roughly two hundred years after the Peace of Westphalia.[19]

With the growth of nationalism—in Europe during the nineteenth century and in the colonial empires during the twentieth century—sovereignty became a more meaningful concept. Nationalism, which is all about self-determination, says that the people living inside a state's borders have the right to determine their own fate, and no outside power has the right to impose its views on another nation-state. Sovereignty is thus inextricably bound up with the nation as well as the state. In essence, nationalist logic reinforced Westphalian sovereignty. But nationalism had its greatest impact on sovereignty outside Europe, where it helped facilitate decolonization in the twentieth century by focusing great attention on the principles of self-determination and nonintervention.[20] In effect, it helped delegitimize empire. It is no surprise that the countries that were once victims of European imperialism staunchly support the concept of sovereignty today.

The influence of sovereignty was probably at its height in the late 1980s, as the Cold War was coming to an end. States all around the globe embraced it, and it definitely resonated with the Eastern European countries trying to free themselves from the Soviet yoke. And once the Cold War ended, many of the republics that comprised the Soviet Union began talking about gaining their own sovereignty, which they eventually did. But the norm was eroding by the mid-1990s, mainly because the United States took to interfering in the politics of other countries even more than it had in the past. Not only did the sole pole have a truly impressive military that could project power all over the globe, but as a liberal state it had the motive to interfere in other countries' affairs. Britain and most of the countries in Western Europe were eager to help Washington pursue its ambitious foreign policy agenda.

Liberalism, of course, is all about meddling in other countries' politics, whether the aim is protecting the rights of foreigners or seeking to spread liberal democracy. In essence, liberalism and sovereignty are fundamentally at odds with each other. This point is hardly controversial among either policymakers or scholars. In April 1999, for example, British prime minister

Tony Blair said, in a highly publicized speech in Chicago: "On the eve of a new Millennium we are now in a new world. . . . The most pressing foreign policy problem we face is to identify the circumstances in which we should get actively involved in other people's conflicts. Non-interference has long been considered an important principle of international order. And it is not one we would want to jettison too readily. One state should not feel it has the right to change the political system of another or foment subversion or seize pieces of territory to which it feels it should have some claim. But the principle of non-interference must be qualified in important respects."[21]

Five years later, in March 2004, as he was trying to justify the Iraq war, Blair referred back to his Chicago speech: "So, for me, before September 11th, I was already reaching for a different philosophy in international relations from a traditional one that has held sway since the treaty of Westphalia in 1648; namely that a country's internal affairs are for it and you don't interfere unless it threatens you, or breaches a treaty, or triggers an obligation of alliance."[22] In May 2000, the German foreign minister Joschka Fischer told a Berlin audience: "The core concept of Europe after 1945 was and still is a rejection of the European balance-of-power principle and the hegemonic ambitions of individual states that emerged after the Peace of Westphalia in 1648, a rejection that took the form of a closer meshing of vital interests and the transfer of nation-state sovereign rights to supranational European institutions."[23] This theme has resonated widely in the academic world, as reflected in books with titles such as *Beyond Westphalia? State Sovereignty and International Intervention* and *The End of Sovereignty? The Politics of a Shrinking and Fragmenting World.*[24]

Given its power and its deep-seated commitment to liberal principles, the United States has spearheaded the post–Cold War assault on sovereignty. Of course, it jealously guards its own sovereignty.[25] While Washington has occasionally acted unilaterally, it usually has gone to considerable lengths to involve other countries in its interventions so that it can claim that the "international community" has legitimized its actions. One consequence of undermining sovereignty, however, has been to make it easier for American leaders to launch wars against other countries. The erosion of sovereignty is one more reason a powerful state with a liberal foreign policy ends up fighting never-ending wars and fostering militarism at home.

Instability and Costly Failures

Liberal hegemony also brings other costs. For starters, even though its aim is to make the world more peaceful, it creates greater instability in the system. In other words, there are likely to be more rather than fewer wars. This outcome is hardly surprising, given the liberal state's relative power and inherent bellicosity. Furthermore, when a great power is free to pursue a liberal foreign policy, it invariably ends up causing serious trouble—for itself, for its allies, for its target states, and for uninvolved states that end up caught in the crossfire.

Antagonizing the Major Powers

A liberal unipole is unlikely to use military power to protect individual rights or foster regime change in a major power, mainly because the costs are too high. Nevertheless, it is likely to interfere in that country's politics in other ways. Its tactics might include relying on nongovernmental organizations (NGOs) to support certain institutions and politicians inside the target state; linking aid, membership in international institutions, and trade to the major power's human rights record; and shaming the target state by publicly reporting its human rights violations. This approach is unlikely to work, however, because the major power invariably views the liberal power's behavior as illegitimate interference in its internal affairs. It will think its sovereignty is being violated, causing the policy to backfire and poisoning relations between the two countries.

This pattern of behavior appears in recent U.S. actions toward both China and Russia. Washington has been pushing to promote human rights and liberal democracy more generally in China since the government cracked down on protestors in Tiananmen Square in 1989. It has been doing the same in Russia since that state was created in 1991, although American policymakers have become especially concerned about rights there since the early 2000s, when Vladimir Putin became president. American leaders often tell Chinese and Russian audiences that their countries need to become more like the United States.

In the Russian case, Americans have focused not just on Russia but also on its immediate neighbors. Washington vigorously promoted so-called color revolutions in Georgia (Rose Revolution), Ukraine (Orange Revolution), and elsewhere, in the hope of turning them into liberal democracies. Those countries, of course, are of great strategic importance to Moscow because they share borders with Russia. The United States has also hinted that it would like to encourage a color revolution in Russia itself. For example, the head of the National Endowment for Democracy, which is funded by the U.S. government and dedicated to promoting regime change around the world, warned Putin in a September 2013 op-ed in the *Washington Post* that his days in office might be numbered.[26]

When Michael McFaul was the American ambassador in Moscow, from January 2012 to February 2014, he made clear by both actions and words his long-standing commitment to promoting democracy in Russia. Predictably, the Russian political establishment recoiled at McFaul's behavior, which helped poison relations between Moscow and Washington. As he acknowledges, his activities led the Russian press to describe him as "an agent sent by Obama to lead another color revolution."[27] And who can blame them? Americans abhor the idea of foreign interference in their politics, as the huge controversy about Russian involvement in the 2016 U.S. presidential election makes clear. When they find themselves the target nation, Americans become deeply committed to the principle of self-determination. Not surprisingly, so do the Russians.

Chinese leaders are no different when it comes to guarding their own sovereignty. They resent the frequent American harangues about human rights, which they see as part of a hidden agenda whose ultimate goal is regime change. Their suspicions of America's intentions run so deep that when there are pro-democracy protests in Hong Kong, Chinese leaders are sure the United States is behind them, even when there is no evidence to support that belief.[28] The Chinese have responded to American criticism about human rights by issuing an annual human rights report of their own in which they severely criticize the U.S. record.[29] In short, Washington's efforts to push Beijing to liberalize have worsened relations between the two countries, just as they did with Russia. At the same time, neither country has made any improvement on human rights, and there is no evidence either one will become a liberal democracy anytime soon.

There are significant limits on how much social engineering the United States can do inside major powers like China and Russia. It certainly cannot invade to stop human rights violations or promote regime change. It cannot achieve much with economic sanctions and other diplomatic tools, partly because major powers are not that vulnerable to coercion, but also because they usually can retaliate. Weaker states, which lack the material capabilities to defend themselves, make easier targets. Not surprisingly, great powers that go down the liberal hegemony road do their most serious social engineering in weak states, thinking the costs will be low and the benefits great.

Even Weak States Are Tough Nuts to Crack

Yet interventions in minor powers often fail too. The American effort to topple authoritarian rulers in the greater Middle East and replace them with democratic regimes, which began in earnest after 9/11 and continued throughout both the Bush and Obama administrations, is a textbook case of the limits of social engineering. The United States has taken aim at five countries: Afghanistan, Egypt, Iraq, Libya, and Syria. It used its own military to help topple the regimes in Afghanistan, Iraq, and Libya but did not do so in Egypt or Syria. Nevertheless, regime change worked twice in Egypt, although not for the better. In Syria, it helped produce a bloody and disastrous civil war.

In each case, American policymakers thought they could put in place a stable democracy that would be friendly to the United States and help it deal with serious problems like nuclear proliferation and terrorism. It is quite striking how much confidence Washington's leaders had in their capacity to transform the politics of those five countries, and the region more generally. But they failed every time, bringing killing and destruction to the greater Middle East and committing the United States to what appear to be endless wars in Afghanistan, Iraq, and Syria.

The United States went to war against Afghanistan in mid-October 2001, about one month after the 9/11 attacks. By early December, it appeared that the American military had won a spectacular victory. The Taliban was routed and a leader who seemed committed to democracy, Hamid Karzai, was installed in Kabul. That apparent success led the Bush administration to think it could produce the same outcome in Iraq, and eventually in the region's other countries as well. This was the genesis of the Bush Doctrine. The United States invaded Iraq in March 2003 and quickly removed Saddam Hussein from power, making it look as though Washington had found the magic formula for transforming the region into a sea of stable democracies. But by late summer, Iraq had descended into civil war, and the American military was beginning to face a major insurgency.

While the Bush administration was preoccupied with Iraq, which was spinning out of control by 2004, the Taliban began to come back from the dead. Afghanistan too found itself consumed by civil war. To make sure the Taliban and its allies did not topple the Karzai government and once again take control, the United States moved large numbers of troops into that country. It was now fighting major conflicts in both Afghanistan and Iraq. Contrary to earlier expectations, Washington had not found the way to pacify the greater Middle East and instead was trying to rescue the situation in two countries.

Both wars, however, now look like lost causes. The Obama administration pulled all American fighting forces out of Iraq in December 2011, leaving behind a broken country that quickly fell into a civil war between the Shia-dominated government in Baghdad and ISIS, a formidable group of militant Sunnis the Bush administration helped create by toppling Saddam and precipitating a civil war between Iraq's Shias and Sunnis. ISIS was initially so successful on the battlefield in Iraq and Syria that it claimed its own de facto state, which the United States went to war against in August 2014, albeit mainly with airpower.[30] Moreover, the Iraqi Kurds, who do not want to be part of a unified Iraq, have created their own de facto state in the north. Given the apparent strength of the Iraqi Kurds and Sunnis, coupled with the weakness of the Baghdad government, the Iraq that existed in 2003 is no more. Still, the United States is back in the fight in that fractured and wrecked country.

One month after taking office in January 2009, President Obama announced that he would send an additional 17,000 troops to Afghanistan on top of the 36,000 who were already there. Later that year, he decided to commit 30,000 more. At the same time, Obama promised that those forces would not stay indefinitely and would be completely out of Afghanistan by the time he left office in January 2017.[31] That plan went awry because the Taliban stood its ground and even conquered more territory as the American forces were drawn down. Moreover, the army commanded by the pro-American regime in Kabul proved incapable of standing up to the Taliban unaided, and ISIS is now a growing force in the country. There were 8,400 U.S. troops remaining in Afghanistan when Obama departed the White House,[32] and President Trump is under pressure from his commanders there to increase U.S. troop levels in what has become the longest war in American history.

Whatever policy the Trump administration pursues in Afghanistan, there is no chance it will defeat the Taliban and turn that country into a stable democracy. The best it can do is delay the day that the Taliban, which now controls roughly 30 percent of the country, regains control of the rest. In short, the United States is destined to lose in Afghanistan, despite the Herculean efforts of the American military and having invested more money in its reconstruction than was committed to Europe with the Marshall Plan in the aftermath of World War II.[33]

Libya represents another failed effort to alter a weak state's politics. In March 2011, the United States and its European allies launched an air campaign aimed at toppling Colonel Muammar Gaddafi from power. The Libyan leader was dealing with a formidable insurrection, and the Western powers used the false pretext that he was about to engage in mass murder to help end his rule. In July, more than thirty countries recognized the rebel-led National Transitional Council as the legitimate government of Libya. Gaddafi was murdered in October 2011, and Libya has since been consumed by a bloody civil war with no end in sight. There is no reason to think it will become a stable democracy in the near future.[34]

At the time the United States was upending the Gaddafi regime in Libya, protests broke out in Syria against its authoritarian ruler, Bashar al-Assad. The government overreacted and used violence to suppress the protests, helping to turn that conflict into a deadly civil war that continues today. But the United States also played a central role in escalating the conflict, although it did not intervene directly.[35] In August 2011, a few months after the trouble started, the Obama administration sided with the anti-government forces and demanded that Assad step down from power.[36] After he refused, Washington joined forces with Qatar, Saudi Arabia, and Turkey in an effort to topple him. The United States provided support to "moderate" rebel groups, for whom the Central Intelligence Agency (CIA) and the Pentagon ultimately spent more than $1.5 billion on weaponry and training.[37]

The strategy has failed completely. Assad is still in power, more than four hundred thousand people (many of them civilians) have died in Syria's civil war, and almost half of the population has been forced to flee their homes.[38] But even if the Assad government had fallen, a radical insurgent group like the Nusra Front, which is affiliated with al Qaeda, almost certainly would have replaced it. If that group or any other like-minded group were to come to power, it would almost certainly embark on a bloody rampage against the many members and supporters of the Assad regime. Moreover, the new regime would be deeply hostile to the United States. The Syrian government is not likely to fall, however, because Russia, Iran, and Hezbollah have directly intervened to keep Assad in power. The civil war will probably drag on for several years, wreaking more havoc and destruction.

There is another terrible consequence of the Syrian conflict. Huge numbers of Syrians have fled their homeland and are trying to settle in Europe, joined by refugees from the ongoing conflicts in Afghanistan, Iraq, and Libya. Most European countries welcomed these exiles at first, but the numbers eventually grew so large that some countries, as well as the European Union (EU) itself, erected significant barriers to keep them out. These moves are contrary to Europe's cherished principle of open borders as well as its enlightened policies on asylum. The huge influx of refugees is fueling the growth of Europe's far-right political parties, which are committed to keeping immigrants and refugees out of their countries. In short, the war in Syria, which the United States helped start, has the potential to do serious damage to the EU in addition to the horrendous costs it has inflicted on the Syrian people.

Finally, there is the case of Egypt, where protests broke out against President Hosni Mubarak in January 2011. As these protests gained momentum, the Obama administration stepped in and helped oust the Egyptian leader from power.[39] Obama welcomed Egypt's move toward democracy and supported the newly elected government that came to power in June 2012, even though the Muslim Brotherhood was in charge. But after one year in office, President Mohamed Morsi, a member of the Brotherhood, was being pressed hard by the Egyptian military and much of the public to resign. The Obama administration, never enthusiastic about Morsi, stepped into this messy situation and gently hinted that it was time for the Egyptian leader to go, which helped facilitate his overthrow.[40] He was replaced by General Abdel Fattah el-Sisi, a military strongman in the Mubarak tradition.

In taking this step, the United States helped foster a coup against a democratically elected leader who was not a threat to the United States. The new Egyptian dictator then turned against the Brotherhood and its supporters, killing over one thousand people and sentencing Morsi to death, although he remains in jail at this writing. The Obama administration lamely tried to prevent this bloody crackdown but failed. It was not willing to withhold the entire $1.5 billion the United States gives Egypt each year, even though American law mandates that all foreign aid be cut to any country "whose duly elected head of government is deposed by military coup or decree."[41]

Washington's performance in Afghanistan, Egypt, Iraq, Libya, and Syria has been dismal. Not only has the United States failed to protect human rights and promote liberal democracy in those countries, it has played a major role in spreading death and disorder across the greater Middle East.[42] Terrorism is a much greater problem in the region today, and the Iran nuclear deal notwithstanding, the incentives for countries around the world to either acquire or keep their nuclear weapons have increased in the face of America's policy of forcible regime change. Policymakers in countries that have serious differences with the United States surely remember that Colonel Gaddafi gave up his programs to create weapons of mass destruction in December 2003 on the promise that Washington would not try to remove him from power.[43] Eight years later, the Obama administration played a key role in removing him from power; soon thereafter he was murdered. It is likely he would still rule Libya today if he had possessed a nuclear deterrent.

The Limits and Perils of Social Engineering

This abysmal record of failure should have been foreseen. Doing large-scale social engineering in any society, including one's own, is an enormously complicated task. What is amazing is that so many American policymakers and pundits were confident they could fundamentally alter the political landscape in a host of Middle Eastern countries and turn them into democracies. The United States was intervening in countries it knew astonishingly little about—few government officials even spoke Arabic or knew that Sunni and Shi'a were different branches of Islam—and its violation of those states' right of self-determination was bound to generate resentment. Furthermore, the countries were all riven with factions and were likely to be in turmoil once the government was brought down. Doing social engineering in a foreign country while fighting to control it is a wickedly hard task.

The problem is particularly acute when the United States invades another country, because the American military forces occupying that country inevitably end up tasked with the nation- and state-building necessary to produce a functioning liberal democracy. In the age of nationalism, however, occupation almost always breeds an insurgency, as the United States discovered long ago in the Philippines and later in Vietnam, long before it entered Afghanistan and Iraq. The occupier must then engage in counterinsurgency, which means fighting a long and bloody military campaign with high odds of failure. The difficulty of winning at counterinsurgency is clearly reflected in the December 2006 edition of the U.S. Army and Marine Corps *Counterinsurgency Field Manual 3-24*. It not only warns that "insurgencies are protracted by nature" but also cautions that "political and military leaders and planners should never underestimate [their] scale and complexity."[44]

It is clear from the historical record that the effort to impose democracy on another country usually fails.[45] Andrew Enterline and J. Michael Greig, for example, examined forty-three cases of imposed democratic regimes between 1800 and 1994 and found that nearly 63 percent failed.[46] Jeffrey Pickering and Mark Peceny, who investigated the democratizing consequences of interventions by liberal states from 1946 to 1996, conclude that "liberal intervention . . . has only very rarely played a role in democratization since 1945."[47] As Alexander Downes and Jonathan Monten point out, imposing democracy on another country is likely to work "if favorable internal preconditions are present. These conditions, unfortunately, are relatively rare in countries where the costs of intervention are low."[48] Great powers like the United States, however, do not invade to attempt regime change unless the costs are low, which means the necessary preconditions for liberal democracy will not be present.

Predictably, the United States has a rich history of failing to impose democracy on other countries. New York University professors Bruce Bueno de Mesquita and George Downs report that between World War II and 2004, "the United States intervened more than 35 times in developing countries around the world. . . . In only one case—Colombia after the American decision in 1989 to engage in the war on drugs—did a full-fledged, stable democracy . . . emerge within 10 years. That's a success rate of less than 3%."[49] Pickering and Peceny find only one case—Panama after the removal of Manuel Noriega—in which American intervention clearly resulted in the emergence of a consolidated democracy.[50] William Easterly and two colleagues at New York University looked at how U.S. and Soviet interventions during the Cold War affected the prospects for a liberal form of government, and found that "superpower interventions are followed by significant declines in democracy, and that the substantive effects are large."[51]

One might argue that events in Eastern Europe circa 1989 provide an encouraging precedent. But that claim is wrong. Democracy sprouted in that region when communism collapsed and the ruling autocrats fell from power, but these cases have little relevance to what the United States has been trying to do in the greater Middle East. Democracy was not imposed on the countries of Eastern Europe. It was homegrown in every instance, and the countries already possessed many of the necessary preconditions for democratization. There is no question the United States has helped nurture these nascent democracies, but these are not cases of Washington successfully exporting popular rule to foreign lands, which is what the Bush Doctrine was all about.[52]

It is not impossible for the United States to impose liberal democracy abroad. But successes are the exception, not the rule, and they usually occur in countries with a particular set of internal characteristics. It helps greatly, for example, if the target state is ethnically and religiously homogeneous and has a strong central government, reasonably high levels of prosperity, and some experience with democracy. Post–World War II Germany and Japan, which are often held up as evidence that the United States can export liberal democracy to the Middle East, fit these criteria. But they are highly unusual.

The Costs of Ignoring Geopolitics

Putting aside the difficulty of interfering successfully in other countries' domestic politics, there is an additional problem that has more to do with realism than nationalism. When a powerful country pursues liberal hegemony, it runs the risk that other states will follow the dictates of realpolitik. This greatly increases the likelihood of miscalculation, which could lead to a crisis or even a war. For example, a liberal state might genuinely believe that its policy is benign or even noble, while another state, operating according to realist principles, might view the same policy as threatening. The liberal state, simply because it acts under a different ism, would probably fail to understand this.

What makes this situation so dangerous for a liberal great power is that most states, most of the time, follow balance-of-power logic. Liberal great powers typically act this way as well, especially toward other great powers. But occasionally they are free to embrace liberal hegemony. Should they forget that they are still operating in a largely realist world, they may cause a lot of trouble for themselves and other states. The ongoing crisis over Ukraine is a case in point. According to the prevailing wisdom in the West, this problem is largely the result of Russian aggression. President Vladimir Putin, the argument goes, is bent on creating a greater Russia akin to the former Soviet Union, which means controlling the governments in its "near abroad"—its neighboring states—including Ukraine, the Baltic states, and possibly other Eastern European countries. The coup against Ukrainian president Viktor Yanukovych on February 22, 2014, provided Putin with a pretext for annexing Crimea and starting a war in eastern Ukraine.

This account is false. The United States and its European allies are mainly responsible for the crisis.[53] The taproot of the trouble is NATO expansion, the central element in a larger strategy to move all of Eastern Europe, including Ukraine, out of Russia's orbit and integrate it into the West. One might think this policy is a classic deterrence strategy aimed at containing a potentially aggressive Russia, but it is not.[54] The West's strategy was based mainly on liberal principles, and its chief architects did not think Moscow should have seen it as threatening.[55] The aim was to integrate Ukraine into the "security community" that had developed in western Europe during the Cold War and had been moving eastward since its conclusion. But the Russians were using a realist playbook. The major crisis that resulted left many Western leaders feeling blindsided.

Taking Aim at Ukraine

The strategy for making Ukraine part of the West consists of three linked components: NATO enlargement, EU expansion, and the Orange Revolution, which aimed at fostering democracy and Western values in Ukraine and thus presumably produce pro-Western leaders in Kiev. From Moscow's perspective, the most threatening aspect of that strategy is NATO's movement eastward.

When the Cold War was ending, the Soviet Union made it clear that it favored keeping the U.S. military in Europe and maintaining NATO. The Soviet leaders understood that this arrangement had kept Germany pacified since World War II and would continue doing so after the country reunified and became much more powerful. But Moscow was deeply opposed to NATO enlargement. The Russians believed their Western counterparts understood their fears and that the alliance would not expand toward the Soviet Union.[56] But the Clinton administration thought otherwise and in the 1990s began pushing NATO expansion.

The first extension, in 1999, brought Poland, Hungary, and the Czech Republic into the alliance. The second tranche, which occurred in 2004, included Bulgaria, Romania, Slovakia, Slovenia, and the three Baltic countries. Russian leaders complained bitterly from the start. Boris Yeltsin, for example, said during NATO's 1995 bombing campaign against Serbia: "This is the first sign of what could happen when NATO comes right up to the Russian Federation's borders. . . . The flame of war could burst out across the whole of Europe."[57] The Russians, however, were too weak to derail either expansion. Moreover, save for the tiny Baltic countries, none of NATO's new members shared a border with Russia.

The real trouble began at the NATO summit in Bucharest in April 2008, when Ukraine's and Georgia's membership came up for discussion. France and Germany were opposed out of fear that admitting them would unduly antagonize Russia, but the Bush administration was committed to bringing these countries into NATO. The outcome of this standoff was that NATO did not initiate the process necessary to bring Ukraine and Georgia into the alliance, but the summit's final declaration included the news that "NATO welcomes Ukraine's and Georgia's Euro Atlantic aspirations for membership in NATO. We agreed today that these countries will become members of NATO."[58] Moscow reacted immediately and angrily. Russia's deputy foreign minister warned that "Georgia's and Ukraine's membership in the alliance is a huge strategic mistake which would have most serious consequences for pan-European security." Putin maintained that admitting those two countries would represent a "direct threat" to Russia. One Russian newspaper reported that Putin, speaking directly to Bush, "very transparently hinted that if Ukraine was accepted into NATO, it would cease to exist."[59]

Any doubts about Russia's determination to prevent Ukraine and Georgia from joining NATO should have been dispelled by the Russia-Georgia war in August 2008. Georgian president Mikheil Saakashvili, who was deeply committed to bringing his country into NATO, decided after the Budapest summit to reincorporate two separatist regions, Abkhazia and South Ossetia, which together make up about 20 percent of Georgia's territory. NATO membership required that these outstanding territorial disputes be resolved, but Putin was not about to let that happen. He preferred to keep Georgia weak and divided and decided to humiliate Saakashvili.[60] After fighting broke out between Georgia and the Ossetian separatists, Russia invaded Georgia under the pretense of a "humanitarian intervention" and gained control over Abkhazia and South Ossetia. The West did little in response, leaving Saakashvili in the lurch. Russia had made its point, yet NATO refused to give up on bringing Ukraine and Georgia into the alliance.

Integrating Ukraine into the West also involved the EU, which like NATO had been expanding eastward since the Cold War ended. Austria, Finland,

and Sweden joined the EU in 1995, and eight Central and Eastern European countries (Czech Republic, Estonia, Hungary, Latvia, Lithuania, Poland, Slovakia, and Slovenia) joined in May 2004 along with Cyprus and Malta. Bulgaria and Romania joined in 2007. In May 2009, just over a year after NATO announced Ukraine would become a member, the EU unveiled its Eastern Partnership initiative, which it described as "an ambitious new chapter in the EU's relations with its Eastern neighbors." Its aim was to foster prosperity and stability in Eastern European countries and promote "far reaching integration into the EU economy."[61] Russian leaders, not surprisingly, viewed the Eastern Partnership as hostile to their country's interests. The Russian foreign minister, Sergei Lavrov, complained that the EU was trying to create a "sphere of influence" in Eastern Europe and hinted that it was engaging in "blackmail."[62] In fact, Moscow sees EU expansion as a stalking horse for NATO enlargement.[63] EU leaders dismiss these claims and argue that Russia too would benefit from the Eastern Partnership.

The final tool for peeling Ukraine away from Russia was the effort to promote the Orange Revolution. The United States and its European allies are deeply committed to fostering social and political change in countries formerly under Soviet control. They aim to spread Western values and promote liberal democracy, which means supporting pro-Western individuals and organizations in those countries—efforts that are funded by official government agencies as well as NGOs.[64] Of course, Russian leaders worry about social engineering in Ukraine, not just because of what it means for Ukraine but also because they think Russia might be the next target.

NATO enlargement, EU expansion, and democracy promotion are a close-knit package of policies designed to integrate Ukraine into the West without antagonizing Russia. But they inadvertently turned Moscow into an enemy, leading directly to the Ukraine crisis.

The Immediate Causes

The crisis began in late November 2013, when President Yanukovych rejected a major economic deal he had been negotiating with the EU and decided instead to accept a Russian counteroffer. That decision led to protests against the government that escalated over the following three months. Two protestors were killed on January 22, 2014, and about one hundred more died in mid-February. Western emissaries, hurriedly flown to Kiev to resolve the crisis, struck a deal on February 21 that would have allowed Yanukovych to stay in power until new elections were held sometime before year's end. But the protestors demanded that he leave office immediately, and he fled to Russia the next day.[65]

The new government in Kiev was thoroughly pro-Western and anti-Russian. Moreover, it contained four members who could legitimately be labeled neofascists. Most importantly, the U.S. government backed the coup, although the full extent of its involvement is unknown. Victoria Nuland, the assistant secretary of state for European and Eurasian Affairs, and Senator John McCain (R-AZ), for example, participated in anti-government demonstrations, while the U.S. ambassador in Kiev proclaimed after the coup that it was "a day for the history books."[66] A leaked transcript of a phone conversation revealed that Nuland advocated regime change and wanted Arseniy Yatsenyuk, who was pro-Western, to become prime minister in the new government, which he did. It is hardly surprising that Russians of all persuasions think Western provocateurs, especially the CIA, helped overthrow Yanukovych.

For Putin, the time to act had arrived. Shortly after the February 22 coup, he set the forces in motion to take Crimea from Ukraine and incorporate it into Russia. This was not difficult given that Russia already had thousands of troops at its naval base in the Crimean port of Sevastopol. Those forces were augmented with additional troops from Russia, many of them not in uniform. Crimea was an easy target because roughly 60 percent of the people living there were ethnic Russians, and most preferred to become part of Russia.

Putin also put massive pressure on the Kiev government to discourage it from siding with the West against Moscow. He made it clear that he would wreck Ukraine as a functioning society before allowing a Western stronghold to exist on Russia's doorstep. Toward that end, he has supported the Russian separatists in eastern Ukraine with weapons and covert troops, helping to push the country into civil war. He has also maintained substantial ground forces on Russia's border with Ukraine and threatened to invade if Kiev cracks down on the rebels. Finally, he has raised the price of gas Russia sells to Ukraine, demanded immediate remittance of overdue payments, and at one point even cut off the supply of gas to Ukraine. As he did with Georgia, Putin is playing hardball with Ukraine, and he has the means to subvert the country indefinitely if it does not abandon its plans to join the West.

Liberal Blinders

Anyone with a rudimentary understanding of geopolitics should have seen this coming. The West was moving into Russia's backyard and threatening its core strategic interests. A huge expanse of flat land that Napoleonic France, Imperial Germany, and Nazi Germany have all crossed to strike at Russia itself, Ukraine serves as an enormously important strategic buffer to Russia. No Russian leader would tolerate a former enemy's military alliance moving into Ukraine. Nor would any Russian leader stand idly by while the West helped install a government in Kiev that was determined to join that alliance.

Washington may not like Moscow's position, but it should understand the logic behind it. Great powers are always sensitive to threats near their home territory. The United States, for instance, under the Monroe Doctrine does not tolerate distant great powers deploying military forces anywhere in the Western Hemisphere, much less on its borders. Imagine the outrage in Washington if China built an impressive alliance and tried to install governments in Canada and Mexico that wanted to join. Logic aside, Russian leaders have told their Western counterparts many times that they will not tolerate NATO expansion into Ukraine and Georgia, or any effort to turn those countries against Russia—a message the 2008 Russia-Georgia War should have made crystal clear.

Western officials contend that they tried hard to assuage Russian fears and that Moscow should have understood NATO has no hostile intentions toward Russia. In addition to denying that its expansion was aimed at containing Russia, the alliance had not permanently deployed military forces on the territory of any new member state. In 2002, hoping to foster cooperation with Moscow, it even created a body called the NATO-Russia Council. To further mollify Russia, the United States announced in 2009 that its new missile defense system would be deployed on warships in European waters, at least initially, not on Czech or Polish territory. None of these measures worked; Russia remained steadfastly opposed to NATO enlargement, especially into Ukraine and Georgia. And it is the Russians, not the West, who ultimately get to decide what counts as a threat to them.

Western elites were surprised by events in Ukraine because most of them have a flawed understanding of international politics. They believe that realism and geopolitics have little relevance in the twenty-first century and that a "Europe whole and free" can be constructed entirely on the basis of liberal principles. These principles include the rule of law, economic interdependence, and democratization. The United States is well suited to lead the creation of this new world, goes the story, because it is a benign hegemon that does not threaten Russia or any other country.

This grand scheme to turn Europe into a giant security community went awry over Ukraine, but the seeds of this disaster were sown in the mid-1990s, when the Clinton administration began pushing for NATO expansion.[67] Pundits and policymakers advanced a variety of arguments for and against enlargement, but they never reached a consensus. Most Eastern European émigrés in the United States and their relatives strongly supported expansion because they wanted NATO protection for countries like Poland and Hungary. A few realists favored the policy because they thought it was still necessary to contain Russia. But most realists opposed expansion because they thought a declining power with an aging population and a one-dimensional economy did not need to be contained, and they feared that enlargement would strongly motivate Moscow to cause trouble. The legendary U.S. diplomat and strategic thinker George Kennan said in a 1998 interview, shortly after the Senate approved the first round of NATO expansion, that "I think the Russians will gradually react quite adversely and it will affect their policies. I think it is a tragic mistake. There was no reason for this whatsoever. No one was threatening anyone else."[68]

Most liberals, including many key members of the Clinton administration, favored enlargement. They believed the end of the Cold War had transformed international politics, and in the new post-national order, the realist logic that had guided state behavior for centuries no longer applied. In this new world, the United States was not only the "indispensable nation," to quote Secretary of State Madeleine Albright, but also a force for good that should not strike fear in the heart of any rational leader. A Voice of America reporter commented in February 2004 that "most analysts agree the enlargement of NATO and the EU should not pose a long-term threat to Russian interests. They point out that having stable and secure neighbors may increase stability and prosperity in Russia, as well as help overcome old Cold War fears and encourage former Soviet satellites to engage Russia in a more positive, cooperative way."[69]

By the late 1990s, the liberals within the Clinton administration had won the battle for NATO expansion. They then had little difficulty convincing their European allies to support enlargement. Given the EU's success during the 1990s, in fact, Western European elites may have been even more wedded than the Americans to the notion that geopolitics no longer matter and that an all-inclusive liberal order could maintain long-term peace in Europe. The common aim of the United States and its liberal European allies as the twentieth century ended was to promote democracy in the countries of Eastern Europe, increase economic interdependence among them, and embed them in international institutions. The ultimate goal was to make the entire continent look like Western Europe.

Liberals came to dominate the discourse about European security so thoroughly during the first decade of the twenty-first century that further NATO expansion faced little opposition in the West from realists or anyone else, even after the alliance had effectively adopted an open-door policy regarding future membership.[70] The liberal worldview dominated the thinking of both the Bush and Obama administrations. In a March 2014 speech about the Ukraine crisis, for example, President Obama talked repeatedly about "the ideals" that motivate Western policy and how those ideals "have often been threatened by an older, more traditional view of power." Secretary of State John Kerry's response to the Russian annexation of Crimea reflected the same perspective: "You just don't in the twenty-first century behave in nineteenth-century fashion by invading another country on completely trumped up pretext."[71]

In sum, Russia and the West have been operating with different handbooks. Putin and his compatriots have been thinking and acting like realists, while Western leaders have adhered to textbook liberal ideas about international politics. The result is that the United States and its allies unwittingly provoked a major crisis that shows no sign of ending, in large part because liberal democracies find it so difficult to engage in diplomacy with authoritarian states.

Liberalism Abroad Undermines Liberalism at Home

States that pursue liberal hegemony invariably damage the fabric of liberalism inside their own borders. The main reason is straightforward: a country pursuing this ambitious strategy abroad has little choice but to create a powerful national security bureaucracy to fight its endless wars and monitor and shape the world in its own image. But a formidable national security state almost always threatens liberal values and institutions at home. The Founding Fathers understood this problem well: as James Madison observed, "No nation can preserve its freedom in the midst of continual warfare."[72]

Militarized liberal states must rely on secrecy and must even deceive their own people when the country's interest requires it, which turns out to be surprisingly often in the eyes of their national security operatives. This same instinct gives way to violating individual rights and undermining the rule of law when those operatives deem it essential for making a liberal foreign policy work. Liberal states that fight frequent wars also routinely end up treating their adversaries with ruthless policies that conflict with their own laws and liberal values.[73]

The United States has waged seven wars since the Cold War ended and has been at war continuously since the month after 9/11, and the wars show no sign of stopping. All of this conflict has made the formidable national security state that existed in 1991, when the Soviet Union collapsed, even more powerful today.

Secrecy and Deception

At the domestic level, transparency is indispensable if liberal democracies are to function effectively. It not only allows voters to make informed decisions but also allows the media and outside experts to assess government policies and participate in a workable marketplace of ideas. It is an essential ingredient of any successful liberal democracy. It helps citizens hold policymakers accountable when they make mistakes or engage in criminal behavior. Secrecy, by definition, is all about limiting transparency, which means too much of it can easily undermine a liberal democratic regime.

There is no question that every country's foreign policy requires some secrecy. For a liberal democracy, however, it is imperative to minimize the amount of secrecy and maximize the amount of transparency. But pursuing liberal hegemony has the opposite effect, in part because any country that does so is powerfully motivated to limit the amount of information that adversaries have about its policies, strategies, and weaponry. Sometimes it makes sense to hide information even from allies. The more ambitious a country's foreign policy, the more reason it has to hide secrets from friends and foes alike. Liberal states also like secrecy because it helps protect leaders from criticism at home, making it easier to pursue policies that might be controversial. It is hard for journalists and academics to criticize a policy, and perhaps ultimately check it, if they know nothing about it. Finally, policymakers want to avoid accountability if their chosen policy goes awry or if pursuing it leads them to break the law. The best way to accomplish this is to keep the public in the dark.

The deep affection for secrecy shown by both the Bush and Obama administrations is not surprising in light of their illegal or at least questionable surveillance of American citizens, which they tried to hide from the public, Congress, and the courts.[74] This is one reason President Obama was so determined to punish Bradley Manning and Edward Snowden, and more generally why he went to war with unprecedented fervor against reporters and whistleblowers.[75] He also went to great lengths to disguise how deeply involved the United States was in the Syrian civil war, and to divulge as little information as possible about drone strikes. Obama was given to claiming that he ran "the most transparent administration in history."[76] If true, the credit should go to the reporters and whistleblowers who defied his deep commitment to government secrecy.

Another harmful consequence of a highly interventionist foreign policy is that it gives leaders numerous occasions to lie, or at least distort the truth, when trying to motivate the public to support military action abroad. This behavior was clearly on display during World War I, when the Wilson administration unleashed a comprehensive propaganda campaign to stir up public sentiment in support of the fight against Imperial Germany. Inflating the Soviet threat was commonplace during the Cold War, and the George W. Bush administration waged a highly effective deception campaign in the run-up to the 2003 Iraq war.

Deception campaigns involve three kinds of behavior: lying, spinning, and concealment. Lying is where a policymaker makes a statement that he knows to be false in the hope that others will think it is true. Spinning, a more common form of deception, is where a leader tells a story that emphasizes certain facts and either deemphasizes or omits other facts, for the purpose of selling or defending some policy. No attempt is made to render a fully accurate account. Spinning, in other words, involves exaggeration and distortion but not prevarication. Concealment is withholding information from the public that might undermine or weaken a favored policy. Obviously, this form of deception is most closely related to secrecy.[77]

Liberal states with ambitious foreign policy agendas are prone to engage in deception campaigns, because inspiring people to fight and die in a war is not easy. Individuals, like states, are deeply motivated to survive. It is especially challenging to sell liberal wars because they are ultimately not about fighting off threats to a country's survival but about protecting the rights of foreigners or spreading liberal democracy. Getting people to fight and die for these liberal goals is not an easy sell. Leaders are always tempted to deceive their publics to get them on board for wars of choice.[78]

Governments also deceive their publics when they are trying to hide illegal or constitutionally suspect activities. For example, James Clapper, the director of national intelligence, appeared before Congress on March 12, 2013, and was asked: "Does the NSA [National Security Agency] collect any type of data at all on millions or hundreds of millions of Americans?" He answered no. It quickly became apparent that he was lying, which he was forced to admit to Congress in June: "My response was clearly erroneous—for which I apologize." Later, he said he responded to that question in the "least untruthful" manner possible. Although lying to Congress is a felony, Clapper was not charged and was not fired from his job.[79]

Pervasive obfuscation inevitably creates a poisonous culture of dishonesty, which gravely damages any body politic but especially a liberal democracy.

Not only does lying make it difficult for citizens to make informed choices about candidates and issues, it also undermines policymaking. If government officials cannot trust each other, the transaction costs of doing business are greatly increased. Furthermore, in a world where distorting or hiding the truth is commonplace, the rule of law is severely weakened. Any legal system, to work effectively, demands public honesty and trust. Finally, if lying becomes pervasive in a liberal democracy, it may alienate the public to the point where it loses faith in that political order and becomes open to authoritarian rule.

Eroding Civil Liberties

A liberal democracy that is constantly preparing for and fighting wars, as well as extolling the benefits of using force, is likely to end up violating the individual rights and rule of law that are at the heart of a liberal society. In times of national emergency such as war, leaders may think they have good reasons to stifle criticism of their policies by curtailing freedom of speech and freedom of the press. They are apt to have deep concerns about an enemy within, which might include disloyal citizens or even aliens. Fear is the order of the day. The atmosphere of suspicion invariably leads to restricting individual rights and monitoring citizens in illiberal ways, often with wide public support.

Leaders do not act this way because they are evil. Given the trade-off between security and civil liberties in dire times, or what are perceived to be dire times, policymakers almost always choose security. A country's highest goal has to be its survival, because if it does not survive, it cannot pursue any other goals. The ample evidence of this kind of behavior in American history includes Lincoln's illiberal policies during the U.S. Civil War, the silencing of anti-war voices during World War I, the infamous "Red Scare" immediately after that conflict, the imprisonment of Japanese American citizens in World War II, and McCarthyism in the late 1940s and early 1950s.

Given the exaggerated fear of foreign threats that has permeated the American foreign policy establishment since 9/11, it is unsurprising that both Presidents Bush and Obama pursued policies that diminished civil liberties at home. Three examples are in order, the first of which involves the right to privacy as it relates to the Fourth Amendment's warrant re-

quirements. Generally speaking, the government cannot gather information on American citizens without a judge's authorization. Normally, to
obtain a search warrant, investigators must show there is probable cause to
think an individual is engaging in illegal activity. Even when the government thinks someone is dangerous or behaving unlawfully, it ordinarily
cannot act without judicial approval.

There is little doubt the Bush administration was engaged in warrantless
surveillance of American citizens from shortly after 9/11 until January 2007.[80]
We also know, thanks to Edward Snowden, that the government, mainly the
NSA, also searches and stores vast amounts of emails and text-based messages.[81] While limited by law to monitoring international communications
for foreign intelligence purposes, the NSA nevertheless collected domestic
communications between American citizens. The government also regularly collects telephone records of millions of Americans and keeps track of
"telephony metadata" that includes the phone numbers of parties to a call,
its duration, location, and time. It is hard to disagree with Senator Ron
Wyden's (D-OR) comment that "the government's authority to collect information on law-abiding American citizens is essentially limitless."[82]

To do this surveillance, the government often gets a warrant from a secret court known as the Foreign Intelligence Surveillance Court (or FISA
court). But this process has significant transparency and credibility problems. The FISA court is a virtual rubber stamp:[83] between 1979 and 2012,
it received almost thirty-four thousand requests to conduct electronic surveillance within the United States and denied eleven.[84] Moreover, it is virtually impossible to challenge FISA court rulings, not only because they are
secret but because no one but the government is a party to the proceedings.
And when FISA evidence is used in federal criminal prosecutions, neither
the defendant nor his attorney can obtain access to the warrant application
if the attorney general certifies, as he routinely does, that disclosure would
endanger national security.[85] When a federal appeals court ruled that the
NSA's collection of bulk data was illegal, the Obama administration instructed the FISA court to ignore the ruling.[86]

The second example of policies that undermine civil liberties concerns
due process, which lies at the very core of America's constitutional protec-
tions and is the backbone of the rule of law. It is no exaggeration to say that

as it applies to so-called enemy combatants in the global war on terror, the traditional notion of due process has become laughable. In January 2002, when the United States began sweeping up suspected terrorists in Afghanistan and elsewhere after 9/11, the Bush administration created a virtual gulag at Guantanamo Bay and strongly resisted the detainees' efforts to obtain due process. Since it was opened, 779 men have been imprisoned there. President Obama vowed to close it but could not, and it remains a due process quagmire. Of the 41 individuals still imprisoned at Guantanamo as of January 2017, 5 have been cleared for release but remain imprisoned, which has been a common pattern at the prison. Twenty-six prisoners cannot be prosecuted, because of insufficient evidence; but the government refuses to release them because it considers them security threats.[87] This arbitrary and unprecedented policy of indefinite detention blatantly violates most commonly held notions of due process.

Worse yet, the Bush administration devised the infamous policy of extraordinary rendition, in which high-value prisoners were sent to countries that cared little about human rights, like Egypt and Syria, to be tortured and interrogated. It appears the CIA also tortured prisoners at its "black sites" in Europe as well as at Bagram Air Base in Afghanistan and Abu Ghraib in Iraq.[88] This policy clearly violated American and international law, both of which forbid torture. Not surprisingly, as Amrit Singh, who directs the project on national security and counterterrorism at the Open Society Justice Initiative, reported, "The secret detention program and the extraordinary rendition program were highly classified, conducted outside the United States, and designed to place detainee interrogations beyond the reach of the law."[89] Taken together, the policies of illegal detention and illegal torture not only subvert the rule of law but conspire to prevent its restoration in the future.

This disgraceful situation brings to mind yet a third example. Because the Obama administration could neither prosecute nor release the detainees at Guantanamo, it had little interest in capturing new prisoners and subjecting them to indefinite detention. So Obama and his advisors apparently decided instead to assassinate suspected enemy combatants wherever they were found.[90] While it is surely easier to kill suspects than bring them to Guantanamo and perpetuate its legal morass, the effects of this new policy may be even more poisonous.

Drones, of course, play a central role in these assassinations. Obama had a kill list known as the "disposition matrix," and every Tuesday there was a meeting in the White House—it was called "Terror Tuesday"—where the next victims were selected.[91] The extent to which the Obama administration bought into this strategy is reflected in the distribution of drone strikes between November 2002, when they began, and May 2013. Micah Zenko reports that there were "approximately 425 non-battlefield targeted killings (more than 95 percent by drones). Roughly 50 took place during Mr. Bush's tenure, and 375 (and counting) under Mr. Obama's."[92] As the journalist Tom Engelhardt writes, "Once upon a time, off-the-books assassination was generally a rare act of state that presidents could deny. Now, it is part of everyday life in the White House and at the CIA. The president's role as assassin in chief has been all but publicly promoted as a political plus."[93]

This assassination strategy leaves hardly any room for due process under the law. The CIA is even authorized to kill young men who are not known to be terrorists but are merely exhibiting suspicious behavior, whatever that might be. It is also difficult to clearly identify targets from thousands of feet above. Thus it is hardly surprising that there are many cases where drones have killed innocent civilians. While it is hard to get firm numbers, at least 10 to 15 percent of the victims appear to have been civilians. A comment by former CIA director Michael Hayden in 2012 captures just how misguided Obama's assassination strategy was: "Right now, there isn't a government on the planet that agrees with our legal rationale for these operations, except for Afghanistan and maybe Israel."[94] Individual rights and the rule of law do not fare well in a country that maintains a large and powerful military and is addicted to fighting wars.[95]

The High-Modernist Ideology

In *Seeing Like a State,* James Scott sets out to determine "why so many well-intended schemes to improve the human condition have gone so tragically awry."[96] His focus is on disastrous domestic programs like China's

Great Leap Forward (1958–62) and collectivization in Russia (1928–40). But I believe Scott's thesis can also be applied to international politics.[97] One could argue that the chances of failure are even higher with liberal hegemony, because it involves social engineering in a foreign country, not at home.

Scott maintains that many of the great disasters in modern history are caused by "great utopian social engineering schemes" that depend on a "high-modernist ideology." Liberal hegemony appears to qualify on both counts. It calls for doing social engineering all across the globe, which is nothing if not utopian. A high-modernist ideology, Scott says, "is best conceived as a strong, one might even say muscle-bound, version of the self-confidence about scientific and technical progress, the expansion of production, the growing satisfaction of human needs, the mastery of nature (including human nature), and, above all, the rational design of social order commensurate with the scientific understanding of natural laws." Again, liberal hegemony, with its confidence in the virtues of liberal democracy and open economic markets and its use of international institutions to purvey standard metrics that make states more legible, fits the bill well.

According to Scott, disastrous failure requires two additional ingredients: "an authoritarian state that is willing and able to use the full weight of its coercive power to bring these high-modernist designs into being" and "a prostrate civil society that lacks the capacity to resist these plans." Liberal democracies and authoritarian states represent fundamentally different political forms, but this distinction is largely moot in the international realm. A powerful liberal state can be intensely single-minded and willing to coerce other countries when it thinks this is not only morally correct but also good for its own security. When liberal democracies feel seriously threatened, they are likely to declare a state of emergency, allowing themselves to take on many of the features of an authoritarian state.

Moreover, civil society simply has no international equivalent. All the talk one hears about the "international community," which implies that the citizens of the world might come together and stand up to a great power, is ultimately empty rhetoric. The international community is prostrate from the outset. There is little danger that popular opposition will stop a liberal great power from trying to impose its high-modernist ideology on weaker states. Of course, the crusading state may run into opposition from other states, but there will not be enough to prevent it from trying to fulfill its ambition to make the world safe for liberal democracy.

All of Scott's ingredients were firmly in place in the United States as the dust was settling after 9/11. The Bush administration adopted a policy of using the American military to topple regimes and bring democracy to the greater Middle East, an area that had little experience with democracy. The Bush Doctrine was a radical strategy that has no parallel in American history. President Obama, though more cautious than his predecessor, nonetheless continued Bush's policy of toppling illiberal regimes and trying to promote democracy across the Middle East. Not only did both presidents fail at almost every turn, their policies brought widespread killing and devastation to the region.

We have seen that a liberal foreign policy is likely to fail and that the costs of failure are high. Yet even those who recognize the risks sometimes argue that the effort can be justified.

7

Liberal Theories of Peace

LIBERAL HEGEMONY IS BUILT AROUND three missions: increasing the number of liberal democracies in the world, facilitating an open economic order, and building international institutions. The assumption is that achieving these goals, especially the first one, is a formula for international peace. I argued in the previous two chapters that such a policy is not only enormously costly both at home and abroad but also likely to fail. States that pursue a liberal foreign policy invariably find themselves worse off.

In this chapter I will examine liberal hegemony's purported benefit: that it will bring peace and wealth and effectively end problems like nuclear proliferation and terrorism. One might argue that it makes sense to try to realize those aims even if the costs are great, simply because the benefits are even greater. To determine whether that might be true, I examine the three main liberal theories of international politics—democratic peace theory, economic interdependence theory, and liberal institutionalism—to see how well each works. These three theories correspond with the three principal missions of a liberal foreign policy. My bottom line is that none of these theories provides a formula for peace. Not only is liberal hegemony prone to costly failures, it would not bring us a world without war even if it achieved its goals.

Each liberal theory takes dead aim at realism, which takes security competition among the great powers and war to be a normal part of life in the international system. Liberal theorists seek a compelling story that trumps

realism and leads to a more peaceful world. But none of these liberal theories makes the case for world government, which might seem to make
sense given that political liberalism can work inside a country only when
there is a higher authority that maintains order. Instead, each theory assumes that the existing state system is here to stay and that we need a
strategy for producing peace under international anarchy.

Furthermore, none of the three theories assumes that states no longer
have reasons to go to war. They are not positing a world such as Francis
Fukuyama describes in his famous 1989 article "The End of History?" Instead, each theory acknowledges that states sometimes have fundamental
political differences, which may cause them to consider military action. Yet
liberalism's proponents maintain that other, more powerful factors cut
against realist logic and ultimately overwhelm it when there is a serious
possibility of war. States will sometimes be tempted, for one reason or another, to unsheathe the sword; but one or more of the liberal logics will
outweigh that temptation, and there will be no war.

Democratic peace theory maintains that liberal democracies do not fight
wars with each other, but it does not predict any decrease in wars between
democracies and non-democracies. The principal explanation for peace
among liberal democracies is that their deep-seated respect for individual
rights, coupled with their emphasis on tolerance and peaceful conflict resolution, overwhelms any rationale they might have to initiate a war. Other
accounts maintain that specific institutional and normative characteristics
of democracy, not liberal rights, prevent war between liberal democracies.

Economic interdependence theory grows out of the liberal emphasis on
the right to own and exchange property, which inexorably leads to promoting investment and trade among states. The ensuing economic intercourse
not only leads to greater prosperity for the trading states but also makes
them dependent on each other for their prosperity. This economic interdependence, the theory says, militates against war, simply because the costs
of fighting become unacceptable. In the end, concerns about prosperity
trump political as well as security considerations.

Liberal institutionalism stems from the importance liberals place on
acting according to well-established rules that stipulate the rights and obligations of individuals. According to the theory, states voluntarily come

together and establish international institutions, which are effectively a set of rules that states agree to obey even when they are tempted to disregard them and act aggressively. When push comes to shove, a deep-seated commitment to the rule of law will quash any temptation a state might have to start a war.

These theories are well known in both the academic and policy worlds. Liberal theorists and policymakers often bundle them together, arguing that they complement each other and thus work in tandem to foster peace. Kant, for example, maintained that the best way to maximize the prospects for "perpetual peace" is to foster commerce, which makes war unprofitable; promote republican constitutions; and create a confederation of republican states, which would be an international institution.[1] More recently, two liberal scholars, Bruce Russett and John Oneal, wrote a book whose title captures their commitment to tying these theories together: *Triangulating Peace: Democracy, Interdependence, and International Organizations*.[2] For these scholars, each strand of liberalism reinforces the others to increase the chances of peace. Two strands cause more peace than one, and all three strands cause even more. Another prominent liberal theorist, Michael Doyle, has a different take: he maintains that all three theories must work together at once for liberalism to produce peace.[3] For Doyle, the liberal case for peace collapses if just one of the theories either does not apply or does not work as expected. For Russett and Oneal, however, all three theories need to be knocked out to make a convincing case that liberalism does not produce peace.

Liberal policymakers are also fond of packaging these theories together. Consider how President Bill Clinton's administration sold two of its most important policies, NATO expansion and engagement with China. Deputy Secretary of State Strobe Talbott argued in 1995 that embedding the countries of Eastern Europe in both NATO and the EU was the key to producing stability in the region. "Enlargement of NATO," he wrote, "would be a force for the rule of law both within Europe's new democracies and among them." Moreover, it would "promote and consolidate democratic and freemarket values," further contributing to peace.[4] At the same time, Secretary of State Madeleine Albright claimed that the key to sustaining peaceful relations with a rising China is to engage with it, not try to contain it the way the

United States contained the Soviet Union during the Cold War. Engagement would help democratize China, integrate it into the American-led economic order, and lead to its membership in some of the world's major institutions. As a "responsible stakeholder" in the international system, China would be highly motivated to maintain peaceful relations with other countries.[5]

I take issue with the claim that these liberal theories offer a formula for a peaceful world. Each theory is fatally flawed, and packaging them together does not remedy the problem. To make my case, I will examine each theory in detail, asking two questions. First, how well do its predictions fit the empirical record? Is there good evidence that any of the liberal theories have actually caused peace? Second, is the causal logic behind the theory sound? Does the theory offer a compelling story about why peace breaks out?

But before assessing each theory in detail, I want to consider two features that are common to all of them: scope conditions and claims about the certainty of peace. The aim is to show that even if you accept these theories on their own terms, they still do not provide a formula for leaving realism behind. The problem is that the case for liberalism, including all three theories, is structured in a way that makes it impossible to diminish the importance that countries place on the survival motive, which sits at the core of realism.

The Primacy of Survival

In the realist story, states worry about their survival above all else, and this motivates them to pursue power at each other's expense. To supersede realism, therefore, a liberal theory must offer an alternative consideration that figures more prominently in policymakers' minds than survival. For democratic peace theory, respect for individual rights, coupled with tolerance and norms of peaceful conflict resolution, dominates concerns about survival. With economic interdependence theory, a deep-seated interest in prosperity overshadows fears about survival; and liberal institutionalists see adherence to rules as the key to alleviating those fears.

None of these factors, however, can eclipse concerns about survival and take realist logic off the table. They come up short for two reasons, both of which involve limitations that are common to all the liberal theories. First, they all have restricted scope, in that they do not apply unless the necessary conditions are present. International institutions, for example, cannot promote peace if they do not exist, and there must be economic interdependence for prosperity to trump security. But these conditions do not always exist. The world has never been populated with democracies alone, which significantly restricts the scope of democratic peace theory. For theorists like Doyle, who maintain that all three theories must be operative to achieve peace, the range of relevant circumstances is even more restricted. Of course, in the absence of institutions and economic interdependence, states follow the dictates of realpolitik, just as democracies do when confronting non-democracies.

Consider, for instance, that none of the liberal theories was relevant to the superpower competition during the Cold War. The Soviet Union was not a democracy, the two sides had little economic intercourse, and few international institutions had both sides as members. Or think about how most liberals talk about the prospects of China's rising peacefully. China is not a democracy today and shows little prospect of becoming one. One rarely hears the argument that democratic peace theory can provide the basis for peace in Asia. But one frequently hears that economic interdependence theory can explain why China's rise will be peaceful. China's economy is tied to the economies of its rivals, and this linkage means not only that China and its trading partners depend on each other to keep prospering, but also that prosperity depends on their peaceful relations. A war involving China would be tantamount to mutual assured destruction at the economic level. Hence, economic interdependence will keep the peace in Asia as China rises.

It is possible to hypothesize a world in which one or more of the liberal theories apply universally, and one where none of them applies at all. But those are not our world. In our world, those theories are likely to cover certain situations but not others. Consider, for example, how democratic peace theory would apply to a scenario in which the United States removes its military forces from Europe and NATO disappears. There would then be three major powers on the Continent: France, Germany, and Russia. According to the theory, France and Germany would not fight each other, because they are both liberal democracies and thus would not compete with each other for power. But they would have a fundamentally different relationship with non-democratic Russia: they would be guided by realist logic, with its emphasis on the survival motive. In that situation, all three countries would end up trying to maximize their positions in the global balance of power.

Let us assume that Russia becomes a democracy. Democratic peace theory would then apply to relations among all three major powers. Yet democratic Russia would have to fear a rising China, which is not a democracy, on its southern border, and so would have to act according to balance-of-power logic in its dealings with China. France and Germany do not share a border with China, but they would still have to worry about a possible threat if China became a superpower. As long as there is one powerful non-democracy in the system, no democracy can escape from acting according to realist logic. As Alexander Wendt notes, "One predator will best a hundred pacifists because anarchy provides no guarantees. This argument is powerful in part because it is so weak: rather than making the strong assumption that all states are inherently power-seeking . . . it assumes that just one is power-seeking and that the others have to follow suit because anarchy permits the one to exploit them."[6] This logic applies even though the democracies in the system would still behave peacefully toward each other, at least according to the theory.

A second and even more fundamental problem inherent in the three liberal theories concerns what they say about the likelihood of peace. For any of these theories to dominate realism, its proponents have to argue that it makes war certain not to occur. It is not enough for them to argue that their theories lead to enhanced interstate cooperation or make war much less likely. One might think I am setting the bar too high. But as long as there is some chance of war between any two states in the system, every state has little choice but to privilege survival and act in accordance with realist principles. Even if the likelihood of war is judged to be only 1 or 2 percent, states must think and act according to balance-of-power logic because the dire consequences of losing a major war require them to worry about their survival. This situation resembles nuclear deterrence. The likelihood that any nuclear-armed state would use those incredibly destructive weapons is low, but the consequences would be horrendous. This is what makes nuclear weapons the ultimate deterrent.

There is no question that cooperation can ameliorate conflict. Yet it can also increase the likelihood of war, since two states can cooperate to launch a war against a third country, as the Germans and Soviets did against Poland in 1939 or as Egypt and Syria did against Israel in 1973. Furthermore, powerful states sometimes cooperate to exploit the resources of weaker regions, as Britain and France did during World War I, when they arranged via the Sykes-Picot agreement of 1916 to divide up much of the Middle East between themselves. Cooperation and peace are certainly related, but they are not the same thing. What liberal theorists must explain is not why their theories produce more cooperation but why they eliminate the possibility of war.

Hardly any liberal theorists argue that war is taken off the table when their theories are operative. They make bold claims but do not rule out war as a possibility. They sometimes emphasize enhanced cooperation among states or say that war becomes highly unlikely. Democratic peace theorists, who make the boldest claims, stress that democracies "seldom" or "rarely" fight each other."[7] As Michael Doyle puts it, "No one should argue that such wars are impossible; but preliminary evidence does appear to indicate that there exists a significant predisposition against warfare between liberal states."[8] Peace, in other words, is not guaranteed. But moving the needle toward peace, even substantially, is not enough. As long as war remains a serious possibility, states have little choice but to put survival above all other considerations, including rights, prosperity, and rules.

So far I have taken the liberal theories on their own terms and assumed they work as advertised. It is time to examine that assumption.

Democratic Peace Theory

The words *democratic peace theory* imply that it offers a story about how democracy, not liberalism, brings peace. But the title is a misnomer, because the arguments underpinning democratic peace theory emphasize liberalism as well as democracy. A number of scholars in this tradition even refer to "liberal peace." It would be more accurate to call it liberal-democratic peace theory. Moreover, liberal states are almost always democratic as well, mainly because the centrality of freedom and inalienable rights clearly implies that all citizens have the right to determine who governs them. As I emphasized in the introduction, this is why I focus on liberal democracies, not simply liberal states. Hence, I will examine both the democracy-based and liberalism-based logics behind democratic peace theory.

Democratic peace theory was remarkably popular in the two decades after the Cold War ended. Michael Doyle introduced it to the academic and policy worlds in a pair of seminal articles published in 1983.[9] When the superpower rivalry ended in 1989, it was widely believed that liberal democracy would steadily sweep across the globe, spreading peace everywhere. This perspective, of course, is the central theme in Fukuyama's "The End of History?" But time has not been kind to Fukuyama's argument. Authoritarianism has become a viable alternative, and there are few signs that liberal democracy will conquer the globe anytime soon. Freedom House maintains that the world's share of democracies actually declined between 2006 and 2016, which naturally reduces the scope of the theory.[10]

Even if liberal democracy were on the march, however, it would not enhance the prospects for peace, because the theory is seriously flawed. Consider its central finding. Some of its proponents argue that there has never been a war between two democracies. But this is wrong: there are at least four cases in the modern era where democracies waged war against each other. Contrary to what democratic peace theorists say, Germany was a liberal democracy during World War I (1914–18), and it fought against four other liberal democracies: Britain, France, Italy, and the United States.[11] In the Boer War (1899–1902) Britain fought against the South African Republic and the Orange Free State, both of which were democracies.[12] The Spanish-American War (1898) and the 1999 Kargil War between India and Pakistan are also cases of democracies fighting each other.[13]

Other cases come close to qualifying as wars between democracies.[14] The American Civil War is usually not counted because it is considered a civil war rather than an interstate war. One might argue, however, that the distinction is not meaningful here. The Confederacy was established on February 4, 1861, but the war did not begin until April, by which time the Confederacy was effectively a sovereign state. It is also worth noting that there have been a host of militarized disputes between democracies, including some cases where fighting broke out and people died, but that fell short of actual war.[15] There are also many cases of democracies, especially the United States, overthrowing democratically elected leaders in other countries, a behavior that seems at odds with the claim that democracies behave peacefully toward one another.

But let us get back to my four cases of actual wars between democracies. One might concede that I am right yet still argue that this tiny number of wars does not substantially challenge the theory. This conclusion would be wrong, however, for reasons clearly laid out by the democratic peace theorist James L. Ray: "Since wars between states are so rare statistically . . . the existence of even a few wars between democratic states would wipe out entirely the statistical and therefore arguably the substantive significance of the difference in the historical rates of warfare between pairs of democratic states, on the one hand, and pairs of states in general, on the other."[16] Those four wars between democracies, in other words, undermine the central claim of democratic peace theorists.

The second major problem with democratic peace theory is that it offers no good explanation for why liberal democracies should not fight each other. Democratic peace theorists have put forward various explanations, some of which focus on democratic institutions and norms and others that emphasize liberal norms. But none are compelling.

Democratic Institutions and Peace

There are three institutional explanations for why liberal democracies do not go to war with each other. The first emphasizes that publics are pacific by nature, and if asked whether to initiate a war they will almost certainly say no. Kant articulates this argument in *Perpetual Peace*: "If the consent of the citizens is required in order to decide that war should be declared . . . nothing is more natural than that they would be very cautious in commencing such a poor game, decreeing for themselves all the calamities of war."[17] This argument was popular during the Cold War among neoconservatives, who believed that liberal democracies were inclined to appease authoritarian states because democratic peoples were not only soft but influential, because they could vote.[18]

The fatal flaw in this argument is that it proves too much. If the citizens of a liberal democracy were so averse to war, they would be disinclined to fight against non-democracies as well as democracies. They would not want to fight any wars at all. It is clear from the historical record, however, that this is not the case. The United States, for instance, has fought seven wars since the Cold War ended, and it initiated all seven. During that period it has been at war for two out of every three years. It is no exaggeration to say that the United States is addicted to war. Moreover, Britain, another liberal democracy, has been at America's side throughout those wars. This helps explain why democratic peace theorists do not argue that democracies are generally more peaceful than non-democracies.

Several factors explain why democratic peoples sometimes favor starting wars. For one, there are sometimes good strategic reasons for war and most citizens will recognize them. Furthermore, democratic leaders are often adept at convincing reticent publics that war is necessary, even when it is not.[19] Sometimes not much convincing is necessary, because the people's nationalist fervor is so great that, if anything, they are pushing their leaders to go to war, whether necessary or not.[20] Finally, it is wrong to assume that the public axiomatically pays a big price when its country goes to war. Wealthy countries often have a highly capitalized military, which means that only a small slice of the population actually serves. Moreover, liberal democracies are often adept at finding ways to minimize their casualties—for example, by using drones against an adversary. As for the financial costs, a state has many ways to pay for a war without seriously burdening its public.[21]

The second institutional explanation is that it is more difficult for government leaders to mobilize a democracy to start a war. This cumbersome decision making is partly a function of the need to get public permission, which is time-consuming given the public's natural reluctance to fight wars and risk death. The institutional obstacles built into democracies, like checks and balances, slow down the process. These problems make it difficult not only to start a war but also to formulate and execute a smart foreign policy.

If these claims were true, again, democracies would not initiate wars against non-democracies. But they do. There may be instances where democratic inefficiencies prevent governing elites from taking their country to war, although as I noted above, that will happen infrequently. Moreover, the institutional impediments that might thwart leaders bent on starting a war usually count for little, because the decision to start a war is often made during a serious crisis, in which the executive takes charge and checks and balances, as well as individual rights, are subordinated to national security concerns. In an extreme emergency, liberal democracies are fully capable of reacting swiftly and decisively, and initiating a war if necessary.

Finally, some argue that "audience costs" are the key to explaining the democratic peace.[22] This claim rests on the belief that democratically elected leaders are especially good at signaling their resolve in crises because they can make public commitments to act in particular circumstances, which they are then obligated to follow through on. In other words, they can tie their own hands. If they renege on their commitments, the public will punish them by voting them out of office. Once a leader draws a red line, the argument goes, his audience will hold his feet to the fire. Two democracies can thus make it clear to each other what exactly they would fight over, which allows them to avoid miscalculation and negotiate a settlement.

The audience-costs story is intuitively attractive, but empirical studies have shown that it has little explanatory power.[23] There is hardly any evidence that audience costs have worked as advertised in actual crises. Moreover, there are many reasons to question the theory's underlying logic. For example, leaders are usually wary about drawing red lines, preferring instead to keep their threats vague so as to maximize their bargaining space. In such cases, audience-costs logic does not even come into play. But even if a leader draws a red line and then fails to follow through, the public is unlikely to punish her if she ends the crisis on favorable terms. Moreover, one should never underestimate political leaders' ability to spin a story so that it appears they did not renege on a commitment when they actually did. And even if a leader gives a signal, there is no guarantee the other side will read it correctly.

In sum, none of the mechanisms involving democratic institutions provides a satisfactory explanation for why democracies rarely fight wars with each other.[24] Some prominent democratic peace theorists recognize the limits of these institutional explanations and instead rely on normative arguments linked to democracy and liberalism.[25]

The Normative Logics

There is substantial overlap between the normative logic that flows from democracy and the one that flows from liberalism. Both emphasize four key concepts: peaceful conflict resolution, respect for others, tolerance, and trust. Democracy and liberalism, however, rivet on those concepts for different reasons, and each emphasizes some more than others.

The central feature of democracy is the electoral process, which is how citizens settle their differences and determine whose vision of the political order will prevail. This way of doing business has the effect of promoting peaceful conflict resolution. "The basic norm of liberal democratic theory," Russett writes, is "that disputes can be resolved without force through democratic political processes."[26] Furthermore, he maintains that "the norms of regulated political competition, compromise solutions to political conflicts, and peaceful transfer of power are externalized by democracies in their dealing with other national actors in world politics." Most importantly, "when two democracies come into a conflict of interest, they are able to apply democratic norms in their interaction."[27]

In a world where even bitter disputes are routinely settled peacefully, there is likely to be significant trust among the relevant actors, since they do not have to worry that their opponents may employ violence against them. There should also be a modicum of respect for those on the opposing side in big political fights. The fact that everyone is willing to accept election results surely means they are willing to tolerate the possibility their rivals might win. And if they are going to pursue compromise solutions with their opponents, both sides have to show some respect toward the other; otherwise it would be difficult to find agreement. Thus, in addition to being wedded to settling their differences via elections, individuals living in a democracy tend to be trustful, tolerant, and respectful of others. These same beliefs, the argument goes, carry over to relations between democracies.

Unlike democracy, which emphasizes the importance of elections, liberalism tells a story of individual rights. Of course, this is by now familiar to readers of this book. Political liberals maintain that rights and tolerance work together to encourage people to respect each other, even when they have fundamental disagreements, and to settle their differences peacefully. There is hardly any place for violence in a liberal world.

Because individual rights are universal, liberal logic applies not just to daily life inside liberal democracies but to interactions between them as well. To quote Michael Doyle, "The basic postulate of liberal international theory holds that states have the right to be free from foreign intervention. Since morally autonomous citizens hold rights to liberty, the states that represent them have the right to exercise political independence. Mutual respect for these rights then becomes the touchstone of international liberal theory."[28] Those inalienable rights include the right to life, which precludes liberal countries from initiating wars against each other since they would be taking the lives of fellow liberals.

Tolerance, too, extends beyond borders when liberal states are dealing with each other. Liberal countries should trust and respect each other and never go to war to settle their differences. "These conventions of mutual respect," Doyle writes, "have formed a cooperative foundation for relations among liberal democracies of a remarkably effective kind."[29] Liberal norms, in other words, explain the democratic peace. John Owen sums up the basic argument: "Liberals believe that individuals everywhere are fundamentally the same, and are best off pursuing self-preservation and material well-being. Freedom is required for these pursuits, and peace is required for freedom; coercion and violence are counter-productive. Thus all individuals share an interest in peace, and should want war only as an instrument to bring about peace."[30]

It should be clear that democracy and liberalism provide separate but complementary logics that explain why liberal democracies do not fight each other, even when they have a profound disagreement that provokes a major crisis. Wars do not break out, according to democratic peace theory, because these logics work either separately or in tandem to promote a formidable set of norms that favor peaceful conflict resolution, respect for the other, tolerance, and trust.

Why Norms Are Ineffectual

There are five problems with the claim that liberal democratic norms are a powerful force for peace. As I argued in chapter 5, without a higher authority to maintain order, liberalism cannot work as advertised. The reason is simple: liberalism accepts that individuals will sometimes have profound differences over first principles and also recognizes that respect for rights and tolerance cannot guarantee that one side, or even both sides, will not turn to violence. There is no assurance that conflicts will be resolved peacefully. This is why virtually every liberal recognizes the need for a state—including John Rawls, who is especially optimistic about the hexing power of tolerance.

Democracy faces the same problem. It too is predicated on the assumption that citizens will sometimes have fierce differences about core political and social issues. Citizens in a democracy are heavily socialized to settle their disputes at the ballot box, but that socialization has its limits, and democracies always maintain formidable police forces to keep order. The norm of peaceful conflict resolution alone cannot ensure peace in a democracy; like liberalism, it requires a strong state to deal with people who feel compelled to back up their views with violence.

Since there is no world state, there is no higher authority in the international system to which countries can turn when another state threatens them. That simple fact of life, coupled with the fact that liberal democracies are not always tolerant, respectful, and peaceful toward each other, means they must worry about their survival even when dealing with other liberal democracies. Once this logic is at play, they have no choice but to engage in balance-of-power politics with each other.

Nationalism is another problem for claims about liberal democratic norms. It is an enormously influential ideology that causes countries to emphasize the differences among them. Each nation-state tends to think it is superior to the others, and sometimes there is genuine hatred between them. That animosity—what I call hypernationalism—exists because nation-states sometimes differ profoundly on first principles, and sometimes engage in harsh security competition that leads to war. Liberal democracies are hardly immune from nationalism, which can undermine tolerance and mutual trust, and even cause them to resolve their disagreements violently. Nor is there a deep-seated worldwide respect for the liberal principle of inalienable rights, whose importance liberals often exaggerate. Especially when it confronts nationalism, liberalism's universalist dimension holds less sway than liberals assume.

Furthermore, there is considerable empirical evidence to contradict the claim that liberal democratic norms are a potent force for peace. The United States, for example, has a rich history of toppling democratically elected governments, especially during the Cold War. The more prominent cases include Iran in 1953, Guatemala in 1954, Brazil in 1964, and Chile in 1973.[31] Following the January 2006 Palestinian elections, in which Hamas defeated the U.S.-supported Fatah, the United States and Israel (another democracy) moved to destabilize the new government and marginalize Hamas. They treated Fatah as the legitimate representative of the Palestinian people, even though it had lost the election.[32] The United States, as we saw, also played a role in toppling the democratically elected Muslim Brotherhood in Egypt in 2013. "The record of American interventions in the developing world," Sebastian Rosato notes, "suggests that democratic trust and respect has often been subordinated to security and economic interests."[33]

Perhaps the most damning evidence against the case for liberal democratic norms is found in Christopher Layne's careful examination of four cases where a pair of liberal democracies marched to the brink of war, but one side pulled back and ended the crisis. He carefully examines the decision-making process in both Britain and the United States during the 1861 Trent Affair and the Venezuelan Crisis of 1895–96, the Fashoda Crisis between Britain and France in 1898, and the 1923 Ruhr Crisis involving France and Germany, and convincingly argues that liberal norms had little to do with settling these crises. There was substantial nationalist fervor on each side, and all four outcomes were primarily determined by strategic calculations involving the balance of power.[34]

A final, albeit indirect, reason to doubt that liberal norms carry much weight in international politics is that there is little evidence that liberal democracies fight wars in especially virtuous ways. Given the emphasis liberalism places on inalienable rights, one would expect liberal democracies to go to some lengths to avoid killing civilians, or at least do better than authoritarian states. This is one of the central tenets of just war theory, a quintessentially liberal theory that has individual rights at its core.[35] Michael Doyle, for instance, urges that all sides in a conflict maintain "a scrupulous respect for the laws of war."[36]

But when Alexander Downes did his groundbreaking study of civilian victimization in war, he found that "democracies are somewhat more likely than nondemocracies to target civilians."[37] John Tirman shows in his detailed analysis of how the United States fights its wars that it has killed millions of civilians, many on purpose.[38] And although Geoffrey Wallace shows autocracies are more likely than democracies to abuse prisoners of war, he provides plenty of evidence that democracies mistreat their prisoners.[39] The widespread use of torture by the United States in the wake of 9/11 is just one example. Both Downes and Wallace show that when states get desperate in wartime, they quickly forget the enemy's humanity and begin to value rights far less than effective fighting. Liberal democracies are no exception.

In short, the norms of liberal democracies provide no persuasive explanation for why they would never fight against each other. There is neither a compelling institutional story nor a normative story underpinning democratic peace theory.

Another reason to doubt this theory is the problem of backsliding. A democracy may always become an authoritarian state.[40] It has happened many times, and as I noted, Freedom House reports that in recent years democracy has been in worldwide retreat. There is no guarantee democracy will last forever even where it is well established.[41] If China were to become a democracy in, say, the next ten years, we could not be highly confident it would retain that political system over the long term. The United States would have to be prepared for the eventuality that it might not, which means that just to be safe, it would try to maximize its power relative to China.

Liberal democracies tend to have more staying power than illiberal democracies, because the former are buttressed by liberal as well as democratic values—a formidable one-two punch. Still, there is no guarantee that any liberal democracy will last. Remember that Weimar Germany, which was a liberal democracy, lasted a little over a decade before giving way in 1933 to one of the most aggressive and evil regimes in recorded history. Thus, even in their relations with each other, liberal democracies must be prepared for the possibility of backsliding, which means they should deal with each other according to the dictates of realism.

Economic Interdependence Theory

According to economic interdependence theory, two countries that are highly dependent on each other for their economic well-being will not go to war even over intense political differences. They will avoid war even if there are good strategic reasons for starting a fight, because a war would have disastrous economic consequences for both sides. In essence, the economic costs of war will outweigh the political benefits, including potential strategic gains. The theory assumes that prosperity, not survival, is the number one goal of states. Economic considerations, in other words, trump strategic concerns.

The theory's emphasis on prosperity is based largely on the belief that publics demand that their leaders promote and protect their economic welfare, and if those leaders fail to deliver, they will be thrown out of office. There might even be significant unrest. This imperative to generate wealth means no rational leader is likely to start a war. There are also apt to be interest groups opposed to war because it might undermine their ability to make money.[42] Some scholars argue, for example, that bankers are invariably a powerful force for peace, because leaders who want to stay in power are unlikely to risk crossing them. All of this is to say that in a world of economically interdependent states, leaders have a marked aversion to conflict, for fear it will endanger prosperity and thus their political careers. Even security competition among these countries is likely to be moderate, not just because leaders prefer to concentrate on maximizing their country's wealth but because an intense rivalry might inadvertently lead to war and economic disaster.

Different scholars refine this basic logic in various ways. In its early incarnation, the theory described economic interdependence in terms of trading relations among countries. Norman Angell's name is famously attached to this perspective, even though he makes a somewhat different argument in his classic 1910 book *The Great Illusion*.[43] More recently, Richard Rosecrance argued for the pacifying effects of trade in his 1986 book *The Rise of the Trading State*.[44] Erik Gartzke contends, however, that trade is the wrong factor to look at when assessing economic interdependence, and instead argues for focusing on capital markets.[45] "Integrated capital markets," he maintains, foster peaceful relations among states. Patrick McDonald, on the other hand, claims that it is trade underpinned by "the presence of liberal economic institutions . . . market-promoting institutions." He stresses that "the predominance of private property and competitive market structures within domestic economies . . . produce peace."[46]

Not all economic interdependence theorists believe that trade and capital flows thwart armed conflict. Stephen Brooks, for example, argues that the key to peace in today's globalized world is the fact that the production facilities of multinational corporations are dispersed all over the globe, which means that virtually every major country is dependent on many other countries for the products it consumes.[47] Thus no developed country can afford to go to war for fear this would paralyze its multinational corporations and ultimately its own economy. Finally, Dale Copeland, who is usually regarded as a realist, makes an argument that has both liberal and realist strands.[48] He maintains that when any two states expect the high levels of trade between them to continue, the logic of basic economic interdependence will facilitate peaceful relations. But when they do not expect to sustain that trade over time, realist logic kicks in and may push the two sides toward war.

Finally, economic interdependence theorists sometimes argue that conquest does not pay in the modern world. Before the Industrial Revolution, the economic benefits of territorial expansion were real, but today a country's economy hardly benefits from conquering another state. This is actually Angell's main point in *The Great Illusion* as well as an important theme in *The Rise of the Trading State*. When we include this additional argument, the overarching claim is that economic interdependence makes war prohibitively costly, while conquest provides few benefits. I will focus mainly on the argument that economic interdependence brings peace by driving up the costs of war, which is the theory's core assertion.

The Limits of Economic Interdependence Theory

It would be wrong to say that economic interdependence does not matter at all. There will surely be cases where it tips the balance away from war, especially when the economic costs of fighting are great but the political stakes are not. Nevertheless, in many circumstances it will not sway policy-makers, and thus it does not come close to guaranteeing peace between economically interdependent states. To render realpolitik irrelevant, that guarantee is necessary.

Economic interdependence theory has three main problems. First, the costs of going to war for economically interdependent countries are not al-ways high, and often when they prove to be high, they are underestimated before the fighting starts. Moreover, wars sometimes lead to economic gains. Second, even when states recognize that there will be significant costs, the political urge to go to war usually trumps economics, especially when core security interests are at stake. Finally, there is little empirical evidence that economic interdependence is a major force for international peace.

Economically interdependent countries can sometimes fight wars while avoiding significant economic costs. A country might take aim at a single ri-val, come up with a clever military strategy, and win a quick and decisive victory. Or it might pick a fight with a much weaker adversary that it de-feats rapidly and easily. Most states go to war anticipating a swift triumph, not that they always get it.[49] When they do, however, the economic costs are often small.[50] The costliest wars are protracted ones involving multiple countries, such as the two World Wars. But again, most leaders do not take their countries to war expecting that outcome.

Furthermore, nuclear weapons make it highly unlikely that contemporary great powers will fight a major conventional conflict like World War II. Wars between them are likely to be limited in both means and goals. It is hard to imagine, for example, that China and the United States would engage in an all-out conventional war in Asia; but it is not difficult to envision them fighting a limited conflict in the South China Sea or over Taiwan with the thought that the economic costs of such a war could be kept manageable.

There is also abundant evidence that states at war with each other do not always break off economic relations. Sometimes they trade with the enemy in wartime because each side believes it benefits from the continued intercourse. Jack Levy and Katherine Barbieri, two of the leading experts on this subject, write: "It is clear that trading with the enemy occurs frequently enough to contradict the conventional wisdom that war will systematically and significantly disrupt trade between adversaries." They add, "Trading with the enemy occurs during all-out wars fought for national independence or global dominance as well as during more limited military encounters."[51] In short, a country may fight a war against a rival with which it remains economically interdependent and not threaten its own prosperity.[52]

Finally, as Peter Liberman explains in his important book *Does Conquest Pay?*, sometimes it does.[53] For example, if China fought and won a war for control of the South China Sea, it would end up owning the abundant natural resources on the sea floor that would surely help fuel Chinese economic growth. States occasionally start wars with the expectation that victory will bring economic and strategic benefits that outweigh the costs of undermining interdependence.

The Primacy of Politics over Economics

But even if one assumes significant costs of war between two economically interdependent states, war remains a real possibility. Proponents of the theory disagree, because they believe the high cost of war will outweigh the expected political benefits. They assume in effect that the principal goal of states is prosperity, not survival. But this is wrong. Political calculations often trump economic ones. This is certainly true when matters of national security are at stake, because survival is ultimately more important than prosperity. A country cannot prosper if it does not survive, but even countries impoverished by war can recover and become rich. Europe was quite prosperous before 1914, yet World War I happened. Germany, which was principally responsible for that conflict, was bent on preventing Russia from growing more powerful and also wanted to establish its own hegemony in Europe.[54] Politics overwhelmed economics.

One might argue that not every dispute involving security is a matter of national survival. Not every crisis is the equivalent of the July crisis in 1914. There is certainly truth in this claim, and it is one reason economic interdependence logic sometimes works as advertised. But ultimately it is not a compelling argument, largely because of what I call "want of a nail" logic. States often worry that if they fail to address minor security problems, their adversary will continue to take advantage and the balance of power will eventually shift profoundly against them. It is better to nip the problem in the bud than wait until survival really is at stake. The power of this viewpoint is magnified by the degree to which survival matters for states.[55]

I should say a brief word about Copeland's argument. He claims that economic interdependence trumps realpolitik when there is the prospect of future trade among rivals. This does not make sense. One problem is that it is impossible to know for sure how long any mutual dependence will last, and thus states have powerful incentives to prepare for its end. When it stops, according to Copeland, those states are back in a realist world, and it is always best to plan for that "rainy day" by following realist dictates before it arrives. Furthermore, as Copeland himself emphasizes, it is impossible to know the future intentions of states.[56] Ignorance about intentions means that a state deeply committed to peace and prosperity today might someday find reasons to start a war, despite the economic consequences. Again, it is best to act according to rainy day logic.[57]

Politics also wins out over prosperity when nationalism is at play. Consider Beijing's position on Taiwan. Chinese leaders have repeatedly emphasized that they will go to war against Taiwan if it declares its independence, even at the cost of damaging China's economy. Chinese thinking about Taiwan is deeply influenced by nationalism; almost everyone in China considers that island sacred territory that must eventually be reintegrated into the mainland.[58] I should also note that history is littered with civil wars, and in almost every instance the combatants had been economically interdependent before the fighting broke out. Nevertheless, political calculations proved more influential.

To drive home the point that political and strategic factors often outweigh economic ones, consider the effectiveness of economic sanctions. The historical record clearly shows that sanctions usually do not achieve their goal. One reason they fail is that the target states can absorb enormous punishment and still not bend to the coercer's demands.[59] This toughness is driven in good part by nationalism, which invariably causes the people in the targeted state to rally around their leaders, not to revolt against them. Britain and the United States discovered this in World War II, when their bombing campaigns against German and Japanese cities failed to spur uprisings by the target populations.[60] It is no surprise that the Russian people have responded to the West's sanctions on Russia over the Ukraine crisis by rallying around Vladimir Putin.

The Ukraine crisis points up the other reason sanctions regularly fail in the face of political or strategic calculations. For Russia, Ukraine is a core strategic interest, and the West's efforts to peel Ukraine away from Moscow's orbit and incorporate it into Western institutions is categorically unacceptable. From Putin's perspective, the policy of the United States and its European allies is a threat to Russia's survival. This viewpoint motivates Russia to go to enormous lengths to prevent Ukraine from joining the West.[61]

We should not be surprised that a theory that is undermined by both balance-of-power logic and nationalism finds little support in the historical record. For sure there are studies that claim economic interdependence makes conflict less likely, although no proponent of the theory argues that it effectively rules out war between countries whose economies are tied closely together.[62] There are other studies, however, showing no effect one way or the other.[63] Some scholars even claim that it makes war *more* likely because it has the potential in troubled economic times to fuel tensions between trading partners.[64] Consider, for example, how the crisis over the euro is fueling nationalism in Europe. Iraq invaded Kuwait in August 1990, despite their close economic ties, in part because Kuwait was violating production limits set by the Organization of Petroleum Exporting States (OPEC) and driving down Iraq's oil profits.

In sum, there is no basis for believing that economic interdependence makes a firm foundation for international peace, even if it may occasionally serve as a brake on war.

Liberal Institutionalism

Liberal institutionalism is probably the weakest of the three major liberal theories.[65] Its chief proponents make modest claims about what international institutions can actually do to bring peace, and the historical record shows clearly that for any great power on the road to war, they are little more than a speed bump. That includes liberal democracies like Britain and the United States.

Institutions are the set of rules that describe how states should cooperate and compete with each other. They prescribe acceptable forms of behavior and proscribe unacceptable behavior. The rules are negotiated by states; they are not imposed. The great powers dominate the writing of these rules and pledge to obey them, even where they think it is not in their interest to do so. In effect, countries voluntarily tie their hands when they join an international institution. The rules are typically formalized in international agreements and administered by organizations with their own personnel and budgets. It is important to emphasize, however, that those organizations per se do not compel states to obey the rules. International institutions are not powerful bodies, which are independent of the states that comprise the system, and they are not capable of forcing states to follow the rules. They are not a form of world government. States themselves must choose to obey the rules they created. Institutions, in short, call for the "decentralized cooperation of individual sovereign states, without any effective mechanism of command."[66]

This emphasis on voluntary obedience also captures how international law works, which tells us there is no meaningful difference between institutions and law at the international level. International institutions are sometimes called "regimes," and many scholars use those terms interchangeably. Thus the analysis here is as applicable to international law and regimes as it is to international institutions.[67]

The Ultimate Goal: Cooperation among States

Liberal institutionalists rarely argue that international institutions are a powerful force for peace. Instead, they make the less ambitious claim that institutions help settle disputes peacefully by promoting interstate cooperation. This emphasis on cooperation is clearly evident in Robert Keohane's *After Hegemony: Cooperation and Discord in the World Political Economy*, probably the most influential work on international institutions.[68] But as his title indicates, Keohane concentrates on explaining how to enhance economic cooperation among states. He says little about war and peace. Some liberal institutionalists do deal directly with security issues, but they too mainly talk about how those security institutions enhance cooperation.[69] This focus on cooperation is found throughout the institutionalist literature, where many of the key pieces have "cooperation" in the title, and where hardly anyone elaborates on how cooperation causes peace.[70]

It is important to specify the particular circumstances in which institutions foster cooperation. They work only when states have mutual interests but cannot realize them because the structure of the situation gives them incentives to take advantage of each other. An example of this problem is the classic prisoner's dilemma, where two individuals have a vested interest in cooperating but cannot because each fears the other might take advantage of him. Instead, they try to exploit each other, which leaves them both worse off than if they had made the deal. Collective action logic is another instance where individuals have common interests but do not realize them because there are powerful incentives for them to take advantage of each other. Institutions, the argument goes, can help individuals in these situations realize their common interests.

The theory has little relevance when states have conflicting interests and neither side thinks it has much to gain from cooperation. In these circumstances, states will almost certainly aim to take advantage of each other, and that will sometimes involve violence. In other words, if the differences are profound and involve important issues, countries will think in terms of winning and losing, which will invariably lead to intense security competition and sometimes war. International institutions have little influence on state behavior in such conditions, mainly because the theory does not address how institutions can resolve or even ameliorate deep conflicts between great powers.[71] It is thus not surprising that liberal institutionalists have little to say about the causes of war and peace.

There is another way to show the limits of institutions. Some liberal institutionalists argue that international politics can be divided into two realms—political economy and security—and that their theory applies mainly to the former. Charles Lipson, for instance, writes that "significantly different institutional arrangements are associated with international economic and security issues."[72] Moreover, the likelihood of cooperation in these realms is markedly different. When economic relations are at stake, "cooperation can be sustained among several self-interested states," whereas the prospects for cooperation are "more impoverished . . . in security affairs."[73]

The same thinking is reflected in Keohane's *After Hegemony,* where he emphasizes that he is concentrating "on relations among the advanced market-economy countries . . . the area where common interests are greatest and where the benefits of international cooperation may be easiest to realize."[74] One example of this important distinction is the contrast between the United Nations' ineffectiveness at resolving political disputes between the great powers and the effectiveness of the International Monetary Fund and the World Bank at facilitating economic cooperation among the major powers. What this means in practice is that liberal institutionalists focus mainly on fostering cooperation in the economic and environmental realms, because those are the domains where states are most likely to need the help of institutions to realize their common interests. Liberal institutionalists devote much less attention to security regimes.

One might argue that military alliances are security institutions, and they certainly have an important effect on international politics. There is no question that alliances are useful for coordinating the actions of the member states in both peace and war, which makes their collective efforts more efficient and effective. NATO is a case in point. It was hugely important during the Cold War in helping the West deter Soviet ambitions in Europe. But the alliance was among states with powerful incentives to cooperate in the face of a common threat, not states that had fundamental disagreements. Thus the general point stands: liberal institutionalists pay little attention to questions about war and peace.

Some might say that John Ikenberry, probably the most prominent liberal institutionalist besides Keohane, is an exception. He has developed a theory that is truly international in scope and can explain how to achieve cooperation in both the economic and security realms. In his seminal book *After Victory: Institutions, Strategic Restraint, and the Rebuilding of Order after Major Wars,* he explains the circumstances under which states can build international orders, which seems to imply an order that covers the entire globe.[75] Ikenberry is particularly interested in the international order that came into being after World War II, for which the United States was principally responsible. That order, of course, was heavily institutionalized.

On close inspection, however, we see that Ikenberry's story is all about the Cold War order within the West, where the major countries had few profound disputes. He pays little attention to the security competition between the United States and the Soviet Union. Nor does he say much about the United Nations—a truly international institution, but almost useless for managing superpower relations. In the end, Ikenberry is not dealing with international order; he is dealing with economic and military relations among the advanced industrial countries of the West. His focus is similar to Keohane's in *After Hegemony,* and although they offer somewhat different theories, neither explains what causes security competition and war or how institutions prevent rival great powers from fighting each other.

The Anarchy Problem

It might seem surprising, but the major liberal institutionalist thinkers do not claim, at least most of the time, to be offering a clear alternative to realism. They seem to want to retain significant elements of realpolitik in their arguments while yet going beyond it. Ikenberry, for example, writes that his theory "draws upon both realist and liberal theoretical traditions," while Keohane writes that "we need to go beyond Realism, not discard it."[76] Helga Haftendorn, Keohane, and Celeste Wallander, the editors of a book dealing directly with security institutions, write: "As we see it, security studies, still dominated by realist thinking, will greatly benefit by incorporating institutionalist approaches."[77] It is hard to understand how any theory that is based in good part on realist logic can possibly leave balance-of-power politics behind. But let us put that matter aside and instead concentrate on explaining why international institutions hold out little hope of significantly enhancing the prospects for peace, even if they enhance the prospects for cooperation.

Liberal institutionalism is predicated on the belief that the main inhibitor of international cooperation is the threat of cheating, which is largely a consequence of intractable uncertainty. A state can never know what other states will think and do in the future. Institutions, so the argument goes, can ameliorate that problem in four ways.

First, they can increase the number of transactions among countries over time. This iteration raises the cost of cheating by creating the prospect of future gains through cooperation. The "shadow of the future" deters cheating today, since a state caught cheating jeopardizes its prospects of benefiting from future cooperation. Iteration gives the victim the opportunity to retaliate against the cheater: it facilitates a tit-for-tat strategy, which works to prevent cheaters from getting away with their transgression. In addition to punishing states that gain a reputation for cheating, it also rewards those that develop a reputation for adherence to agreements.

Second, rules can tie together interactions between states in different issue areas. The aim of issue linkage is to create greater interdependence between states, which will make them more reluctant to cheat in one issue area for fear that the victim, and perhaps other states, will retaliate in another area. Like iteration, linkage raises the costs of double-dealing and provides ways for victims to retaliate against the cheater.

Third, a system of rules can increase the amount of information available to the participants in cooperative agreements, which permits close monitoring. Raising the level of information discourages cheating by increasing the likelihood cheaters will be caught. It also provides victims with early warning of possible cheating, enabling them to take protective measures before they are badly hurt.

Finally, rules can reduce the transaction costs of individual agreements. When institutions perform the tasks described above, states are able to devote less effort to negotiating and monitoring agreements, and to hedging against possible defections. By increasing the efficiency of international cooperation, institutions make it more profitable and thus more attractive.

There is no question that the fear of a rival state breaking the rules, either covertly or openly, is a central element in the realist story, and one of the driving forces behind security competition and war.[78] States are deeply concerned about the balance of power because they can never be certain they will not fall victim to another state cheating. If they do, there is no night watchman they can turn to for help. The key question for our purposes is whether international institutions solve the cheating problem in any way that challenges basic realist logic. Almost certainly, they do not.

The central problem, of course, is the absence of a higher authority that can credibly threaten to punish states if they disobey the rules. International institutions are not autonomous actors that can force a state to obey the rules when it thinks that doing so is not in its national interest. There is no evidence of any institution coercing a great power into acting against realist dictates. Instead, institutions depend on their member states to stick to the rules, because they think it serves their long-term interests. In the institutionalist story, member states have to police themselves.[79]

But we know from the historical record that states will cheat or disobey when they think that adhering to the rules is not in their interest. Consider, for example, that the United States—the quintessential liberal democratic state—violated international law to initiate wars against Serbia in 1999 and Iraq in 2003.[80] In both cases, Washington failed to secure the required United Nations Security Council resolution sanctioning those wars. Still, the United States opted to ignore international law in both cases because it felt there were strong moral and strategic imperatives for doing so. Naturally, it was never punished. One could also point to instances when France and Germany violated well-established EU rules because they believed doing so was in their interest.[81] They were not punished either. It is hard to find a case where an international institution punished a great power in any serious way for breaking the rules.

Given that states sometimes have fundamental differences and international institutions cannot meaningfully constrain them, those states recognize that they are operating in a self-help world where it makes eminently good sense to control as large a share of global power as possible, regardless of whether they gain that control by following the rules. After all, if a state obeys the law but sacrifices its security, who will come to its rescue if it is attacked by a rival state? Probably nobody. This logic explains why liberal institutionalism has so little to say about matters of war and peace, and why it does not offer a serious challenge to realism.

I would add a final word about cheating. Fear of cheating is generally considered a more formidable obstacle to cooperation when security issues are at stake:[82] betrayal in such circumstances could bring a devastating military defeat. This threat of "swift, decisive defection," as Charles Lipson writes, is simply not present in international economics. Given that "the costs of betrayal" are potentially much graver in the military sphere, it is hardly surprising that liberal institutionalism has little to say about security affairs but much to say about economic and environmental cooperation. As we saw, the other reason liberal institutionalism is relevant in the economic realm is that states often have common interests that institutions can help realize. In the security realm, where rival states often have fundamental differences, institutions are largely irrelevant, save for alliances.

In sum, international institutions are useful tools of statecraft when states have common interests and need help realizing them. They can facilitate cooperation among states, although that cooperation is not always for peaceful ends. The more important point, however, is that there is no reason to think institutions can push states away from war.

Why I Am a Realist

This discussion of the main liberal theories of international politics brings me to the reason I am a realist and why I think states, especially great powers, are strongly inclined to act according to balance-of-power logic. Simply put, no country can ever be certain that a potential rival will hew to liberal dictates during a serious dispute, especially given the powerful influence of nationalism. If that rival opts to start a war, there is no supreme authority to rescue the target country from defeat. States operate in a self-help world in which the best way to survive is to be as powerful as possible, even if that requires pursuing ruthless policies. This is not a pretty story, but there is no better alternative if survival is a country's paramount goal.

8

The Case for Restraint

MY CENTRAL MISSION IN THIS BOOK has been to examine what happens
when a powerful state pursues liberal hegemony. That mission was motivated, of course, by U.S. foreign policy in the post–Cold War era. But to understand how liberalism works in international politics, it is necessary to
understand how it relates to nationalism and realism, both of which profoundly affect the interactions among states. At its core, therefore, this
book is about the relationship among those three isms.

The analysis in the preceding chapters implies a number of recommen-
dations for the future conduct of American foreign policy. First, the United
States should jettison its grand ambitions of liberal hegemony. Not only is
this policy prone to failure, it tends to embroil the American military in
costly wars that it ultimately loses. Second, Washington should adopt a
more restrained foreign policy based on realism and a clear understanding
of how nationalism limits a great power's room to maneuver. Although realism is not a formula for perpetual peace, a foreign policy informed by
realism will mean fewer American wars and more diplomatic successes
than will a policy guided by liberalism. Nationalism works to make an ambitious policy abroad even less necessary. In brief, the United States should
learn the virtue of restraint.

What is the likelihood that the United States will move away from liberal
hegemony and adopt a realist foreign policy? The answer to this question
depends on two closely related considerations: the future structure of the

international system—or to put it in more concrete terms, the global distribution of power—and the degree of agency or freedom liberal states have in choosing a foreign policy.

A powerful state can pursue liberal hegemony only in a unipolar system in which it need not worry about threats from other great powers. When the world is bipolar or multipolar, on the other hand, great powers have little choice but to act according to realist dictates, because of the presence of rival great powers. There is good reason to think unipolarity is coming to an end, mainly because of China's impressive rise. If so, American policymakers will have to abandon liberal hegemony. But there is a serious downside: the United States will have to compete with a potential peer.

Perhaps China will run into significant economic problems and suffer a precipitous slowdown in its growth, in which case the system will remain unipolar. If that happens, it will be difficult for the United States to abandon liberal hegemony. A crusader impulse is deeply wired into liberal democracies, especially their elites, and it is difficult for them not to try to remake the world in their own image. Liberal regimes, in other words, have little agency when presented with the chance to embrace liberal hegemony. Nevertheless, once it becomes clear that liberal hegemony leads to one policy failure after another, we may reasonably hope that the liberal unipole will wise up and abandon that flawed strategy in favor of a more restrained strategy based on realism and a sound appreciation of nationalism. Countries do sometimes learn from their mistakes.

The Folly of Liberalism Abroad

As I emphasized at the start of this book, I believe liberal democracy is the best political order. It is not perfect, but it beats the competition by a long shot. Yet in the realm of international politics, liberalism is a source of endless trouble. Powerful states that embrace liberal hegemony invariably get themselves into serious trouble both at home and abroad. Moreover, they usually end up harming other countries, including the ones they sought to help. Contrary to the conventional wisdom in the West, liberalism is not a force for peace among states. Despite its numerous virtues as a political system, it is a poor guide for foreign policy.

The principal source of the problem is that liberalism has an activist mentality woven into its core. The belief that all humans have a set of inalienable rights, and that protecting these rights should override other concerns, creates a powerful incentive for liberal states to intervene when other countries—as they do on a regular basis—violate their citizens' rights. Some liberals believe that illiberal states are by definition at war with their people. This logic pushes liberal states to favor using force to turn autocracies into liberal democracies, not only because doing so would ensure that individual rights are never again trampled in those countries, but also because they believe liberal democracies do not fight wars with each other. Thus the key to safeguarding human rights and bringing about world peace is to build an international system consisting solely of liberal democracies. Liberalism calls as well for building international institutions and cultivating an open international economy, measures also thought to be conducive to peace.

But liberalism has another important strand that should discourage liberal democracies from interfering in other states' politics, and certainly from invading them. Most liberals maintain that it is impossible to reach a universal consensus on first principles, and thus individuals should be as free as possible to decide for themselves what constitutes the good life and to live their lives accordingly. This fundamental belief is the reason for liberalism's great emphasis on tolerance, which is all about respecting the rights of others to think and act in ways that one considers wrongheaded.

One might think this basic logic would also apply to international politics and so would incline liberal states to stay out of other states' internal affairs. Liberal powers, in this telling, should even respect the sovereignty of illiberal states. But they do not, mainly because liberals actually believe they know a great deal about what constitutes the good life, although they do not acknowledge or maybe even recognize that fact. Liberalism effectively mandates the creation and maintenance of liberal states across the globe, because there is no way under an illiberal state that individual rights can enjoy the prominence liberalism assigns them and the protection they warrant. In effect, liberals are saying they have a universally valid and enduring insight about what constitutes the good life: having a liberal state that guarantees the inalienable rights of all its citizens. Given this conviction, it is not surprising that powerful liberal states adopt highly interventionist policies abroad.[1]

States pursuing liberal hegemony, however, run into serious trouble. One reason is that support for individual rights does not run deep in most countries, which means that turning an autocracy into a liberal democracy is usually a colossal task. Liberal foreign policies also end up clashing with nationalism and balance-of-power politics. Liberalism is no match for either of those other isms when they clash, in large part because they are more in line with human nature than liberalism is. Nationalism is an exceptionally influential political ideology that holds much greater sway than liberalism. It is no accident that the international system is populated by nation-states, not liberal democracies. Moreover, the great powers that dominate the system typically follow realist principles, causing major problems for countries exporting liberal values.

In short, liberalism is a fool's guide for powerful states operating on the world stage. It would make eminently good sense for the United States to abandon liberal hegemony, which has served it so poorly, and pursue a more restrained policy abroad. In practice that means American policymakers should embrace realism.

Realism and Restraint

Most students of international politics associate realism with rivalry and conflict. This, of course, is one reason realism is so unpopular in liberal societies.[2] It is also disliked because realists consider war a legitimate tool of statecraft that can be employed to either maintain the balance of power or shift it in an advantageous way. Advocates of realpolitik downplay the prospects for cooperation among states, moreover, because they think countries have to provide for their own security, given that they operate in a world with no higher authority to protect them. To maximize their survival prospects, those states have little choice but to compete for power, which can be a ruthless and bloody business. Realism does not inspire a hopeful outlook for the future.

Nevertheless, realists are generally less warlike than liberals, who have a strong inclination to use force to promote international peace, even while they dismiss the argument that war is a legitimate instrument of statecraft. This point is illustrated by Valerie Morkevičius's observation, in her comparison of the two bodies of theory, that most realists opposed the U.S. invasion of Iraq in 2003, while America's three most prominent just war theorists (Jean Elshtain, James Turner Johnson, and Michael Walzer) "viewed the war more positively." She concludes that "conventional wisdom holds that realists support the recourse to war more than just war theorists. I argue that the opposite is true: just war theory produces a more bellicose orientation than realism."[3]

Many realists actually believe that if states acted according to balance-of-power logic, there would be hardly any wars between the great powers. These "defensive realists" maintain that the structure of the international system usually punishes aggressors and that the push toward war usually comes from domestic political forces. Great powers, in other words, most often go to war for non-realist reasons. This perspective is nicely captured in the title of Charles Glaser's important article "Realists as Optimists."[4] Other prominent defensive realists include Jack Snyder, Stephen Van Evera, and even Kenneth Waltz, who is sometimes mistakenly said to argue that international anarchy causes states to act aggressively to gain power.[5] Two other realists, Sebastian Rosato and John Schuessler, advocate a realist foreign policy for the United States that they describe as a "recipe for security without war."[6]

The historian Marc Trachtenberg, who looks at the world from the perspective of a defensive realist, explicitly argues that following the dictates of realism leads to a relatively peaceful world, while acting according to what he calls "impractical idealism" leads to endless trouble. His reading of history tells him that "serious trouble developed only when states failed to act in a way that made sense in power-political terms." Conflict occurs when states "squander [power] on moralistic, imperialistic, or ideological enterprises." Realism, he maintains, is "at heart a theory of peace, and it is important that it be recognized as such." In brief, "power is not unstable."[7]

I do not share this sanguine understanding of realism. The structure of the international system often forces great powers to engage in intense security competition and sometimes initiate wars. International politics is a nasty and brutish business, and not just because misguided liberal ideas or other malevolent domestic political forces influence states' foreign policies. Great powers occasionally start wars for sound realist reasons.

Still, even if states act according to my harsher version of realism, they are likely to fight fewer international wars than if they follow liberal principles. There are three reasons why even hard-nosed offensive realists like me are less likely to advocate war than liberals. First, because great powers operating under realist dictates are principally concerned with maximizing their share of global power, there are only a limited number of regions where they should be willing to risk a war. Those places include the great power's own neighborhood and distant areas that are either home to another great power or the site of a critically important resource. For the United States, three regions outside the Western Hemisphere are of vital strategic importance today: Europe and East Asia, because that is where the other great powers are located; and the Persian Gulf, because it is the main source of an exceptionally important resource, oil.

This means the United States should not fight wars in Africa, Central Asia, or areas of the Middle East that lie outside the Persian Gulf. During the Cold War, for example, realists maintained that American policymakers should avoid wars in the "Third World" or "Developing World" because it was populated with minor powers that were of little strategic significance.[8] Almost every realist opposed the Vietnam War, because Vietnam's fate held little strategic consequence for the global balance of power.[9]

Liberals, on the other hand, tend to think of every area of the world as a potential battlefield, because they are committed to protecting human rights everywhere and spreading liberal democracy far and wide. They would naturally prefer to achieve these goals peacefully, but they are usually willing to countenance using military force if necessary. In short, while realists place strict limits on where they are willing to employ force, liberals have no such limits. For them, vital interests are everywhere.

Second, realists are inclined to be cautious about using force or even the threat of force because they recognize that balance-of-power logic will compel other states to contain aggressors, even if they are liberal democracies. Of course, balancing does not always work, which is why wars sometimes occur. Great powers are especially vigilant about their security, and when they feel threatened, they invariably take measures to protect themselves. This wariness explains why Russian leaders have stubbornly opposed NATO enlargement since the mid-1990s and why most American realists opposed it as well. Liberals, however, tend to dismiss balance-of-power logic as irrelevant in the twenty-first century. This kind of thinking helps to make liberals less restrained than realists about using military force.

Third, realists are Clausewitzians in the sense they understand that going to war takes a country into a realm of unintended consequences.[10] Occasionally those consequences are disastrous. Virtually all realists appreciate this basic fact of life because they study war closely and learn that leaders who take their countries to war are sometimes surprised by the results.[11] The mere fact that it is hard to be certain about how a war will turn out makes realists cautious about starting them, which is not to say war never makes sense. Circumstances sometimes call for unsheathing the sword. Liberals, on the other hand, are usually not serious students of war at an intellectual level, probably because they are not inclined to treat war as a normal instrument of statecraft. Clausewitz's *On War* is unlikely to be on their reading lists. Thus they tend to have little appreciation of war's complexities and its potential for unwelcome outcomes.

To be clear, realism is not a recipe for peace. The theory portrays a world where the possibility of war is part of the warp and woof of daily life. Moreover, realism dictates that the United States should seek to remain the most powerful state on the planet. It should maintain hegemony in the Western Hemisphere and make sure that no other great power dominates its region of the world, thus becoming a peer competitor. Still, a foreign policy based on realism is likely to be less warlike than one based on liberalism.

Finally, a proper understanding of how nationalism constrains great powers, especially in their relations with minor powers, provides further reason for the United States to adopt a policy of restraint. A brief analysis of how American policymakers thought about interacting with smaller powers during the Cold War shows that they not only failed to appreciate how nationalism limits Washington's ability to intervene in other states, but also did not understand how that ism works to America's advantage. If the United States had to run the Cold War all over again, or had to engage in a similar security competition in the future, it would make good sense to pursue containment in a markedly different way.[12]

Nationalism and Restraint

For much of the Cold War, American leaders worried about who ruled the minor powers in every region of the world. The great fear was that any country governed by communists would help promote communism in neighboring states, which, in turn, would cause additional states to follow suit. The Soviet Union, of course, played a central role in this story. As a great power committed to spreading communism across the globe via institutions like the Comintern, it was thought to have a relatively easy task. Communism was a universalist ideology with broad appeal. With Soviet sponsorship, more and more states would jump on that bandwagon until, at some point, Moscow would dominate the international system. This phenomenon was known as the domino theory.[13]

The American response to this perceived threat was to do everything possible to prevent minor powers from "going communist." Washington intervened in the politics of virtually every country whose politics showed signs of moving leftward, which led the United States into hard-nosed social engineering on a global scale. In practice, this approach meant (1) giving money, weapons, and other resources to friendly governments to keep them in power; (2) fostering coups against perceived foes, including democratically elected rulers; and (3) intervening directly with American troops.

This strategy was doomed to fail. Social engineering in any country, even one's own, is difficult. The problems are multifaceted and complex, resistance is inevitable, and there are always unintended consequences, some of them bad. The task is even more demanding when social engineering is imposed from outside because nationalism, which is ever present, makes the local population want to determine its own fate without foreigners interfering in its politics. These interventions also fail because the intervening power hardly ever understands the target country's culture and politics. In many cases, the foreigners do not even speak the local language. The problems are even worse when a country tries to use military force to alter another country's social and political landscape, as the United States has rediscovered in Afghanistan and Iraq after previously discovering it in Vietnam during the Cold War. The ensuing violence will make the invading country look like an oppressor, further complicating its efforts to promote positive change.

This is not to deny that during the Cold War the United States sometimes successfully interfered in the politics of minor countries. But even some of those successes came back to haunt American leaders. For example, the 1953 coup in Iran that put the shah back in power gave the United States an important ally for about twenty-five years. But it poisoned relations between Tehran and Washington after the shah was toppled in 1979 and Ayatollah Khomeini came to power. Indeed, memories of the 1953 coup continue to mar relations today, more than sixty years later. And that was a success! As Lindsey O'Rourke shows, most U.S. coup attempts did not even achieve their short-term goals.[14] American interventions could also prove remarkably costly for the target states. The number of citizens of other countries killed by the United States and its allies during the Cold War is stunning.[15]

Worst of all, these interventions were unnecessary. The domino theory did not describe any serious threat: it assumed that universalist ideologies like Marxism would dominate local identities and desire for self-determination. They do not. Proponents of the domino theory failed to understand that nationalism is a far more powerful ideology than communism, just as it is far more powerful than liberalism. Nationalism is all about self-determination. Nations want to control their own fates, and where sovereignty is concerned their political leaders are jealous gods. They want to do what they think is in their country's interest and not be pushed around by other states, even those with which they share an ideology. It is not surprising that communist countries across Eastern Europe deeply resented taking orders from Moscow during the Cold War. So did China. Nor is it an accident that the Soviet Union disintegrated in good part because Ukrainians, Azeris, Armenians, Georgians, Estonians, and many others wanted independence. Minor powers are likely to pursue independent foreign policies and resist the influence of the great powers unless it suits their interests, which it sometimes does but mostly does not. "Puppet states" exist more often in name than in reality.

America's Cold War policy of hyper involvement in the affairs of minor powers was exactly the wrong strategy. Instead of trying to control their political orientation, Washington should have adopted a hands-off policy. The ideological orientation of a country's leaders matters little for working with or against them. What matters is whether both sides' interests are aligned. In almost all of the Cold War cases where the United States had serious dealings with minor powers, the smart strategy would have been to do little to influence who came to power and concentrate instead on working with whoever was in charge to promote America's interests. In the face of a rigidly controlling communist ideology, this strategy might have accomplished what decades of armed interventions could not: move popular sentiment to favor America.

During the Cold War, in short, the United States should have been much more open to seeking friendly relations with communist states, just as it occasionally made sense to have unfriendly relations with democracies. In fact, Washington did have good relations with a few communist countries during the Cold War, because it made good strategic sense for both sides to get along. Chinese-American relations are a case in point. The United States and communist China were deeply antagonistic for the first twenty-plus years of the Cold War, but that changed in the early 1970s, largely as a consequence of the Sino-Soviet split, which meant that both Beijing and Washington were hostile to the Soviet Union and thus well positioned to join forces. The United States ended up working well with a communist state that it had earlier identified as a fallen domino.

The case of Vietnam provides more evidence of the limits of universal ideologies like communism and the power of national interests, which, of course, are tightly bound up with nationalism. Ho Chi Minh, the Vietnamese leader, was both a communist and a fervent nationalist. He was seriously interested in befriending the United States after World War II, but the Truman administration foolishly rejected his overtures because he was a communist. America ended up fighting a long and brutal war against Vietnam mainly because of misguided fears based on the domino theory.[16] After the United States suffered a decisive defeat in that unnecessary war, communist Vietnam fought wars against communist Cambodia and communist China. Moreover, once the Cold War ended, relations between Hanoi and Washington improved significantly and today are better than ever, mainly because both fear a rising China.

If the United States had not been deeply involved in the developing world, might the Soviet Union have invaded a host of minor powers and turned them into puppet states? Perhaps the Soviets might have attacked a few smaller countries, but the result would not have been a steady string of communist victories. On the contrary, the Soviets would have ended up in one quagmire after another. Just look at what happened when the Soviet military moved into Afghanistan in 1979. They were stuck for ten years and ultimately suffered a humiliating defeat. U.S. interests would have been well served if the Soviets had had more Afghanistans, just as Moscow would have been well served if the United States had had more Vietnams. Baiting and bleeding the other side was a smart strategy for both super-powers.[17]

Yet it is still difficult for American policymakers to think along these lines. Most of them fail to appreciate the power of nationalism and instead overestimate universal ideologies like communism and liberalism. Nevertheless, the historical record shows that the best strategy for a great power dealing with minor powers is to avoid getting involved in their domestic politics—and certainly not to invade and occupy them unless it is absolutely necessary. Aggressive intervention is what great powers should try to draw their rivals into doing. U.S. policymakers should keep this lesson in mind if the Sino-American security competition continues to heat up.

A proper understanding of the relationship between liberalism, nationalism, and realism suggests that even the mightiest powers on the planet—including the United States—should pursue a foreign policy of restraint. Any country that fails to understand that basic message and tries instead to shape the world in its own image is likely to face unending trouble.

Where Is the United States Headed?

The American foreign policy establishment would surely resist any move to abandon the pursuit of liberal hegemony and adopt a foreign policy based

on realism. Both the Democratic and Republican parties are deeply wedded to promoting liberalism abroad, even though that policy has been a
failure at almost every turn.[18] Although the American public tends to favor
restraint, the governing elites pay little attention to public opinion—until
they have to—when formulating foreign policy.

Nevertheless, there is good reason to think this situation is about to
change, for reasons beyond the control of the foreign policy establishment.
It appears that the structure of the international system is moving toward
multipolarity, because of China's striking rise and the resurrection of Russian power. This development is likely to bring realism back to the fore in
Washington, since it is impossible to pursue liberal hegemony when there
are other great powers in the international system. American policymakers
have not had to concern themselves with the global balance of power since
the Cold War ended and the Soviet Union collapsed, but the unipolar system seems to have been short-lived, which means that the United States
will once again have to worry about other great powers. Indeed, the Trump
administration has made it clear, to quote Secretary of Defense James
Mattis, that "great power competition between nations is a reality once
again," and "great power competition, not terrorism, is now the primary
focus of U.S. national security strategy."[19]

In a world of three great powers, especially when one of them has China's potential military might, there is sure to be security competition and
maybe even war.[20] The United States will have little choice but to adopt a
realist foreign policy, simply because it must prevent China from becoming a regional hegemon in Asia. That task will not be easy if China continues to grow economically and militarily. Still, liberalism will most likely
continue to influence U.S. policy abroad in small ways, as the impulse to
spread democracy is by now hardwired into the foreign policy establishment's DNA. Although great-power competition will prevent Washington
from fully embracing liberal hegemony, the temptation to pursue liberal
policies abroad will be ever present.

In addition to this lingering tendency to adopt liberal strategies on the
margins of a largely realist foreign policy, there is also the danger that U.S.
policymakers will not fully grasp that nationalism limits their ability to intervene in other countries just as much as it limits their adversaries' ability

to conquer other states. They failed to understand the effects of nationalism both during the Cold War and in the post–Cold War world, and there is
no assurance they will get it in the future. Even with the return of realism
and the demise of liberal hegemony, it will still be imperative to sound the
tocsins about the dangers of a liberal foreign policy and the importance of
understanding how nationalism limits great powers' ability to act.

There is also an alternative scenario. The Chinese economy could encounter serious problems that markedly slow its growth over the long term,
while the American economy grows at a solid pace.[21] In that situation, the
present power gap, which clearly favors the United States, would widen
even further and make it impossible for China to challenge American
power. One might wonder whether Russia is likely to pose a future challenge to the United States, even if China does not. America's three principal great-power rivals from the twentieth century—Germany, Japan, and
Russia—are all depopulating and the United States is likely to become increasingly powerful relative to each of them over the next few decades.[22]
China is the only country on the planet with the potential to challenge U.S.
power in a meaningful way, but if it does not realize that potential, the
United States will remain by far the most powerful state in the international
system. In other words, the system will not remain multipolar for long before reverting back to unipolarity.

In that event, American policymakers would be free to continue pursuing liberal hegemony, since they would again have little reason to worry
about the U.S. position in the global balance of power. Even the further
foreign policy disasters that would surely follow would not endanger the
security of the United States because no other great power could threaten
it. Should this scenario pan out, is there any hope that Washington might
abandon liberal hegemony and adopt a foreign policy that emphasizes restraint rather than permanent war?

There is no question that it would be difficult to get the United States to
stop pursuing liberalism abroad, simply because liberal democracies reflexively want to create a world populated solely with liberal states. Barack
Obama's experience is instructive here. During the 2008 presidential campaign, he emphasized that he would end America's involvement in the Afghanistan and Iraq wars, avoid getting the United States tangled in new

conflicts, and concentrate on nation-building at home instead of abroad. But he failed to change the direction of U.S. foreign policy in any meaningful way. American troops were still fighting in Afghanistan when he left office, and he oversaw American involvement in regime change in Egypt, Libya, and Syria. He removed U.S. troops from Iraq in 2011 but sent them back in 2014 to wage war against ISIS, which had overrun large parts of Iraq and Syria. It is clear from a series of wistful interviews he gave the *Atlantic* before leaving office in January 2017 that he understood "the Washington playbook" was deeply flawed, yet he had operated according to its rules and strategies.[23] He was ultimately no match for the foreign policy establishment.

Still, there is a glimmer of hope that a unipolar United States could be persuaded to move away from liberal hegemony. Powerful liberal states do have agency and are not doomed to follow a misguided strategy, even though the pressure to do so is enormous.[24] The main reason to think the United States can move beyond liberal hegemony revolves around the distinction between the decision to adopt that strategy when the opportunity first presents itself and the decision to forsake it after seeing the long-term results. It is almost impossible to stop a liberal state, when it first gains unipolar status, from embracing that extraordinarily ambitious policy. It promises great benefits and its costs are not yet apparent. But once the strategy has been tried and its flaws become clear, derailing it becomes possible.

The 2016 presidential election shows that liberal hegemony is vulnerable. Donald Trump challenged almost every aspect of the strategy, reminding voters time after time that it had been bad for America. Most importantly, he promised that if he were elected president, the United States would get out of the business of spreading democracy around the world. He emphasized that his administration would have friendly relations with authoritarian leaders, including Vladimir Putin, the current bête noire of the liberal foreign policy establishment. He was also critical of international institutions, going so far as to call NATO obsolete. And he advocated protectionist policies that were at odds with the open international order the United States had spearheaded since the end of World War II. Hillary Clinton, meanwhile, vigorously defended liberal hegemony and left no doubt she favored the status quo. Although foreign policy was not the central issue in the election, Trump's opposition to liberal hegemony undoubtedly helped him with many voters.

One might argue that Trump's campaign rhetoric is irrelevant because the foreign policy elites will tame him just as they tamed his predecessor. After all, Obama challenged liberal hegemony when he was a candidate, yet as president he was forced to stick to the Washington playbook. The same will happen to Trump. Indeed, there is already some evidence that efforts by the foreign policy establishment to tame Trump have at least partly succeeded and that his initial policies show considerable continuity with his predecessors' policies.[25]

To help ensure that the United States does not go back to liberal hegemony, should neither China nor Russia prove a sufficient rival, it is essential to come up with a game plan that is independent of Donald Trump or any particular successor. For starters, the best way to undermine liberal hegemony is to build a counter-elite that can make the case for a realist-based foreign policy.[26] The good news is that there is already a small and vocal core of restrainers that can serve as the foundation for that select group.[27] Still it is essential to win over others in the foreign policy establishment. That task should be feasible because most people do learn, and it should be manifestly clear by now that doing social engineering on a global scale does not work. We have run the experiment and it failed. People with the capacity to learn should be open to at least considering an alternative foreign policy. Although many members of the elite will no doubt want to stick with liberal hegemony and try to implement it more successfully, its fundamental flaws cannot be overcome.

The historical record provides reason to think that much of the foreign policy establishment can be convinced of the virtues of realism and restraint. The United States, after all, has a rich tradition of elite-level restrainers, as the journalist Stephen Kinzer makes clear in *The New Flag*, where he describes the great debate that took place between American imperialists and anti-imperialists at the close of the nineteenth century.[28] Although the expansionists carried the day, they barely won, and the restrainers remained a formidable presence in debates about American foreign policy throughout the twentieth century. Thus, as Kinzer notes: "Those of us who are trying to push America to a more prudent and restrained foreign policy are standing on the shoulders of titans—great figures of American history who first enunciated the view and to continue to make their argument is something quintessentially American."[29]

It is also crucial to win over young people who are likely to become part of the foreign policy establishment. That should be possible because those newcomers are not heavily invested in liberal hegemony and thus more likely than their elders to be open to new ideas.

The first order of business for the counter-elite hoping to rein in American foreign policy is to build formidable institutions from which they can make the case. This message should be aimed at the broader public as well as politicians and policymakers. The public is an especially important target because it is likely to be receptive to arguments for restraint. Most Americans prefer to address problems at home rather than fight endless wars and try to run the world. Unlike the foreign policy establishment, they are not deeply committed to liberal hegemony, so it should be possible to persuade many of them to abandon it. The best evidence of the public's dissatisfaction with liberal hegemony is that the last three U.S. presidents all gained the office by campaigning against it.[30] Hillary Clinton, on the other hand, defended liberal hegemony to the hilt in 2008 and again in 2016 and lost both times, first to Obama and then to Trump.

The central message that restrainers should drive home is that liberal hegemony does not satisfy the principal criterion for assessing any foreign policy: it is not in America's national interest. In other words, selling a realist foreign policy requires an appeal to nationalism, which means asking Americans to think hard about what makes the most sense for them and their fellow citizens. This is not a call for adopting a hard-edged nationalism that demonizes other groups and countries. The emphasis instead is on pursuing policies based almost exclusively on one criterion: what is best for the American people? To make their case, restrainers should emphasize three points. First, the United States is the most secure great power in recorded history and thus does not need to interfere in the politics of every country on the planet. It is a hegemon in the Western Hemisphere, and it is separated from East Asia and Europe—the regions where other great powers have historically been located—by two giant moats, the Atlantic and Pacific Oceans. It has thousands of nuclear weapons, and in the scenario we are considering here, it is the only great power in the international system.

Second, liberal hegemony simply does not work. It was tried for twenty-five years and left a legacy of futile wars, failed diplomacy, and diminished prestige.

Finally, liberal hegemony involves significant costs for the American people, in both lives and money. The ongoing wars in Afghanistan and Iraq are expected to cost more than $5 trillion.[31] Surely if we were intent on adding that much to America's huge national debt, the money could have been better spent on education, public health, transportation infrastructure, and scientific research, just to name a few areas where additional investment would have made the United States a more prosperous and livable country. Perhaps the greatest cost of liberal hegemony, however, is something else: the damage it does to the American political and social fabric. Individual rights and the rule of law will not fare well in a country addicted to fighting wars.

Restrainers will surely encounter the argument that appealing to American nationalism is selfish and that a powerful country like the United States has the resources and the responsibility to help people in trouble around the world. This argument might make sense if liberal hegemony worked as advertised. But it does not. The people who have paid the greatest cost for Washington's failed policies in the post–Cold War period are foreigners who had the misfortune of living in countries that American policymakers targeted for regime change. Just look at the greater Middle East today, which the United States, pursuing liberal hegemony, has helped turn into a giant disaster zone. If Americans want to facilitate the spread of democracy around the world, the best way to achieve that goal is to concentrate on building a vibrant democracy at home that other states will want to emulate.

The case for a realist-based foreign policy is straightforward and powerful, and it should be compelling to a large majority of Americans. But it is still a tough sell, mainly because many in the foreign policy elite are deeply committed to liberal hegemony and will go to enormous lengths to defend it. Of course, the best way to put an end to liberal hegemony would be for

China to continue rising, thus ending unipolarity and making the question moot. But then the United States would have to compete with a potential peer competitor, a situation no great power wants to face. It would be preferable to retain the unipolar world, even though it would tempt American policymakers to stick with liberal hegemony. For that not to happen, Americans must understand the dangers of a liberal foreign policy and the virtues of restraint. I hope this book will help that cause.

NOTES

Chapter 1. The Impossible Dream

1. It is commonplace in everyday American discourse to distinguish between liberals and conservatives. Liberals are usually identified with the Democratic Party, while conservatives are identified with the Republican Party. Given that distinction, it would make little sense to describe the United States as a deeply liberal country. I am using the term *liberal*, however, in what Louis Hartz called the "classic Lockean sense," which allows him and me to say that America is liberal at its core, and that although there are important differences between the Democratic and Republican Parties, in essence, they are both liberal institutions. Louis Hartz, *The Liberal Tradition in America: An Interpretation of American Political Thought since the Revolution* (New York: Harcourt Brace, 1955), p. 4.

2. The United States actively promoted democracy abroad throughout the twentieth century, as Tony Smith makes clear in *America's Mission: The United States and the Worldwide Struggle for Democracy in the Twentieth Century* (Princeton, NJ: Princeton University Press, 1994). Until the Cold War ended, however, spreading liberal democracy always took a backseat to hard-nosed policies based on power politics, which sometimes involved overthrowing democratically elected leaders and having cozy relations with brutal autocrats. The United States, in other words, was not in a position to adopt liberal hegemony until 1989.

3. Francis Fukuyama, "The End of History?," *National Interest*, no. 16 (Summer 1989), pp. 3–18. Also see Francis Fukuyama, *The End of History and the Last Man* (New York: Free Press, 1992).

4. "The 1992 Campaign; Excerpts from Speech by Clinton on U.S. Role," *New York Times*, October 2, 1992.

5. "President Discusses the Future of Iraq," Hilton Hotel, Washington, DC, February 26, 2003. For the White House transcript see https://georgewbush-whitehouse.archives.gov/news/releases/2003/02/print/20030226-11.html.

6. "President Bush Discusses Freedom in Iraq and Middle East," remarks at the 20th Anniversary of the National Endowment for Democracy, Washington, DC, September 6, 2003. For the White House transcript see https://georgewbush -whitehouse.archives.gov/news/releases/2003/11/20031106-2.html.

7. John Locke, *The Second Treatise of Government*, ed. Thomas P. Peardon (Indianapolis: Bobbs-Merrill, 1952), p. 4. Also see Fukuyama, *The End of History and the Last Man*, pp. 138–39; John Rawls, *The Law of Peoples: With "The Idea of Public Reason Revisited"* (Cambridge, MA: Harvard University Press, 1999), pp. 12–13, 17, 19. As Alan Ryan notes, "To found one's politics on a view of human nature that most people find implausible is to found one's politics on quicksand." Alan Ryan, *The Making of Modern Liberalism* (Princeton, NJ: Princeton University Press, 2012), p. 26.

8. Given that I have written a theoretical tract on realism—*The Tragedy of Great Power Politics*, updated ed. (New York: Norton, 2014)—one might wonder how *The Great Delusion* relates to *Tragedy*. They complement each other in two ways. For starters, little attention is paid to liberalism and hardly any attention is paid to nationalism in *Tragedy*. The focus is instead on developing and testing a theory of realism. Nevertheless, how realism relates to these other two isms helps provide a fuller understanding of how the international system works. Furthermore, this new book presents an opportunity to say more about the roots of realism. There is no discussion of human nature in *Tragedy*, whereas it is a central part of the story in *The Great Delusion*. Digging a level deeper and examining human nature will hopefully shed light on some of the key assumptions that underpin realism.

9. The three isms that are at the center of this book—liberalism, nationalism, and realism—are treated as both political ideologies and theories, as they all fit squarely into these two overlapping categories. For me, a theory is a simplified picture of reality that attempts to explain how the world *actually works* in particular domains. A theory relies on concepts or variables that are tied together to tell a causal story that leads to a specific outcome. Theories are explanatory in nature. See John J. Mearsheimer and Stephen M. Walt, "Leaving Theory Behind: Why Simplistic Hypothesis Testing Is Bad for International Relations," *European Journal of International Relations* 19, no. 3 (September 2013): 427–57. A political ideology, on the other hand, is a systematic body of concepts and principles that explain how a particular society, or the international system more generally, *should work*. In other words, it is prescriptive; it provides a blueprint for how a political order should operate. Ideologies are inherently normative in nature, although every ideology has theory behind it, which explains in good part the significant overlap between these two concepts. Ideology, for that reason, might be called normative theory, as opposed to explanatory theory.

10. Samuel Moyn, *The Last Utopia: Human Rights in History* (Cambridge, MA: Harvard University Press, 2010), p. 1. In his review of Moyn's book, John Gray refers to "the contemporary cult of human rights." See Gray, "What Rawls Hath Wrought," *National Interest*, no. 111 (January/February 2011), p. 81.

11. These two kinds of liberalism—modus vivendi and progressive—are ideal types, and thus the writings of most liberal theorists do not fit perfectly into one category or the other, although some do. John Locke, for example, is clearly a modus vivendi liberal, while John Rawls fits squarely in the progressive liberal category. Regardless, my main concern is not to categorize particular liberal scholars according to one school of thought or the other, but instead to understand the main dividing lines within liberalism and how they relate to politics at home and abroad. Furthermore, my distinction between these two types of political liberalism is not novel. In fact, I have learned much from reading the works of other scholars who employ a similar dichotomy, although they use somewhat different names and make somewhat different arguments about the content of each kind of liberalism. John Gray, for example, distinguishes between "modus vivendi liberalism" and "liberal legalism" in his aptly titled book *The Two Faces of Liberalism,* while Alan Ryan contrasts "classical liberalism" with "modern liberalism." Judith Shklar, who is well known for her writings about the "liberalism of fear," also writes about "legalism," which is akin to progressive liberalism. John Gray, *The Two Faces of Liberalism* (New York: New Press, 2000); Ryan, *The Making of Modern Liberalism,* chap. 1; Judith N. Shklar, *Political Thought and Political Thinkers,* ed. Stanley Hoffmann (Chicago: University of Chicago Press, 1998), chap. 1.

12. Quoted in David Armitage, *The Declaration of Independence: A Global History* (Cambridge, MA: Harvard University Press, 2008), p. 80.

13. E. H. Carr, *The Twenty Years' Crisis, 1919–1939: An Introduction to the Study of International Relations,* 2nd ed. (London: Macmillan, 1962).

14. This point is developed in Jeanne Morefield, *Covenants without Swords: Idealist Liberalism and the Spirit of Empire* (Princeton, NJ: Princeton University Press, 2005).

15. Markus Fischer, "The Liberal Peace: Ethical, Historical, and Philosophical Aspects" (BCSIA Discussion Paper 2000-07, Kennedy School of Government, Harvard University, April 2000), p. 5.

16. See Fischer, "The Liberal Peace," pp. 1–6; Stephen Holmes, *Passions and Constraint: On the Theory of Liberal Democracy* (Chicago: University of Chicago Press, 1995), pp. 8–10, 31–36.

17. Kenneth N. Waltz, *Man, the State and War: A Theoretical Analysis* (New York: Columbia University Press, 1965).

Chapter 2. Human Nature and Politics

1. Joseph de Maistre, *Considerations on France,* trans. Richard A. Lebrun (Montreal: McGill–Queen's University Press, 1974), p. 97.

2. Mark Pagel, *Wired for Culture: Origins of the Human Social Mind* (New York: Norton, 2012), p. 12.

3. Pierre Bourdieu, *Outline of a Theory of Practice* (New York: Cambridge University Press, 1977).

4. James D. Fearon, "What Is Identity (as We Now Use the Word)?" (unpublished paper, Stanford University, November 3, 1999); Samuel P. Huntington, *Who Are We? The Challenges to American National Identity* (New York: Simon & Schuster, 2004), chap. 2.

5. Jeanne E. Arnold, "The Archaeology of Complex Hunter-Gatherers," *Journal of Archaeological Method and Theory* 3, no. 2 (March 1996): 77–126; T. Douglas Price and James A. Brown, eds., *Prehistoric Hunter-Gatherers: The Emergence of Cultural Complexity* (San Diego, CA: Academic Press, 1985).

6. Leo Strauss, *An Introduction to Political Philosophy: Ten Essays by Leo Strauss*, ed. Hilail Gildin (Detroit: Wayne State University Press, 1989), p. 3.

7. Richard A. Posner, *The Problematics of Moral and Legal Theory* (Cambridge, MA: Harvard University Press, 1999), p. 137. Also see p. 36, where he writes: "The most important rules of cooperation in a human society are embedded in its moral code."

8. The phrase—"Reason Rules the World"—is from Hegel's *Introduction to the Philosophy of History*, trans. Leo Rauch (Indianapolis: Hackett Publishing, 1988), p. 12. For an example of a scholar who believes that people everywhere can agree on a body of first principles, see Derek Parfit, *On What Matters*, 2 vols. (New York: Oxford University Press, 2011). Also consider Louise Antony's comment in the introduction to a book of essays by "twenty leading philosophers from Great Britain and the United States, all of whom abjure traditional religious faith." Noting that atheists are routinely said to have "no moral values," she notes, "The essays in this volume should serve to roundly refute this. Every writer in this volume adamantly affirms the objectivity of right and wrong." Louise M. Antony, ed., *Philosophers without Gods: Meditations on Atheism and the Secular Life* (New York: Oxford University Press, 2007), pp. x, xii. This optimistic perspective on objective truth is also clearly reflected in J. L. Mackie, *Ethics: Inventing Right and Wrong* (London: Penguin Books, 1990), although Mackie himself argues against it.

9. One might argue that there are absolute truths when it comes to core questions about what constitutes the good life, but our critical faculties are simply inadequate for helping us discern them. That line of argument, however, is consistent with my claims about the limits of our critical faculties.

10. Peter Gay, *The Enlightenment: The Rise of Modern Paganism* (New York: Norton, 1966); Peter Gay, *The Enlightenment: The Science of Freedom* (New York: Norton, 1996); Isaac Kramnick, ed., *The Portable Enlightenment Reader* (New York: Penguin Books, 1995); Anthony Pagden, *The Enlightenment: And Why It Still Matters* (New York: Random House, 2013).

11. Quoted in Kramnick, *The Portable Enlightenment Reader*, p. 388.

12. William Godwin, *An Enquiry concerning Political Justice, and Its Influence on General Virtue and Happiness* (Harmondsworth, UK: Penguin Books, 1976), pp. 140, 168.

13. Frederick C. Beiser, *The Fate of Reason: German Philosophy from Kant to Fichte* (Cambridge, MA: Harvard University Press, 1987); Isaiah Berlin, *The Proper Study of Mankind: An Anthology of Essays* (New York: Farrar, Straus and Giroux,

1998), pp. 243–68; Max Horkheimer, *Eclipse of Reason* (New York: Continuum, 2004).

14. Alasdair MacIntyre, *After Virtue: A Study in Moral Theory* (Notre Dame, IN: University of Notre Dame Press, 1981), p. 6. Other works that emphasize our inability to reach agreement on ethical or moral principles include Stuart Hampshire, *Morality and Conflict* (Cambridge, MA: Harvard University Press, 1984); Bernard Williams, *Ethics and the Limits of Philosophy* (Cambridge, MA: Harvard University Press, 1985).

15. Max Weber makes a related point when he notes, "I do not know how one might wish to decide 'scientifically' the value of French and German culture; for here, too, different gods struggle with one another, now and for all time to come." Max Weber, "Science as a Vocation," in *From Max Weber: Essays in Sociology*, ed. and trans. H. H. Gerth and C. Wright Mills (New York: Oxford University Press, 1971), p. 148.

16. All the quotes in this paragraph are from Brad S. Gregory, *The Unintended Reformation: How a Religious Revolution Secularized Society* (Cambridge, MA: Harvard University Press, 2012), p. 21.

17. Brian Leiter, "Legal Realism and Legal Positivism Reconsidered," *Ethics* III, no. 2 (January 2001): 285.

18. Richard A. Posner, *Economic Analysis of Law*, 9th ed. (New York: Wolters Kluwer Law & Business, 2014).

19. The quotes in this paragraph are from Ronald Dworkin, *A Matter of Principle* (Cambridge, MA: Harvard University Press, 2000), pp. 3, 69.

20. Dworkin, *A Matter of Principle*, p. 162.

21. *The Essential Holmes: Selections from the Letters, Speeches, Judicial Opinions, and Other Writings of Oliver Wendell Holmes, Jr.*, ed. Richard A. Posner (Chicago: University of Chicago Press, 1992), p. 107.

22. "Why Obama Voted against Roberts," *Wall Street Journal*, June 2, 2009.

23. Irving Kristol, "Some Personal Reflections on Economic Well-Being and Income Distribution," in *The American Economy in Transition*, ed. Martin Feldstein (Chicago: University of Chicago Press, 1980), p. 486. The British economist Lionel Robins similarly remarked that economics "is unconcerned with norms and ends; it is concerned strictly with constructing patterns for the appropriation of scarce means to given purposes." Quoted in S. M. Amadae, *Rationalizing Capitalist Democracy: The Cold War Origins of Rational Choice Liberalism* (Chicago: University of Chicago Press, 2003), p. 91.

24. C. Bradley Thompson with Yaron Brook, *Neoconservatism: An Obituary for an Idea* (Boulder, CO: Paradigm Publishers, 2010), pp. 68, 106.

25. Leo Strauss, *Natural Right and History* (Chicago: University of Chicago Press, 1953), p. 5.

26. Strauss, *An Introduction to Political Philosophy*, p. 5.

27. Strauss, *Natural Right and History*, p. 6.

28. Strauss, *Natural Right and History*, pp. 26–27, 253; Strauss, *An Introduction to Political Philosophy*, pp. 94–98. Also see John G. Gunnell, "Strauss before Straussianism:

Reason, Revelation, and Nature," *Review of Politics,* special issue on the thought of Leo Strauss, 53, no. 1 (Winter 1991): 72–73; and Laurence Lampert, *Leo Strauss and Nietzsche* (Chicago: University of Chicago Press, 1996), who argues that Nietzsche, Plato, and Strauss all understood that reason could not provide final truths, but what distinguishes them from each other is that Plato and Strauss preferred to hide this critical fact of life from the public, while Nietzsche proclaimed it loudly and clearly in his writings.

29. Jonathan Haidt, "The Emotional Dog and Its Rational Tail: A Social Intuitionist Approach to Moral Judgment," *Psychological Review* 108, no. 4 (October 2001): 827.

30. Individuals sometimes have little time for reflection and thus have no choice but to make a snap judgment based on their intuitions. Alternatively, some people might not have any interest in reasoning through an issue, because it involves hard work and might lead to unwelcome conclusions. Alan Jacobs, *How to Think: A Survival Guide for a World at Odds* (New York: Currency, 2017).

31. Daniel Kahneman maintains that there are two systems that influence the way we think: System 1, which involves fast thinking and relies mainly on intuition; and System 2, where thinking is slower and relies on careful reasoning. Kahneman, *Thinking Fast and Slow* (New York: Farrar, Straus and Giroux, 2011), especially part I. Also see Richard H. Thaler and Cass R. Sunstein, *Nudge: Improving Decisions about Health, Wealth, and Happiness,* rev. ed. (New York: Penguin, 2009), which distinguishes between the Automatic and Reflective Systems. This distinction between these two cognitive processes is widely reflected in the psychology literature.

32. Antonio Damasio, *Descartes' Error: Emotion, Reason, and the Human Brain* (New York: Penguin Books, 2005).

33. Haidt writes, for example, "The central claim of the social intuitionist model is that moral judgment is caused by quick moral intuitions and is followed (when needed) by slow, ex post facto moral reasoning." Haidt, "The Emotional Dog and Its Rational Tail," p. 817. Some scholars believe that our critical faculties have evolved over time, not to help us discover truth and make smart decisions, but instead to help us win arguments with other people. See Patricia Cohen, "Reason Seen More as Weapon than Path to Truth," *New York Times,* June 14, 2011; Hugo Mercier and Dan Sperber, "Why Do Humans Reason? Arguments for an Argumentative Theory," *Behavioral and Brain Sciences* 34, no. 2 (April 2011): 57–74.

34. David Hume, *A Treatise of Human Nature* (London: Clarendon Press, 1896), pp. 415, 457.

35. John Dewey, *Liberalism and Social Action* (New York: Capricorn Books, 1963), p. 70.

36. Dewey, *Liberalism and Social Action,* p. 79.

37. John J. Mearsheimer, "The Aims of Education," *Philosophy and Literature* 22, no. 1 (April 1998): 137–55.

38. Michael Powell, "A Redoubt of Learning Holds Firm," *New York Times*, September 3, 2012.

39. Jean-Jacques Rousseau, *The First and Second Discourses*, ed. Roger D. Masters, trans. Roger D. Masters and Judith R. Masters (New York: St. Martin's Press, 1964), p. 79.

40. Liberals and others who emphasize individualism and downplay the importance of society or community usually concede that humans could never have been atomistic individuals in the state of nature, and that everyone had to be raised by others in a society. Nevertheless, they believe this invented story is a useful theoretical device for thinking about the human condition. While this approach has its virtues, its great flaw is that the social nature of humans, which is so important for understanding how the world works, gets left on the cutting room floor. Jean Hampton, "Contract and Consent," in *A Companion to Contemporary Political Philosophy*, ed. Robert E. Goodin and Philip Pettit (Malden, MA: Blackwell, 2007), pp. 379–82.

41. Daniel Defoe, *Robinson Crusoe: An Authoritative Text, Contexts, Criticism*, ed. Michael Shinagel, 2nd ed. (New York: Norton, 1994), p. 310.

42. Pagel, *Wired for Culture*.

43. Hume argues that "the passions of lust and natural affection" made human society "unavoidable." Hume, *A Treatise of Human Nature*, p. 486.

44. Emile Durkheim, *The Rules of Sociological Method*, trans. Sarah A. Solovay and John H. Mueller, 8th ed. (New York: Free Press, 1938), p. 103.

45. Antonio Gramsci, *Selections from the Prison Notebooks*, trans. and ed. Quintin Hoare and Geoffrey Nowell-Smith (New York: International Publishers, 1971), p. 324.

46. Yael Tamir stresses the importance of allowing individuals maximum flexibility to choose the culture that satisfies their needs and desires. Tamir, *Liberalism and Nationalism* (Princeton, NJ: Princeton University Press, 1993).

47. See Christoph Frei, *Hans J. Morgenthau: An Intellectual Biography* (Baton Rouge: Louisiana State University Press, 2001); Peter Graf Kielmansegg, Horst Mewes, and Elisabeth Glaser-Schmidt, eds., *Hannah Arendt and Leo Strauss: German Emigrés and American Political Thought after World War II* (New York: Cambridge University Press, 1997), chaps. 4–8; Mark Lilla, "Leo Strauss: The European," *New York Review of Books*, October 21, 2004; William E. Scheuerman, *Morgenthau* (Malden, MA: Polity Press, 2009); Michael C. Williams, ed., *Realism Reconsidered: The Legacy of Hans J. Morgenthau in International Relations* (New York: Oxford University Press, 2007).

48. Edmund Burke, *Reflections on the Revolution in France*, ed. J. G. A. Pocock (Indianapolis: Hackett Publishing, 1987), p. 85.

49. Rule of law is a concept that is sometimes associated with liberal democracies. All societies, however, require a system of rules to function effectively. Even Nazi Germany had a well-established body of rules, which is not to say those rules were just. See Alan E. Steinweis and Robert D. Rachlin, eds., *The Law in Nazi*

Germany: Ideology, Opportunism, and the Perversion of Justice (New York: Berghahn, 2013); Michael Stolleis and Thomas Dunlap, eds., *The Law under the Swastika: Studies on Legal History under Nazi Germany* (Chicago: University of Chicago Press, 1998).

50. Anarchy does not mean disorder or chaos in my story, but instead is an ordering principle, which conveys that a social or political system contains no higher authority. With hierarchy, there is an overarching authority. See Kenneth N. Waltz, *Theory of International Politics* (Reading, MA: Addison-Wesley, 1979), pp. 102–16.

51. Quoted in Sarah Boseley, "Power to the People," *Guardian*, August 11, 2008. Barack Obama made the same comment. See William Finnegan, "The Candidate: How the Son of a Kenyan Economist Became an Illinois Everyman," *New Yorker*, May 31, 2004.

52. Jack Knight, *Institutions and Social Conflict* (New York: Cambridge University Press, 1992).

53. Harold D. Lasswell, *Politics: Who Gets What, When, How* (New York: Whittlesey House, 1936).

54. I discuss the limits of rules under anarchy in John J. Mearsheimer, "The False Promise of International Institutions," *International Security* 19, no. 3 (Winter 1994/95): 5–49.

55. Steven Pinker, *The Better Angels of Our Nature: Why Violence Has Declined* (New York: Viking, 2011), chaps. 2–3.

56. *The Landmark Thucydides: A Comprehensive Guide to the Peloponnesian War*, ed. Robert B. Strassler (New York: Simon & Schuster, 1998), p. 352.

57. Joseph M. Parent, *Uniting States: Voluntary Union in World Politics* (New York: Oxford University Press, 2011); Sebastian Rosato, *Europe United: Power Politics and the Making of the European Community* (Ithaca, NY: Cornell University Press, 2011); Ashley J. Tellis, "The Drive to Domination: Toward a Pure Realist Theory of Politics" (PhD diss., University of Chicago, 1994).

58. This basic fact of life is a core theme in *The Prince*. Machiavelli was deeply committed to finding a talented prince who could unite Italy's various city-states and turn Italy into a great power that could stand up to Austria and France, which frequently interfered, sometimes militarily, in Italian politics. To achieve this goal, the prince of one city-state would have to conquer and subdue the other Italian city-states. Machiavelli was fully aware that winning over defeated rivals would be an especially difficult task. He writes, for example, "But when one acquires states in a province disparate in language, customs, and orders, here are the difficulties, and here one needs to have great fortune and great industry to hold them." Niccolò Machiavelli, *The Prince*, trans. Harvey C. Mansfield, 2nd ed. (Chicago: University of Chicago Press, 1998), pp. 9–10. Not surprisingly, this classic book is filled with advice from Machiavelli about how the prince should deal with resistance from hostile populations and leaders. Although Machiavelli wrote *The Prince* in 1513, Italy was not fully unified until 1870.

59. A study of what causes schisms in American Protestant denominations found that "the most powerful single predictor of schism is size as measured by deno-

minational membership: the larger the denomination, the greater the tendency to schism." Robert C. Liebman, John R. Sutton, and Robert Wuthnow, "Exploring the Social Sources of Denominationalism: Schisms in American Protestant Denominations, 1890–1980," *American Sociological Review* 53, no. 3 (June 1988): 343–52. Also see James R. Lewis and Sarah M. Lewis, eds., *Sacred Schisms: How Religions Divide* (New York: Cambridge University Press, 2009).

60. On the problem of projecting power in the modern world, see Patrick Porter, *The Global Village Myth: Distance, War, and the Limits of Power* (Washington, DC: Georgetown University Press, 2015). On the "stopping power of water," see John J. Mearsheimer, *The Tragedy of Great Power Politics*, updated ed. (New York: Norton, 2014), pp. 114–28.

61. Schmitt writes: "One could test all theories of state and political ideas according to their anthropology and thereby classify these as to whether they consciously or unconsciously presuppose man to be by nature evil or by nature good." Carl Schmitt, *The Concept of the Political*, trans. George Schwab (New Brunswick, NJ: Rutgers University Press, 1976), p. 58.

62. This is one of the central themes in Rousseau's "Discourse on the Origin and Foundations of Inequality among Men," where he writes that "most of our ills are our own work and . . . we would have avoided almost all of them by preserving the simple, uniform, and solitary way of life prescribed to us by nature." Rousseau, *The First and Second Discourses*, p. 110.

63. John Patrick Diggins, *Why Niebuhr Now?* (Chicago: University of Chicago Press, 2011).

64. Carl N. Degler, *In Search of Human Nature: The Decline and Revival of Darwinism in American Social Thought* (New York: Oxford University Press, 1991); Dominic D. P. Johnson and Bradley A. Thayer, "The Evolution of Offensive Realism: Survival under Anarchy from the Pleistocene to the Present," *Politics and the Life Sciences* 35, no. 1 (Spring 2016): 1–26; Hans J. Morgenthau, *Scientific Man vs. Power Politics* (London: Latimer House, 1947), pp. 165–67; Hans J. Morgenthau, *Politics among Nations*, 5th ed. (New York: Knopf, 1973), pp. 34–35; Edward O. Wilson, *Sociobiology: The New Synthesis*, 2nd ed. (Cambridge, MA: Harvard University Press, 2004), chap. 27; Edward O. Wilson, *On Human Nature*, rev. ed. (Cambridge, MA: Harvard University Press, 2004).

Chapter 3. Political Liberalism

1. John Locke, *The Second Treatise of Government*, ed. Thomas P. Peardon (Indianapolis: Bobbs-Merrill, 1952), p. 4.

2. Alexis de Tocqueville, *The Ancien Régime and the French Revolution*, trans. and ed. Gerald Bevan (New York: Penguin Books, 2008), p. 102.

3. Sanford A. Lakoff, *Equality in Political Philosophy* (Cambridge, MA: Harvard University Press, 1964).

4. Hobbes is not a liberal for two reasons. First, he pays hardly any attention to natural rights, which are at the heart of liberalism. Second, he calls for an especially

powerful state, which runs counter to liberal thinking about the need to limit state power as much as possible.

5. Locke, *The Second Treatise of Government*, p. 56. Also see pp. 11–14, 70–73.

6. Alan Ryan notes: "The advocacy or denial of toleration as a matter of right divides the liberal and non-liberal more sharply than anything else." Ryan, *The Making of Modern Liberalism* (Princeton, NJ: Princeton University Press, 2012), p. 31. Also see pp. 22–23.

7. This perspective is reflected in John Stuart Mill, *On Liberty* (Indianapolis: Bobbs-Merrill, 1956).

8. Max Weber, "Politics as a Vocation," in *From Max Weber: Essays in Sociology*, ed. and trans. H. H. Gerth and C. Wright Mills (New York: Routledge, 2009), p. 78.

9. Quoted in John Dewey, *Liberalism and Social Action* (New York: Capricorn Books, 1963), p. 22.

10. The importance of the state as an impartial umpire in liberal thinking is a central theme in Paul Kelly, *Liberalism* (Malden, MA: Polity Press, 2005).

11. Judith N. Shklar, *Political Thought and Political Thinkers*, ed. Stanley Hoffmann (Chicago: University of Chicago Press, 1998), p. 3.

12. Paine's full quote is: "Society in every state is a blessing, but Government, even in its best state, is but a necessary evil; in its worst state an intolerable one." Thomas Paine, *Common Sense*, ed. Isaac Kramnick (London: Penguin, 1986), p. 61.

13. Aristotle, *Nicomachean Ethics*, trans. C. D. C. Reeve (Indianapolis: Hackett Publishing, 2014), p. 13.

14. As discussed in the next chapter, nationalism produces the deep ties that a liberal state has with its citizens. Indeed, no liberal democracy could survive for long without nationalism, which is why every liberal state is also a nation-state.

15. See Sheldon S. Wolin, *Politics and Vision: Continuity and Innovation in Western Political Thought*, expanded ed. (Princeton, NJ: Princeton University Press, 2004), chap. 9. Also see Karl Marx, "On the Jewish Question," in *The Marx-Engels Reader*, ed. Robert C. Tucker (New York: Norton, 1972), pp. 24–51; Mill, *On Liberty*.

16. Quoted in Wolin, *Politics and Vision*, p. 280.

17. Markus Fischer, "The Liberal Peace: Ethical, Historical, and Philosophical Aspects" (BCSIA Discussion Paper 2000-07, Kennedy School of Government, Harvard University, April 2000), p. 18. Fischer also talks about the "emptiness of liberalism" (p. 59). John Rawls is well aware of the charge that liberalism is "distraught by spiritual emptiness." While he notes that "spiritual questions" are certainly important, he believes that dealing with them is not the government's business; instead "it leaves them for each citizen to decide for himself or herself." John Rawls, *The Law of Peoples: With "The Idea of Public Reason Revisited"* (Cambridge, MA: Harvard University Press, 1999), p. 127.

18. Stephen Holmes, *Passions and Constraint: On the Theory of Liberal Democracy* (Chicago: University of Chicago Press, 1995), p. 10.

19. Wolin, *Politics and Vision*, chap. 9. Also see Carl Schmitt, *The Concept of the Political*, trans. George Schwab (Chicago: University of Chicago Press, 2007); Francis

Fukuyama, "The End of History?," *National Interest,* no. 16 (Summer 1989), pp. 3, 16, 18. John Dewey maintained that the great transformation within liberalism took place when politics was subordinated to economics. Dewey, *Liberalism and Social Action,* pp. 7–11.

20. John Gray, *Two Faces of Liberalism* (New York: New Press, 2000), p. 16. Also see John Gray, *Endgames: Questions in Late Modern Political Thought* (Cambridge: Polity Press, 2004), pp. 51–54. Ronald Dworkin, who was a liberal legal theorist, naturally focused on courts, not politics, as the main vehicle for pushing forward his progressive liberal agenda.

21. Niccolò Machiavelli, *Discourses on Livy,* trans. Julia C. Bondanella and Peter Bondanella (New York: Oxford University Press, 2009).

22. On Locke's intolerance toward atheists and Catholics, see David J. Lorenzo, "Tradition and Prudence in Locke's Exceptions to Toleration," *American Journal of Political Science* 47, no. 2 (April 2003): 248–58. Judith Shklar writes that liberalism "must reject only those political doctrines that do not recognize any difference between the spheres of the personal and the public. Because of the primacy of toleration as the irreducible limit on public agents, liberals must always draw such a line." Shklar, *Political Thought and Political Thinkers,* p. 6.

23. Gray, *Two Faces of Liberalism,* p. 3.

24. Holmes, *Passions and Constraint,* p. 2. The term *classical liberalism* is synonymous with *modus vivendi liberalism.*

25. Alan Ryan notes that classical (modus vivendi) liberals, unlike modern (progressive) liberals, "do not display any particular attachment to the ideal of moral and cultural progress." Ryan, *The Making of Modern Liberalism,* p. 24.

26. Isaac Kramnick, ed., *The Portable Enlightenment Reader* (New York: Penguin Books, 1995), pp. xi–xii.

27. Jeremy Waldron, "Theoretical Foundations of Liberalism," *Philosophical Quarterly* 37, no. 147 (April 1987): 134.

28. Quoted in Kramnick, *The Portable Enlightenment Reader,* p. xi.

29. Ronald Dworkin, *A Matter of Principle* (Cambridge, MA: Harvard University Press, 2000), p. 203.

30. The quotes in this paragraph are from Dworkin, *A Matter of Principle,* pp. 119, 145, 187, 203. To be fair, Dworkin understands that applying moral principles to hard cases will be an especially difficult task, which is why he calls his ideal judge "Hercules." Ronald Dworkin, *Law's Empire* (Cambridge, MA: Harvard University Press, 1986), pp. 238–40.

31. Francis Fukuyama, *The End of History and the Last Man* (New York: Free Press, 1992), p. xii. The remaining quotes in this paragraph are from Fukuyama, "The End of History?," pp. 4, 5, 18.

32. The quotes in this paragraph are from Steven Pinker, *The Better Angels of Our Nature: Why Violence Has Declined* (New York: Viking, 2011), pp. 182, 650, 662, 690–91. On page 692, Pinker, sounding like Fukuyama talking about the ineluctable spread of liberal democracy, writes that "many liberalizing reforms that

originated in Western Europe or on the American coasts have been emulated, after a time lag, by the more conservative parts of the world."

33. Jeremy Waldron, "How Judges Should Judge," review of *Justice in Robes*, by Ronald Dworkin, *New York Review of Books*, August 10, 2006.

34. Quotes in this paragraph are from Fukuyama, *The End of History and the Last Man*, pp. 296, 298, 338.

35. Quotes in this paragraph are from Fukuyama, *The End of History and the Last Man*, pp. 128, 294, 332, 334. Not surprisingly, Fukuyama is even less confident today about his 1989 predictions than he was when he wrote *The End of History and the Last Man* in 1992. See, for example, Francis Fukuyama, "At the 'End of History' Still Stands Democracy," *Wall Street Journal*, June 6, 2014.

36. Stephen Holmes, "The Scowl of Minerva," *New Republic*, March 23, 1992, p. 28. Dworkin and Pinker also sometimes pull back from their bold claims about where reason can take us, although not as emphatically as Fukuyama. Dworkin, for example, concedes that his optimistic views on the power of reason are clearly in the minority among lawyers, which undermines his claim that reason can lead lawyers and judges to a consensus regarding "right answers" in hard cases. To put the matter in Dworkin's own words, "If lawyers and judges disagree about what the law is, and no one has a knockdown argument either way, then what sense does it make to insist that one opinion is right and others are wrong?" Dworkin, *A Matter of Principle*, p. 3. Of course, the answer is that it makes little sense. Regarding Pinker, despite his emphasis on the "escalator of reason," he makes it clear that a continuing decline in violence is not inevitable. For example, he writes: "The decline, to be sure, has not been smooth; it has not brought violence down to zero; and it is not guaranteed to continue." Moreover, he minces no words in stressing that human beings remain highly aggressive, writing that "most of us—including you, dear reader—are wired for violence." He further notes that there is still a powerful strategic logic at play—he calls it the Pacifist's Dilemma—that is potentially an important cause of conflict. Thus, he concludes: "Motives like greed, fear, dominance, and lust keep drawing us toward aggression." His hope, of course, is that the better angels of our nature will continue to trump the darker side of our nature, but he acknowledges that there is no guarantee that will happen in the future. Pinker, *Better Angels*, pp. xxi, 483, 678–80, 695.

37. Deborah Boucoyannis, "The International Wanderings of a Liberal Idea, or Why Liberals Can Learn to Stop Worrying and Love the Balance of Power," *Perspectives on Politics* 5, no. 4 (December 2007): 707–8; Michael C. Desch, "America's Liberal Illiberalism: The Ideological Origins of Overreaction in U.S. Foreign Policy," *International Security* 32, no. 3 (Winter 2007/8): 11–15; Gray, *Two Faces of Liberalism*, pp. 2, 19, 27–29, 34, 70, 137; Kenneth N. Waltz, "Kant, Liberalism, and War," *American Political Science Review* 56, no. 2 (June 1962): 331–40.

38. Waltz, "Kant, Liberalism, and War," p. 331.

39. Rawls, *The Law of Peoples*, pp. 34, 85.

40. This quote and the subsequent one are from John Rawls, *Political Liberalism*, expanded ed. (New York: Columbia University Press, 2005), p. xxxvii.

41. Rawls, *The Law of Peoples*, pp. 25, 125. For an elaboration of Rawls's views on public reason, see *Political Liberalism*, pp. xlviii–lviii, 212–54, 440–90. Also see his discussion of "deliberative rationality" in *A Theory of Justice* (Cambridge, MA: Harvard University Press, 1971), pp. 416–24.

42. George Klosko, *Democratic Procedures and Liberal Consensus* (New York: Oxford University Press, 2004), p. vii. Also see George Klosko, "Rawls's 'Political' Philosophy and American Democracy," *American Political Science Review* 87, no. 2 (June 1993): 348–59; Gerald N. Rosenberg, "Much Ado about Nothing? The Emptiness of Rights' Claims in the Twenty-First Century United States," in "Revisiting Rights," ed. Austin Sarat, special issue, *Studies in Law, Politics, and Society* (Bingley, UK: Emerald Group, 2009), pp. 1–41; Shaun P. Young, "Rawlsian Reasonableness: A Problematic Presumption?," *Canadian Journal of Political Science* 39, no. 1 (March 2006): 159–80.

43. Quotes in this paragraph are from Rawls, *The Law of Peoples*, pp. 74, 81.

44. Quotes in this paragraph are from Rawls, *Political Liberalism*, p. xxv.

45. Rawls, *Political Liberalism*, p. xl.

46. Quoted in Young, "Rawlsian Reasonableness," p. 162. Sounding that same theme, Rawls writes: "Peoples may often have final ends that require them to oppose one another without compromise. And if these ends are regarded as fundamental enough, and if one or more societies should refuse to accept the idea of the politically reasonable and the family of ideas that go with it, an impasse may arise between them, and war comes as it did between North and South in the American Civil War." Rawls, *The Law of Peoples*, p. 123.

47. Rawls, *The Law of Peoples*, p. 126.

48. Rawls, *The Law of Peoples*, pp. 98–105.

49. Harold J. Laski, *The Rise of European Liberalism: An Essay in Interpretation* (London: Allen & Unwin, 1947); C. B. Macpherson, *The Political Theory of Possessive Individualism: Hobbes to Locke* (New York: Oxford University Press, 1975).

50. F. A. Hayek, *The Constitution of Liberty: The Definitive Edition* (Chicago: University of Chicago Press, 2011), p. 57.

51. Hayek, *The Constitution of Liberty*, p. 148. See chap. 6 more generally. William Graham Sumner held similar views on liberty. See Robert C. Bannister, ed., *On Liberty, Society, and Politics: The Essential Essays of William Graham Sumner* (Indianapolis: Liberty Fund, 1992); William Graham Sumner, *The Forgotten Man and Other Essays* (New Haven, CT: Yale University Press, 1919).

52. Also see Brian Barry, *Why Social Justice Matters* (Malden, MA: Polity Press, 2005); Michael Walzer, *Spheres of Justice: A Defense of Pluralism and Equality* (New York: Basic Books, 1983). Kelly emphasizes the importance of promoting equal opportunity for progressive liberals in *Liberalism*.

53. Dworkin, *A Matter of Principle*, pp. 4, 179; Rawls, *A Theory of Justice*.

54. Dworkin, *A Matter of Principle*, p. 188.

55. For a discussion of how social scientists served the United States during the Cold War, see Joy Rohde, *Armed with Expertise: The Militarization of American Social Research during the Cold War* (Ithaca, NY: Cornell University Press, 2013); Mark Solovey and Hamilton Cravens, eds., *Cold War Science: Knowledge Production, Liberal Democracy, and Human Nature* (New York: Palgrave Macmillan, 2012).

56. Rawls's reluctance to embrace the state is on display in *The Law of Peoples,* where he purposefully avoids focusing on states, which are usually considered the principal actors in international politics, and instead talks mainly about peoples, which are usually given short shrift by international relations scholars.

57. See Gary Gerstle, *Liberty and Coercion: The Paradox of American Government from the Founding to the Present* (Princeton, NJ: Princeton University Press, 2015), which describes the growing power of the American interventionist state over time and how modus vivendi liberalism affects it in limited ways.

58. Michael McGerr, *A Fierce Discontent: The Rise and Fall of the Progressive Movement in America, 1870–1920* (New York: Oxford University Press, 2003); Charles Postel, *The Populist Vision* (New York: Oxford University Press, 2007); Stephen Skowronek, Stephen M. Engel, and Bruce Ackerman, eds., *The Progressives' Century: Political Reform, Constitutional Government, and the Modern American State* (New Haven, CT: Yale University Press, 2016); Alan Trachtenberg, *The Incorporation of America: Culture and Society in the Gilded Age* (New York: Hill and Wang, 1982); Robert H. Wiebe, *The Search for Order, 1877–1920* (New York: Hill and Wang, 1967).

59. David Burner, *Herbert Hoover: A Public Life* (New York: Knopf, 1978); Ellis W. Hawley, "Neo-institutional History and the Understanding of Herbert Hoover," in *Understanding Herbert Hoover: Ten Perspectives,* ed. Lee Nash (Stanford, CA: Hoover Institution Press, 1987), pp. 65–84; Glen Jeansonne, *Herbert Hoover: A Life* (New York: New American Library, 2016); Joan Hoff Wilson, *Herbert Hoover: Forgotten Progressive* (Long Grove, IL: Waveland Press, 1992).

60. Alan Brinkley, *The End of Reform: New Deal Liberalism in Recession and War* (New York: Knopf, 1995); Alan Brinkley, *Liberalism and Its Discontents* (Cambridge, MA: Harvard University Press, 1998), chap. 7; David Ciepley, *Liberalism in the Shadow of Totalitarianism* (Cambridge, MA: Harvard University Press, 2006); Richard Hofstadter, *The Age of Reform: From Bryan to F.D.R.* (New York: Knopf, 1981).

61. Rick Unger, "Who Is the Smallest Government Spender since Eisenhower? Would You Believe It's Barack Obama?," *Forbes,* May 24, 2012. Christopher Faricy writes that when he takes into account both direct and indirect government spending between 1967 and 2006, he finds "no statistically conclusive evidence that Democratic control of the federal government results in higher levels of total social spending." Christopher Faricy, "The Politics of Social Policy in America: The Causes and Effects of Indirect versus Direct Social Spending," *Journal of Politics* 73, no. 1 (January 2011): 74. Also see Robert X. Browning, "Presidents, Congress, and Policy Outcomes: U.S. Social Welfare Expenditures, 1949–77," *American Journal of Political Science* 29, no. 2 (May 1985): 197–216; Andrew C.

Pickering and James Rockey, "Ideology and the Size of US State Government," *Public Choice* 156, nos. 3/4 (September 2013): 443–65.

62. Quoted in Henry Olsen, "Here's How Ronald Reagan Would Fix the GOP's Health-Care Mess," *Washington Post,* June 22, 2017.

63. Libertarian Party, "2016 Platform," adopted May 2016, https://www.lp.org /platform/. The Libertarian Party's emphasis on "individual sovereignty" illustrates how deeply suspicious, if not hostile to, it is of the state. Sovereignty connotes who has supreme authority, which means that if individuals were "sovereign over their own lives," those individuals would have the ultimate authority to approve or disapprove every decision the state made. This situation would make it virtually impossible, by definition, to have a sovereign state that could effectively govern those individuals. Mariya Grinberg, "Indivisible Sovereignty: Delegation of Authority and Exit Option" (unpublished paper, University of Chicago, April 24, 2017).

64. Walter Lippmann, *Drift and Mastery: An Attempt to Diagnose the Current Unrest* (Englewood Cliffs, NJ: Prentice-Hall, 1961), p. 147.

65. John Dewey, *The Public and Its Promises: An Essay in Political Inquiry* (University Park: Pennsylvania State University Press, 2012), p. 94. See chapter 4 of that work for a more detailed discussion of this phenomenon. Also see Gillis J. Harp, *Positivist Republic: Auguste Comte and the Reconstruction of American Liberalism, 1865–1920* (University Park: Pennsylvania State University Press, 1995).

66. Britain was the first country to industrialize in a serious way, and the British state was deeply involved in managing its economy in the early stages of industrialization. See Peer Vries, *State, Economy and the Great Divergence: Great Britain and China, 1650s–1850s* (New York: Bloomsbury Academic, 2015). The American state played a similar role when the Industrial Revolution hit the United States with full force in the late nineteenth century. That state's influence, however, had grown in substantial ways throughout that century. See Brian Balogh, *A Government Out of Sight: The Mystery of National Authority in Nineteenth-Century America* (New York: Cambridge University Press, 2009).

67. Bernard E. Harcourt, *The Illusion of Free Markets: Punishment and the Myth of Natural Order* (Cambridge, MA: Harvard University Press, 2011).

68. See Daniel Deudney's discussion of how nuclear weapons increase "violence interdependence" among states, which has significant effects on both domestic and international politics. Deudney, *Bounding Power: Republican Security Theory from the Polis to the Global Village* (Princeton, NJ: Princeton University Press, 2007).

69. Jennifer Mittelstadt, *The Rise of the Military Welfare State* (Cambridge, MA: Harvard University Press, 2015).

70. Morris Janowitz, *Social Control of the Welfare State* (New York: Elsevier, 1976), pp. 37–38. Also see Ellis W. Hawley, *The Great War and the Search for a Modern Order: A History of the American People and Their Institutions, 1917–1933* (New York: St. Martin's Press, 1979).

71. Irwin F. Gellman, *The President and the Apprentice: Eisenhower and Nixon, 1952–1961* (New Haven, CT: Yale University Press, 2015), p. 478.

72. All quotes in this paragraph are from Mary L. Dudziak, *Cold War Civil Rights: Race and the Image of American Democracy* (Princeton, NJ: Princeton University Press, 2000), p. 12. Also see Thomas Borstelmann, *The Cold War and the Color Line: American Race Relations in the Global Arena* (Cambridge, MA: Harvard University Press, 2001).

73. Alexander Keyssar, *The Right to Vote: The Contested History of Democracy in the United States* (New York: Basic Books, 2000), p. xxi.

74. Theda Skocpol, *Protecting Soldiers and Mothers: The Political Origins of Social Policy in the United States* (Cambridge, MA: Harvard University Press, 1992), pp. 59–60.

75. Glenn C. Altschuler and Stuart M. Blumin, *The GI Bill: A New Deal for Veterans* (New York: Oxford University Press, 2009); Edward Humes, *Over Here: How the G.I. Bill Transformed the American Dream* (New York: Harcourt, 2006).

76. John Troyer, ed., *The Classical Utilitarians: Bentham and Mill* (Indianapolis: Hackett Publishing, 2003), p. 92.

77. Dewey, *Liberalism and Social Action*, p. 19.

78. David Armitage, *The Declaration of Independence: A Global History* (Cambridge, MA: Harvard University Press, 2008), p. 80. For more on Bentham's views on individual rights, see pp. 78–81, 173–86.

79. Troyer, *The Classical Utilitarians*, p. 92.

80. Boucoyannis, "The International Wanderings of a Liberal Idea," p. 709.

81. Quoted in Wolin, *Politics and Vision*, p. 298.

82. Quoted in E. H. Carr, *The Twenty Years' Crisis: An Introduction to the Study of International Relations* (London: Macmillan, 1962), p. 24.

83. Mill, *On Liberty*, p. 14.

84. There is a utilitarian theory in the international relations literature that is commonly referred to as bargaining theory. See James Fearon, "Rationalist Explanations for War," *International Organization* 49, no. 3 (Summer 1995): 379–414; Dan Reiter, "Exploring the Bargaining Model of War," *Perspectives on Politics* 1, no. 1 (March 2003): 27–43; Thomas C. Schelling, *The Strategy of Conflict* (Cambridge, MA: Harvard University Press, 1960), chaps. 2–3. This literature starts with the observation that war is an inefficient and costly way of settling disputes, and therefore it makes eminently good sense for states to settle their disagreements peacefully by negotiating a deal rather than fighting it out on the battlefield. Bargaining theorists maintain that three factors determine the likelihood that rival states will strike a deal rather than fight with each other. There must be "issue divisibility," which effectively means the differences between the two sides must be amenable to compromise. Both parties must be willing to give up something important to them in the bargain. Furthermore, each side must have a good understanding of the actual balance of power between them, so they know who will prevail if fighting breaks out. Finally, both actors must be able to credibly commit to the agreed bargain. Each side needs to be confident the other side will not

welch on the deal. This is not the place to evaluate bargaining theory, which, like all theories, has pluses and minuses. The key point is that bargaining theory, like utilitarianism, is not a liberal theory, and thus it falls outside the scope of this book.

85. Liberal idealism is sometimes referred to as the "new liberalism."

86. Alan Ryan refers to Dewey as a "mid-western T. H. Green." Alan Ryan, *John Dewey and the High Tide of American Liberalism* (New York: Norton, 1995), p. 12.

87. Jack Crittenden, *Beyond Individualism: Reconstituting the Liberal Self* (New York: Oxford University Press, 1992), p. 154. Also see Gerald F. Gaus, *The Modern Liberal Theory of Man* (New York: St. Martin's Press, 1983); Stephen Macedo, *Liberal Virtues: Citizenship, Virtue, and Community in Liberal Constitutionalism* (New York: Oxford University Press, 1990); Avital Simhony and D. Weinstein, eds., *The New Liberalism: Reconciling Liberty and Community* (New York: Cambridge University Press, 2001). It is worth noting that the communitarian critique of Rawlsian liberalism—which I call progressive liberalism—played a key role in fostering the growth of liberal idealist work in recent decades. See Simhony and Weinstein, *The New Liberalism.*

88. T. H. Green, *Prolegomena to Ethics*, 3rd ed. (Oxford: Clarendon Press, 1890), p. 311.

89. Dewey, *Liberalism and Social Action*, p. 25.

90. G. W. F. Hegel, *Hegel: Elements of the Philosophy of Right*, ed. Allen W. Wood (Cambridge: Cambridge University Press, 1991).

91. In direct contrast to the concept of natural rights, T. H. Green writes: "No one therefore can have a right except (1) as a member of a society, and (2) of a society in which some common good is recognized by the members of the society as their own ideal good, as that which should be for each of them." Green, *Lectures on the Principles of Political Obligation* (Ann Arbor: University of Michigan Press, 1967), p. 45. For more on this point, see Simhony and Weinstein, *The New Liberalism*, p. 16.

92. Liberal idealists effectively believe that liberalism and nationalism can be integrated into a single coherent ideology. My argument is that they are separate isms with different core logics, and thus they cannot be unified. Nevertheless, they can coexist within states, although there is always the possibility that those two isms will come into conflict with each other.

93. The Bosanquet quote is from Jeanne Morefield, *Covenants without Swords: Idealist Liberalism and the Spirit of Empire* (Princeton, NJ: Princeton University Press, 2005), p. 46. The Green quote is from his *Lectures on the Principles of Political Obligation*, p. 175. Regarding Green's views on "cosmopolitan nationalism," see Duncan Bell and Casper Sylvest, "International Society in Victorian Political Thought: T. H. Green, Herbert Spencer and Henry Sidgwick," *Modern Intellectual History* 3, no. 2 (August 2006): 220–21.

94. Carr, *The Twenty Years' Crisis*, p. 46.

95. Erez Manela, *The Wilsonian Moment: Self-Determination and the International Origins of Anticolonial Nationalism* (New York: Oxford University Press, 2007).

96. John Dewey, "Nationalizing Education," in *John Dewey: The Middle Works, 1899–1924*, vol. 10 (Carbondale: Southern Illinois University Press, 1980), p. 202. For a discussion of how nationalism was viewed in the latter part of the nineteenth century and early twentieth century, see Mark Mazower, *Governing the World: The History of an Idea, 1815 to the Present* (New York: Penguin Books, 2012), pp. 48–54, 60–67; Casper Sylvest, "James Bryce and the Two Faces of Nationalism," in *British International Thinkers from Hobbes to Namier*, ed. Ian Hall and Lisa Hill (New York: Palgrave Macmillan, 2009), pp. 161–79.

97. Dewey, "Nationalizing Education," p. 203; Alfred E. Zimmern, *Nationality and Government with Other War-Time Essays* (New York: Robert M. McBride, 1918), pp. 61–86. That chapter is based on a speech Zimmern gave in June 1915.

98. Zimmern, *Nationality and Government with Other War-Time Essays*, p. 100.

99. Hegel, *Hegel: Elements of the Philosophy of Right*, p. 282.

100. Liberal idealism's ambivalence toward the state is clearly reflected in Green, *Lectures on the Principles of Political Obligation*. Another reason British theorists could not fully embrace Hegel was the growing Anglo-German antagonism in the late nineteenth and early twentieth centuries, which culminated in World War I. See Morefield, *Covenants without Swords*, pp. 57–72.

101. Green, *Lectures on the Principles of Political Obligation*, p. 2.

102. Green, *Prolegomena to Ethics*, p. 388.

103. Green, *Lectures on the Principles of Political Obligation*, p. 29.

104. Green, *Prolegomena to Ethics*, p. 311.

105. L. T. Hobhouse, *Liberalism* (London: Butterworth, 1911), p. 136.

106. Green, *Prolegomena to Ethics*, p. 311.

107. A. D. Lindsay, "Introduction," in Green, *Lectures on the Principles of Political Obligation*, p. vi.

108. Dewey, *Liberalism and Social Action*, p. 70.

109. Dewey, *Liberalism and Social Action*, p. 69.

110. Dewey, *Liberalism and Social Action*, p. 65.

111. Dewey, *Liberalism and Social Action*, pp. 72, 73, 86, 91.

112. On Murray and Zimmern, see Morefield, *Covenants without Swords*.

113. Zimmern, *Nationality and Government with Other War-Time Essays*, p. 61.

114. Morefield, *Covenants without Swords*, p. 156.

Chapter 4. Cracks in the Liberal Edifice

1. Communitarians have been arch critics of liberalism's assumption that humans are naturally "unencumbered" individuals, to use Michael Sandel's wording. For a sampling of the debate between communitarians and liberals on this and other matters, see Shlomo Avineri and Avner de-Shalit, *Communitarianism and Individualism* (New York: Oxford University Press, 2011). The Sandel quote is from p. 18.

2. A *nation* is an abstract concept and cannot act, but I use the term as a shorthand reference for its members, especially its elites, who do have agency and are capable of acting to advance their political goals, such as statehood. The same logic applies when I use the term *state*, in which case it is the political leaders who have agency.

3. See Ernest Gellner, *Nations and Nationalism* (Ithaca, NY: Cornell University Press, 1983), p. 1. My definition of nationalism is similar to that of many scholars. See, for example, John Breuilly, *Nationalism and the State* (Chicago: University of Chicago Press, 1985), pp. 1–3; Ernst B. Haas, "What Is Nationalism and Why Should We Study It?," *International Organization* 40, no. 3 (Summer 1986): 726; E. J. Hobsbawm, *Nations and Nationalism since 1780: Programme, Myth, Reality* (New York: Cambridge University Press, 1991), p. 9; Anthony D. Smith, *Nations and Nationalism in a Global Era* (Malden, MA: Polity Press, 1995), pp. 55, 150.

4. Benedict Anderson, *Imagined Communities: Reflections on the Origin and Spread of Nationalism* (London: Verso, 1990); David A. Bell, *The Cult of the Nation in France: Inventing Nationalism, 1680–1800* (Cambridge, MA: Harvard University Press, 2001); William H. Sewell Jr., "The French Revolution and the Emergence of the Nation Form," in *Revolutionary Currents: Nation Building in the Transatlantic World*, ed. Michael A. Morrison and Melinda Zook (Lanham, MD: Rowman and Littlefield, 2004), pp. 91–125.

5. Some of the large groups that preceded the nation were rather well defined and quite easily morphed into nations. For example, the Dutch, the English, the French, the Poles, and the Russians had developed a distinct identity before each group became a nation, which made the transition to nationhood relatively straightforward. To put the matter in Ronald Suny's language, they went from "cultural or ethnic awareness" to "full-blown political nationalism—that is, an active commitment to realizing a national agenda." Ronald G. Suny, *The Revenge of the Past: Nationalism, Revolution, and the Collapse of the Soviet Union* (Stanford, CA: Stanford University Press, 1993), p. 48. There are other cases, however, where the links between the nations that eventually emerged and their predecessors are more tenuous. Examples include Azerbaijanis, Belorussians, Italians, and Lithuanians, who did not have that particular identity before they became nations. Other local and social identities were key for them, which invariably meant that the state had to go to great lengths to fashion them into nations. Some key works dealing with the links between nations and their predecessors include John Armstrong, *Nations before Nationalism* (Chapel Hill: University of North Carolina Press, 1982); Patrick J. Geary, *The Myth of Nations: The Medieval Origins of Europe* (Princeton, NJ: Princeton University Press, 2003); Philip S. Gorski, "The Mosaic Moment: An Early Modernist Critique of Modernist Theories of Nationalism," *American Journal of Sociology* 105, no. 5 (March 2000): 1428–68; Anthony W. Marx, *Faith in Nation: Exclusionary Origins of Nationalism* (New York: Oxford University Press, 2003); Miroslav Hroch, *European Nations: Explaining Their Formation*, trans. Karolina Graham (New York: Verso, 2015), chap. 3; Philip G. Roeder, *Where Nation-States*

Come From: Institutional Change in the Age of Nationalism (Princeton, NJ: Princeton University Press, 2007); Anthony D. Smith, *The Ethnic Origins of Nations* (New York: Basil Blackwell, 1989).

6. Anderson, *Imagined Communities*.

7. On how boundaries between social groups have become less fluid and harder to penetrate with the coming of nationalism, see Fredrik Barth, ed., *Ethnic Groups and Boundaries: The Social Organization of Culture Difference* (Long Grove, IL: Waveland Press, 1998). James Scott writes about the "utter plasticity of social structure" outside nation-states. In that world, "group boundaries are porous and identities are flexible." James Scott, *The Art of Not Being Governed: An Anarchist History of Upland Southeast Asia* (New Haven, CT: Yale University Press, 2009), pp. 219, 249.

8. For a discussion of the close links between nationalism and "claims for the equality and liberty of all citizens," see Dominique Schnapper, "Citizenship and National Identity in Europe," *Nations and Nationalism* 8, no. 1 (January 2002): 1–14. The quote is from p. 2.

9. Anderson, *Imagined Communities*, p. 16.

10. Geary, *The Myth of Nations*, p. 118. He also writes: "With the constant shifting of allegiances, intermarriages, transformations, and appropriations, it appears that all that remained constant were names, and these were vessels that could hold different contents at different times" (ibid.). Also see Norman Davies, *Vanished Kingdoms: The Rise and Fall of States and Nations* (New York: Penguin Books, 2011), especially chaps. 1–6.

11. One might think the Roman Empire contradicts my claim, but this would be wrong. The Roman Empire was a sprawling political entity that was home to numerous social groups. It was hardly a unified culture. "Roman," as Geary notes, was not a "primary self-identifier for the millions of people who inhabited, permanently or temporarily, the Roman Empire. Rather than sharing a national or ethnic identity, individuals were more likely to feel a primary attachment to class, occupation, or city." Indeed, "in the pluralistic religious and cultural tradition of Rome, the central state had never demanded exclusive adherence to Roman values." Geary, *The Myth of Nations*, pp. 64, 67. The primary loyalty of the inhabitants of the Roman Empire was to their particular social group, which invariably occupied a particular slice of territory within the empire. Thus, it is no surprise that the concept of "Roman identity" virtually disappeared from Europe in the Middle Ages, save for the inhabitants of the city of Rome. Of course, there was a Holy Roman Empire from 962 to 1806, but like its predecessor, it comprised numerous social groups, and hardly any of the people who came under its sway identified themselves as Romans. It is worth noting that nationalism played the key role in destroying what remained of that loosely knit empire in the early nineteenth century.

12. Patrick Geary writes, for example, "Among the free citizens of the [Roman] Empire, the gulfs separating the elite and the masses of the population were enormous," a situation that did not change after the collapse of the empire. Geary, *The Myth of Nations*, p. 66. In addition to the two dominant classes in pre-nationalist

Europe—the aristocracy and the peasantry—there was a small bourgeoisie and a small working class, although they were largely concentrated in England and France. Neither the peasantry nor the aristocracy had a powerful sense it was part of a large social group, much less a distinct nation. Peasants tended to think in local terms and not conceive of themselves as part of an extended family that spread across a large expanse of territory. They usually spoke in local dialects and knew little about other peasants who lived a few days' travel from them. A peasant living in Prussia, for example, was not likely to think of himself as a Prussian peasant and compare himself with French or Polish peasants. His identity was more likely to be wrapped up in comparisons with his immediate neighbors. Aristocrats were remarkably cosmopolitan and had nothing like a national identity. This point is illustrated by looking at marriages among the European nobility, which were often between individuals from different countries. And consider that Frederick the Great of Prussia greatly admired French culture and preferred speaking French rather than German. Tim Blanning, *Frederick the Great: King of Prussia* (New York: Random House, 2016), pp. 342–46, 352–53, 357–61, 444. In short, "the idea that the aristocracy belonged to the same culture as the peasants must have seemed abominable to the former and incomprehensible to the latter before nationalism." Thomas H. Eriksen, *Ethnicity and Nationalism: Anthropological Perspectives,* 3rd ed. (London: Pluto Press, 2010), p. 123.

13. Bell, *The Cult of the Nation in France,* p. 6.

14. Karl Marx and Friedrich Engels, "Manifesto of the Communist Party," in *The Marx-Engels Reader,* ed. Robert C. Ticker (New York: Norton, 1979), pp. 331–62. Marx and Engels write, "working men have no country," that industrialization and the attendant exploitation of the average worker "has stripped him of every trace of national character," and thus workers "have no interests separate and apart from those of the proletariat as a whole" (pp. 344–45, 350).

15. Michael Howard, *War in European History* (New York: Oxford University Press, 1979), p. 110.

16. The terms *core nation* and *minority nation* are from Harris Mylonas, *The Politics of Nation-Building: Making Co-nationals, Refugees, and Minorities* (New York: Cambridge University Press, 2012).

17. There is always the danger with multinational states that one or more of the minor nations will be committed to breaking away and forming their own nation-states. In such unstable states, it makes little sense to talk about a common national identity at the level of the state.

18. Alfred Stepan, Juan J. Linz, and Yogendra Yadav, *Crafting State-Nations: India and Other Multinational Democracies* (Baltimore: Johns Hopkins University Press, 2011), p. 38. Stepan, Linz, and Yadav do not employ the terms *thick* and *thin cultures,* but instead use the terms *state-nation* and *nation-state,* respectively. Also see Sener Akturk, *Regimes of Ethnicity and Nationhood in Germany, Russia, and Turkey* (New York: Cambridge University Press, 2012).

19. Sigmund Freud, *Civilization and Its Discontents,* ed. and trans. James Strachey (New York: Norton, 1961), p. 61.

20. Quoted in Roeder, *Where Nation-States Come From*, p. 29.

21. Max Weber, *Economy and Society: An Outline of Interpretive Sociology*, vol. 1, ed. Guenther Roth and Claus Wittich (Berkeley: University of California Press, 1978), p. 389.

22. Walker Connor, "A Nation Is a Nation, Is a State, Is an Ethnic Group Is a. . . ." *Ethnic and Racial Studies* 1, no. 4 (October 1978): 379.

23. Hobsbawm writes, "Any sufficiently large body of people whose members regard themselves as members of a 'nation,' will be treated as such." Hobsbawm, *Nations and Nationalism since 1780*, p. 8. Hugh Seton-Watson writes, "A nation exists when a significant number of people in a community consider themselves to form a nation, or behave as if they formed one." Seton-Watson, *Nations and States: An Enquiry into the Origins of Nations and the Politics of Nationalism* (Boulder, CO: Westview Press, 1977), p. 5.

24. Scott, *The Art of Not Being Governed*, p. 227. Also see Keith A. Darden, *Resisting Occupation in Eurasia* (New York: Cambridge University Press, forthcoming); Adrian Hastings, *The Construction of Nationhood: Ethnicity, Religion and Nationalism* (New York: Cambridge University Press, 1997).

25. This chauvinism is in good part a consequence of the sense of oneness that characterizes nations. In particular, the tight bonds among nationals and the firm boundaries between nations promote narrow-mindedness. Chauvinism is less likely in a world where identities are more flexible and people can envision themselves moving rather easily across the boundaries that separate social groups. Greater social fluidity, in short, tends to enhance tolerance. This is not to say, however, that the large social groups that existed before the coming of nations were paragons of tolerance, because they were not. But they were more tolerant and less chauvinistic than nations, where the bonds among members are tight and identities are difficult to change, considerations that lend themselves to seeing the "other" as alien and inferior, and even evil. Polish-Jewish relations provide a good example of this phenomenon at work. Poland, which was a tolerant place by European standards before the rise of nationalism, was a haven for Jews during the Middle Ages. Some estimate that roughly 80 percent of world Jewry lived in Poland by the middle of the sixteenth century, and those Jews did well for themselves by the standards of the time. This situation changed dramatically in the nineteenth and twentieth centuries as nationalism swept across Europe, and Poland became one of the most anti-Semitic countries in that region. See Brian Porter, *When Nationalism Began to Hate: Imagining Modern Politics in Nineteenth-Century Poland* (New York: Oxford University Press, 2000). This general pattern was not restricted to Poland. See Shmuel Almog, *Nationalism and Antisemitism in Modern Europe, 1815–1945* (Elmsford, NY: Pergamon Press, 1990); Timothy Snyder, *The Reconstruction of Nations: Poland, Ukraine, Lithuania, Belarus, 1569–1999* (New Haven, CT: Yale University Press, 2004).

26. Quoted in Anatol Lieven, *America Right or Wrong: An Anatomy of American Nationalism* (New York: Oxford University Press, 2004), p. 34.

27. Quoted in Ronald Hyam, *Britain's Imperial Century, 1815–1914: A Study of Empire and Expansion*, 2nd ed. (London: Macmillan, 1993), p. 89.

28. Quoted in Joan Beaumont and Matthew Jordan, *Australia and the World: A Festschrift for Neville Meaney* (Sydney, Australia: Sydney University Press, 2013), p. 276.

29. Albright made this statement on NBC's *Today* show on February 19, 1998.

30. Reinhold Niebuhr, *The Irony of American History* (Chicago: University of Chicago Press, 2008), p. 71.

31. This is surely why the political philosopher John Dunn described nationalism as "the starkest political shame of the twentieth century, the deepest, most intractable and yet most unanticipated blot on the history of the world since the year 1900." John Dunn, *Western Political Theory in the Face of the Future*, 2nd ed. (New York: Cambridge University Press, 1993), p. 59.

32. Stephen Van Evera, "Hypotheses on Nationalism and War," *International Security* 18, no. 4 (Spring 1994): 27.

33. Geary, *The Myth of Nations*, p. 15. Two other useful sources on this phenomenon are Christopher B. Krebs, *A Most Dangerous Book: Tacitus's Germania from the Roman Empire to the Third Reich* (New York: Norton, 2011); and Shlomo Sand, *The Invention of the Jewish People*, trans. Yael Lotan (London: Verso, 2009).

34. Ernest Renan, "What Is a Nation?," in *On the Nation and the "Jewish People,"* ed. Shlomo Sand, trans. David Fernbach (London: Verso, 2010), p. 45.

35. C. Burak Kadercan, "Politics of Survival, Nationalism, and War for Territory: 1648–2003" (PhD diss., University of Chicago, 2011); Tamar Meisels, *Territorial Rights*, 2nd ed. (Dordrecht, The Netherlands: Springer, 2009); David Miller, *Citizenship and National Identity* (Malden, MA: Polity Press, 2005); Margaret Moore, *The Ethics of Nationalism* (New York: Oxford University Press, 2001); Peter Sahlins, *Boundaries: The Making of France and Spain in the Pyrenees* (Berkeley: University of California Press, 1991).

36. During the 2017 dispute between China and India over thirty-four square miles of land in the Himalayan Mountains, China's president, Xi Jinping, said: "We will never permit anybody, any organization, any political party to split off any piece of Chinese territory from China at any time or in any form. . . . Nobody should nurse any hope that we will swallow the bitter fruit of harm to our national sovereignty, security and development interests." Quoted in Chris Buckley and Ellen Barry, "China Tells India That It Won't Back Down in Border Dispute," *New York Times*, August 4, 2017. This is not to say that all the territory a nation occupies or seeks to conquer is holy land. There are exceptions. China, for example, has settled a number of territorial disputes with its neighbors, and in each case China made compromises that involved surrendering territory to other countries. See M. Taylor Fravel, *Strong Borders, Secure Nation: Cooperation and Conflict in China's Territorial Disputes* (Princeton, NJ: Princeton University Press, 2008). There are large swaths of territory, however, that China would never surrender willingly, because they are considered sacred lands that rightfully belong to the Chinese nation.

37. Kadercan, "Politics of Survival, Nationalism, and War for Territory." Of course, nations still care about territory for practical reasons, although controlling territory is not as important today for economic and security reasons as it was before the coming of the Industrial Revolution and nuclear weapons. But ironically, people in the age of nationalism appear to care more about territory than did their predecessors, because they care greatly about their homeland at a deep emotional level (p. 21).

38. As Mariya Grinberg notes, although the concept of sovereignty is invariably linked with the state, it can be applied to other political forms as well. The key is that it can be applied only to the highest-level forms of political organization in the international system, be they empires, city-states, or whatever. The discussion here, however, is limited to states, because the focus is on nationalism, which is identified with nation-states. Grinberg, "Indivisible Sovereignty: Delegation of Authority and Exit Option" (unpublished paper, University of Chicago, April 24, 2017).

39. Robert Jackson, *Sovereignty: Evolution of an Idea* (Malden, MA: Polity Press, 2007), p. 6.

40. Jackson, *Sovereignty*, p. 93.

41. Quoted in Bell, *The Cult of the Nation in France*, p. 59.

42. Jackson, *Sovereignty*, p. 104.

43. Carl Schmitt, *Political Theology: Four Chapters on the Concept of Sovereignty*, trans. George Schwab (Cambridge, MA: MIT Press, 1988), pp. 5–15.

44. Bernard Yack, "Popular Sovereignty and Nationalism," *Political Theory* 29, no. 4 (August 2001): 518.

45. This democratic impulse built into nationalism is reflected in Renan's famous comment: "The existence of a nation is, if you will pardon me the metaphor, a daily plebiscite." Renan, "What Is a Nation?," p. 64. Also see Schnapper, "Citizenship and National Identity in Europe"; Liah Greenfield, *Nationalism: Five Roads to Modernity* (Cambridge, MA: Harvard University Press, 1992); and Yack, "Popular Sovereignty and Nationalism." Greenfield writes on p. 10: "The location of sovereignty within the people and the recognition of the fundamental equality among its various strata, which constitute the essence of the modern national idea, are at the same time the basic tenets of democracy. Democracy was born with the sense of nationality. The two are inherently linked, and neither can be fully understood apart from this connection. Nationalism was the form in which democracy appeared in the world, contained in the idea of the nation as a butterfly in a cocoon. Originally, nationalism developed as democracy; where the conditions of such original development persisted, the identity between the two was maintained."

46. Maximilien Robespierre, "Report on the Principles of Political Morality," *French Revolution and Napoleon*, http://www.indiana.edu/~b356/texts/polit-moral.html.

47. Russell Hardin, *One for All: The Logic of Group Conflict* (Princeton, NJ: Princeton University Press, 1997); Mark Pagel, *Wired for Culture: Origins of the Human Social Mind* (New York: Norton, 2012).

48. Bernard Yack, *Nationalism and the Moral Psychology of Community* (Chicago: University of Chicago Press, 2012).

49. Renan, "What Is a Nation?," p. 63.

50. Nationalism is sometimes said to be a substitute for religion, which began losing influence in Europe after the Thirty Years' War ended in 1648. This process has accelerated over the ensuing centuries. This perspective is wrong, however. Although religion's influence has waned over this long period, it cetainly has not disappeared. More importantly, religion is effectively an element of national culture, where it has the potential to act as a powerful unifying force for group members. Ernest Barker, *Christianity and Nationality: Being the Burge Memorial Lecture for the Year 1927* (Oxford: Clarendon Press, 1927), p. 31. Other works that show how religion can act as a force multiplier for nationalism include Samuel P. Huntington, *Who Are We? The Challenges to American National Identity* (New York: Simon & Schuster, 2005); and Marx, *Faith in Nation*.

51. Charles Tilly, *Coercion, Capital, and European States, AD 990–1992* (Cambridge, MA: Blackwell, 1992), p. 1.

52. Perry Anderson, *Lineages of the Absolutist State* (London: Verso, 1980), p. 20.

53. Andreas Osiander, *Before the State: Systemic Political Change in the West from the Greeks to the French Revolution* (New York: Oxford University Press, 2007), p. 5.

54. Sewell, "The French Revolution and the Emergence of the Nation Form," p. 98.

55. Jackson, *Sovereignty*, p. 32.

56. Joseph R. Strayer and Dana C. Munro, *The Middle Ages: 395–1500* (New York: Appleton-Century-Crofts, 1942), pp. 113, 270.

57. On the limits of power projection over long distances, see Scott, *The Art of Not Being Governed*, chaps. 1–2; and David Stasavage, "When Distance Mattered: Geographic Scale and the Development of European Representative Assemblies," *American Political Science Review* 104, no. 4 (November 2010): 625–43.

58. Yael Tamir, *Liberal Nationalism* (Princeton, NJ: Princeton University Press, 1993), pp. xiv, 74.

59. Eugen Weber, *Peasants into Frenchmen* (Stanford, CA: Stanford University Press, 1976).

60. Walker Connor, "Nation-Building or Nation-Destroying?," *World Politics* 24, no. 3 (April 1972): 319–55.

61. It is clear from Scott's *The Art of Not Being Governed* that a similar logic applies to groups that live outside states and are trying to avoid being incorporated into them. He writes: "Where they could . . . all states in the region have tried to bring such peoples under their routine administration, to encourage and, more rarely, to insist upon linguistic, cultural, and religious alignment with the majority population at the state core" (p. 12). The state's reach is so great today that very few groups continue to live outside a state.

62. Benjamin A. Valentino, *Final Solutions: Mass Killing and Genocide in the 20th Century* (Ithaca, NY: Cornell University Press, 2004), pp. 157–66.

63. Partha Chatterjee, *The Nation and Its Fragments: Colonial and Postcolonial Histories* (Princeton, NJ: Princeton University Press, 1993); Partha Chatterjee, *The*

Black Hole of Empire: History of a Global Practice of Power (Princeton, NJ: Princeton University Press, 2012).

64. Ernest Gellner, *Nations and Nationalism* (Ithaca, NY: Cornell University Press, 1983), p. 34.

65. The economic logic described in the previous paragraph has important military consequences. Since wealth is one of the two main building blocks of military power, any measures taken to grow the economy contribute to building a more powerful military. See John J. Mearsheimer, *The Tragedy of Great Power Politics*, updated ed. (New York: Norton, 2014), chap. 3.

66. Barry R. Posen, "Nationalism, the Mass Army, and Military Power," *International Security* 18, no. 2 (Fall 1993): 85.

67. The negative consequences that flow from having a multinational state in which the constituent groups are poorly integrated are reflected in the performance of the Austro-Hungarian military in the late nineteenth and early twentieth centuries. See Gunther E. Rothenberg, *The Army of Francis Joseph* (West Lafayette, IN: Purdue University Press, 1998), p. 108; Spencer C. Tucker, *The European Powers in the First World War: An Encyclopedia* (New York: Garland Publishing, 1996), p. 86. Also see Posen, "Nationalism, the Mass Army, and Military Power."

68. David Bell explains how nationalism made it much easier for French leaders to mobilize their populations during the Seven Years' War (1756–63) and the French Revolutionary and Napoleonic Wars (1792–1815) than was the case in wars fought during the pre-national era. Bell, *The Cult of the Nation in France*, chap. 3; David A. Bell, *The First Total War: Napoleon's Europe and the Birth of Warfare as We Knew It* (Boston: Houghton Mifflin, 2007), chaps. 4, 6, 7. Also see Michael Howard, *War in European History* (New York: Oxford University Press, 2009), chap. 6.

69. Geoffrey Best, *War and Society in Revolutionary Europe, 1770–1870* (London: Fontana Paperbacks, 1982), p. 30.

70. Quoted in J. F. C. Fuller, *Conduct of War: 1789–1961* (London: Eyre and Spottiswoode, 1961), p. 46. Also see Peter Paret, "Nationalism and the Sense of Military Obligation," in *Understanding War: Essays on Clausewitz and the History of Military Power*, ed. Peter Paret (Princeton, NJ: Princeton University Press, 1993), pp. 39–52.

71. Carl von Clausewitz, *On War*, ed. and trans. Michael Howard and Peter Paret (Princeton, NJ: Princeton University Press, 1976), p. 592.

72. Posen, "Nationalism, the Mass Army, and Military Power."

73. Marx, *Faith in Nation*, p. 9.

74. James C. Scott, *Seeing Like a State: How Certain Schemes to Improve the Human Condition Have Failed* (New Haven, CT: Yale University Press, 1998), pp. 72, 78.

75. Judith N. Shklar, *Political Thought and Political Thinkers*, ed. Stanley Hoffmann (Chicago: University of Chicago Press, 1998), p. 4. Also see Markus Fischer, "The Liberal Peace: Ethical, Historical, and Philosophical Aspects" (BCSIA Discussion Paper 2000-07, Kennedy School of Government, Harvard University, April 2000), pp. 22–27, 56.

76. Arch Puddington and Tyler Roylance, "Populists and Autocrats: The Dual Threat to Global Democracy," in *Freedom in the World, 2017* (Washington, DC: Freedom House, 2017), p. 4.

77. Jeanne Morefield, *Covenants without Swords: Idealist Liberalism and the Spirit of Empire* (Princeton, NJ: Princeton University Press, 2005), p. 208.

78. Stephen Holmes, *Passions and Constraint: On the Theory of Liberal Democracy* (Chicago: University of Chicago Press, 1995), p. 39.

79. Will Kymlicka, *Multicultural Citizenship: A Liberal Theory of Minority Rights* (New York: Oxford University Press, 1995), pp. 90–91.

80. Louis Hartz, *The Liberal Tradition in America: An Interpretation of American Political Thought since the Revolution* (New York: Harcourt Brace, 1955); Gunner Myrdal, *An American Dilemma: The Negro Problem and Modern Democracy*, 2 vols. (New Brunswick, NJ: Transaction Publishers, 1995, 1996); Alexis de Tocqueville, *Democracy in America and Two Essays on America*, ed. Isaac Kramnick, trans. Gerald Bevan (New York: Penguin, 2003). For a discussion of the parallels between these two books and Hartz's *The Liberal Tradition in America*, see Rogers M. Smith, *Civic Ideals: Conflicting Visions of Citizenship in U.S. History* (New Haven, CT: Yale University Press, 1997), introduction and chap. 1.

81. Smith, *Civic Ideals*, p. 14.

82. Smith, *Civic Ideals*, p. 6.

83. Smith, *Civic Ideals*, p. 9.

84. Smith, *Civic Ideals*, pp. 9–12, 38–39.

85. Huntington, *Who Are We?*; Lieven, *America Right or Wrong*.

86. All the quotes in this paragraph are from David Armitage, "The Declaration of Independence: The Words Heard around the World," *Wall Street Journal*, July 3, 2014. For an elaboration on these points, see David Armitage, *The Declaration of Independence: A Global History* (Cambridge, MA: Harvard University Press, 2008).

87. This perspective is captured in Hans Kohn, *The Idea of Nationalism* (New York: Macmillan, 1945); and John Plamenatz, "Two Types of Nationalism," in *Nationalism: The Nature and Evolution of an Idea*, ed. Eugene Kamenka (London: Edward Arnold, 1976), pp. 22–36.

88. See Gregory Jusdanis, *The Necessary Nation* (Princeton, NJ: Princeton University Press, 2001), chap. 5; Taras Kuzio, "The Myth of the Civic State: A Critical Survey of Hans Kohn's Framework for Understanding Nationalism," *Ethnic and Racial Studies* 25, no. 1 (January 2002): 20–39; Marx, *Faith in Nation*, pp. 113–17; Smith, *Civic Ideals*; Ken Wolf, "Hans Kohn's Liberal Nationalism: The Historian as Prophet," *Journal of the History of Ideas* 37, no. 4 (October–December 1976): 651–72; Bernard Yack, "The Myth of the Civic Nation," *Critical Review* 10, no. 2 (Spring 1996): 193–211.

89. On Israel, see Richard Falk and Virginia Tilley, "Israeli Practices toward the Palestinian People and the Question of Apartheid," *Palestine and the Israeli Occupation*, Issue No. 1 (Beirut: United Nations, 2017); Yitzhak Laor, *The Myths of Liberal*

Zionism (New York: Verso, 2009); Gideon Levy, "Israel's Minister of Truth," *Haaretz*, September 2, 2017; Yakov M. Rabkin, *What Is Modern Israel?*, trans. Fred A. Reed (London: Pluto Press, 2016). Regarding India, see Sumit Ganguly and Rajan Menon, "Democracy à la Modi," *National Interest*, no. 153 (January/February 2018), pp. 12–24; Christopher Jaffrelot, *The Hindu Nationalist Movement in India* (New York: Columbia University Press, 1998); Pankaj Mishra, "Narendra Modi and the New Face of India," *Guardian*, May 16, 2014; Martha C. Nussbaum, *The Clash Within: Democracy, Violence, and India's Future* (Cambridge, MA: Harvard University Press, 2009).

90. For a good example of the extent to which liberalism treats individuals as utility maximizers, see S. M. Amadae, *Rationalizing Capitalist Democracy: The Cold War Origins of Rational Choice Liberalism* (Chicago: University of Chicago Press, 2003).

91. Although they are not concerned with nationalism per se, Christopher H. Achen and Larry M. Bartels make an argument about the workings of American politics that dovetails with my claims about the relationship between liberalism and nationalism. Specifically, they argue in *Democracy for Realists: Why Elections Do Not Produce Responsive Government* (Princeton, NJ: Princeton University Press, 2016) that the voting behavior of Americans can best be explained by their social and group identities, not by how each individual assesses a politician's position on the issues he cares about most.

92. Most liberal theorists acknowledge that individuals have important social ties. John Rawls, for example, writes: "Each person finds himself placed at birth in some particular position in some particular society, and the nature of his position materially affects his life prospects." John Rawls, *A Theory of Justice* (Cambridge, MA: Harvard University Press, 1971), p. 13. Moreover, in *The Law of Peoples: With "The Idea of Public Reason Revisited"* (Cambridge, MA: Harvard University Press, 1999), Rawls focuses directly on peoples, which is a synonym for nations. Still, much of the analysis in *The Law of Peoples* focuses on the individual, which is certainly the focus of attention in his other two seminal book, *A Theory of Justice* and *Political Liberalism*, expanded ed. (New York: Columbia University Press, 2005). Nevertheless, a theory based on individualism cannot at the same time emphasize that people are profoundly social, because the two perspectives are at odds with each other. In fact, Rawls has been criticized on this point. For example, see Andrew Kuper, "Rawlsian Global Justice: Beyond the Law of Peoples to a Cosmopolitan Law of Persons," *Political Theory* 28, no. 5 (October 2000): 640–74; Thomas W. Pogge, "The Incoherence between Rawls's Theories of Justice," *Fordham Law Review* 72, no. 5 (April 2004): 1739–59. For an overview of the debate between Rawls's critics and defenders, see Gillian Brock, *Global Justice: A Cosmopolitan Account* (New York: Oxford University Press, 2009), chap. 2.

93. See Paul W. Kahn, *Putting Liberalism in Its Place* (Princeton, NJ: Princeton University Press, 2005).

94. Uday Singh Mehta, *Liberalism and Empire: A Study in Nineteenth-Century British Liberal Thought* (Chicago: University of Chicago Press, 1999), pp. 117–18.

95. It reads: "The rights and liberties asserted and claimed in the said declaration are the true, ancient and indubitable rights and liberties of the people of this kingdom." "English Bill of Rights 1689," The Avalon Project at the Yale Law School, http://avalon.law.yale.edu/17th_century/england.asp.

96. Hartz, *The Liberal Tradition in America*; Rawls, *The Law of Peoples*.

97. See Otto Hintze, "The Formation of States and Constitutional Development: A Study in History and Politics," and "Military Organization and the Organization of the State," in *The Historical Essays of Otto Hintze*, ed. Felix Gilbert (New York: Oxford University Press, 1975), pp. 157–215; Harold D. Lasswell, "The Garrison State," *American Journal of Sociology* 46, no. 4 (January 1941): 455–68.

98. Hannah Arendt, *The Origins of Totalitarianism* (San Diego: Harcourt, 1973), pp. 291–92.

99. Arendt, *The Origins of Totalitarianism*, p. 300.

100. Arendt, *The Origins of Totalitarianism*, pp. 269, 299.

101. Lynn Hunt calls this "the Paradox of Self-Evidence." She writes, "If equality of rights is so self-evident, then why did this assertion have to [be] made and why was it only made in specific times and places? How can human rights be universal if they are not universally recognized?" Hunt, *Inventing Human Rights: A History* (New York: Norton, 2007), pp. 19–20.

102. H. L. A. Hart, "Rawls on Liberty and Its Priority," in *Essays in Jurisprudence and Philosophy* (Oxford: Clarendon Press, 1983), pp. 223–47.

103. John Rawls, *Political Liberalism*, expanded ed. (New York: Columbia University Press, 2005), p. 162.

104. Contrast the views of Jeremy Waldron, *The Harm in Hate Speech* (Cambridge, MA: Harvard University Press, 2012) with Michael W. McConnell's review of that book: "You Can't Say That: A Legal Philosopher Urges Americans to Punish Hate Speech," *New York Times*, June 24, 2012; and John Paul Stevens's review of the book: "Should Hate Speech Be Outlawed?," *New York Review of Books*, June 7, 2012, pp. 18–22.

105. John Gray, *Two Faces of Liberalism* (New York: New Press, 2000), p. 82.

106. John Stuart Mill, *On Liberty* (Indianapolis: Bobbs-Merrill, 1956), p. 13.

107. Michael Walzer, *Just and Unjust Wars: A Moral Argument with Historical Illustrations* (New York: Basic Books, 2007), p. 268.

108. Rawls, *The Law of Peoples*, p. 105. Also see Giorgio Agamben, *State of Exception*, trans. Kevin Attell (Chicago: University of Chicago Press, 2005); Carl J. Friedrich, *Constitutional Government and Democracy: Theory and Practice in Europe and America* (Boston: Ginn and Company, 1946), chap. 13; Clinton L. Rossiter, *Constitutional Dictatorship: Crisis Government in the Modern Democracies* (Princeton, NJ: Princeton University Press, 1948); Fredrick M. Watkins, "The Problem of Constitutional Dictatorship," in *Public Policy: A Yearbook of the Graduate School of Public Administration, Harvard University*, ed. C. J. Friedrich and Edward S. Mason (Cambridge, MA: Harvard University Press, 1940).

109. "Inside the Hearts and Minds of Arab Youth," 8th Annual ASDA'A Burson-Marsteller Arab Youth Survey, 2016, p. 26.

110. Stephen Kinzer, "Rwanda and the Dangers of Democracy," *Boston Globe*, July 22, 2017. Also see Stephen Kinzer, *A Thousand Hills: Rwanda's Rebirth and the Man Who Dreamed It* (Hoboken, NJ: Wiley, 2008).

111. "Stability and Comfort over Democracy: Russians Share Preferences in Poll," *RT News*, April 3, 2014.

112. The difficulty of spreading liberal rights in the West is a central theme in two recent books dealing with the history of human rights: Hunt, *Inventing Human Rights*; and Samuel Moyn, *The Last Utopia: Human Rights in History* (Cambridge, MA: Harvard University Press, 2010). Both authors make it clear that the concept of inalienable rights first gained widespread attention in the latter part of the eighteenth century with the American Declaration of Independence (1776) and the French Declaration of the Rights of Man and of the Citizen (1789). But for roughly the next 150 years, individual rights were not paid great attention within the West. Hunt argues they once again became a subject of marked importance in 1948, while Moyn maintains that this did not happen until 1977. Also see Markus Fischer, "The Liberal Peace: Ethical, Historical, and Philosophical Aspects" (BCSIA Discussion Paper 2000-07, Kennedy School of Government, Harvard University, April 2000), pp. 20–22. It is worth noting that contingency is at the core of both Hunt's and Moyn's stories. Hunt writes, for example: "Yet even naturalness, equality, and universality are not quite enough. Human rights only become meaningful when they gain political content. They are not the rights of humans in a state of nature; they are the rights of humans in society" (p. 21). In other words, she is arguing against natural rights. For Moyn, human rights were "only one appealing ideology among others" (p. 5).

113. An indication of how difficult it is to spread liberalism is the trouble Britain had exporting that ideology to its colonial empire, especially India. See Karuna Mantena, *Alibis of Empire: Henry Maine and the Ends of Liberal Imperialism* (Princeton, NJ: Princeton University Press, 2010); Mehta, *Liberalism and Empire*.

114. Rossiter, *Constitutional Dictatorship*, p. 228. For a more detailed discussion of Lincoln's actions, see pp. 223–39.

115. Aristide R. Zolberg, *A Nation by Design: Immigration Policy in the Fashioning of America* (Cambridge, MA: Harvard University Press, 2006), p. 192.

116. This discrimination against European immigrants is reflected in the titles of these three books: Karen Brodkin, *How Jews Became White Folks and What That Says about Race in America* (New Brunswick, NJ: Rutgers University Press, 1998); Noel Ignatiev, *How the Irish Became White* (New York: Routledge, 2008); David R. Roediger, *Working toward Whiteness: How America's Immigrants Became White* (New York: Basic Books, 2005).

117. David M. Kennedy, *Over Here: The First World War and American Society* (New York: Oxford University Press, 1982), chap. 1; Frederick C. Luebke, *Bonds of Loyalty: German Americans and World War I* (DeKalb: Northern Illinois University Press, 1974); Carl Wittke, *German-Americans and the World War* (Columbus: Ohio State Archaeological and Historical Society, 1936).

118. Armitage, *The Declaration of Independence*, p. 18; Gerald N. Rosenberg, "Much Ado about Nothing? The Emptiness of Rights' Claims in the Twenty-First Century United States," in "Revisiting Rights," ed. Austin Sarat, special issue, *Studies in Law, Politics, and Society* (Bingley, UK: Emerald Group, 2009), pp. 1–41.

119. Rosenberg, "Much Ado about Nothing?," pp. 20, 23–28. Also see George Klosko, "Rawls's 'Political' Philosophy and American Democracy," *American Political Science Review* 87, no. 2 (June 1993): 348–59; George Klosko, *Democratic Procedures and Liberal Consensus* (New York: Oxford University Press, 2004), p. vii; Shaun P. Young, "Rawlsian Reasonableness: A Problematic Presumption?," *Canadian Journal of Political Science* 39, no. 1 (March 2006): 159–80.

120. All three quotes are from Rosenberg, "Much Ado about Nothing?," p. 33.

121. James Madison, Alexander Hamilton, and John Jay, *The Federalist Papers*, ed. Isaac Kramnick (New York: Penguin, 1987), pp. 122–28.

122. Lisa Blaydes and James Lo, "One Man, One Vote, One Time? A Model of Democratization in the Middle East," *Journal of Theoretical Politics* 24, no. 1 (January 2012): 110–46; Paul Pillar, "One Person, One Vote, One Time," *National Interest Blog*, October 3, 2017, http://nationalinterest.org/blog/paul-pillar/one-person-one-vote-one-time-22583.

123. There is worrisome evidence that the various cleavages in the American public are beginning to line up. Alan Abramowitz, *The Great Alignment: Race, Party Transformation and the Rise of Donald Trump* (New Haven, CT: Yale University Press, 2018). Not surprisingly, there is good reason to worry about the authoritarian temptation in the United States today. See Steven Levitsky and Daniel Ziblatt, *How Democracies Die* (New York: Crown, 2018).

124. Emile Durkheim, *The Division of Labor in Society* (New York: Free Press, 1964).

125. Michael J. Glennon, *National Security and Double Government* (New York: Oxford University Press, 2016). Also see Michael Lofgren, *The Fall of the Constitution and the Rise of a Shadow Government* (New York: Penguin, 2016).

Chapter 5. Liberalism Goes Abroad

1. Concerning the claim that liberal democracy promotes prosperity, see Michael C. Desch, *Power and Military Effectiveness: The Fallacy of Democratic Triumphalism* (Baltimore: Johns Hopkins University Press, 2008), pp. 52–53; Yi Feng, "Democracy, Political Stability, and Economic Growth," *British Journal of Political Science* 27, no. 3 (July 1997): 391–418; David A. Lake, "Powerful Pacifists: Democratic States and War," *American Political Science Review* 86, no. 1 (March 1992): 24–37.

2. Most foreign policy analysts and scholars believe that the international system has been unipolar since the Cold War ended, and the United States is the sole pole. The other states can be categorized as either major or minor powers, but not great powers. See Nuno P. Monteiro, *Theory of Unipolar Politics* (New York: Cambridge University Press, 2014). In contrast, I believe the world has been multipolar, as China and Russia are also great powers. John J. Mearsheimer,

The Tragedy of Great Power Politics, updated ed. (New York: Norton, 2014). There is no question, however, that the United States is far more powerful than those other two great powers. Indeed, it is the only superpower among the three. Thus, there is little daylight between my view of the global balance of power and those who see unipolarity. Given this fact, coupled with how the popular lexicon has evolved, I use the term *unipolarity,* not *unbalanced multipolarity,* to describe the architecture of the system since 1989. Nevertheless, I believe that a great power that is far stronger than its rivals in multipolarity would also be free to pursue liberal hegemony, mainly because the weaker great powers would have few capabilities that could be used to challenge the dominant state outside their own borders.

3. Michael W. Doyle, "Liberalism and World Politics," *American Political Science Review* 80, no. 4 (December 1986): 1161.

4. Some scholars maintain that particular features of democracy, not liberalism, account for why liberal democracies do not war with each other. Those alternative accounts, in other words, do not emphasize the importance of inalienable rights, which is the liberal explanation for this purported phenomenon. In chapter 7, I assess those particular attributes of democracies that are said to prevent war between liberal democracies.

5. Quoted in G. John Ikenberry, "Liberal Internationalism 3.0: America and the Dilemmas of Liberal World Order," *Perspectives on Politics* 7, no. 1 (March 2009): 75.

6. Michael W. Doyle, "Kant, Liberal Legacies, and Foreign Affairs," part 2, *Philosophy and Public Affairs* 12, no. 4 (Fall 1983): 324. Also see Doyle, "Liberalism and World Politics," pp. 1156–63.

7. Quoted in Kenneth N. Waltz, *Man, the State and War: A Theoretical Analysis* (New York: Columbia University Press, 1965), p. 111. Relatedly, Doyle writes: "Liberal wars are only fought for popular, liberal purposes." Doyle, "Liberalism and World Politics," p. 1160. John Owen writes: "All individuals share an interest in peace, and should want war only as an instrument to bring about peace." John M. Owen, "How Liberalism Produces Democratic Peace," *International Security* 19, no. 2 (Fall 1994): 89.

8. Ikenberry, "Liberal Internationalism 3.0," p. 72.

9. John Rawls, *The Law of Peoples: With "The Idea of Public Reason Revisited"* (Cambridge, MA: Harvard University Press, 1999), p. 35.

10. Rawls, *The Law of Peoples,* p. 24.

11. Bertrand Russell, *Portraits from Memory and Other Essays* (New York: Simon & Schuster, 1956), p. 45.

12. See, for example, Seyla Benhabib, "Claiming Rights across Borders: International Human Rights and Democratic Sovereignty," *American Political Science Review* 103, no. 4 (November 2009): 691–704.

13. Rawls, *The Law of Peoples,* pp. 5, 93, 113.

14. John M. Owen, *The Clash of Ideas in World Politics: Transnational Networks, States, and Regime Change, 1510–2010* (Princeton, NJ: Princeton University Press, 2010), p. 4.

15. See Nicolas Guilhot, *The Democracy Makers: Human Rights and the Politics of Global Order* (New York: Columbia University Press, 2005).

16. Charles R. Beitz, "International Liberalism and Distributive Justice: A Survey of Recent Thought," *World Politics* 51, no. 2 (January 1999): 270. Also see Brian Barry, "Humanity and Justice in Global Perspective," in *Ethics, Economics, and the Law; Nomos XXIV*, ed. J. Roland Pennock and John W. Chapman (New York: New York University Press, 1982), chap. 11; Brian Barry, "International Society from a Cosmopolitan Perspective," in *International Society: Diverse Ethical Perspectives*, ed. David R. Mapel and Terry Nardin (Princeton, NJ: Princeton University Press, 1998), pp. 144–63; Charles R. Beitz, *Political Theory and International Relations* (Princeton, NJ: Princeton University Press, 1999), part 3; Richard W. Miller, *Globalizing Justice: The Ethics of Poverty and Power* (New York: Oxford University Press, 2010); Thomas W. Pogge, *Realizing Rawls* (Ithaca, NY: Cornell University Press, 1989), part 3.

17. Doyle, "Kant, Liberal Legacies, and Foreign Affairs," part 2, pp. 338–43; Eric Mack, "The Uneasy Case for Global Redistribution," in *Problems of International Justice*, ed. Steven Luper-Foy (Boulder, CO: Westview Press, 1988), pp. 55–66. Great powers are sometimes willing to allow an important ally to gain economic advantage at their expense because it is necessary to deter or fight against an especially powerful adversary. Mearsheimer, *The Tragedy of Great Power Politics*, pp. 159, 292, 324–25. This realist logic, however, has nothing to do with promoting global justice.

18. Samuel P. Huntington, *Who Are We? The Challenges to America's National Identity* (New York: Simon & Schuster, 2004), p. 268. Also see Samuel P. Huntington, *The Clash of Civilizations and the Remaking of World Order* (New York: Simon & Schuster, 1996), chap. 3.

19. Stephen M. Walt, *The Hell of Good Intentions: America's Foreign Policy Elite and the Decline of U.S. Primacy* (New York: Farrar, Straus and Giroux, 2018), chap. 3. Also see Christopher Layne, "The US Foreign Policy Establishment and Grand Strategy: How American Elites Obstruct Adjustment," *International Politics* 54, no. 3 (May 2017): 260–75; Kevin Narizny, *The Political Economy of Grand Strategy* (Ithaca, NY: Cornell University Press, 2007).

20. Realism comes in two basic forms: human nature and structural. The theory presented here clearly falls in the latter category, as it emphasizes that the overarching design of the international system causes states to pursue power. For human nature realists, on the other hand, states want power largely because most people are born with a will to power hardwired into them, which effectively means countries are led by individuals bent on having their state dominate its rivals. Hans Morgenthau, for example, maintained that individuals have an *animus dominandi*, which is the driving force behind human behavior as well as state behavior. Hans J. Morgenthau, *Scientific Man vs. Power Politics* (London: Latimer House, 1947), pp. 165–67. Also see Hans J. Morgenthau, *Politics among Nations*, 5th ed. (New York: Knopf, 1973), pp. 34–35. For realists of this persuasion, power is principally an end in itself, not a means to survival, as it is for structural

realists. Nevertheless, human nature realists do incorporate survival logic into their story, in large part because states operating in a world filled with aggressive and potentially dangerous neighbors have no choice but to worry about their survival, even if their ultimate goal is to gain power for its own sake. On the evolution of realist thinking in the United States, see Nicolas Guilhot, *After the Enlightenment: Political Realism and International Relations in the Mid-twentieth Century* (New York: Cambridge University Press, 2017); Brian C. Schmidt, *The Political Discourse of Anarchy: A Disciplinary History of International Relations* (Albany, NY: State University of New York Press, 1998).

21. The following discussion of realism draws heavily on Mearsheimer, *The Tragedy of Great Power Politics*, pp. 29–54, 363–65.

22. Sebastian Rosato, "The Inscrutable Intentions of Great Powers," *International Security* 39, no. 3 (Winter 2014/15): 48–88.

23. Joseph M. Parent and Sebastian Rosato, "Balancing in Neorealism," *International Security* 40, no. 2 (Fall 2015): 51–86.

24. Quoted in Evan Luard, *Basic Texts in International Relations: The Evolution of Ideas about International Society* (London: Macmillan, 1992), p. 166.

25. No state can be a global hegemon, mainly because of geographical constraints. The sheer size of the planet, coupled with the presence of a handful of huge oceans, makes it impossible to dominate in its entirety. The best a state can hope for is to be a regional hegemon, which means dominating its own region of the world. The United States, for example, has been a regional hegemon in the Western Hemisphere since the late nineteenth century. For further elaboration, see Mearsheimer, *The Tragedy of Great Power Politics*, pp. 40–42. As discussed below, the same factors that rule out a global hegemon make a world state impossible.

26. Robert B. Strassler, ed., *The Landmark Thucydides: A Comprehensive Guide to the Peloponnesian War* (New York: Simon & Schuster, 1998).

27. Markus Fischer, "Feudal Europe, 800–1300: Communal Discourse and Conflictual Practices," *International Organization* 46, no. 2 (Spring 1992): 427–66.

28. Steven Pinker, *The Better Angels of Our Nature: Why Violence Has Declined* (New York: Viking, 2011), p. 55.

29. Thomas Hobbes, *Leviathan*, ed. C. B. Macpherson (Harmondsworth, UK: Penguin, 1986), p. 186.

30. As emphasized in the previous chapter, one of the main weaknesses of liberalism is that it treats the people living inside a state as atomistic individuals, when, in fact, they are social beings at their core. This weakness does not apply at the international level, however, because states are not social entities in any meaningful way. They are individual political actors that are self-regarding at their core. Of course, this is precisely how realism treats states, which helps explain why states acting according to the dictates of liberalism in the international system end up acting according to balance-of-power logic.

31. Charles L. Glaser, *Rational Theory of International Politics: The Logic of Competition and Cooperation* (Princeton, NJ: Princeton University Press, 2010), pp. 38–39;

Mearsheimer, *The Tragedy of Great Power Politics*, pp. 31, 363; Rosato, "The Inscrutable Intentions of Great Powers," pp. 52–53.

32. John Locke, *The Second Treatise of Government* (Indianapolis: Bobbs-Merrill, 1952), p. 83.

33. Stephen Holmes, *Passions and Constraint: On the Theory of Liberal Democracy* (Chicago: University of Chicago Press, 1997), p. 39.

34. Deborah Boucoyannis, "The International Wanderings of a Liberal Idea, or Why Liberals Can Learn to Stop Worrying and Love the Balance of Power," *Perspectives on Politics* 5, no. 4 (December 2007): 708; G. Lowes Dickinson, *The European Anarchy* (New York: Macmillan, 1916).

35. For different perspectives on the distinction between liberalism at the domestic and international levels, see Charles R. Beitz, *Political Theory and International Relations* (Princeton, NJ: Princeton University Press, 1979); and Hidemi Suganami, *The Domestic Analogy and World Order Proposals* (New York: Cambridge University Press, 1989).

36. Monteiro, *Theory of Unipolar Politics*, chap. 3.

37. This is not to deny that the constituent nations in some multinational states do not treat each other as equals that deserve the same rights. But there are numerous cases where this is not a significant problem, cases where the different nations get along quite well in the context of a larger nation-state.

38. Quoted in Gerald N. Rosenberg, "Much Ado about Nothing? The Emptiness of Rights' Claims in the Twenty-First Century United States," in "Revisiting Rights," ed. Austin Sarat, special issue, *Studies in Law, Politics, and Society* (Bingley, UK: Emerald Group, 2009), p. 20.

39. Michael Barnett, *Eyewitness to a Genocide: The United Nations and Rwanda* (Ithaca, NY: Cornell University Press, 2002), pp. 12–13, 34–39, 68, 85, 116–17, 163; Samantha Power, *"A Problem from Hell": America and the Age of Genocide* (New York: Basic Books, 2002), pp. 366–67, 374–75.

40. Scott D. Sagan and Benjamin A. Valentino, "Use of Force: The American Public and the Ethics of War," *Open Democracy*, July 2, 2015, https://www.opendemocracy.net/openglobalrights/scott-d-sagan-benjamin-valentino/use-of-force-american-public-and-ethics-of-war.

41. Julia Hirschfeld Davis, "After Beheading of Steven Sotloff, Obama Pledges to Punish ISIS," *New York Times*, September 3, 2014; White House Press Office, "Statement by the President on ISIL," September 10, 2014.

42. John Tirman, *The Deaths of Others: The Fate of Civilians in America's Wars* (New York: Oxford University Press, 2011), pp. 295–302. Also see Michal R. Belknap, *The Vietnam War on Trial: The My Lai Massacre and the Court-Martial of Lieutenant Calley* (Lawrence: University Press of Kansas, 2002); Kendrick Oliver, *The My Lai Massacre in American History and Memory* (Manchester, UK: Manchester University Press, 2006).

43. John Mueller, *War and Ideas: Selected Essays* (New York: Routledge, 2011), p. 174.

44. Tirman, *The Deaths of Others*, p. 3.

45. This case is discussed at greater length in chapter 6.

46. Rawls, *The Law of Peoples*, pp. 4–5, 80–81, 90.

47. Rawls, *The Law of Peoples*, p. 126.

48. John J. Mearsheimer, "The False Promise of International Institutions," *International Security* 19, no. 3 (Winter 1994/1995): 5–49.

49. Within the United States, the strongest advocates of pursuing a foreign policy based largely on modus vivendi liberalism are probably found in the Libertarian Party and at the CATO Institute. Christopher A. Preble, *The Power Problem: How American Military Dominance Makes Us Less Safe, Less Prosperous, and Less Free* (Ithaca, NY: Cornell University Press, 2009); Libertarian Party, "2016 Platform," adopted May 2016, https://www.lp.org/platform/. It is worth noting that Preble and other experts who share his views believe that the United States operates in a largely benign strategic environment, which means that pursuing a foreign policy based on modus vivendi liberalism is consistent with balance-of-power logic.

50. See Charles Tilly, *Coercion, Capital, and European States, AD 990–1992* (Cambridge, MA: Blackwell, 1992), chaps. 1–2.

51. David Armitage, "The Contagion of Sovereignty: Declarations of Independence since 1776," *South African Historical Journal* 52, no. 1 (January 2005): 1. Also see Robert Jackson, *Sovereignty: The Evolution of an Idea* (Cambridge: Polity Press, 2007); Andreas Wimmer, *Waves of War: Nationalism, State Formation, and Ethnic Exclusion in the Modern World* (New York: Cambridge University Press, 2013).

52. Some words are in order about the compatibility of nationalism and realism at the international level. As noted, realism is a timeless theory, which means it does not matter what kind of political units make up the system, as long as it is anarchic and the threat of violence is ever present. The existing international system, however, is populated almost exclusively with nation-states, which means that the nation-state is the principal unit of analysis for contemporary realism. The nation-state is also the key unit of analysis for nationalism. Indeed, as I argued in chapter 4, the nation-state is the embodiment of nationalism. Nationalism and realism also tell a similar story about what motivates the behavior of those nation-states in the international system. Both are particularistic theories in which the key actors are autonomous units that interact with each other as a matter of course and sometimes have fundamentally different interests. Because those interactions can be either beneficial or harmful, the units—and here we are talking about nation-states—pay careful attention to how the behavior of other units affects their own interests. In the end, they pursue policies aimed at maximizing their own interests, sometimes at the expense of the other units' interests. Privileging one's own well-being occasionally leads nation-states to seek to harm or even destroy their rivals. This selfish behavior notwithstanding, the units are not hostile toward each other in all instances, and they certainly are not in a constant state of war. In fact, they sometimes cooperate with each other. Nevertheless, every nation-state knows that another might threaten it at some point. Because the potential for conflict is always present, the units worry about their survival,

even when there is no imminent threat. Thus, survival is at the core of each theory. Of course, survival is not the only goal for nation-states, but it must be their
highest goal for the obvious reason that if they do not survive, they cannot pursue
their other goals. In short, both nationalism and realism are consistent with my
sparse theory of politics laid out in chapter 2.

53. Fischer, "Feudal Europe: 800–1300." Also see Robert Bartlett, *The Making of Europe: Conquest, Colonization, and Cultural Change, 950–1350* (Princeton, NJ: Princeton University Press, 1994); Tilly, *Coercion, Capital, and European States.*

54. Tilly, *Coercion, Capital, and European States.* Also see Otto Hintze, "The Formation of States and Constitutional Development: A Study in History and Politics,"
and "Military Organization and the Organization of the State," in *The Historical
Essays of Otto Hintze,* ed. Felix Gilbert (New York: Oxford University Press, 1975),
pp. 157–215.

55. Niccolò Machiavelli, *The Prince,* trans. Harvey C. Mansfield, 2nd ed. (Chicago:
University of Chicago Press, 1998), pp. 53, 84, 105.

56. See especially Machiavelli, *The Prince,* p. 102, and, more generally, pp. 101–5.

57. For an overview of France's military might and its military campaigns between
1792 and 1815, see Mearsheimer, *The Tragedy of Great Power Politics,* pp. 272–88.

58. Barry R. Posen, "Nationalism, the Mass Army, and Military Power," *International
Security* 18, no. 2 (Fall 1993): 89–99. Also see Peter Paret, *Yorck and the Era of
Prussian Reform, 1807–1815* (Princeton, NJ: Princeton University Press, 1966);
Peter Paret, *Clausewitz and the State* (New York: Oxford University Press, 1976).

59. Jackson, *Sovereignty,* chaps. 3–4.

60. John Gray, *Black Mass: Apocalyptic Religion and the Death of Utopia* (New York:
Farrar, Straus and Giroux, 2007), p. 30. Also see Reinhold Niebuhr, *The Irony of
American History* (Chicago: University of Chicago Press, 2008).

61. Ronald Suny, *The Revenge of the Past: Nationalism, Revolution, and the Collapse of the
Soviet Union* (Stanford, CA: Stanford University Press, 1993).

62. Benedict Anderson, *Imagined Communities: Reflections on the Origin and Spread of
Nationalism* (London: Verso, 1983), pp. 1–3. Anderson turns to nationalism to
help explain those conflicts between communist states.

63. See Luis Cabrera, *Global Governance, Global Government: Institutional Visions for
an Evolving World System* (Albany: State University of New York Press, 2011), chap. 2;
Daniel Deudney, *Bounding Power: Republican Security Theory from the Polis to the
Global Village* (Princeton, NJ: Princeton University Press, 2007); Alexander Wendt,
"Why a World State Is Inevitable," *European Journal of International Relations* 9,
no. 4 (December 2003): 491–542. There has been considerable interest in the
possibility of a world state in the United States at different points in the past. In
fact, realists such as Hans Morgenthau and Reinhold Niebuhr maintained that
the development of nuclear weapons necessitated a world state. For background
on American thinking about a world state, see inter alia Luis Cabrera, "World
Government: Renewed Debate, Persistent Challenges," *European Journal of International Relations* 16, no. 3 (2010): 511–30; Campbell Craig, "The Resurgent Idea

of World Government," *Ethics & International Affairs* 22, no. 2 (Summer 2008): 133–42; Thomas G. Weiss, "What Happened to the Idea of World Government?," *International Studies Quarterly* 53, no. 2 (June 2009): 253–71.

64. This is the central theme in Dickinson, *The European Anarchy*. It is important to note that a unipolar international system is fundamentally different from a world state. With unipolarity, the system is anarchic, as it is composed of multiple states, although one state is much more powerful than the others. Each of those states is a sovereign entity. With a world state, there is by definition only one sovereign state on the planet, and thus the system is hierarchic.

65. Rawls, *The Law of Peoples*, p. 36. Also see Ian Shapiro, *Politics against Domination* (Cambridge, MA: Harvard University Press, 2016), chap. 5.

Chapter 6. Liberalism as a Source of Trouble

1. The Congressional Research Service published a report in October 2017 that lists the "instances in which the United States has used its Armed Forces abroad in situations of military conflict or potential conflict or for other than normal peacetime purposes" from 1798 to 2017. Barbara Salazar Torreon, "Instances of Use of United States Armed Forces Abroad, 1798–2017," Congressional Research Service Report, R42738, Washington, DC, October 12, 2017. It shows that the frequency of U.S. military deployments for those purposes in the post–Cold War period (1990–2017) has been more than six times greater than in the period between 1798 and 1989.

2. Alex J. Bellamy, *Responsibility to Protect* (Malden, MA: Polity Press, 2009); Alex J. Bellamy and Tim Dunne, eds., *The Oxford Handbook of the Responsibility to Protect* (New York: Oxford University Press, 2016); Gareth Evans, *The Responsibility to Protect: Ending Mass Atrocity Crimes Once and for All* (Washington, DC: Brookings Institution, 2009); Roland Paris, "The 'Responsibility to Protect' and the Structural Problems of Preventive Humanitarian Intervention," *International Peacekeeping* 21, no. 5 (October 2014): 569–603; Ramesh Thakur and William Maley, eds., *Theorizing the Responsibility to Protect* (New York: Cambridge University Press, 2015).

3. The two quotes in this paragraph are from Christopher Layne, "Kant or Cant: The Myth of the Democratic Peace," *International Security* 19, no. 2 (Fall 1994): 46.

4. John Rawls, *The Law of Peoples: With "The Idea of Public Reason Revisited"* (Cambridge, MA: Harvard University Press, 1999), pp. 93, 113.

5. Rawls, *The Law of Peoples*, pp. 89–93.

6. John M. Owen, "How Liberalism Produces Democratic Peace," *International Security* 19, no. 2 (Fall 1994): 88–89.

7. President Bush said shortly before the invasion of Iraq in March 2003 that "the greatest danger in the war on terror [is] outlaw regimes arming with weapons of mass destruction." George W. Bush, speech at the American Enterprise Institute (AEI) Annual Dinner, Washington, DC, February 28, 2003. On the Bush Doctrine, see *The National Security Strategy of the United States* (Washington, DC: White House, September 17, 2002).

8. Bush, speech at the AEI Annual Dinner. On the Bush Doctrine, see *The National Security Strategy of the United States;* George W. Bush, address to the West Point Graduating Class, June 1, 2002; Robert Jervis, "Understanding the Bush Doctrine," *Political Science Quarterly* 118, no. 3 (Fall 2003): 365–88; Jonathan Monten, "The Roots of the Bush Doctrine: Power, Nationalism, and Democracy Promotion in U.S. Strategy," *International Security* 29, no. 4 (Spring 2005): 112–56.

9. Bush, speech at the AEI Annual Dinner.

10. Henry A. Kissinger, *A World Restored: Metternich, Castlereagh, and the Problems of Peace, 1812–22* (Boston: Houghton Mifflin, 1957), p. 2.

11. W. H. Lawrence, "Churchill Urges Patience in Coping with Red Dangers," *New York Times,* June 27, 1954.

12. Carl Schmitt captures this point: "To confiscate the word humanity, to invoke and monopolize such a term probably has certain incalculable effects, such as denying the enemy the quality of being human and declaring him to be an outlaw of humanity; and a war can thereby be driven to the most extreme inhumanity." Schmitt, *The Concept of the Political,* trans. George Schwab (New Brunswick, NJ: Rutgers University Press, 1976), p. 54. The political philosopher Michael Walzer clearly acknowledges this tendency in *Just and Unjust Wars,* although he is determined to combat it, since his aim is to put limits on war and not engage in crusades. Walzer, *Just and Unjust Wars: A Moral Argument with Historical Illustrations* (New York: Basic Books, 2007), chap. 7.

13. The quotes in this paragraph are from Marc Trachtenberg, "The Question of Realism: A Historian's View," *Security Studies* 13, no. 1 (Autumn 2003): 168–69.

14. Robert Jackson, *Sovereignty: Evolution of an Idea* (Malden, MA: Polity Press, 2007).

15. Stephen D. Krasner, *Sovereignty: Organized Hypocrisy* (Princeton, NJ: Princeton University Press, 1999).

16. See John J. Mearsheimer, "The False Promise of International Institutions," *International Security* 19, no. 3 (Winter 1994/95): 5–49.

17. On the Thirty Years' War, see Geoffrey Parker, ed., *The Thirty Years' War,* 2nd ed. (New York: Routledge, 1998); C. V. Wedgwood, *The Thirty Years War* (London: Jonathan Cape, 1938); Peter H. Wilson, *The Thirty Years War: Europe's Tragedy* (Cambridge, MA: Harvard University Press, 2011). Regarding the importance of the Treaty of Westphalia for beginning the age of sovereignty, see Leo Gross, "The Peace of Westphalia, 1648–1948," *American Journal of International Law* 42, no. 1 (January 1948): 20–41. Some scholars, however, challenge Gross's interpretation. See Andreas Osiander, "Sovereignty, International Relations, and the Westphalian Myth," *International Organization* 55, no. 2 (April 2001): 251–87; Derek Croxton, "The Peace of Westphalia of 1648 and the Origins of Sovereignty," *International History Review* 21, no. 3 (September 1999): 569–91. I agree with Daniel Philpott's assessment "that Westphalia signals the consolidation, not the creation ex nihilo, of the modern system. It was not an instant metamorphosis, as elements of sovereign statehood had indeed been accumulating for three centuries." Daniel Philpott, "The Religious Roots of Modern International Relations," *World Politics* 52, no. 2 (January 2000): 209.

18. Wilson, *The Thirty Years War*, p. 787.

19. Marc Trachtenberg, "Intervention in Historical Perspective," in *Emerging Norms of Justified Intervention*, ed. Laura W. Reed and Carl Kaysen (Cambridge, MA: American Academy of Arts and Sciences, 1993), pp. 15–36.

20. For a discussion of how the norms of sovereignty and decolonization helped put an end to the European empires, see Neta C. Crawford, "Decolonization as an International Norm: The Evolution of Practices, Arguments, and Beliefs," in Reed and Kaysen, *Emerging Norms of Justified Intervention*, pp. 37–61. Crawford, however, emphasizes that the changing interests and capabilities of the imperial powers as well as the local populations also helped determine the final outcome.

21. For Blair's 1999 speech, see https://www.globalpolicy.org/component/content /article/154/26026.html.

22. "Full Text: Tony Blair's Speech," *Guardian,* March 5, 2004, http://www.theguardian .com/politics/2004/mar/05/iraq.iraq.

23. Joschka Fischer, "From Confederacy to Federation—Thoughts on the Finality of European Integration" (speech at Humboldt University, Berlin, May 12, 2000), http://germanhistorydocs.ghi-dc.org/sub_document.cfm?document_id=3745.

24. Gene M. Lyons and Michael Mastanduno, eds., *Beyond Westphalia? National Sovereignty and International Intervention* (Baltimore: Johns Hopkins University Press, 1995); Joseph A. Camilleri and Jim Falk, *The End of Sovereignty? The Politics of a Shrinking and Fragmenting World* (Cheltenham, UK: Edward Elgar, 1992). Also see A. Claire Cutler, "Critical Reflections on the Westphalian Assumptions of International Law and Organization: A Crisis of Legitimacy," *Review of International Studies* 27, no. 2 (April 2001): 133–50.

25. One might argue that this tension between liberalism and sovereignty will eventually disappear, because once the world is populated solely with liberal democracies, there will be no need for them to intervene in each other's domestic affairs. After all, liberal democracies are not serious human rights violators, and they do not fight wars against each other. Thus, sovereignty would once again be venerated, since there would be no conflict between liberal principles and Westphalian sovereignty. This outcome, however, assumes that countries like Britain and the United States can successfully spread liberal democracy across the globe, sometimes at the end of a rifle barrel. But this assumption is wrong, as doing social engineering in foreign countries ends up failing more often than not, sometimes disastrously, as was the case with the Bush Doctrine.

26. Carl Gershman, "Former Soviet States Stand Up to Russia. Will the U.S.?," *Washington Post*, September 26, 2013.

27. Michael McFaul, "Moscow's Choice," *Foreign Affairs* 93, no. 6 (November/ December 2014): 170. Also see David Remnick, "Letter from Moscow: Watching the Eclipse," *New Yorker,* August 11 and 18, 2014.

28. Keith Bradsher, "Some Chinese Leaders Claim U.S. and Britain Are behind Hong Kong Protests," *New York Times,* October 10, 2014; Zachary Keck, "China Claims US behind Hong Kong Protests," *The Diplomat,* October 12, 2014. Also see Chris Buckley, "China Takes Aim at Western Ideas," *New York Times,* Au-

gust 19, 2013, which makes clear that President Xi Jinping and his lieutenants believe that "Western anti-China forces led by the United States have joined in one after the other, and colluded with dissidents within the country to make slanderous attacks on us in the name of so-called press freedom and constitutional democracy. . . . They are trying to break through our political system."

29. Michael Forsythe, "China Issues Report on U.S. Human Rights Record, in Annual Tit for Tat," *New York Times*, June 26, 2015.

30. According to the Pentagon, there were about 8,900 American troops in Iraq in September 2017. Christopher Woody, "There's Confusion about US Troop Levels in the Middle East and Trump May Keep It That Way," *Business Insider*, November 28, 2017.

31. Helene Cooper, "Putting Stamp on Afghan War, Obama Will Send 17,000 Troops," *New York Times*, February 17, 2009; Eric Schmitt, "Obama Issues Order for More Troops in Afghanistan," *New York Times*, November 30, 2009; Sheryl Gay Stolberg and Helene Cooper, "Obama Adds Troops, but Maps Exit Plan," *New York Times*, December 1, 2009; Mark Landler, "U.S. Troops to Leave Afghanistan by End of 2016," *New York Times*, May 27, 2014.

32. Mark Landler, "Obama Says He Will Keep More Troops in Afghanistan than Planned," *New York Times*, July 6, 2016.

33. As of 2014, the United States had committed $109 billion to the reconstruction of Afghanistan. The Truman administration committed $103.4 billion (adjusted for inflation) to the Marshall Plan. Of that $109 billion spent in Afghanistan, $62 billion was used to build up its security forces. Special Inspector General for Afghanistan Reconstruction, *Quarterly Report to the United States Congress*, July 30, 2014, https://www.sigar.mil/pdf/quarterlyreports/2014-07-30qr.pdf. By the end of 2016, the United States had spent $117 billion on reconstruction in Afghanistan. Special Inspector General for Afghanistan Reconstruction, *Quarterly Report to the United States Congress*, January 30, 2017, https://www.sigar.mil/pdf/quarterlyreports/2017-01-30qr.pdf. This report cites a study that estimates that "at least $30 billion, and possibly as much as $60 billion, has been lost to contract waste and fraud" in the Afghanistan and Iraq conflicts.

34. For a detailed discussion of the Libya fiasco, see Foreign Affairs Committee, British House of Commons, "Libya: Examination of Intervention and Collapse and the UK's Future Policy Options," September 9, 2016. Also see Jo Becker and Scott Shane, "The Libya Gamble," Parts 1 and 2, *New York Times*, February 27, 2016, https://www.nytimes.com/2016/02/28/us/politics/hillary-clinton-libya.html and https://www.nytimes.com/2016/02/28/us/politics/libya-isis-hillary-clinton.html; Alan J. Kuperman, "A Model Humanitarian Intervention? Reassessing NATO's Libya Campaign," *International Security* 38, no. 1 (Summer 2013): 105–36; Dominic Tierney, "The Legacy of Obama's 'Worst Mistake,'" *Atlantic Monthly*, April 15, 2016.

35. Tim Anderson, *The Dirty War on Syria: Washington, Regime Change and Resistance* (Montreal: Global Research Publishers, 2016); Stephen Gowns, *Washington's Long War on Syria* (Montreal: Baraka Books, 2017); Mark Mazzetti, Adam Goldman,

and Michael S. Schmidt, "Behind the Death of a $1 Billion Secret C.I.A. War in Syria," *New York Times*, August 2, 2017; Jeffrey D. Sachs, "America's True Role in Syria," *Project Syndicate*, August 30, 2016.

36. Scott Wilson and Joby Warrick, "Assad Must Go, Obama Says," *Washington Post*, August 18, 2011; Steven Mufson, "'Assad Must Go': These 3 Little Words Are Huge Obstacle for Obama on Syria," *Washington Post*, October 19, 2015.

37. Mazzetti, Goldman, and Schmidt, "Behind the Death of a $1 Billion Secret C.I.A. War in Syria."

38. Syria's population is 23 million, of which roughly 6.1 million are internally displaced, and 4.8 million are refugees living outside Syria. Approximately 13.5 million Syrians require humanitarian assistance. United Nations Office for the Coordination of Humanitarian Affairs, "Syrian Arab Republic," http://www.unocha.org/syria.

39. Helene Cooper and Mark Landler, "White House and Egypt Discuss Plan for Mubarak's Exit," *New York Times*, February 3, 2011; Tim Ross, Matthew Moore, and Steven Swinford, "Egypt Protests: America's Secret Backing for Rebel Leaders behind Uprising," *Telegraph*, January 28, 2011; Anthony Shadid, "Obama Urges Faster Shift of Power in Egypt," *New York Times*, February 1, 2011.

40. Shadi Hamid, "Islamism, the Arab Spring, and the Failure of America's Do-Nothing Policy in the Middle East," *Atlantic Monthly*, October 9, 2015; Emad Mekay, "Exclusive: US Bankrolled Anti-Morsi Activists, *Al Jazeera*, July 10, 2013; Dan Roberts, "US in Bind over Egypt after Supporting Morsi but Encouraging Protesters," *Guardian*, July 3, 2013.

41. On the killings of Brotherhood members and their allies, see "All According to Plan: The Rab'a Massacre and Mass Killings of Protestors in Egypt," *Human Rights Watch*, August 12, 2014, https://www.hrw.org/report/2014/08/12/all-according -plan/raba-massacre-and-mass-killings-protesters-egypt. On U.S. law and the coup in Egypt, see Max Fischer, "Law Says the U.S. Is Required to Cut Aid after Coups. Will It?," *Washington Post*, July 3, 2013; Peter Baker, "A Coup? Or Something Else? $1.5 Billion in U.S. Aid Is on the Line," *New York Times*, July 4, 2013. On the U.S. response to the coup, see Amy Hawthorne, "Congress and the Reluctance to Stop US Aid to Egypt," MENASource, Atlantic Council, Washington, DC, January 14, 2014.

42. Hamid, "Islamism, the Arab Spring, and the Failure of America's Do-Nothing Policy in the Middle East." The United States has also provided critical assistance (aerial refueling, intelligence, supplying bombs) to Saudi Arabia for its brutal military intervention in the Yemeni civil war (2015–present). The Saudi Air Force's widespread bombing campaign against civilian targets has been a major cause of the enormous suffering inflicted on the people of Yemen.

43. David E. Sanger and Judith Miller, "Libya to Give Up Arms Programs, Bush Announces," *New York Times*, December 20, 2003.

44. U.S. Army and Marine Corps, *Counterinsurgency Field Manual 3-24* (Chicago: University of Chicago Press, 2007), pp. 2, 43.

45. See inter alia Bruce Bueno de Mesquita and George W. Downes, "Intervention and Democracy," *International Organization* 60, no. 3 (Summer 2006): 627–49;

William Easterly, Shanker Satyanath, and Daniel Berger, "Superpower Interventions and Their Consequences for Democracy: An Empirical Inquiry" (National Bureau of Economic Research Working Paper No. 13992, Cambridge, MA, May 2008); Andrew Enterline and J. Michael Greig, "The History of Imposed Democracy and the Future of Iraq and Afghanistan," *Foreign Policy Analysis* 4, no. 4 (October 2008): 321–47; Nils Petter Gleditsch, Lene Siljeholm Christiansen, and Havard Hegre, "Democratic Jihad? Military Intervention and Democracy" (World Bank Research Policy Paper No. 4242, Washington, DC, June 2007); Arthur A. Goldsmith, "Making the World Safe for Partial Democracy? Questioning the Premises of Democracy Promotion," *International Security* 33, no. 2 (Fall 2008): 120–47; Jeffrey Pickering and Mark Peceny, "Forging Democracy at Gunpoint," *International Studies Quarterly* 50, no. 3 (September 2006): 556.

46. Enterline and Greig, "The History of Imposed Democracy," p. 341.

47. Pickering and Peceny, "Forging Democracy at Gunpoint," p. 556.

48. Alexander B. Downes and Jonathan Monten, "Forced to Be Free: Why Foreign-Imposed Regime Change Rarely Leads to Democratization," *International Security* 37, no. 4 (Spring 2013): 94.

49. George W. Downes and Bruce Bueno de Mesquita, "Gun-Barrel Diplomacy Has Failed Time and Again," *Los Angeles Times*, February 4, 2004.

50. Pickering and Peceny, "Forging Democracy at Gunpoint," p. 554.

51. Easterly, Satyanath, and Berger, "Superpower Interventions and Their Consequences for Democracy," p. 1.

52. The United States and its European allies sometimes tout Bosnia as a successful intervention. While there is no question the West brought the bloody conflict in Bosnia to a halt in 1995, it is not an independent country today, because the Office of the High Representative, a creation largely of the EU and the United States, plays a central role in governing it. Moreover, even if Bosnia were independent, it would not qualify as a democracy, in large part because its constitution violates the European Convention on Human Rights. Finally, the EU maintains a military presence in Bosnia to keep the rival factions from starting their war anew.

53. For a fuller description of this case, see John J. Mearsheimer, "Why the Ukraine Crisis Is the West's Fault," *Foreign Affairs* 93, no. 5 (September/October 2014): 77–89; John J. Mearsheimer, "Moscow's Choice," *Foreign Affairs* 93, no. 6 (November/December 2014): 175–78.

54. This is an argument that some analysts made after the crisis broke out, but hardly anyone made before the crisis began. Stephen Sestanovich, for example, claims that "today's aggressive Russian policy was in place" in the early 1990s and "power calculations undergirded" American policy toward Russia from that point forward. Stephen Sestanovich, "How the West Has Won," *Foreign Affairs* 93, no. 6 (November/December 2014): 171, 173. NATO enlargement, in this view, is a realist policy. The available evidence, however, contradicts this interpretation of events. Russia was in no position to take the offensive in the 1990s, and although its economy and military improved somewhat after 2000, hardly anyone

in the West saw it as a serious threat to invade its neighbors—especially Ukraine—before the February 22 coup. In fact, Russia had hardly any large-scale combat units on or near its western border, and no serious Russian policymaker or pundit talked about conquering territory in eastern Europe. Thus, it is unsurprising that U.S. leaders rarely invoked the threat of Russian aggression to justify NATO expansion.

55. G. John Ikenberry, *After Victory: Institutions, Strategic Restraint, and the Rebuilding of Order after Major Wars* (Princeton, NJ: Princeton University Press, 2001), pp. 235–39, 245–46, 270–73. Six months after the Ukraine crisis began, President Obama told an audience in Estonia that "our NATO Alliance is not aimed 'against' any other nation; we're an alliance of democracies dedicated to our own collective defense." Official transcript of "Remarks by the President to the People of Estonia," Nordea Concert Hall, Tallinn, Estonia, September 3, 2014 (Washington, DC: White House).

56. Mary Elise Sarotte, "A Broken Promise? What the West Really Told Moscow about NATO Expansion," *Foreign Affairs* 93, no. 5 (September/October 2014): 90–97; Joshua R. I. Shifrinson, "Deal or No Deal? The End of the Cold War and the U.S. Offer to Limit NATO Expansion," *International Security* 40, no. 4 (Spring 2016): 7–44.

57. "Yeltsin Sees War Threat in NATO Enlargement," Jamestown Foundation *Monitor* 1, no. 91 (September 8, 1995). Also see Roger Cohen, "Yeltsin Opposes Expansion of NATO in Eastern Europe," *New York Times,* October 2, 1993; Steven Erlanger, "In a New Attack against NATO, Yeltsin Talks of a 'Conflagration of War,'" *New York Times,* September 9, 1995.

58. "Bucharest Summit Declaration Issued by the Heads of State and Government Participating in the Meeting of the North Atlantic Council in Bucharest on 3 April 2008," http://www.summitbucharest.ro/en/doc_201.html.

59. "NATO Denies Georgia and Ukraine," *BBC News,* April 3, 2008; Adrian Blomfield and James Kirkup, "Stay Away, Vladimir Putin Tells NATO," *Telegraph,* April 5, 2008; International Crisis Group, "Ukraine: Running Out of Time" (Europe Report No. 231, May 14, 2014).

60. On the Russia-Georgia war, see Ronald D. Asmus, *A Little War That Shook the World: Georgia, Russia, and the Future of the West* (New York: Palgrave, 2009); Andrew A. Michta, "NATO Enlargement Post-1989: Successful Adaptation or Decline?," *Contemporary European History* 18, no. 3 (August 2009): 363–76; Paul B. Rich, ed., *Crisis in the Caucasus: Russia, Georgia and the West* (New York: Routledge, 2012).

61. "The Eastern Partnership—an Ambitious New Chapter in the Relations with Its Eastern Neighbors," *European Commission,* press release, Brussels, December 3, 2008, http://europa.eu/rapid/press-release_IP-08-1858_en.htm?locale=FR%3E. For a discussion of the EU's European Neighborhood Policy, which was aimed at Eastern Europe and preceded the Eastern Partnership, see Stefan Lehne, "Time to Reset the European Neighborhood Policy," *Carnegie Europe,* February 4, 2014, http://carnegieeurope.eu/publications/?fa=54420.

62. Valentina Pop, "EU Expanding Its 'Sphere of Influence,' Russia Says," *euobserver,* March 21, 2009.

63. The Association Agreement the EU was pushing Ukraine to sign in 2013 did not deal just with economic matters. It also had an important security dimension. Specifically, it called for all parties to "promote gradual convergence on foreign and security matters with the aim of Ukraine's ever deeper involvement in the European security area." It also called for "taking full and timely advantage of all diplomatic and military channels between the Parties, including appropriate contacts in third countries and within the United Nations, the OSCE [Organization for Security and Co-operation in Europe] and other international fora." This certainly sounds like a back door to NATO membership, and no prudent Russian leader would interpret it any other way. For background information and a copy of the Association Agreement, which the Ukrainian president signed in parts on March 21, 2014, and June 27, 2014, see "A Look at the EU-Ukraine Association Agreement," *European Union External Action,* April 27, 2015, http://collections .internetmemory.org/haeu/content/20160313172652/http://eeas.europa.eu/top _stories/2012/140912_ukraine_en.htm. The above quotes are from Title II, Article 4, 1; Title II, Article 5, 3b.

64. Victoria Nuland, the assistant secretary of state for Europe, estimated in December 2013 that the United States has invested over $5 billion since 1991 to help Ukraine achieve "the future that it deserves." Nuland, "Remarks at the U.S.-Ukraine Foundation Conference," Washington, DC, December 13, 2013, https:// www.youtube.com/watch?x-yt-ts=1422411861&v=2y0y-JUsPTU&x-yt-cl =84924572. A key organization spearheading that effort is the National Endowment for Democracy (NED), a private, nonprofit foundation heavily funded by the U.S. government. Robert Parry, "A Shadow US Foreign Policy," *Consortium News,* February 27, 2014; Robert Parry, "CIA's Hidden Hand in 'Democracy' Groups," *Consortium News,* January 10, 2015. The NED has funded more than sixty projects aimed at promoting civil society in Ukraine, which its president, Carl Gershman, sees as the "biggest prize" for his organization. Gershman, "Former Soviet States Stand Up to Russia"; William Blum, "US Policy toward Ukraine: Hypocrisy of This Magnitude Has to Be Respected," *Foreign Policy Journal,* March 8, 2014. Regarding the NED-funded projects, see National Endowment for Democracy, "Ukraine 2014," http://www.ned.org/region/central-and-eastern-europe/ukraine -2014/. After Viktor Yanukovych won Ukraine's presidential election in February 2010, the NED decided he was undermining its movement toward democracy. So, the NED moved to support the opposition to Yanukovych and also to strengthen Ukraine's democratic institutions.

65. For a detailed discussion of the events leading up to the February 22, 2014, coup, see Richard Sakwa, *Frontline Ukraine: Crisis in the Borderlands* (London: I. B. Tauris, 2015), chaps. 1–4. Also see Rajan Menon and Eugene Rumer, *Conflict in Ukraine: The Unwinding of the Post–Cold War Order* (Cambridge, MA: MIT Press, 2015), chap. 2.

66. Geoffrey Pyatt (@USAmbGreece), Twitter, February 22, 2014, 2:31 p.m., https:// mobile.twitter.com/GeoffPyatt/status/437308686810492929.

67. On the initial decision to expand NATO eastward, see Ronald D. Asmus, *Opening NATO's Door: How the Alliance Remade Itself for a New Era* (New York: Columbia University Press, 2002); James M. Goldgeier, *Not Whether but When: The U.S. Decision to Enlarge NATO* (Washington, DC: Brookings Institution Press, 1999).

68. Quoted in Thomas L. Friedman, "Foreign Affairs; Now a Word from X," *New York Times,* May 2, 1998.

69. "Moscow Looks with Concern at NATO, EU Enlargement—2004-02-17," Voice of America English News, October 26, 2009.

70. One reason there was so little resistance to NATO expansion is that liberals assumed the alliance would never have to honor its new security guarantees, because the nature of international politics, at least in Europe, had fundamentally changed. War has been burned out of Europe. It is worth noting that the United States and its European allies do not consider Ukraine to be a core strategic interest, as their unwillingness to use military force to come to its aid in the ongoing crisis shows. From a realist perspective, it would be the height of folly to bring Ukraine into NATO when the alliance's members have no intention of defending it. Liberals, however, thought there was no need to worry about defending Ukraine, given their understanding of how the contemporary world works. So they were willing to give a security guarantee to a country that they were ultimately unwilling to defend.

71. "Full Transcript: President Obama Gives Speech Addressing Europe, Russia on March 26," *Washington Post,* March 26, 2014; "Face the Nation Transcripts March 2 2014: Kerry Hagel," CBS News, March 2, 2014. Also see the official transcript of "Remarks by the President at the New Economic School Graduation," Moscow, July 7, 2009 (Washington, DC: White House).

72. James Madison, "Political Observations. April 20, 1795," in *Letters and Other Writings of James Madison,* vol. 4 (New York: Worthington, 1884), p. 492. Also see Michael C. Desch, "America's Liberal Illiberalism: The Ideological Origins of Overreaction in U.S. Foreign Policy," *International Security* 32, no. 3 (Winter 2007/8): 7–43; David C. Hendrickson, *Republic in Peril: American Empire and the Liberal Tradition* (New York: Oxford University Press, 2018), especially chap. 4.

73. For a discussion of how militarized liberal states end up pursuing militarized policies at home, see Radley Balko, *Rise of the Warrior Cop: The Militarization of America's Police Forces* (New York: PublicAffairs, 2013), especially chaps. 7–8; Bernard E. Harcourt, *The Counterrevolution: How Our Government Went to War against Its Own Citizens* (New York: Basic Books, 2018).

74. James Risen, *State of War: The Secret History of the CIA and the Bush Administration* (New York: Free Press, 2006); James Risen, *Pay Any Price: Greed, Power, and Endless War* (New York: Houghton Mifflin Harcourt, 2014). Also see Dana Priest and William M. Arkin, *Top Secret America: The Rise of the New American Security State* (New York: Back Bay Books, 2011); Charlie Savage, *Power Wars: The Relentless Rise of Presidential Authority and Secrecy* (New York: Back Bay, 2017).

75. Glenn Greenwald, *No Place to Hide: Edward Snowden, the NSA, and the U.S. Surveillance State* (New York: Picador, 2015), chap. 5.

76. Jonathan Easley, "Obama Says His Is 'Most Transparent Administration' Ever," *The Hill,* February 14, 2013.

77. These definitions are taken from John J. Mearsheimer, *Why Leaders Lie: The Truth about Lying in International Politics* (New York: Oxford University Press, 2011), chap. 1.

78. This problem is particularly acute in the case of the United States because its huge size and providential geography make it a remarkably secure country. Thus, the American public will be strongly inclined to avoid wars of choice.

79. Lee Ferran, "America's Top Spy James Clapper: 'I Made a Mistake but I Did Not Lie,'" ABC News, February 17, 2016; Glenn Kessler, "Clapper's 'Least Untruthful' Statement to the Senate," *Washington Post,* June 12, 2013; Abby D. Phillip, "James Clapper Apologizes to Congress for 'Clearly Erroneous' Testimony," ABC News, July 2, 2013.

80. Risen, *State of War.*

81. Greenwald, *No Place to Hide.*

82. Jennifer Martinez, "Wyden Warns Data Collection under Patriot Act Is 'Limitless,'" *The Hill,* July 23, 2013.

83. Greenwald, *No Place to Hide,* pp. 27–30, 127–30, 229–30, 251.

84. Siobhan Gorman, "Secret Court's Oversight Gets Scrutiny," *Wall Street Journal,* June 9, 2013.

85. Thomas A. Durkin, "Permanent States of Exception: A Two-Tiered System of Criminal Justice Courtesy of the Double Government Wars on Crime, Drugs & Terror," *Valparaiso University Law Review* 50, no 2 (Winter 2016): 419–92.

86. Spencer Ackerman, "Obama Lawyers Asked Secret Court to Ignore Public Court's Decision on Spying," *Guardian,* June 9, 2015; Charlie Savage and Jonathan Weisman, "NSA Collection of Bulk Call Data Is Ruled Illegal," *New York Times,* May 7, 2015.

87. "Guantanamo by the Numbers," *American Civil Liberties Union,* March 2017, https://www.aclu.org/infographic/guantanamo-numbers. For purposes of comparison, on August 12, 2013, there were 149 detainees on Guantanamo, of which 37 were designated for indefinite detention and 79 were cleared for release but were still being held. "By the Numbers," *Miami Herald,* August 12, 2013, http://www.miamiherald.com/news/nation-world/world/americas/guantanamo/article1928628.html.

88. Mark Fallon, *Unjustifiable Means: The Inside Story of How the CIA, Pentagon, and US Government Conspired to Torture* (New York: Regan Arts, 2017).

89. Amrit Singh, *Globalizing Torture: CIA Secret Detention and Extraordinary Rendition* (New York: Open Society Foundation, 2013).

90. This is not to deny there are cases where it is not feasible to capture a suspected terrorist, thus leaving American decision makers with no choice but to either assassinate the individual or let him go. The focus here, however, is on cases where it is possible to capture the suspect but the decision is made instead to kill him because of all the legal problems that attend dealing with detainees.

91. Jo Becker and Scott Shane, "Secret 'Kill List' Proves a Test of Obama's Principles and Will," *New York Times*, May 29, 2012; Clive Stafford Smith, "Who's Getting Killed Today?," *Times Literary Supplement*, June 28, 2017.

92. Micah Zenko, "How Barack Obama Has Tried to Open Up the One-Sided Drone War," *Financial Times*, May 23, 2013. Writing in January 2016, Zenko says: "Whereas President George W. Bush authorized approximately 50 drone strikes that killed 296 terrorists and 195 civilians in Yemen, Pakistan and Somalia, Obama has authorized 506 strikes that have killed 3,040 terrorists and 391 civilians." Micah Zenko, "Obama's Embrace of Drone Strikes Will Be a Lasting Legacy," *New York Times*, January 12, 2016. Also see Micah Zenko, "Do Not Believe the U.S. Government's Official Numbers on Drone Strike Civilian Casualties: It's Way, Way Too Low," *Foreign Policy*, July 5, 2016; "Get the Data: Drone Wars," *The Bureau of Investigative Journalism*, September 13, 2016, https://www.thebureauinvestigates.com /category/projects/drones/drones-graphs/.

93. Tom Engelhardt, *Shadow Government: Surveillance, Secret Wars, and a Global Security State in a Single-Superpower World* (Chicago: Haymarket Books, 2014), pp. 88–89.

94. Quoted in Doyle McManus, "Who Reviews the U.S. Kill List?," *Los Angeles Times*, February 5, 2012.

95. This is not to deny that competition among the great powers in either bipolarity or multipolarity leaves them little choice but to retain large military forces in peacetime and certainly in wartime, which can pose a threat to civil liberties. In unipolarity, however, the single great power has the option of reducing the size of its military and refraining from fighting wars, simply because it is so powerful. In that event, the sole pole's foreign policy would not threaten liberalism at home. Liberal hegemony, on the other hand, guarantees that the unipole will end up building a huge military establishment and hooked on war.

96. All the quotes in this paragraph and the next two are from James C. Scott, *Seeing Like a State: How Certain Schemes to Improve the Human Condition Have Failed* (New Haven, CT: Yale University Press, 1998), pp. 4–5.

97. Also see John Gray, *Black Mass: Apocalyptic Religion and the Death of Utopia* (New York: Farrar, Straus and Giroux, 2007), who does not reference Scott but makes an argument similar to mine.

Chapter 7. Liberal Theories of Peace

1. Immanuel Kant, *Perpetual Peace* (Minneapolis: Filiquarian, 2007), pp. 13–32.

2. Bruce Russett and John R. Oneal, *Triangulating Peace: Democracy, Interdependence, and International Organizations* (New York: Norton, 2000).

3. Michael W. Doyle, "Three Pillars of the Liberal Peace," *American Political Science Review* 99, no. 3 (August 2005): 463. For other examples of these theories being bundled together, see Dale C. Copeland, *Economic Interdependence and War* (Princeton, NJ: Princeton University Press, 2015), pp. 24–25.

4. Strobe Talbott, "Why NATO Should Grow," *New York Review of Books,* August 10, 1995. Talbott's views on NATO expansion were widely shared in the upper echelons of the Clinton administration. See Warren Christopher, "Reinforcing NATO's Strength in the West and Deepening Cooperation with the East" (opening statement at the North Atlantic Council Ministerial Meeting, Noordwijk, Netherlands, May 30, 1995); Madeleine Albright, "A Presidential Tribute to Gerald Ford" (Ford Museum Auditorium, Grand Rapids, MI, April 17, 1997); Madeleine Albright, Commencement Address, Harvard University, Cambridge, MA, June 5, 1997.

5. Madeleine Albright, "American Principle and Purpose in East Asia" (1997 Forrestal Lecture, U.S. Naval Academy, Annapolis, MD, April 15, 1997). Also see Warren Christopher, "America and the Asia-Pacific Future" (address to the Asia Society, New York City, May 27, 1994); "A National Security Strategy of Engagement and Enlargement," The White House, February 1995, pp. 28–29; "A National Security Strategy for a New Century," The White House, October 1998, pp. 41–47. Deputy Secretary of State Robert Zoellick first introduced the term *responsible stakeholder* in 2005. Zoellick, "Whither China? From Membership to Responsibility" (remarks to the National Committee on U.S.-China Relations, New York City, September 21, 2005).

6. Alexander Wendt, "Anarchy Is What States Make of It: The Social Construction of Power Politics," *International Organization* 46, no. 2 (Spring 1992): 408.

7. John M. Owen, "How Liberalism Produces Democratic Peace," *International Security* 19, no. 2 (Fall 1994): 87; Bruce Russett, *Grasping the Democratic Peace: Principles for a Post–Cold War World* (Princeton, NJ: Princeton University Press, 1993), p. 4.

8. Michael W. Doyle, "Kant, Liberal Legacies, and Foreign Affairs," part 1, *Philosophy and Public Affairs* 12, no. 3 (Summer 1983): 213. On that same page, he writes: "There appear to be some exceptions to the tendency for liberal states not to engage in a war with each other."

9. Doyle, "Kant, Liberal Legacies, and Foreign Affairs," part 1, pp. 205–35; Michael W. Doyle, "Kant, Liberal Legacies, and Foreign Affairs," part 2, *Philosophy and Public Affairs* 12, no. 4 (Fall 1983): 323–53. Also see Michael W. Doyle, "Liberalism and World Politics," *American Political Science Review* 80, no. 4 (December 1986): 1151–69.

10. Arch Puddington and Tyler Roylance, "Populists and Autocrats: The Dual Threat to Global Democracy," in *Freedom in the World, 2017* (Washington, DC: Freedom House, 2017), p. 4. Also see *Anxious Dictators, Wavering Democracies: Global Freedom under Pressure,* Freedom House's Annual Report on Political Rights and Civil Liberties (Washington, DC: Freedom House, 2016); Larry Diamond and Marc F. Plattner, eds., *Democracy in Decline?* (Baltimore: Johns Hopkins University Press, 2015); Larry Diamond, Marc F. Plattner, and Christopher Walker, eds., *Authoritarianism Goes Global: The Challenge to Democracy* (Baltimore: Johns Hopkins University Press, 2016).

11. For an excellent discussion of why Germany qualifies as a liberal democracy, see Christopher Layne, "Shell Games, Shallow Gains, and the Democratic Peace," *International History Review* 23, no. 4 (December 2001): 803–7. Also see Ido Oren, "The Subjectivity of the 'Democratic' Peace: Changing U.S. Perceptions of Imperial Germany," *International Security* 20, no. 2 (Fall 1995): 147–84. In Britain in 1900, 18 percent of the population was enfranchised to vote for the lower chamber of Parliament, while in Germany the figure was 22 percent. Niall Ferguson, *Pity of War: Explaining World War I* (New York: Basic Books, 1999), p. 29. Even Michael Doyle acknowledges that "Imperial Germany is a difficult case." Doyle, "Kant, Liberal Legacies, and Foreign Affairs," part 1, p. 216.

12. Democratic peace theorists rule this case out, either because they believe these two South African states were not sufficiently independent of Britain or because the South African Republic was not democratic enough. But they are wrong on both counts. Both states had clearly established their independence, even if Britain did not want to grant them full sovereignty, and although the South African Republic did exclude certain groups from voting, so did virtually every other democracy at the time.

13. Kargil is an uncontested case. The Spanish-American War is a disputed case; Layne explains why it should be treated as a case of two democracies fighting against each other. Layne, "Shell Games," p. 802.

14. James L. Ray, for example, examines twenty cases that are "alleged" to be examples of democracies at war with each other. See James L. Ray, *Democracy and International Conflict: An Evaluation of the Democratic Peace Proposition* (Columbia: University of South Carolina Press, 2009), chap. 3. Also see Russett, *Grasping the Democratic Peace*, pp. 16–23; Spencer R. Weart, *Never at War: Why Democracies Will Not Fight One Another* (New Haven, CT: Yale University Press, 1998). Whether a state is an "alleged" democracy depends on how one defines democracy, which is sometimes subject to the bias of the observer. Sarah S. Bush, "The Politics of Rating Freedom: Ideological Affinity, Private Authority, and the Freedom in the World Ratings," *Perspectives on Politics* 15, no. 3 (September 2017): 711–31; Oren, "The Subjectivity of the 'Democratic' Peace."

15. A militarized conflict is where the threat, display, or use of military force short of war (one thousand battle deaths) is employed by one state against another. Bruce Russett maintains that although democratic states do engage in militarized conflicts with each other, they do so less often than is the case when at least one of the disputants is a non-democracy. Russett, *Grasping the Democratic Peace*, pp. 20–21, 72–93. He may be right, but the point is they do fight with each other, even if those conflicts are not deadly enough to qualify as a war.

16. Ray, *Democracy and International Conflict*, p. 42. Not surprisingly, Ray attempts to knock down every case that might be seen as an example of democracies fighting against each other. Thus, he concludes his key chapter on those cases: "Skeptical, or perhaps even simply disinterested readers may conclude, by this point, that the sheer number of ostensible exceptions to the proposition that democratic states *never* fight international wars against each other undermines its credibility.

'Where there is so much smoke, there must be at least a little fire' would be an understandable reaction" (p. 124).

17. Kant, *Perpetual Peace*, p. 14.

18. See, for example, Donald Kagan, "World War I, World War II, World War III," *Commentary*, March 1987, pp. 21–40.

19. Chaim Kaufmann, "Threat Inflation and the Failure of the Marketplace of Ideas: The Selling of the Iraq War," *International Security* 29, no. 1 (Summer 2004): 5–48; Walter Lippmann, *Public Opinion* (New York: Harcourt, Brace, 1922); John J. Mearsheimer, *Why Leaders Lie: The Truth about Lying in International Politics* (New York: Oxford University Press, 2012); John M. Schuessler, *Deceit on the Road to War: Presidents, Politics, and American Democracy* (Ithaca, NY: Cornell University Press, 2015); Marc Trachtenberg, *The Craft of International History: A Guide to Method* (Princeton, NJ: Princeton University Press, 2006), chap. 4.

20. Nationalist sentiment, for example, played a key role in pushing Britain's governing elites to enter the Crimean War in 1853, even though they were reluctant to do so. See Gavin B. Henderson, "The Foreign Policy of Lord Palmerston," *History* 22, no. 88 (March 1938): 335–44; Kingsley Martin, *The Triumph of Lord Palmerston: A Study of Public Opinion in England before the Crimean War* (London: Allen & Unwin, 1924), chap. 2; Norman Rich, *Why the Crimean War? A Cautionary Tale* (Hanover, NH: University Press of New England, 1985), pp. 4, 10. Chinese nationalism helped push Chiang Kai-shek and his lieutenants to declare war against Japan in 1937, even though they thought doing so was not in China's best interest. See James M. Bertram, *Crisis in China: The Story of the Sian Mutiny* (London: Macmillan, 1937), pp. 117–23, 127–29; John Israel, *Student Nationalism in China, 1927–1937* (Stanford, CA: Stanford University Press, 1966), pp. 170–71. Austin Carson shows that warring states sometimes subtly work together to hide facets of the ongoing war from their publics, for fear that the citizenry finding out about them would fuel nationalist sentiment that would lead to unwanted escalation. Carson, "Facing Off and Saving Face: Covert Intervention and Escalation Management in the Korean War," *International Organization* 71, no. 1 (January 2016): 103–31. On the close connection between nationalism and war, see Andreas Wimmer, *Waves of War: Nationalism, State Formation, and Ethnic Exclusion in the Modern World* (New York: Cambridge University Press, 2013).

21. Jeff Carter and Glenn Palmer, "Regime Type and Interstate War Finance," *Foreign Policy Analysis* 12, no. 4 (October 2016): 695–719; Jonathan D. Caverley, *Democratic Militarism: Voting, Wealth, and War* (New York: Cambridge University Press, 2014); Gustavo A. Flores-Macias and Sarah E. Kreps, "Borrowing Support for War: The Effect of War Finance on Public Attitudes toward Conflict," *Journal of Conflict Resolution* 61, no. 5 (May 2017): 997–1020; Matthew Fuhrmann and Michael C. Horowitz, "Droning On: Explaining the Proliferation of Unmanned Aerial Vehicles," *International Organization* 71, no. 2 (April 2017): 397–418; Benjamin A. Valentino, Paul K. Huth, and Sarah E. Croco, "Bear Any Burden? How Democracies Minimize the Costs of War," *Journal of Politics* 72, no. 2 (April 2010): 528–44;

Rosella Cappella Zielinski, *How States Pay for Wars* (Ithaca, NY: Cornell University Press, 2016).

22. The key works on audience costs include James D. Fearon, "Domestic Political Audiences and the Escalation of International Disputes," *American Political Science Review* 88, no. 3 (September 1994): 577–92; James D. Fearon, "Signaling Foreign Policy Interests: Tying Hands versus Sinking Costs," *Journal of Conflict Resolution* 41, no. 1 (February 1997): 68–90; Kenneth Schultz, *Democracy and Coercive Diplomacy* (New York: Cambridge University Press, 2001). Also see Matthew Baum, "Going Private: Public Opinion, Presidential Rhetoric, and the Domestic Politics of Audience Costs in U.S. Foreign Policy Crises," *International Studies Quarterly* 48, no. 5 (October 2004): 603–31; Charles Lipson, *Reliable Partners: How Democracies Have Made a Separate Peace* (Princeton, NJ: Princeton University Press, 2003); Alastair Smith, "International Crises and Domestic Politics," *American Political Science Review* 92, no. 3 (September 1998): 623–38.

23. The major critiques of audience costs include Alexander B. Downes and Todd S. Sechser, "The Illusion of Democratic Credibility," *International Organization* 66, no. 3 (July 2012): 457–89; Jack Snyder and Erica D. Borghard, "The Cost of Empty Threats: A Penny, Not a Pound," *American Political Science Review* 105, no. 3 (August 2011): 437–56; Marc Trachtenberg, "Audience Costs: An Historical Analysis," *Security Studies* 21, no. 1 (January 2012): 3–42. Also see Bronwyn Lewis, "Nixon, Vietnam, and Audience Costs," H-Diplo/ISSF Forum, no. 3 (November 7, 2014), pp. 42–69; Marc Trachtenberg, "Kennedy, Vietnam, and Audience Costs," H-Diplo/ISSF Forum, no. 3 (November 7, 2014), pp. 6–42.

24. I have discussed the three main institutional explanations for the democratic peace. Sebastian Rosato points out three others that bear mentioning, although none provides a compelling causal story. First, democratic leaders are said to be more cautious than authoritarian leaders, because the former are more accountable to their publics and thus suffer greater costs if they lose a war. Using the work of Hein Goemans and others, Rosato shows that leaders of both kinds pay roughly the same price when they take their country into a losing war. Second, anti-war interest groups throw significant hurdles in the path of democratic leaders bent on war. There is little evidence, however, that anti-war groups are more likely to influence policymakers in a liberal democracy than pro-war groups. Plus, autocrats have powerful incentives not to start wars, because they normally represent a narrow slice of the population and going to war usually unleashes forces that empower other slices of the population, if not most of the population, all of which is likely to threaten the autocrat's rule. Third, democracies are said to be incapable of launching surprise attacks because their decision-making process is so transparent. As Rosato notes, the 1956 Suez War shows this is not true: three democracies (Britain, France, and Israel) planned a coordinated attack on Egypt that surprised not only the Egyptians but the United States as well. Moreover, most wars are not initiated with a surprise attack. Sebastian Rosato, "The Flawed Logic of Democratic Peace Theory," *American Political Science Review* 97, no. 4 (November 2003): 585–602.

25. John Owen writes: "I found that democratic structures were nearly as likely to drive states to war as to restrain them from it." Owen, "How Liberalism Produces Democratic Peace," p. 91. Also see Bruce Russett, *Controlling the Sword: The Democratic Governance of National Security* (Cambridge, MA: Harvard University Press, 1990), p. 124.

26. Russett, *Controlling the Sword*, p. 124. Also see William J. Dixon, "Democracy and Peaceful Settlement of International Settlement," *American Political Science Review* 88, no. 1 (March 1994): 14–32; Zeev Maoz and Bruce Russett, "Normative and Structural Causes of Democratic Peace, 1946–1986," *American Political Science Review* 87, no. 3 (September 1993): 624–38; Russett, *Grasping the Democratic Peace*; Weart, *Never at War*.

27. Russett, *Grasping the Democratic Peace*, p. 33.

28. Doyle, "Kant, Liberal Legacies, and Foreign Affairs," part 1, p. 213.

29. Doyle, "Kant, Liberal Legacies, and Foreign Affairs," part 1, p. 213.

30. Owen, "How Liberalism Produces Democratic Peace," p. 89.

31. Stephen Van Evera, "American Intervention in the Third World: Less Would Be Better," *Security Studies* 1, no. 1 (August 1991): 1–24.

32. John B. Judis, "Clueless in Gaza: New Evidence That Bush Undermined a Two-State Solution," *New Republic*, February 18, 2013; David Rose, "The Gaza Bombshell," *Vanity Fair*, March 3, 2008; Graham Usher, "The Democratic Resistance: Hamas, Fatah, and the Palestinian Elections," *Journal of Palestine Studies* 35, no. 3 (Spring 2006): 20–36.

33. Rosato, "The Flawed Logic of Democratic Peace Theory," p. 591. Rosato notes that one reason the U.S. government engages in covert interventions around the world is because it is trying to hide that interference from its own public (ibid.). Lindsey O'Rourke makes the same point in *Covert Regime Change: America's Secret Cold War* (Ithaca, NY: Cornell University Press, 2018).

34. Christopher Layne, "Kant or Cant: The Myth of the Democratic Peace," *International Security* 19, no. 2 (Fall 1994): 5–49.

35. Michael Walzer, *Just and Unjust Wars: A Moral Argument with Historical Illustrations* (New York: Basic Books, 2007).

36. Doyle is approvingly paraphrasing Kant in making this point. Doyle, "Kant, Liberal Legacies, and Foreign Affairs," part 2, p. 344. The overlap between just war theory and democratic peace theory is reflected in John Rawls, *The Law of Peoples: With "The Idea of Public Reason Revisited"* (Cambridge, MA: Harvard University Press, 1991). Rawls's discussion of just war theory, for example, depends heavily on Walzer's *Just and Unjust Wars*. See Rawls, *The Law of Peoples*, pp. 94–105.

37. Alexander B. Downes, *Targeting Civilians in War* (Ithaca, NY: Cornell University Press, 2008), p. 3. For further evidence of democracies killing large numbers of civilians, see Robert A. Pape, *Bombing to Win: Air Power and Coercion in War* (Ithaca, NY: Cornell University Press, 1996); Benjamin Valentino, Paul Huth, and Dylan Balch-Lindsay, "'Draining the Sea': Mass Killing and Guerrilla Warfare," *International Organization* 58, no. 2 (Spring 2004): 375–407.

38. John Tirman, *The Deaths of Others: The Fate of Civilians in America's Wars* (New York: Oxford University Press, 2011), quoted on back cover.

39. Geoffrey P. R. Wallace, *Life and Death in Captivity: The Abuse of Prisoners during War* (Ithaca, NY: Cornell University Press, 2015).

40. Doyle, "Liberalism and World Politics," p. 1159. Also see Larry Diamond, "Facing Up to the Democratic Recession," *Journal of Democracy* 26, no. 1 (January 2015): 141–55; Ethan B. Kapstein and Nathan Converse, *The Fate of Young Democracies* (New York: Cambridge University Press, 2008); Juan J. Linz and Alfred Stepan, *Problems of Democratic Transition and Consolidation: Southern Europe, South America, and Post-Communist Europe* (Baltimore: Johns Hopkins University Press, 1996); Ko Maeda, "Two Modes of Democratic Breakdown: A Competing Risk Analysis of Democratic Durability," *Journal of Politics* 72, no. 4 (October 2010): 1129–43; Dan Slater, Benjamin Smith, and Gautam Nair, "Economic Origins of Democratic Breakdown? The Redistributive Model and the Postcolonial State," *Perspectives on Politics* 12, no. 2 (June 2014): 353–74.

41. In fact, three prominent scholars argue that the contemporary "United States is in danger of backsliding." Robert Mickey, Steven Levitsky, and Lucan A. Way, "Is America Still Safe for Democracy?," *Foreign Affairs* 96, no. 3 (May/June 2017): 20–29. Also see Steven Levitsky and Daniel Ziblatt, *How Democracies Die* (New York: Crown, 2018).

42. Jonathan Kirshner, *Appeasing Bankers: Financial Caution on the Road to War* (Princeton, NJ: Princeton University Press, 2007); Beth Simmons, "Pax Mercatoria and the Theory of the State," in *Economic Interdependence and International Conflict*, ed. Edward D. Mansfield and Brian M. Pollins (Ann Arbor: University of Michigan Press, 2003), pp. 31–43; Etel Solingen, "Internationalization, Coalitions, and Regional Conflict and Cooperation," in Mansfield and Pollins, *Economic Interdependence and International Conflict*, pp. 60–68.

43. Norman Angell, *The Great Illusion: A Study of the Relationship of Military Power in Nations to Their Economic and Social Advantage* (London: William Heinemann, 1910).

44. Richard N. Rosecrance, *The Rise of the Trading State: Commerce and Conquest in the Modern World* (New York: Basic Books, 1986).

45. Erik Gartzke, "The Capitalist Peace," *American Journal of Political Science* 51, no. 1 (January 2007): 166–91; Erik Gartzke, Quan Li, and Charles Boehmer, "Investing in the Peace: Economic Interdependence and International Conflict," *International Organization* 55, no. 2 (Spring 2001): 391–438.

46. Patrick J. McDonald, *The Invisible Hand of Peace: Capitalism, the War Machine, and International Relations Theory* (New York: Cambridge University Press, 2009), p. 5.

47. Stephen G. Brooks, *Producing Security: Multinational Corporations, Globalization, and the Changing Calculus of Conflict* (Princeton, NJ: Princeton University Press, 2005).

48. Dale C. Copeland, "Economic Interdependence and War: A Theory of Trade Expectations," *International Security* 20, no. 4 (Spring 1996): 5–41; Copeland, *Economic Interdependence and War.*

49. John J. Mearsheimer, *Conventional Deterrence* (Ithaca, NY: Cornell University Press, 1983).

50. One might argue that the other economically interdependent states in the system would work hard to prevent those two rivals from fighting with each other out of fear the ensuing war would damage the economies of the neutral countries. However, as Eugene Gholz and Daryl Press note, "The costs that wars impose on neutral countries are usually greatly exaggerated; in fact many neutrals profit slightly from the economic changes caused by war." Eugene Gholz and Darryl G. Press, "The Effects of Wars on Neutral Counties: Why It Doesn't Pay to Preserve the Peace," *Security Studies* 10, no. 4 (Summer 2001): 3.

51. Jack S. Levy and Katherine Barbieri, "Trading with the Enemy during Wartime," *Security Studies* 13, no. 3 (Spring 2004): 2, 7. Also see Charles H. Anderton and John R. Carter, "The Impact of War on Trade: An Interrupted Time-Series Study," *Journal of Peace Research* 38, no. 4 (July 2001): 445–57; Katherine Barbieri and Jack S. Levy, "Sleeping with the Enemy: The Impact of War on Trade," *Journal of Peace Research* 36, no. 4 (July 1999): 463–79; Katherine Barbieri and Jack S. Levy, "The Trade-Disruption Hypothesis and the Liberal Economic Theory of Peace," in *Globalization and Armed Conflict*, ed. Gerald Schneider, Katherine Barbieri, and Nils Petter Gleditsch (Lanham, MD: Rowman & Littlefield, 2003), pp. 277–98.

52. It is worth noting that any country that is economically dependent on a country it fears it might fight can reduce that dependency to protect itself in the event of war. James Morrow, "How Could Trade Affect Conflict?," *Journal of Peace Research* 36, no. 4 (July 1999): 481–89. Also see Albert O. Hirschman, *National Power and the Structure of Foreign Trade* (Berkeley: University of California Press, 1980), pp. v–xii.

53. Peter Liberman, *Does Conquest Pay? The Exploitation of Occupied Industrial Societies* (Princeton, NJ: Princeton University Press, 1998).

54. Dale C. Copeland, *The Origins of Major War* (Ithaca, NY: Cornell University Press, 2000), chaps. 3–4.

55. The phrase "want of a nail" comes from the famous "Rhineland Parable," which is usually attributed to Benjamin Franklin:

For the want of a nail the shoe was lost
For the want of a shoe the horse was lost
For the want of a horse the rider was lost
For the want of a rider the battle was lost
For the want of a battle the kingdom was lost
And all for the want of a horseshoe-nail

To give an example, one could argue that Britain and France should have directly confronted Hitler when he remilitarized the Rhineland in 1936, rather than waiting until 1939 to confront him over Poland. After all, the Wehrmacht was a much more formidable fighting force in 1939 than it was in 1936. This example points up that "want of a nail" logic applies to cases involving "supreme emergencies."

Rather than waiting until it finds itself in dire straits, it makes sense for a state to deal with a potentially dangerous foe before it becomes an existential threat.

56. Dale C. Copeland, "The Constructivist Challenge to Structural Realism: A Review Essay," *International Security* 25, no. 2 (Fall 2000): 187–212; Copeland, *Economic Interdependence and War*, pp. 39–42; Copeland, *The Origins of Major War*, pp. 15, 22, 29; Dale C. Copeland, "Rationalist Theories of International Politics and the Problem of the Future," *Security Studies* 20, no. 3 (July–September 2011): 441–50.

57. "Rainy day" logic is different from "want of a nail" logic. With rainy day logic, there is no evidence that a particular country is a threat at the moment, but there is always a possibility it might become one in the future. With "want of a nail" logic, that other country is a threat, but not yet an existential threat. There is some chance, however, it will become a mortal threat. This logic underpins preventive war.

58. Nationalism is an especially powerful force in contemporary China, and is likely to have a marked influence on how Chinese policymakers and the public think about international politics across the board. See William A. Callahan, *China: The Pessoptimist Nation* (New York: Oxford University Press, 2010); Peter Hays Gries, *China's New Nationalism: Pride, Politics, and Diplomacy* (Berkeley: University of California Press, 2004); Christopher R. Hughes, *Chinese Nationalism in the Global Era* (London: Routledge, 2006); Christopher Hughes, "Reclassifying Chinese Nationalism: The *Geopolitik* Turn," *Journal of Contemporary China* 20, no 71 (September 2011): 601–20; Zheng Wang, *Never Forget National Humiliation: Historical Memory in Chinese Politics and Foreign Relations* (New York: Columbia University Press, 2012); Suisheng Zhao, *A Nation-State by Construction: Dynamics of Modern Chinese Nationalism* (Stanford, CA: Stanford University Press, 2004); Suisheng Zhao, "Foreign Policy Implications of Chinese Nationalism Revisited: The Strident Turn," *Journal of Contemporary China* 22, no. 82 (July 2013): 535–53.

59. Robert A. Pape, "Why Economic Sanctions Do Not Work," *International Security* 22, no. 2 (Fall 1997): 90–136.

60. Pape, *Bombing to Win*, chaps. 4, 8.

61. Andrei Kolesnikov, "Russian Ideology after Crimea," Carnegie Moscow Center, September 2015; Alexander Lukin, "What the Kremlin Is Thinking: Putin's Vision for Eurasia," *Foreign Affairs* 93, no. 4 (July/August 2014): 85–93.

62. See Gartzke, "The Capitalist Peace"; Edward D. Mansfield and Jon C. Pevehouse, "Trade Blocs, Trade Flows, and International Conflict," *International Organization* 54, no. 4 (Autumn 2000): 775–808; John R. Oneal and Bruce M. Russett, "The Classical Liberals Were Right: Democracy, Interdependence, and Conflict, 1950–1985," *International Studies Quarterly* 41, no. 2 (June 1997): 267–94.

63. See Barry Buzan, "Economic Structure and International Security: The Limits of the Liberal Case," *International Organization* 38, no. 4 (Autumn 1984): 597–624; Patrick J. McDonald, "The Purse Strings of Peace," *American Journal of Political Science* 51, no. 3 (July 2007): 569–82; James D. Morrow, "How Could Trade Affect Conflict?," *Journal of Peace Research* 36, no. 4 (July 1999): 481–89.

64. See Barbieri and Levy, "Sleeping with the Enemy"; Katherine Barbieri, *The Liberal Illusion: Does Trade Promote Peace?* (Ann Arbor: University of Michigan Press, 2002); Robert Gilpin, *War and Change in World Politics* (New York: Cambridge University Press, 1981); Kenneth N. Waltz, "The Myth of National Interdependence," in *The International Corporation,* ed. Charles P. Kindelberger (Cambridge, MA: MIT Press, 1970), pp. 205–23.

65. The focus here is on examining the liberal perspective on institutions. There is also a separate constructivist story about institutions, which lies outside the scope of this study. See John J. Mearsheimer, "The False Promise of International Institutions," *International Security* 19, no. 3 (Winter 1994/1995): 5–49.

66. Charles Lipson, "Is the Future of Collective Security Like the Past?," in *Collective Security beyond the Cold War,* ed. George W. Downs (Ann Arbor: University of Michigan Press, 1994), p. 114.

67. The fact that there is no difference between institutions and regimes is clearly reflected in Stephen D. Krasner, "Structural Causes and Regime Consequences: Regimes as Intervening Variables," in "International Regimes," ed. Stephen D. Krasner, special issue, *International Organization* 36, no. 2 (Spring 1982): 185–205.

68. Robert O. Keohane, *After Hegemony: Cooperation and Discord in the World Political Economy* (Princeton, NJ: Princeton University Press, 1984).

69. See, for example, Helga Haftendorn, Robert O. Keohane, and Celeste A. Wallander, eds., *Imperfect Unions: Security Institutions over Time and Space* (New York: Oxford University Press, 1999); Celeste A. Wallander, *Mortal Friends, Best Enemies: German-Russian Cooperation after the Cold War* (Ithaca, NY: Cornell University Press, 1999); Seth Weinberger, "Institutional Signaling and the Origins of the Cold War," *Security Studies* 12, no. 4 (Summer 2003): 80–115.

70. See, for example, Robert Axelrod and Robert O. Keohane, "Achieving Cooperation under Anarchy: Strategies and Institutions," *World Politics* 38, no. 1 (October 1985): 226–54; Charles Lipson, "International Cooperation in Economic and Security Affairs," *World Politics* 37, no. 1 (October 1984): 1–23; Lisa L. Martin, "Institutions and Cooperation: Sanctions during the Falkland Islands Conflict," *International Security* 16, no. 4 (Spring 1992): 143–78; Lisa L. Martin, *Coercive Cooperation: Explaining Multilateral Economic Sanctions* (Princeton, NJ: Princeton University Press, 1992); Kenneth A. Oye, "Explaining Cooperation under Anarchy: Hypotheses and Strategies," *World Politics* 38, no. 1 (October 1985): 1–24; Arthur A. Stein, *Why Nations Cooperate: Circumstance and Choice in International Relations* (Ithaca, NY: Cornell University Press, 1990).

71. See Haftendorn, Keohane, and Wallander, *Imperfect Unions*; Krasner, "Structural Causes and Regime Consequences," p. 192; Robert Jervis, "Security Regimes," in Krasner, "International Regimes," special issue, *International Organization,* pp. 357–78; Wallander, *Mortal Friends, Best Enemies,* pp. 5, 20, 22.

72. Lipson, "International Cooperation in Economic and Security Affairs," pp. 2, 12. Also see Axelrod and Keohane, "Achieving Cooperation under Anarchy," pp. 232–33; Keohane, *After Hegemony,* pp. 39–41.

73. Lipson, "International Cooperation in Economic and Security Affairs," p. 18.

74. Keohane, *After Hegemony*, pp. 6–7.

75. G. John Ikenberry, *After Victory: Institutions, Strategic Restraint, and the Rebuilding of Order after Major Wars* (Princeton, NJ: Princeton University Press, 2001). Also see G. John Ikenberry, *Liberal Leviathan: The Origins, Crisis, and Transformation of the American World Order* (Princeton, NJ: Princeton University Press, 2012).

76. Ikenberry, *After Victory*, p. xiii; Keohane, *After Hegemony*, p. 16.

77. Haftendorn, Keohane, and Wallander, *Imperfect Unions*, p. 1. They make the modest claim in the conclusion that "this book has argued that institutional theory can illuminate security issues" (p. 326). Wallander, who focuses on German-Russian relations in *Mortal Friends, Best Enemies*, concludes: "Power and interests remain central to German and Russian security calculations" (p. 6).

78. The other major obstacle to cooperation is relative gains consideration, which I do not address here, mainly because of space constraints. For my views on that matter, see Mearsheimer, "The False Promise of International Institutions," pp. 9–26.

79. We are talking about self-enforcement, which virtually every liberal understands does not work inside a country, and explains why you need a state with coercive power. So why would anyone expect it to work at the international level?

80. Other cases include Grenada (1983), Panama (1989), and Libya (2011).

81. Jan-Werner Muller, "Rule-Breaking," *London Review of Books*, August 27, 2015; Sebastian Rosato, "Europe's Troubles: Power Politics and the State of the European Project," *International Security* 35, no. 4 (Spring 2011): 72–77.

82. This point is clearly articulated in Lipson, "International Cooperation in Economic and Security Affairs," especially pp. 12–18. The subsequent quotations in this paragraph are from ibid. Also see Axelrod and Keohane, "Achieving Cooperation under Anarchy," pp. 232–33.

Chapter 8. The Case for Restraint

1. Scholars such as John Rawls and Michael Walzer are aware of the crusading impulse built into liberal theory, and go to considerable lengths to argue against using force to make the world a better place. See Michael Walzer, *Just and Unjust Wars: A Moral Argument with Historical Illustrations* (New York: Basic Books, 2007); John Rawls, *The Law of Peoples: With "The Idea of Public Reason Revisited"* (Cambridge, MA: Harvard University Press, 1999). This discussion of Walzer's views points up that initiating wars to spread liberal democracy around the world is at odds with just war theory, which is concerned with ruling offensive wars out of bounds except under highly restrictive circumstances, which do not include democracy promotion. In practice, however, it is especially difficult for powerful liberal democracies to resist the compulsion to use force for purposes of making the world a better place.

2. E. H. Carr, *The Twenty Years' Crisis: An Introduction to the Study of International Relations*, 2nd ed. (London: Macmillan, 1962); Robert Gilpin, "Nobody Loves a Political Realist," *Security Studies* 5, no. 3 (Spring 1996): 3–26; John J. Mearsheimer,

"E.H. Carr vs. Idealism: The Battle Rages On," *International Relations* 19, no. 2 (June 2005): 139–52; Mearsheimer, "The Mores Isms the Better," *International Relations* 19, no. 3 (September 2005): 354–59.

3. Valerie Morkevičius, "Power and Order: The Shared Logics of Realism and Just War Theory," *International Studies Quarterly* 59, no. 1 (March 2015): 11. Also see Valerie Morkevičius, *Realist Ethics: Just War Traditions as Power Politics* (New York: Cambridge University Press, 2018).

4. Charles L. Glaser, "Realists as Optimists: Cooperation as Self-Help," *International Security* 19, no. 3 (Winter 1994/95): 50–90. Also see Charles L. Glaser, *Rational Theory of International Politics: The Logic of Competition and Cooperation* (Princeton, NJ: Princeton University Press, 2010).

5. Jack Snyder, *Myths of Empire: Domestic Politics and International Ambition* (Ithaca, NY: Cornell University Press, 1993); Stephen Van Evera, *Causes of War: Power and the Roots of Conflict* (Ithaca, NY: Cornell University Press, 1999); Kenneth N. Waltz, *Theory of International Politics* (Reading, MA: Addison-Wesley, 1979).

6. Sebastian Rosato and John Schuessler, "A Realist Foreign Policy for the United States," *Perspectives on Politics* 9, no. 4 (December 2011): 812. They also write: "Realism as we conceive it offers the prospect of security without war" (p. 804).

7. The quotes in this paragraph are from Marc Trachtenberg, "The Question of Realism: An Historian's View," *Security Studies* 13, no. 1 (Fall 2003): 159–60, 167, 194. Also see Michael C. Desch, "It's Kind to Be Cruel: The Humanity of American Realism," *Review of International Studies* 29, no. 3 (July 2003): 415–26.

8. Stephen M. Walt, "U.S. Grand Strategy: The Case for Finite Containment," *International Security* 14, no. 1 (Summer 1989): 5–49; Stephen Van Evera, "Why Europe Matters, Why the Third World Doesn't: America's Grand Strategy after the Cold War," *Journal of Strategic Studies* 13, no. 2 (June 1990): 1–51. Nevertheless, some minor powers matter greatly to the United States because they are located in strategically important regions. Cuba (Western Hemisphere), Iran (Persian Gulf), and South Korea (Northeast Asia) are three prominent examples.

9. Vietnam is located in Southeast Asia, which was not a strategically important region during the Cold War. The two great powers in Asia that concerned the United States over the course of the twentieth century were Japan and Russia. Both of them are squarely located in Northeast Asia, which is why it was commonplace to describe that region, but not Southeast Asia, as strategically important to the United States. China, which was not a great power for centuries but is now rising rapidly, is located in Northeast as well as Southeast Asia. Thus, it is appropriate today to say that East Asia, not Northeast Asia, is one of the three key strategic regions of the world for the United States.

10. Clausewitz writes, for example, "War is the realm of chance. No other human activity gives it greater scope: no other has such incessant and varied dealings with this intruder. Chance makes everything more uncertain and interferes with the whole course of events." At another point, he says: "War is the realm of uncertainty; three quarters of the factors on which action in war is based are wrapped in a fog of greater or lesser uncertainty." Carl von Clausewitz, *On War*,

ed. and trans. Michael Howard and Peter Paret (Princeton, NJ: Princeton University Press, 1976), p. 101. Also see p. 85.

11. Although realists appreciate that unintended consequences play an important role in international politics, this belief is not derived from realist theory. As noted, it comes largely from studying the conflictual side of international politics.

12. This theme is emphasized in Rosato and Schuessler, "A Realist Foreign Policy for the United States."

13. Robert Jervis and Jack Snyder, eds., *Dominoes and Bandwagons: Strategic Beliefs and Great Power Competition in the Eurasian Rimland* (New York: Oxford University Press, 1991); Jerome Slater, "Dominoes in Central America: Will They Fall? Does it Matter?," *International Security* 12, no. 2 (Fall 1987): 105–34; Jerome Slater, "The Domino Theory and International Politics: The Case of Vietnam," *Security Studies* 3, no. 2 (Winter 1993/94): 186–224; Van Evera, *Causes of War,* chap. 5.

14. Lindsey O'Rourke, *Covert Regime Change: America's Secret Cold War* (Ithaca, NY: Cornell University Press, 2018).

15. Consider, for example, the death and devastation that the United States inflicted on its adversaries in the Korean War (1950–53) and the Vietnam War (1965–72). Although there is little agreement on the exact numbers, it is reasonable to assume that the U.S. military killed about one million North Korean civilians and soldiers, roughly four hundred thousand Chinese soldiers, and about one million Vietnamese civilians and soldiers. As Conrad Crane notes, "Most authors estimate that more than a million civilians died on each side" during the Korean War. Conrad C. Crane, *American Airpower Strategy in Korea, 1950–1953* (Lawrence: University Press of Kansas, 2000), p. 8. Also see Guenter Lewy, *America in Vietnam* (New York: Oxford University Press, 1978), p. 450; John Tirman, *The Deaths of Others: The Fate of Civilians in America's Wars* (New York: Oxford University Press, 2011), p. 92. Since hundreds of thousands of North Korean soldiers died in combat, one million is a conservative estimate for the total number of North Koreans killed by American forces. Regarding the brutality with which the United States waged war against North Korea, see Crane, *American Airpower Strategy in Korea;* Robert A. Pape, *Bombing to Win: Air Power and Coercion in War* (Ithaca, NY: Cornell University Press, 1996), chap. 5. The number of Chinese battle deaths is from Michael Clodfelter, *Warfare and Other Conflicts: A Statistical Encyclopedia of Casualty and Other Figures, 1494–2007,* 3rd ed. (Jefferson, NC: McFarland, 2008); Tirman, *The Deaths of Others,* p. 92. On Vietnam, the "prevailing view of most knowledgeable authorities" is "that close to one million communist combatants lost their lives, in addition to a quarter-million South Vietnamese soldiers and an unknown number of civilian casualties in South and North Vietnam." Charles Hirschman, Samuel Preston, and Vu Manh Loi, "Vietnamese Casualties during the American War: A New Estimate," *Population and Development Review* 21, no. 4 (December 1995): 783–84. This study estimates that there were slightly more than a million war-related deaths in all of Vietnam between 1965 and 1975. U.S. forces obviously did not cause all of those deaths. The study also notes that

the Vietnamese government estimates the number to be 3.1 million war deaths (p. 807). Guenter Lewy places the number at 1.3 million, 28 percent (365,000) of whom he estimates were civilians (Lewy, *America in Vietnam*, pp. 451–53). American forces surely killed a substantial number of those civilians, as the forces were pursuing a firepower-oriented military strategy aimed at inflicting massive punishment on their adversary, which would push it to the breaking point. John E. Mueller, "The Search for the 'Breaking Point' in Vietnam: The Statistics of a Deadly Quarrel," *International Studies Quarterly* 24, no. 4 (December 1980): 497–519. Lewy notes that the Pentagon estimates that North Vietnamese and Viet Cong military deaths alone numbered about 660,000 (Lewy, *America in Vietnam*, p. 450). Also see Tirman, *The Deaths of Others*, pp. 320–22, which provides a variety of estimates that show there is good reason to think the U.S. military killed at least one million Vietnamese. Regarding America's "non-stop" wars in the greater Middle East after the Cold War, former CIA analyst and Middle East expert Graham Fuller maintains that "American military intervention in the Muslim world over the past few decades" has resulted "in the killing of at least two million Muslims." Fuller, "Trump—Blundering into European Truths," *Graham E. Fuller* (blog), June 5, 2017, http://grahamefuller.com/trump-blundering-into-european -truths/. Of course, the U.S. military did not directly cause all those deaths, although it certainly killed many of the victims, and it played a key role in starting and fueling those wars.

16. Fredrik Logevall, *Choosing War: The Lost Chance for Peace and the Escalation of War in Vietnam* (Berkeley: University of California Press, 1999).

17. On bait and bleed strategies, see John J. Mearsheimer, *The Tragedy of Great Power Politics*, updated. ed. (New York: Norton, 2014), pp. 153–54.

18. Stephen M. Walt, *The Hell of Good Intentions: America's Foreign Policy Elite and The Decline of U.S. Primacy* (New York: Farrar, Straus and Giroux, 2018).

19. "Remarks by Secretary Mattis on the National Defense Strategy," Paul H. Nitze School of Advanced International Studies, Washington, DC, January 19, 2018. For the Department of Defense transcript, see https://www.defense.gov/News /Transcripts/Transcript-View/Article/1420042/remarks-by-secretary-mattis-on -the-national-defense-strategy/. Also see "National Security Strategy of the United States of America," White House, Washington, DC, December 2017; "Summary of the 2018 National Defense Strategy of the United States of America," Department of Defense, Washington, DC, January 2018.

20. Mearsheimer, *The Tragedy of Great Power Politics*, chap. 10.

21. Michael Beckley, "China's Century? Why America's Edge Will Endure," *International Security* 36, no. 3 (Winter 2011/12): 41–78.

22. According to the United Nations, the United States had about 310 million people in 2010 and will have 389 million in 2050. For those same years, Germany will go from 80 million to 75 million, Japan will go from 127 million to 107 million, and Russia will go from 143 million to 129 million. United Nations, Department of Economic and Social Affairs, Population Division, *World Population Prospects: The 2015 Revision*, https://esa.un.org/unpd/wpp/DataQuery/.

23. Jeffrey Goldberg, "The Obama Doctrine: The U.S. President Talks Through His Hardest Decisions about America's Role in the World," *Atlantic Monthly*, April 2016.

24. The following discussion on how liberal hegemony might be thwarted benefited greatly from conversations with Eliza Gheorghe, Sean Lynn-Jones, and Stephen Walt.

25. See Walt, *The Hell of Good Intentions*, chap. 6.

26. For a detailed discussion of this idea, see Walt, *The Hell of Good Intentions*, chap. 7.

27. Some of the key works making the case for restraint include Andrew J. Bacevich, *The Limits of Power: The End of American Exceptionalism* (New York: Holt Paperbacks, 2009); Richard K. Betts, *American Force: Dangers, Delusions, and Dilemmas in National Security* (New York: Columbia University Press, 2013); David C. Hendrickson, *Republic in Peril: American Empire and the Liberal Tradition* (New York: Oxford University Press, 2018); Chalmers Johnson, *Dismantling the Empire: America's Last Best Hope* (New York: Metropolitan Books, 2010); Christopher Layne, *The Peace of Illusions: American Grand Strategy from 1940 to the Present* (Ithaca, NY: Cornell University Press, 2007); Anatol Lieven and John Hulsman, *Ethical Realism: A Vision for America's Role in the World* (New York: Pantheon, 2006); Michael Lind, *The American Way of Strategy: U.S. Foreign Policy and the American Way of Life* (New York: Oxford University Press, 2006); Walter A. McDougall, *Promised Land, Crusader State: The American Encounter with the World since 1776* (New York: Houghton Mifflin, 1997); David Mayers, *Dissenting Voices in America's Rise to Power* (New York: Cambridge University Press, 2007); John J. Mearsheimer and Stephen M. Walt, "The Case for Offshore Balancing," *Foreign Affairs* 95, no. 4 (July/August 2016): 70–83; Rajan Menon, *The Conceit of Humanitarian Intervention* (New York: Oxford University Press, 2016); Joseph M. Parent and Paul K. MacDonald, "The Wisdom of Retrenchment: America Must Cut Back to Move Forward," *Foreign Affairs* 90, no. 6 (November/December 2011): 32–47; Barry R. Posen, *Restraint: A New Foundation for U.S. Grand Strategy* (Ithaca, NY: Cornell University Press, 2015); Christopher A. Preble, *The Power Problem: How American Military Dominance Makes Us Less Safe, Less Prosperous, and Less Free* (Ithaca, NY: Cornell University Press, 2009); Rosato and Schuessler, "A Realist Foreign Policy for the United States," pp. 803–19; A. Trevor Thrall and Benjamin H. Friedman, eds., *US Grand Strategy in the 21st Century: The Case for Restraint* (New York: Routledge, 2018); Stephen M. Walt, *Taming American Power: The Global Response to U.S. Primacy* (New York: Norton, 2005). It is important to note that realists are not the only advocates of restraint; there are restrainers who approach foreign policy from non-realist perspectives. Indeed, there are even some liberal internationalists who favor restraint. See, for example, Tony Smith, *Why Wilson Matters: The Origin of American Liberal Internationalism and Its Crisis Today* (Princeton, NJ: Princeton University Press, 2017).

28. Stephen Kinzer, *The True Flag: Theodore Roosevelt, Mark Twain, and the Birth of American Empire* (New York: Henry Holt, 2017).

29. Robin Lindley, "The Origins of American Imperialism: An Interview with Stephen Kinzer," *History News Network*, October 1, 2017.
30. In addition to Obama and Trump, George W. Bush campaigned in 2000 on the promise that he would pursue a more "humble" foreign policy and not do nation-building. Condoleezza Rice, "Promoting the National Interest," *Foreign Affairs* 79, no. 1 (January/February 2000): 45–62. He quickly abandoned that realist policy after 9/11 and enthusiastically embraced liberal hegemony.
31. Neta C. Crawford, "United States Budgetary Costs of Post 9/11 Wars through FY2018: A Summary of the $5.6 Trillion in Costs for the US Wars in Iraq, Syria, Afghanistan," Costs of War Project, Watson Institute, Brown University, November 2017.

INDEX